An Overview of Chinese Translation Studies at the Beginning of the 21st Century

An Overview of Chinese Translation Studies at the Beginning of the 21st Century presents and analyses over 100,000 bibliographic notes contained within a large academic database focusing on translation within China.

Exploring Chinese translation studies two decades before and after the year 2000, the book will introduce aspects of theory, culture, strategy, register, genre, and context to the field of translation in China, and will also take into account the impact of technology, education and research within this field.

Aimed at postgraduate students and researchers of translation studies, the focus of *An Overview of Chinese Translation Studies at the Beginning of the 21st Century* is the theory and practice of translation studies within a fast-paced and growing academic discipline.

Weixiao Wei is currently a Lecturer at Taiyuan University of Technology in China. She obtained her MA in Foreign Languages and Literature from Taiyuan University of Technology in 2010. Her research interests include discourse analysis, language education, and translation studies. She has contributed to multiple Routledge Handbooks, including: *The Routledge Handbook of Chinese Applied Linguistics, The Routledge Handbook of Chinese Discourse Analysis*, and *The Routledge Handbook of Chinese Language Teaching*.

Routledge Studies in Chinese Translation
Series Editor: Chris Shei
Swansea University, UK

This series encompasses scholarly works on every possible translation activity and theory involving the use of the Chinese language. Putting together an important knowledge base for Chinese and Western researchers on translation studies, the series draws on multiple disciplines for essential information and further research that is based on, or relevant to, Chinese translation.

A Discourse Analysis of News Translation in China
Liang Xia

Translating Chinese Art and Modern Literature
Edited by Yifeng Sun and Chris Song

An Overview of Chinese Translation Studies at the Beginning of the 21st Century
Past, Present, Future
Weixiao Wei

For more information about this series, please visit: https://www.routledge.com/languages/series/RSCT

An Overview of Chinese Translation Studies at the Beginning of the 21st Century
Past, Present, Future

Weixiao Wei

LONDON AND NEW YORK

First published 2020
by Routledge
2 Park Square, Milton Park, Abingdon, Oxon OX14 4RN

and by Routledge
52 Vanderbilt Avenue, New York, NY 10017

Routledge is an imprint of the Taylor & Francis Group, an informa business

© 2020 Weixiao Wei

The right of Weixiao Wei to be identified as author of this work has been asserted by her in accordance with sections 77 and 78 of the Copyright, Designs and Patents Act 1988.

All rights reserved. No part of this book may be reprinted or reproduced or utilised in any form or by any electronic, mechanical, or other means, now known or hereafter invented, including photocopying and recording, or in any information storage or retrieval system, without permission in writing from the publishers.

Trademark notice: Product or corporate names may be trademarks or registered trademarks, and are used only for identification and explanation without intent to infringe.

British Library Cataloguing-in-Publication Data
A catalogue record for this book is available from the British Library

Library of Congress Cataloging-in-Publication Data
Names: Wei, Weixiao, author.
Title: An overview of Chinese translation studies at the beginning of the 21st century: past, present, future/Weixiao Wei.
Description: Abingdon, Oxon; New York, NY: Routledge, 2020. | Series: Routledge studies in Chinese translation | Includes bibliographical references and index.
Identifiers: LCCN 2019025072 (print) | LCCN 2019025073 (ebook) | ISBN 9780367209865 (hardback) | ISBN 9780367209872 (paperback) | ISBN 9780429264689 (ebook) | ISBN 9780429555237 (adobe pdf) | ISBN 9780429564178 (mobi) | ISBN 9780429559709 (epub)
Subjects: LCSH: Translating and interpreting—China. | Translating and interpreting—Study and teaching (Higher)—China.
Classification: LCC P306.8.C6 W44 2020 (print) | LCC P306.8.C6 (ebook) | DDC 418/.020951—dc23
LC record available at https://lccn.loc.gov/2019025072
LC ebook record available at https://lccn.loc.gov/2019025073

ISBN: 978-0-367-20986-5 (hbk)
ISBN: 978-0-367-20987-2 (pbk)
ISBN: 978-0-429-26468-9 (ebk)

Typeset in Times New Roman
by Deanta Global Publishing Services, Chennai, India
Printed and bound by CPI Group (UK) Ltd, Croydon, CR0 4YY

Visit the eResources at: www.routledge.com/9780367209872

Contents

List of figures	vii
List of tables	viii
Preface	ix
Foreword	xiii

Introduction 1

Translation studies in the West 1
Research on Chinese translation 6
Chinese discourse on translation studies 12
Contents of the book 24
References 25

1   The inception of Chinese translation theory 28

Philosophical foundation of Chinese translation 28
The development of Chinese translation theory 38
Introducing Western translation theory 43
Reconceptualizing Chinese translation theory 51
References 55

2   The blossoming of Chinese translation theory 59

Equivalence theory 62
Application of Systemic Functional Linguistics in translation 67
Functionalist approaches to translation 70
Postcolonial translation theory 74
Deconstruction 78
Feminism 81
Relevance theory 83
Conclusion 86
References 87

vi *Contents*

3 Chinese translation activities, translators and translation theory   93

The history of Chinese translation 93
Representative Chinese translators 100
Revisiting Chinese translation theory 116
Conclusion 126
References 127

4 The translation of Chinese culture and the culturalization of Chinese translation   132

Cultural problems and strategies in translation 133
Translating the Chinese culture 140
Translating traditional Chinese medicine 144
Conclusion 153
References 154

5 Translating Chinese literature   157

Translated foreign literature in China 158
The translation of Hong Lou Meng 166
Conclusion 189
References 190

6 Chinese translation: from research to teaching   195

Research in translation teaching 196
Translation competence 201
Translation curriculum and pedagogy 207
Translation technology 214
Conclusion 220
References 220

7 Conclusion   224

Index   231

Figures

0.1	Keywords from scientometric analysis of 'translation studies' literature in visualization form	3
0.2	Keywords from scientometric analysis of 翻译 'translation' literature in visualization form	8
2.1	Visualization of bibliographic corpus collected from CNKI with 翻译理论 (translation theory) as search phrase in the topic domain	60
4.1	Keywords in Chinese culture and translation	133
6.1	Keywords from scientometric analysis of 翻译教学 'translation teaching' literature in visualization form	199

Tables

0.1	Keywords from scientometric analysis of 'translation studies' in tabular format	4
0.2	100 keywords with higher frequencies from scientometric analysis of 翻译 'translation' literature in tabular format	9
2.1	100 keywords with higher frequency from CNKI research on the topic of 翻译理论	60
4.1	50 top keywords from scientometric analysis of 翻译 'translation' and 文化 'culture'	134
5.1	50 top keywords from scientometric analysis of 翻译 'translation' and 文学 'literature'	160
5.2	Nine versions of *Hongloumeng* translation	169
5.3	Number and variety of comparative literature studies involving *Hongloumeng*	183
6.1	A list of top 50 keywords from scientometric analysis of 翻译教学 'translation teaching' literature	200

Preface

Translation is a form of learning by which a person, community or culture upgrades or updates itself by crossing the language (or other) barrier, and adds new information to an existing knowledge base. The Bible was translated from Classical Hebrew into Greek, just as Buddhist Scriptures were translated from Sanskrit into Chinese and other languages. In both cases, new information about the religion was transmitted and incorporated into the minds of the believers. As the act of translating was performed, discourse about translation was created, most likely from the translators themselves. By and by, translation theory was formed out of the many discourses contributed by translators and other intellectuals interested in translating as a form of knowledge acquisition and cultural exchange. Eugene Nida was a representative figure in modern Western history who translated the Bible, created a discursive context for the act of translation and developed a theory of translation out of his translating experience. In China, the three phases (or faces) of the business of translation also existed and exist: translating, discoursing about translation, and developing translation theory. Xuan Zang (玄奘), the Chinese Buddhist master who lived during the Tang dynasty (618–907 CE), started translating at age 46 and died at 62, having produced 75 titles with 1335 volumes of high-quality Buddhist Scripture translations. He was alleged to have said 'The differences between the teachings of Buddhism and Taoism are enormous. How can we use Buddhism to explain the meaning of Taoism?' (佛道二教的教理差距悬殊，怎能用佛理通道义？). This piece of discourse from the great Chinese translator Xuan Zang has a lot going for it. When Buddhism was imported into China from the Western Regions (西域), Confucianism and Taoism were already established philosophies and disciplines on Chinese soil. Translators prior to Xuan Zang had used Taoist terms to translate words and phrases in Buddhist sutras in order to make the abstruse concepts understandable to the general public. However, Xuan Zang apparently opposed this convention and advocated maintaining the original characteristics of the Sanskrit. These two oppositional practices were lexicalized into the binary terms of 'domestication' vs. 'foreignization' by Lawrence Venuti, approximately 1350 years later. Obviously, both translation discourse and translation theory have long existed in the Chinese history of translation. However, Chinese thoughts on translation in the past were not explicitly articulated and systematically developed into

x *Preface*

distinct theories and models as they often were in the West. Thus, Chinese translation theory and philosophy have remained mysterious and implicit, hidden among the many practical experiences and uttered or unuttered discourses.

Some people believed that the history of Chinese translation can be divided into five periods.

- Ancient period: Buddhist translation in the Han and Tang Dynasties
- The period of scientific translation during the Ming and Qing dynasties
- Western translation in the late Qing dynasty and the early Republic of China (after the Opium War and before the May Fourth Movement)
- Modern period: social science and literary translation after the May 4th Movement
- Contemporary: after the founding of the People's Republic of China in 1949

The first period of Buddhist Scripture translation climaxed with renowned monk translators like Kumārajīva (鸠摩罗什) and Xuan Zang. Kumarajiva and his disciples translated a total of 74 titles consisting of 384 volumes of sutras including the Diamond Sutra (金刚经), the Fahua Sutra (法华经), the Vimo (维摩经), the Middle View (中观论) and the Bai Theory (百论). In the Tang Dynasty, the Buddhist translation career reached its peak. A large number of famous translators appeared, among whom Xuan Zang was the most representative. In 826 CE, Xuan Zang went to India to seek enlightenment from the Buddhist Scriptures. After 17 years, he returned to China and brought back 657 Buddhist Scriptures. Xuan Zang then hosted larger translation workshops (译场) than ever before and translated 75 titles amounting to 1335 volumes of sutra in 19 years. In addition, Xuan Zang also translated a part of Laozi's work into Sanskrit and became the first person to introduce Chinese works abroad. The second peak of Chinese translation activities did not occur until the late Ming and early Qing dynasties, near 1000 years after Xuan Zang. In this period, a group of Jesuits from Europe came to China and engaged in translation activities, mainly for missionary purposes, but also introducing Western scholarship in the meantime. The most important achievement in this period was the translation of some natural science books, such as astronomy, mathematics, and mechanics. Representative figures of this stage are Chinese scientist Xu Guangqi (徐光启) and the Italian Jesuit priest Matteo Ricci (利玛窦). The two of them co-translated the first six volumes of the famous book *Euclid's Elements* (几何原本). Xu Guangqi was an outstanding scientist, translator, progressive thinker and patriotic politician in the late Ming Dynasty. He was the first translator to expand the scope of Chinese translation from religion and literature to natural science. It is worth mentioning that, in this period, long before Yan Fu published his translation of *Evolution and Ethics*, the linguist Ma Jianzhong (马建忠) already proposed the so-called 'good understanding' (善解) translation norm; that is, the translator must be proficient in both the original and target language, they must know the similarities and differences between the two languages, and master the patterns and regularities of both languages. Before translating a book, the translator must thoroughly understand the original text, reach the point of 'understand by heart and interpret by spirit' (心悟神解), and then start writing, faithfully expressing the original meaning to the point of 'no gap as fine as a hair' (无毫发出入于其间). In addition, Ma also emphasized that a good translation must also emulate the original's style and tone. Ma's advocacy was 'reminiscent' of the equivalent model of Western translation theory when systematic translation studies began in the 1960s. The third peak of Chinese translation occurred between the Opium War and the May Fourth Movement, bringing Western thoughts and literature onto the soil of China. The most prominent translators in this period were Yan Fu (严复) and Lin Shu (林纾 1852–1924). While Yan Fu was proficient in English and became famous for his translation standards of *xin* (信 'faithfulness'), *da* (达 'expressiveness'), *ya* (雅 'elegance'); Lin Shu invented a quite unique and thought-provoking translation method. Lin Shu himself did not know any foreign languages. However, he was very well-learned in classical Chinese and very good at writing. In the process of translating, he had to cooperate with friends who understood foreign languages. The friends first read the contents in Chinese (who were therefore the ones actually doing the translating), and Lin Shu would 'transcribe' what he heard into fluent classical Chinese. Being an accomplished classical Chinese writer, Lin Shu would modify and even rewrite the contents at will when 'translating'. This was a very free translation method indeed, defying the classification of any translation paradigm, although it was reminiscent of the sutra translation method, which also involved oral input. Some of Lin Shu's rewritings had enhanced the literary appeal of the works; others, however, did not properly translate the ST and deviated from the original's meanings and intentions. Despite the general literary appeal of his works, numerous errors had been found in his translations, which was not surprising given the translator's total oblivion of the source text. Lin Shu was a very productive translator. Throughout his life, he translated over 200 novels including Shakespeare, Dickens, Hugo, Dumas and many others. As a trigger for the fourth translation, the May Fourth Movement (1919 CE) was an important turning point in Chinese history. It is a new stage for the Chinese people to access knowledge imported from the West through the translating of literature and science. The post-May Fourth Movement period not only saw the rise of many outstanding translators and translation theorists such as Lun Xun (鲁迅) and Liang Shiqiu (梁实秋), as many literary societies and social groups were also established after the New Youth (新青年) periodical pioneered by Chen Duxiu (陈独秀), which were dedicated to disseminating the knowledge and culture embedded in Western literature. By translating more foreign literary works, these highly motivated Chinese intellectuals hoped that Chinese people could learn more knowledge from the West and dramatically change the domestic state and international status of China. Eventually, we find ourselves at the era of the People's Republic of China from 1949 where Chinese translation entered a new phase, especially after the open door policy initiated by Deng Xiaoping in 1978 and the Chinese culture going out strategy mapped out at the beginning of the 21st century, in which a large quantity of Chinese classical literature was translated into English. Chinese translation history has come a long way.

xii *Preface*

While the practice of Chinese translation continues since it began nearly 2000 years ago sometime in the Eastern Han dynasty (25–220 CE), and while the discourse about translating never ceased to exist in the intellectual history of China, Chinese translation theory only started to materialize in the late 20th century, arguably triggered by the introduction of Nida's translation theory into China by some enthusiastic translation practitioners and scholars in the 1980s. Today, after four decades of continuous research, publication, discussion, debates, speculation, formulation and dissemination, the academic discipline of Chinese translation studies gradually took form. And nowhere is this more evident than in the CNKI (China National Knowledge Infrastructure, 中国知网) database, which indexes virtually the entire range of academic journals in China, including those publishing translation and linguistic articles. A search on CNKI using 翻译 ('translation') as the search word reveals the number of papers published in this area ranging from three figures between 1975 (130) and 1986 (939), to four figures between 1987 (1044) and 2007 (8803), and finally to the five-figure number of papers published, between 10,000 and 13,000, from 2008 to the present. This is now a force that can no longer be ignored by the study of translation as a global enterprise. In this great wealth of intellectual effort in translation research and publishing, there lies the epitome of the Chinese practice of translation, the Chinese discourse about translation and, gradually, the Chinese theory concerning translation as a tradition and a way of pursuing or disseminating knowledge. In that context, this book has been written to offer the reader a cogent summary and discussion of that collective effort by contemporary Chinese intellectuals to establish an emerging academic discipline at the beginning of the 21st century called Chinese translation studies.

This work is funded through Research Project Supported by Shanxi Scholarship Council of China Shanxi Scholarship Council of China.

Foreword

By the Series Editor

When Bible translation took place in the West soon after the beginning of the common era, well-learned monks serving Chinese emperors were also vigorously translating Buddhist Scripture from Sanskrit, often based on memorized text. They left not only a wealth of Buddhist sutras in Chinese but also, occasionally, thoughts on translation equivalent to what we call translation theory today. In a sense, the content and form of Chinese translation roughly 'matched' what happened in the West, up until the second half of the 20th century, when translation studies in the West made a sudden breakthrough. There was a 17-year time lag between Nida's *Toward a science of translating* (1964) and Lin Shuwu's *A brief introduction to Nida's translation theory* published in the Chinese journal *Foreign Linguistics* in 1981. The catching-up was, however, amazing. At the time of writing, at least 100,000 Chinese papers on translation studies have been published in China's journals. The introduction of Western translation theory ignited the big engine of Chinese translation research, and the deep mine of Chinese translation history fueled it endlessly. The field of translation studies in the West, however, so far has little awareness of what translation researchers are writing about in China, as most if not all papers are published in Chinese (with an English abstract, sometimes). In this context, *An Overview of Chinese Translation Studies at the Beginning of the 21st Century* brings a ray of sunshine to everyone interested in knowing more about Chinese translation activities and research. 'Everyone' is not limited to English-speaking students and scholars, though the book is obviously written in English. Even for someone who understands all the Chinese papers cited in this book, they can from nowhere else find a better teacher who summarizes the Chinese translation history and noteworthy theories in such a useful way.

This book uses a core of 100s of Chinese papers on translation studies and radiates in all directions, including language, translation, literature, culture, philosophy, politics, education, etc. It provides knowledge and it provokes thoughts and potential discussions. It explains, since the introduction of Nida's dynamic equivalence theory in the 1980s, how a succession of linguistics and culturally oriented translation theory has been absorbed and reacted to in China's academic circle, including the functionalist approaches, postcolonial theory, deconstructionism, xiv *Foreword*

feminism, relevance theory, systemic functional linguistics and so on. But that is not all. Far from it. The book also goes deep into the root of Chinese translation by examining the philosophical basis of Chinese translation theory (Confucianism, Daoism, Buddhism…) and details the achievements and beliefs of prominent translators throughout Chinese history (Dao'an, Kumārajīva, Yan Fu, Ru Xun…). If that is not enough, the book makes a huge effort in detailing the problems involved in translating traditional Chinese medicine – a sorely needed area for the integration of world medicine. In addition, a substantial block of the book is devoted to the study of the translation of *Dream of the Red Chamber* (a classic Chinese novel) as a fine example of problems involved in translating Chinese literature and in studying the literary translation system itself. Last but not least, regarding the topic of a Chinese translator's education, the author of the book correctly recognizes the pivotal role played by research and technology in translation pedagogy and devotes a cogent chapter to the problem. This book, all things considered, is a gem in Chinese translation studies and a timely input to research in translation on a global scale.

Chris Shei
Swansea University, UK
May 2019

Introduction

Translation studies in the West

In a recent interview carried out by Pal Heltai, Andrew Chesterman was asked 'whether there has been any progress in translation studies' (Chesterman, 2017, p. 315). Chesterman's answer includes some good aspects of progression which are summarized as follows:

- 'There has been a great deal of institutional progress' (p. 316): 'more journals, conferences, associations, etc. than ever before'
- 'many cooperation initiatives in research training': 'international graduate schools and doctoral programmes' (ibid.)
- 'There has also been considerable methodological progress': 'an expansion in the kinds of data elicitation and analysis methods' (ibid.)

Some developments in Chesterman's eyes may not mean straightforward progress. In particular, he noted that '[translation studies has] become an ever broader interdiscipline, but this has also brought more fragmentation, as more and more subfields emerge, sometimes without strong links to other subfields' (p. 316). Conceptually speaking, according to Chesterman, there has also been 'expansion' (note he did not use the word 'progress' or 'progression' here) in that 'we have more and more terms, more and more distinctions'; however, 'they do not all seem to be justified in the sense of giving rise to better testable hypotheses' (ibid.). Thus, the fragmentation of translation studies as an academic discipline and a proliferation of terms and distinctions in the field without sufficient justification seem like a cloud on the horizon for the further development of translation studies. Toward the end of the interview, as the final part of his answer to Heltai's question (whether there has been any progress in translation studies), Chesterman mentioned two areas that are still lacking in translation studies:

- a standardized terminology
- an agreed general theory

The proliferation of terms and the expansion of the discipline seem to jointly point to a general tendency of 'uncontrolled growth'. The impression is further

2 Introduction

strengthened by Chesterman's observation that there is a lack of 'agreed general theory' in translation studies. One may think the Descriptive translation studies initiated by Gideon Toury would be a good candidate for the 'agreed general theory' Chesterman had in mind. However, like descriptive (as opposed to prescriptive) linguistics, Descriptive translation studies is only a general approach that looks into existing texts and describes the rules they seem to follow. It is hardly a well-spelled-out theory. This is why even though Chesterman found himself 'most at home in' Toury's theory (Chesterman, 2017, p. 312), he still does not consider it an 'agreed general theory'. Another candidate is the relevance theory, also originating in linguistic studies and favored by Chesterman. According to him, 'by showing all the things which translation has in common with communication in general, relevance theory can demonstrate how much you can explain of translation behaviour in terms of general communication strategies' (ibid.). Apparently, however, due to its lack of specific reference to translation studies and the lack of universal endorsement by translation scholars, relevance theory is still not taken by Chesterman as a viable 'agreed general theory'.

In an effort to find out what Chesterman's 'agreed general theory' is likely to be, a meta-analysis of the recent translation studies literature is in order. By looking into what translation researchers have produced in the past few decades; by extracting key terms from these works and examining them in some detail, we might be able to take a peep at what translation theories (in plural rather than singular form) work behind these terms and concepts and start to figure out what an 'agreed general theory' may look like. To achieve that goal, I used CiteSpace (Chen, 2016) as a scientometric tool to do the meta-analysis on research work produced by translation scholars in the past few decades. I also used Web of Science as the database to collect source data for analysis (i.e. papers published in translation journals and books over a period of time). By entering 'translation studies' as a key phrase in the topic area in the Web of Science database, and by refining the categories to be linguistics-related (as 'translation' is also a key term in the unrelated biological–medical field), I obtained around 4300 bibliographic notes at the time when this research was conducted (i.e. December 2018) including relevant publications from 1978 to the present. These bibliographic notes were exported and fed into CiteSpace for scientometric processing. The results include a visualization image shown in Figure 0.1, which reveals plenty of keywords extracted from the 4000 or so bibliographic notes (including the titles and abstracts of the articles among other things). The bigger the triangle, the more frequent the keywords appear in the bibliographic corpus.

Concurrently, a keyword list in the form of a table was also generated by CiteSpace along with the visualization image, which is partially reduplicated in Table 0.1. A close examination of Figure 0.1 and Table 0.1 seems to reveal five groups of terms that are often visible in the literature of translation studies:

- general linguistic terms: e.g. expression, sequence
- general translation terms: e.g. equivalence, text
- specific linguistic terms or theory: e.g. contrastive linguistics

Introduction 3

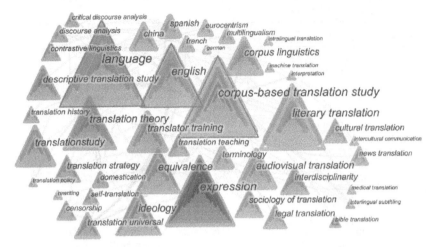

Figure 0.1 Keywords from scientometric analysis of 'translation studies' literature in visualization form (see this image in color at www.routledge.com/9780367209872)

- specific translation terms or theory: e.g. audiovisual translation
- general or specific non-linguistic/translation terms: anthropology, literature

Out of these categories of keywords, terms related to linguistic or translation theories are particularly meaningful, as most likely Chesterman's 'agreed general theory' will be generated one way or another from this bunch of discussions, if that idealized overall theory exists at all. Here we might refer to Dong and Chen's (2015) study, which analyzed Web of Science publications related to translation and interpreting between 2000 and 2015 and found that, among other things, three areas of research can be distinguished within translation studies: **theoretical translation research, translation and interpreting training**, and **linguistics-oriented translation research** (Dong and Chen, 2015, p. 1124). 'Interpreting' came out as a significant research area because Dong and Chen used it as one of the keywords strung by the Boolean connector OR in their search. Compared with translating, interpreting is highly connected to practical training and psycholinguistic processing, and the study of interpreting seems to have its own theoretical orientation. Therefore, if we leave interpreting out of the equation and combine the other two in Dong and Chen's discovery of three areas of translation studies research, the result is 'linguistics-oriented research of translation theory'. This seems to largely coincide with the five (or at least the first four) groups of terms identified from our own scientometric research listed above. More importantly, this seems to indicate that the majority of publications in translation studies so far seem to concentrate their efforts on the familiar linguistics battleground in the hope of finding an answer to the 'agreed general theory' posited by Chesterman.

Table 0.1 Keywords from scientometric analysis of 'translation studies' in tabular format (with 4+ frequency)

Frequency	Keyword	Frequency	Keyword
248	translation	7	cell
207	translation study	7	context
34	language	7	translation history
32	corpus-based translation study	7	self-translation
29	expression	7	corpora
27	literary translation	7	eurocentrism
25	english	7	discourse analysis
22	translation theory	7	domestication
21	messenger rna	7	french
19	ideology	7	multilingualism
19	equivalence	6	history
19	sequence	6	sociology
17	translator training	6	nucleotide sequence
17	audiovisual translation	6	critical discourse analysis
17	translation study	6	escherichia coli
16	corpus linguistics	6	secondary structure
15	linguistics	6	explicitation
14	gene	6	teaching
14	text	6	communication
14	descriptive translation study	6	localization
14	discourse	6	research methodology
13	protein	5	metaphor
12	culture	5	comparative literature
12	china	5	news
12	sociology of translation	5	ethics
12	interdisciplinarity	5	model
11	translation strategy	5	student
11	paratext	5	hybridity
11	translation universal	5	quality
10	cultural translation	5	higher education
10	methodology	5	children's literature
10	globalization	5	doctoral training
10	competence	5	bible translation
10	legal translation	5	parallel corpora
10	spanish	4	interpretation
10	pragmatics	4	interpreting study
10	terminology	4	multimodality
9	identity	4	translation process
9	corpus	4	anthropology
9	adaptation	4	randomized controlled trial
9	translation teaching	4	intercultural communication
8	identification	4	bibliometrics
8	interpreting	4	machine translation
8	contrastive linguistics	4	bilingualism
8	parallel corpus	4	german
8	literature	4	sex
8	censorship	4	world literature

Introduction 5

An interesting piece of information that can be gathered from Table 0.1, the sets of keywords generated from the 4000 or so publications centering around the topic of 'translation studies', is that many language names surface as keywords identified in the field, such as Spanish, French, German and so on. This makes us wonder if translation problems are language-pair specific or if they are general at a certain level (so that they can be solved by the 'agreed general translation theory'). If we turn to the closely associated field of linguistics for inspirations, we can find two likely 'general theories' that have been used to solve problems across many languages: on the one hand, we have Chomsky's generative syntactic theory (Chomsky, 1957, 1965) dwelling on the nature and the cognitive side of language; and, on the other hand, there is Halliday's systemic functional grammar (Halliday, 1994), exploring the meaning and principles of selection in the context of its use. In translation studies, there is a tempting term called 'translation universals' which seems to forecast a likely general theory for translation. However, the idea is refuted by Chesterman (2017) among others, who said that '[the term translation universals] suggests a hypothesis which is too general' (p. 307) and that 'if you suggest that something is a universal, you seem to imply... that it is present in every single translation... and I think that is not reasonable' (p. 308). Indeed, translation studies seems to present an additional layer of complexity in comparison with linguistics when seeking a universal theory because translation involves the presentation of the same message in two languages, whereas linguistic studies compares the same grammatical notion across different languages. Chomsky's universal grammar (see e.g. White, 2003), for example, proposed a principle (applicable to all languages) and parameter (varies among languages) approach. Although we can easily find 'parameters' in translating (e.g. the treatment of passive sentences during translation for different language pairs), it will be harder to identify any 'principles' which can apply to all language pairs when translating. In addition, Chomsky's universal grammar is mostly 'innate' (see e.g. Pinker, 1994), whereas translating is a much more calculated and sophisticated activity. Something like universal grammar would never have existed in translation. Due to the heterogeneous nature of translating, the investigation of translation behaviors and norms between different language pairs is important for translation studies in order to find the closest match to an 'agreed general theory'.

In their memoriam of Gideon Toury, Delabastita et al. (2017) stated:

> During a period of some thirty-five years Toury showed an unwavering commitment to his main project of working out James Holmes's 'map' as an academic programme for translation studies.
>
> (p. 3)

If Descriptive translation studies are of the utmost concern for Toury, then Holmes's map for translation studies, which Toury so endlessly pursued, must be an idealized form of research results for the discipline. In Holmes's (1975) model of translation studies, two broad fields of enquires were distinguished: 'pure' translation studies, including Descriptive translation studies and Theoretical

6 *Introduction*

translation studies, and 'applied' translation studies, including translator training, translation aid, translation policy, and translation criticism. Under the title of 'pure' translation studies, some subfields were further identified such as discourse studies, textual linguistics, contrastive linguistics, psycholinguistics and sociolinguistics, machine-aided translation, cultural studies, literature, and psychology and sociology. These finer distinctions seemed to forecast the proliferation of the discipline later lamented by Chesterman (2017). Thus, there seems to be a tension between the search for an 'agreed general theory' and the fact that so many subfields sorely need to be explored for translation studies to uncover idiosyncratic norms and behaviors.

In Dong and Chen's (2015) work, geographical sources of publication in translation studies were probed, and it was found that the majority of works in their dataset were produced by American scholars, followed by English scholars. This coincides with the fact that most translation research centers around a language pair where English is mandatory. The other pair part, however, may be Spanish, German, or French as Table 0.1 above shows according to our finding. The People's Republic of China was also on the list of Dong and Chen (p. 1115), which occupied the fourth position in the number of papers produced in translation studies within the period being investigated (2000–2015), next to the USA, England, and Spain. This means Chinese translation has become or is becoming very important for translation studies and is contributing to the discovery of the multifaceted truths of a general translation theory. We now turn to an overview of Chinese translation studies including its relevance and possible contribution to a globalized general translation theory.

Research on Chinese translation

In his widely read textbook *Introducing Translation Studies Theories and Applications*, Jeremy Munday brought the importance of Chinese translation to the fore of translation studies. He said: 'Over recent years, there has been increased interest from the West in Chinese and other writing on translation and this has highlighted some important theoretical points' (p. 36). One example Munday cited from Eva Hung (2005) was the need to reconceptualize the distinction between ST (source text) and TT (target text). The object in question was the translation, or transmission, of sutra. Since the original text of sutra was mostly transmitted orally, involving more than one language, and often getting lost after the Chinese TT was produced (often as a team effort), the definition of ST (and that of TT) is really hard to obtain. Conceivably, there must be other modes of translation and other less explored thoughts and theories in Chinese translation studies, ancient or contemporary, that are worthy of exploration in the contemporary setting. The inadequacy of Eurocentrism in modern translation theory is even more clearly articulated by Shadrin (2018), who comments that 'the Eurocentric translation studies were ideally suited to the requirements of the historical development of the Western countries but can no longer be relevant to the changes occurring in the modern globalized world' (p. 937). Instead, Shadrin proposes that 'the modern theory of translation should be based on the truly international character of translation studies' (p. 942). Three aspects of this modern approach to translation are mentioned at the end of Shadrin's proposition: 'new methods of translation', 'methodological principles of the translators' preparation' and 'modern processes of linguistic and cultural interaction of all the peoples of the world' (ibid.).

Dong and Chen (2017) recorded 149 publications in translation-related journals output by researchers from the People's Republic of China between 2000 and 2015. This is not a large number in comparison to the number of similar publications in Chinese journals published in China on issues of translation. In this book, I collected 6000 papers published in China's academic journals in the period between 2000 and 2018 with their topic on 'translation' (翻译). Using CiteSpace again to analyze the corpus of bibliographic notes consisting of the title and abstract of the paper among other things, this time exported from the CNKI (China National Knowledge Infrastructure, aka China Academic Journals Full-Text Database), I obtained the keyword visualization image like that shown in Figure 0.2. Table 0.2, on the other hand, lists 100 or so keywords found by CiteSpace with the highest frequency in the bibliographic corpus extracted from the CNKI database. From the set of keywords identified by the scientometric analysis, we can identify at least nine 'concept groups' as shown in the list below (with some example keywords in Chinese characters shown in each category):

- Translation theory: 翻译理论, 动态对等, 关联理论
- Translation and culture: 文化翻译观, 茶文化, 跨文化交际
- Translation strategies: 翻译技巧, 翻译实践
- Text types: 文本类型, 外宣翻译, 佛经翻译
- Translator: 译者主体性
- Literary translation: 翻译文学, 翻译家
- Translation education: 翻译能力, 翻译过程
- Translation technology: 机器翻译, 计算机辅助翻译, 平行语料库
- The ecology of translation: 生态翻译学

By exploring the relations between these categories, we can discover their internal connections and set up a coherent system for further discussion. Furthermore, in some of the subsequent chapters, I will search the CNKI for a subset of relevant literature and focus on the keywords generated from the individual bundles of published journal papers in a reconfigured subset of the nine subfields and do a corresponding literature review. I will summarize existing findings in each area and show what the Chinese researchers are concerned about and what theories they propose to deal with perceived problems. I will consolidate the findings, foreground the existing achievements of Chinese translation research, and speculate as to their relevance and contribution to translation studies on a global scale; in particular, what implications can Chinese translation carry for the generation of an 'agreed general theory'.

8 *Introduction*

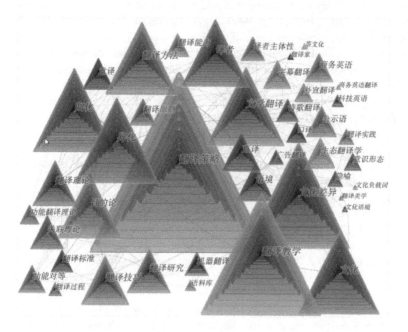

Figure 0.2 Keywords from scientometric analysis of 翻译 'translation' literature in visualization form

What is the nature of 'Chinese translation' and what can it contribute to the existing debates of translation studies? Ding (2016) conducted a fairly interesting interview with Douglas Robinson, Chair Professor of English at Hong Kong Baptist University. During that interview, Ding asked Robinson a very interesting question regarding the quest for 'a translation theory with Chinese characteristics' (中国特色的翻译学). According to Ding (p. 84), some leading scholars in Chinese translation think there is only applied translation theory and no pure translation theory in China. They think it is necessary to introduce translation theory from the West to serve as an analytical framework for Chinese translation, and incrementally test and improve on the theory in an effort to join the conversation with Western scholars and jointly build a global translation theory. Ding wanted to know Robinson's thoughts about this issue. Robinson gave a somewhat surprising and particularly enlightening answer. He said he knew nothing about 'global translation studies' and 'Chinese translation study' was a nationalistic term. According to Robinson:

> 如果你是真心热爱学习和研究，那么你只要满含热情地去研究就是了。你读甚么文献以及如何运用所读文献并不那么重要。('If you really love to learn and do research, just go on with your investigation with a lot of passion. What literature you read and how to use them is not so important.')
>
> (p. 84)

Table 0.2 100 keywords with higher frequencies from scientometric analysis of 翻译 'translation' literature in tabular format

Frequency	Keyword	Frequency	Keyword
20732	翻译 (translation)	373	影响 (influence)
3819	翻译策略 (translation strategy)	363	《红楼梦》 (Dream of the Read Mansion)
2656	翻译教学 (translation teaching)	350	广告翻译 (advertisement translation)
2312	文化差异 (cultural difference)	345	翻译过程 (translation process)
1895	异化 (foreignization)	341	特点 (characteristic)
1844	归化 (domestication)	322	科技英语 (technical English)
1820	文化 (culture)	315	原文 (source text)
1723	文学翻译 (literary translation)	315	问题 (problem)
1631	翻译方法 (translation method)	281	语料库 (corpus)
1509	译者 (translator)	273	对策 (countermeasure)
1399	目的论 (skopos theory)	271	中华人民共和国 (People's Republic of China)
1154	翻译技巧 (translation technique)	224	商标 (trade mark)
1042	翻译理论 (translation theory)	210	文化内涵 (cultural connotation)
1015	翻译研究 (translation research)	206	读者 (reader)
938	英语 (English)	204	词汇 (vocabulary)
926	直译 (literal translation)	201	理解 (comprehension)
903	语境 (context)	194	音译 (transliteration)
808	译文 (target text)	171	翻译家 (scholarly translator)
784	关联理论 (relevance theory)	159	茶文化 (tea culture)
772	策略 (strategy)	153	文化负载词 (culturally loaded word)
741	英译 (English translation)	151	翻译学 (translatology)
733	公示语 (public sign language)	150	教学模式 (teaching model)
733	意译 (semantic translation)	149	商务英语翻译 (business English translation)
705	英汉翻译 (English to Chinese translation)	148	方法 (method)
700	汉英翻译 (Chinese to English translation)	147	翻译美学 (translation aesthetics)
687	功能对等 (functional equivalence)	147	可译性 (translatability)
680	生态翻译学 (ecological translation studies)	140	文化语境 (cultural context)

(*Continued*)

Table 0.2 Continued

Frequency	Keyword	Frequency	Keyword
680	商务英语 (business English)	139	忠实 (loyalty)
649	字幕翻译 (subtitle translation)	134	主体性 (subjectivity)
637	翻译原则 (principle of translation)	134	汉语 (Chinese language)
608	机器翻译 (machine translation)	121	汉译英 (Chinese to English)
599	诗歌翻译 (poetic translation)	116	翻译思想 (translation thinking)
582	译者主体性 (subjectivity of translator)	110	技巧 (technique)
563	语言 (language)	110	原则 (principle)
547	翻译标准 (translation norm)	103	英译汉 (English to Chinese)
542	翻译能力 (translation competence)	94	商标翻译 (trademark translation)
505	习语 (idiom)	94	翻译人才 (translation talent)
496	口译 (interpreting)	89	跨文化 (intercultural)
474	差异 (variation)	84	电影片名 (movie title)
465	功能翻译理论 (functional translation theory)	78	互文性 (Intertextuality)
456	英语翻译 (English translation)	77	教学 (teaching)
437	跨文化交际 (intercultural communication)	75	英文 (English)
436	外宣翻译 (publicity translation)	74	应用 (application)
425	大学英语 (college English)	74	文化意象 (cultural imagery)
418	隐喻 (metaphor)	69	接受美学 (receptive aesthetics)
409	意识形态 (ideology)	68	翻译软件 (translation software)
402	翻译实践 (translation practice)	67	比较 (comparative)

Robinson also dismissed Ding's reference to the widely held assumption that Chinese thoughts on translation were unorthodox (偏论), dispersed (散论), built on experience alone (经验之谈), and lacking in strict reasoning and dialectical logic. According to Robinson, being systematic is not the most important quality of academic research; therefore, whether Chinese translation theories are systematic or not is really not important. Robinson held that human affairs are full of randomness, inadequacies, and overlaps. There is no such thing as a perfect systematic construction in the world of humans. We should not complain about our own imperfection, but should instead concentrate on what we actually do in trying to solve problems. Robinson's position is highly reminiscent of Pym's (2014) words after his brief review of major translation theories such as equivalence theory, skopos theory, descriptive studies, and cultural translation. Pym's advice is that 'there is no need to start in any one paradigm and certainly no need to belong to one' (p. 160). That is, researchers should develop their own translation theory by identifying a problem first and then looking for ideas that can help solve the problem, whichever 'school' they come from.

So far, we have seen two views of translation theory that seem to contradict each other. On one hand, we have Chesterman's (2017) reminder that the field of translation studies still lacks an 'agreed general theory'. Chesterman somehow thinks translation studies has run into difficulties due to inconsistent use of terms and the proliferation of subfields. On the other hand, we have Robinson's view expressed in Ding's (2016) interview that a 'systematic' translation theory is completely unnecessary, which seems to be supported by Pym's (2014) suggestion that one can still do great research in translation studies without being affiliated to any school of thought or theory. In Ding's (2016) interview, Robinson continues to observe that

> 中国拥有非常丰富的哲学文化遗产。但大多数的当代中国翻译学者都没有去探索、去研究、去利用。 (China owns extremely rich philosophical and cultural heritages. But most contemporary Chinese translation scholars have not explored, studied or made use of them.)
>
> (p. 85)

For Robinson, there is no such thing as 世界翻译学 ('world translation studies') or 中国翻译学 ('Chinese translation studies'). Presumably, he thought such a thing as an 'agreed general theory' of translation does not exist. The latter, he thought, was suggestive of nationalistic thinking, which Robinson recommended translators to rid themselves of. A compromised view advocated in this book is a modified version of Shadrin (2018), which, as we recall, says that Eurocentric translation studies are no longer relevant to the changes of the modern world, and recommends that a contemporary theory of translation ought to be based on 'the truly international character of translation studies' (p. 937). This book takes the view that the existing translation theory based on Western thinking patterns still has its merits, but it may benefit from new input from translation discourse from other languages, including Chinese. There is no harm for the field to come up with a general translation theory of some sort, but it does not have to be binding. A theory can be taken as general (such as the Big Bang theory) but it can still continue to evolve, to be modified by new research, to open up new theories, and even to be completely overthrown one day. Arriving at an 'agreed general theory' is a good goal, but exploring the nuances in translation studies by examining different language pairs and investigating the 'translational context' of each language is also a worthy enterprise. It is with this conviction that we turn next to the Chinese discourse on translation studies.

Chinese discourse on translation studies

'Chinese discourse' as described here pertains to academic papers written in Chinese and likely published in China or other Chinese regions such as Taiwan, Hong Kong, Singapore and so on. 'Chinese discourse on translation studies', on the other hand, is taken to mean academic papers written in Chinese sharing the author's research and understanding about the nature and progress of translation studies. This book distinguishes between three kinds of 'Chinese discourse on translation studies': 1. Chinese scholarly discussion on English-based translation studies; 2. Chinese scholarly discussion on classical Chinese discourse on translation; and 3. Chinese scholarly discussion on translation studies without clear reference to English or Chinese works or with an intention to combine both approaches.

The first category of Chinese discourse on translation consists of works which undertake the responsibility to introduce foreign language (mainly English)-based translation studies into China. This kind of introductory work started in the 1980s from the importation of Eugene A. Nida's linguistics-based translation theory (e.g. Qiu, 1984), and then closely shadowed the development of translation studies in the West in a remarkable effort to update the research agenda of Chinese translation studies at the home ground. For example, at the turn of the century, Sun and Zheng (2000) introduced the 'cultural shift' movement of translation studies in the West, following the thoughts of Western scholars like Lambert and Robyns to promote the idea that translation is a communication between cultures rather than simply a transfer of text between languages. Jiang (2002), at about the same time, introduced the skopos theory and mentioned well-known names like Vermeer and Nord. Jiang took the theory as a shift of focus from ST to TT including an emphasis on the function of the translation and a reinterpretation of translation policy. Thereafter, the translator's knowledge and professional ethics became more important in the process of translation. More recently, Li (2007) introduced Pierre Bourdieu's sociological concepts and the application of his theoretical model to translation studies. Li suggested, for example, that the Chinese translation of sutra could be treated as a 'field' in Bourdieu's terms, and the translated sutra as 'cultural capital'.

Another type of discourse in this strand is offering a historical account of the (usually modern) development of translation studies in the West, concentrating on certain iconic figures or representative schools of thoughts across the board. Tan (2005), for example, summarizes the development and prospects of Western translation theory since World War II, presenting the review and analysis of mainstream thinking on translation in the hope of stimulating further investigation and consideration of translation studies in the West. Citing Xie (2003), Tan summarizes three developmental stages of Western translation theory: the first stage started from the 1950s when Western translation studies concentrated on the technical problems of transfer in translation, exploring the issue of equivalence phonetic, syntactic, and semantic angles. The second stage saw translation research moving beyond the act of translating itself, into the problems of the commission and patronage of translation, the translator and the readership. At the third stage, researchers refocused their attentions on other disciplines beyond translation studies, that is, 'to examine translation in an expanded cultural context' (把翻译放到一个宏大的文化语境中去审视) (Tan, 2005, p. 58). Wang (2017) offers another meta-analysis on the history of Western discourse on translation research from 1964 to 2014. Some important figures or 'big names' in translation studies are mentioned in Wang's work; for example, Holmes, for setting up the analytical framework for translation studies; Even-Zohar, for pioneering the Polysystem theory; Toury and his Descriptive translation studies and so on. Referring to Pym (1998), Wang reminds the reader that studying the history of translation can help promote our understanding of the literary history, ideational history and cultural history of a nation, especially how the development of that nation has been influenced by external forces. Knowing this can in turn provide resources and food for thought to the study of international relations.

More recently, in addition to the introduction of mainstream Western translation theory, some Chinese authors also draw on research findings from less represented countries. Chen (2004), for example, introduced the research method of Canadian translation studies, showing how an analytical framework for translation problems can surpass linguistic concerns and go deeper into the fields of gender studies and ideology research, manifesting the full potential of postcolonial translation research and showing how theory and practice can be successfully combined. Other authors dedicate their writings to the introduction of Western classic translation figures or theories. Liu (2016), for example, is set on a course to reconceptualize Marcus Tullius Cicero's contribution to Western translation theory by reexamining the historical contexts of his life and work. According to Liu, Cicero was the creator of the division between literal translation and liberal translation, and the precursor of free translation (based on meaning rather than form). In Liu's eyes, Cicero's identity as a great public speaker is closely connected to his defense of self-expression. Liu argues quite eloquently about how Cicero transcended the meaning of translation:

> 将自己的身份和声音加于译文之中，希望通过翻译重塑希腊文学，形成拉丁语的新范本，并最终取代希腊源本，超越希腊成就。([He] added his own identity and voice into the target text, hoping to recondition Greek literature through translation, thereby forming a new template for Latin and eventually replacing the Greek original, surpassing its achievements.)
>
> (p. 27)

Understandably, the first kind of Chinese discourse on translation as categorized here (that purely introducing imported translation theory from the West) necessarily followed a trajectory of a downward sloping curve as researchers became familiar with Western translation studies. As more and more translation theories were imported into Chinese regions, Chinese thinkers and researchers began to ponder 'what we have' against the background of what had been imported, for example, Martha Cheung's two volumes of 'Anthology of Chinese Discourse on Translation' (Cheung, 2006, 2017), although this book will include only the more contemporary discussions on Chinese translation. Thus, the second category of Chinese discourse on translation is the reverse of the first category, in which Chinese translation scholars are eager to justify the Chinese approach, drawing mostly from Chinese literature and philosophical studies in China's long history. Pan (2012) is a typical example in question where the author strongly and passionately argues for China's 'right of discourse' in the global arena of translation studies. According to Pan, Chinese scholars' 'right of discourse' had been lost due to an excessive degree of Westernization in Chinese translation research for the past 100 years. In Pan's reasoning, the terminology, system and theory used in a discipline can be collectively called 'discourse'. As long as a discourse is accepted by other researchers in the field, the body of theory advocated by that discourse will have been established. When the discourse continues to develop up to a certain stage, it becomes mandatory for other researchers in the field to use the same discourse for discussion. It is at such a point that the discourse creator achieves the 'right of discourse' within the discipline. Therefore, to establish 'translation studies with Chinese characteristics' is to gain the right of discourse for Chinese translation theory (建设"中国特色翻译学"，说到底，就是要取得中国译学的话语权) according to Pan (p. 3). As to how this discourse can be generated for Chinese translation studies, Pan thinks it would be 'abnormal' if such a big country having 2000 years of translation history with an enormous amount of translation jobs done cannot make its own voice heard. He thinks that all the elements of Chinese history, Chinese culture, and the accumulated studies on Chinese discourse and culture will certainly be reflected in Chinese translation theory and generate a different discourse from the translation theory produced in other contexts. Pan especially emphasized the importance of 'theory of letters composition' (文章学, translation copied from the English abstract of Pan's Chinese paper). He thinks this is fundamentally important for establishing Chinese discourse on translation, and explains alongside Yan Fu's famous criteria of 信 (faithfulness), 达 (expressiveness), 雅 (elegance) for translation. According to Pan, the first element of 'theory of letters composition' is the status of the composition and the public's attitudes about the composition (文章的地位和对文章的态度) (p. 6). Because of the heightened status of composition in Chinese history (here Pan quoted a sentence from the Chinese emperor Wei Wendi, who praised the superior status of composition in Chinese society), Yan Fu's criterion of 'faithfulness' raised the status of translation studies to that of composition, in Pan's reasoning. Again, according to Pan (2012), the second element of 'theory of letters composition' is 'the thought or content must be fully expressed' (思想或内容必须得到充分的表达) (ibid.), which corresponds to Yan Fu's second, 'expressiveness' criterion, including the entire process of understanding the ST and rendering the TT. Finally, Pan's third element of 'theory of letters composition' is the 'colorfulness' of composition (文采) which is a rather 'Chinese style' requirement and corresponds to Yan Fu's third criterion, 'elegance', for translation. Finally, Pan summarized his interesting article by claiming that the development of Western translation theory in the past few decades, including the linguistics-oriented theory in the 1960s and 1970s; the cultural turn in the seventies and eighties; the topics of translator's subjectivity in the 1990s and the recent focus on translation process and policy, can all be subsumed under the criterion of 'expressiveness'. So far, there is no dedicated discussion on 'faithfulness' and 'elegance' in the West as explicated in Pan's essay. Pan thinks this is where traditional Chinese translation theory can compensate for the inadequacy of Western translation studies.

Hu (1998) was another example which anchored translation research to the long history of China, where the first translation activities can be traced as far back as the Zhou Dynasty (1046–256 BCE). Hu claimed to have found five characteristics of Chinese translation theory after 2000 years research of translation theory.

1. Translation theory is rooted in the soil of national culture and continues to grow there.
2. Many translation theorists in the past did not know any foreign language.
3. All translation theorists had a strong sense of mission towards the home country.
4. Translator training occupies a significant place in the study of translation theory.
5. Current translation theory is heading toward the direction of multidimensional research.

Drawing from Chen (1992), Hu distinguished between two large categories of translation research: the internal research (内篇 or 内部研究), and the external research (外篇 or 外部研究). The internal problems include 'core contents' of translation studies, such as the basic theoretical models for translation; the essence, principles, norms and thinking patterns of translation; translatability; translation methods; translation process; the aesthetics of translation; the arts, styles and techniques of translating and so on. The external problems concern the relationship between translation and the external world, for example, the position of translation studies within the network of interrelated disciplines (e.g. philosophy, sociology, cultural studies, linguistics, psychology), translation teaching, translation criticism and construction, team building of translator groups, the self-cultivation of translation (翻译工作者修养问题), the compilation of translation tool books and teaching materials and so on. Despite the obvious similarities and overlaps between Chen's (1992) model of translation research and a Western model such as Holmes (1975), Hu (1998) still believed this is a unique Chinese translation research approach and will continue to update itself with the progress of science and technology and the advance of society, 'leading to the establishment of a full system of translation theory for our country' (进而建立我国完整的翻译理论体系) (p. 6).

Jia (2017) represents the work of another vehement advocator of 'translation theory with Chinese characteristics'. What stands out in Jia's work is his condemnation, following Pan (2016), of the common method seen in Chinese universities of applying Western translation theory to the study of translation problems as 'pseudo scholarship' (伪学术) and 'malignant Westernization' (恶性西化). Jia suggests that any importation of advanced concept and cutting-edge technology must go through four stages of '引进 (introduction) →消化 (digestion) →模仿 (imitation) →创新 (innovation)' (p. 4). Chinese translation research, according to Jia, has undergone the stages of introduction and digestion. Now it enters the stages of imitation and creation. In particular, Jia claims that research publications in the rubric of applied translation theory in the West are very scarce. In contrast, battalions of researchers led by Fang Mengzhi (方梦之) in the area of applied translation theory have produced formidable results. According to Jia (2017), this could well be the entry point for Chinese translation studies into the world arena, creating a discourse of Chinese applied translation theory.

Amid these forceful voices calling out for the creation and dissemination of Chinese discourse on translation in the world, there is another kind of quieter voice that has no obvious intention of competing with the foreign discourse on translation studies. This kind of voice seems to focus solely on rejuvenating older Chinese discourse on translation held by certain historical figures or schools, hoping to bring out their contemporary relevance so they can serve as guidelines for future directions. Shi (2017) is a typical example in this strand, which is completely devoted to the explication of the ideas of a late Qing dynasty scholar, Kang Youwei (康有为, 1858–1927), on translation. According to Shi, Kang's thoughts on translation started from cultural nationalism (文化民族主义) and concluded at the state of cultural cosmopolitanism (文化世界主义). Shi suggested that Kang's thinking incorporated the philosophy of Confucianism and Buddhism and came about at a time when the country was extremely weak. Kang took it as his own responsibility to learn from the West and strengthen the nation, making the country prosperous and long-lasting. That is, In Shi's words,

> 以译启民智，以译觉乱世，以译救亡国，以译臻大同，康子翻译思想之文化民族主义与文化世界主义意蕴昭昭明甚矣。(Using translation to open people's mind, using translation to awaken the chaotic society, using translation to save the weakening nation, using translation to achieve world peace, Kang Youwei's thoughts on translation clearly carry the meaning of cultural nationalism and cultural cosmopolitanism.)
>
> (p. 68)

Another remarkable effort aimed at developing cogent argument to rejuvenate ancient Chinese thoughts on translation and invigorate modern translation studies is given by Wang (2016), who offered a very interesting and well-researched account on the meaning of 翻译 ('translate', or literally 'turn over' and 'interpret') in Chinese translation history. According to Wang, Chinese historical thinkers on translation first used the word 译 ('interpret') only to refer to the act of translating, which basically meant a straightforward literal translation (or transliteration) method, or in Wang's words, a 'parallel replacement' (平行性替换) phenomenon (p. 144). It was not until much later when translation scholars encountered the difficulty of 'losing the basis' (失本), or finding the impossibility of the literal translation method in the face of new source texts, that the word 翻 ('turn over') began to be used. Wang suggested that Dao'an (道安 312–385, a Buddhist monk and translation scholar) proposed the term 'losing basis' because he saw that the differences in language and culture could not be overcome by the highly limited translation method of 译 ('interpret'), which essentially used 'oral transfer' and 'transliteration' to do a two-dimensional, parallel transfer. Therefore, another Buddhist monk Sengyou (僧祐 445–518) later proposed the term 翻转 ('turn and flip') to explain a new type of translation strategy. This gradually evolved into the modern usage when yet another Buddhist monk Huijiao (慧皎 497–554) started to use the word 翻译 ('translate'). The change of the term means the act of translating was no longer a simple transfer or interpretation on the basis of the original sutra, but to do a large scale 'turn and flip' (大幅度的"翻转") after a thorough understanding of the original meaning of the ST. Since then, translation began to be seen as a 'three-dimensional' turning and flipping activity as opposed to the previous 'transfer' (传) and 'interpreting' (译) activities. As a result, the term 翻经 ('translating sutra') is more often used at a time than 译经 ('interpreting sutra'). In a nutshell, based on Wang's (2016) understanding,

> "译"本来是一个平面的移动，而"翻"是一个将正面翻为背面的立体的"翻转"后的结果。… 如照镜子的人与镜子里照出来的人… 在这样的状态里，译文与原文应是既相反相成、又若合符契的关系。('Interpreting' is essentially a two-dimensional movement; 'translating' is a stereoscopic act to flip the upside to the downside, just like creating a mirror image. In such a condition, the TT and the ST are opposite and complementary to each other, fulfilling a contract together.)
>
> (p. 148)

Therefore, if there is a large discrepancy existing between two languages, which prevents the ST from moving smoothly to TT in a parallel fashion, the translation method of 'turn and flip' must be applied to make large scale, three-dimensional changes. This means to 'stand firmly in the translator's own language and culture and make creative interpretation of the ST' (p. 149, my translation). On the basis of the above historical account and his understanding of the issue of 'translatability', Wang (2016) proposed that the translation activities conducted within the European countries mostly occur within the same language family, which can be accounted for by the parallel movement theory of 译 ('interpreting'). The translation activities in ancient China, on the other hand, involved the exchange between two dramatically different languages like Sanskrit and Chinese, which had to be dealt with by the 翻转 ('turn and flip') strategy. Therefore, in Wang's reasoning, the Chinese concept of translating and the Chinese recognition of translation activities are much more comprehensive and profound than those of the West. In particular, when dealing with the 'untranslatability' problem in modern translation studies, Wang thinks the traditional Chinese thoughts on the distinction between "译" and "翻" are better placed than Western translation theory to solve the problem. According to Wang, the modern translation problem of 'untranslatability' is mostly associated with the literary domain, especially when translating the 'voices', genre, rhetoric, and style of poetic works. However, Wang thinks the problem is entirely caused by the failure of a translation theory to distinguish between "译" and "翻", or to realize that although some ST cannot be "译" ('interpret' using parallel movement method) it can still be "翻" ('turn and flip' using three-dimensional method). In other words, the problem of untranslatability is caused entirely by the absence of the concept of "翻". As the most difficult text type to be translated, poetic works certainly cannot be dealt with using the simple parallel movement method of 译 ('interpret') but must be accounted for by the much more complicated method of 翻转 ('turn and flip'). This kind of translation method creates fuzzy artistic impressions among the precise control of turning and flipping, fully realizing the translator's potential to regenerate and recreate. Wang (2016) gave a rather cogent conclusion at the end of his essay as follows:

> 在现代翻译的语境下，中国古代的"译"与"翻"的思想及"译"、"翻"之辨，仍具有不灭的生命力和重要的理论价值，不仅可以为我们重构中国特色的翻译学、翻译理论提供出发点，而且也可以将"可译／不可译"这一持续多年的聚讼纷纭的争论画上句号。(In modern translation context, the ancient Chinese thoughts and debate of interpreting' and 'flipping' is still full of vitality and theoretical value. This can not only serve as the basis for our reconstruction of translation studies and theory with Chinese characteristics, it can also put an end to the long lasting dispute of translatability and untranslatability.)
>
> (p. 156)

A final strand of research involving both Chinese and Western translation approaches we will discuss here centers around the concept and practice of 'retranslation'. As explained in Gu (2003, p. 37), 'retranslation' means to translate a work for a second time or for many times on the basis of previous translation(s). Chen (2014) explained why it is necessary for a literary work to be retranslated time and again in human history: 1. Words do not have fixed meanings throughout history; 2. Each translator has their unique subjectivity; 3. Readers are different across different nations and history; 4. Languages change. Gu (2003) proposed a theory which he called 'filtered translational accumulation theory for retranslation' (筛选积淀重译论) as a viable approach to solve the problem of retranslation. The basic tenet of Gu's theory is that the development of human culture and its expansion are intimately related to plagiarism in large quantities. Innovation is made possible only with copying and imitation working at the background. As regards translation, Gu thinks that every translation (of a great literary work) is the result of wisdom and efforts of the previous translator, consisting of not only the translator's understanding and interpretation of the original work, but also their own wisdom and skills. It is unreasonable for new translators of the same work to start from scratch without drawing from all the wisdom and techniques embedded in the previous translations. Thus, Gu defines his 'filtered translational accumulation theory' for retranslation as follows:

> 所谓筛选积淀重译论,指的是在合理利用一切已经产生的译本的基础上,去粗取精,并注入新的更好的表达法,最终合成翻译出最佳度近似于原作的译作。(By 'filtered translational accumulation for retranslation' I mean making reasonable use of all existing translations, keeping the good part and getting rid of the bad portion, while injecting new and better expressions and eventually producing the best translation that is closest to the original work.)
>
> (p. 37)

The filtering process in Gu's theory has two layers of meaning: 1. To extract good examples from previous translations (good sentences, good styles or good handling techniques); 2. To filter through all previous works and find those worth retranslating. In terms of the advantages of the 'filtering and accumulating' process for retranslation, Gu offered five points in question: 1. The achievements of the previous translator(s) are duly honored in this way; 2. The strong points of the existing translation(s) are put to good use; 3. New translations of old works are guaranteed to be upgraded versions (preventing the production of wrong translation, poor translation, lesser translation and so on); 4. A great deal of new translator's pointless labors are saved; 5. Successive translators are given legitimate opportunities to demonstrate their abilities. Gu (2003) went on to challenge the Western law of protecting individual (intellectual) properties at the expense of collective benefits. To Gu, excessive emphasis on the protection of the first translation of a work will prevent the translation from being incrementally improved. For Gu, the Chinese traditional emphasis of learning from the historical saints and the collective wisdom of the forefathers is the correct approach in dealing with the problem of retranslation, a theory he termed 'cultural recreation on filtered cultural accumulation' (人类文化积淀重创). Gu's retranslation theory was later recommended by Gao (2016, p. 100) for creating a new discourse outside the highly limited system of the 'hypothesis-testing' pattern in the Western approach to the problem of retranslation.

The third category of Chinese discourse on translation as defined here refers to works that focus on translation problems per se without distinguishing between Chinese and Western approaches, or works that clearly advocate a synergy between the two approaches. A notable example of the contemporary effort to build a translation theory without referring specifically to a Western or Chinese traditional approach is the 'translation variation' theory (变译论) developed by Huang Zhonglian (黄忠廉). The main tenet of Huang's 'translation variation' theory centers around the 12 variation methods that can be applied to translating various text types. These are stipulated in Huang and Li (2014), for example, as 摘译 (selected translation), 编译 (edited translation), 译述 (narrated translation),

缩译 (condensed translation), 综述 (summarized translation), 述评 (summarized translation plus comment), 译评 (translation plus comment), 译写 (translation plus writing), 阐译 (translation plus explanation), 改译 (translation plus rewriting), 参译 (translation plus quotation), 仿作 (translation plus imitation) (Huang & Li's translation, p. 88). The 12 translation methods are arranged in Huang and Li (2014) on an ST–TT continuum with 'selected translation' closest to the ST and 'translation plus imitation' the most distant from ST and closest to the TT. This is of course reminiscent of Newmark's (1988) diagram of his eight translation methods (word for word translation, literal translation, faithful translation, semantic translation, communicative translation, idiomatic translation, free translation, adaptation), which were also depicted to be on a SL (source language) emphasis to TL (target language) emphasis continuum (Newmark p. 45). Huang and Li's (2014) however, put more emphasis on the concept and measure of 'variation'. They promoted the theory as 'a new category of translation studies' (变译是翻译的新子范畴) (p. 88, the authors' own English translation in Abstract). Therefore, the variation methods presumably occur only when 'normal translation methods' fail to apply. According to Jia and Jia (2018), Huang's translation variation theory is very similar to Lefevere's rewriting theory and they overlap in some translation methods proposed. Both 'translation variation' and 'rewriting' theories, in Jia and Jia's analysis, adopt the techniques of commenting, selecting, editing and so on, and both can be subsumed under the rubric of 'manipulation theory'. Jia and Jia think, however, that the 'rewriting' theory is better grounded in theoretical underpinning as it resorts to ideology, poetics, and patronage as the manipulating factors. Huang's variation theory, on the other hand, seems to stay at the technical level without substantial theoretical explanation, according to Jia and Jia (p. 9). As an 'indigenous' translation theory, however, Jia and Jia think the translation variation theory is highly promising and is capable of creating a Chinese discourse on translation in international forums. They encourage Huang and colleagues to develop it into an applied translation theory and produce "变译论" 2.0 新版 ('the 2.0 version of translation variation theory'), ultimately upgrading "变译论" ('variation translation theory') to "变译学" ('variation translation school') (Jia & Jia, 2018, p. 12).

Most of the Chinese publications that discuss translation seriously nowadays, however, are aware of the Western influences to a certain extent and either adopt the imported research methodology entirely (the first category) or propose that a process of integration be initiated between Western and Chinese translation theories. Chang (2000) made a clear distinction between 'pure translation studies' and 'applied translation studies' and claimed that Chinese translation studies belongs to the latter category; i.e. Chinese translation theory is 'applied' in nature. Chang thought that applied translation studies cannot be well developed and can even go astray without the guidance of pure translation theory (p. 4). He offered a somewhat harsh criticism on the Chinese style of translation research:

> 中国的翻译研究，往往只是进行文本比较,以原文为根据来评价译文；再加上忽视或回避意识形态以及其他社会文化因素，缺乏历史眼光，充分暴露了没有纯理论指导的应用研究的局限性。(Chinese translation studies

often carries out comparative text analysis, using the source text to judge target text. In addition, the problems of ideology and other social cultural factors are often ignored or avoided. There is a lack of historical insights, fully exposing the limitation of applied research without the guidance of pure theory.)

(p. 5)

Ideologically speaking, Chang thought that some Chinese scholars rejected Western translation theory on the grounds that the Chinese culture had a long history. There was an extremely rich collection of translation research publications and a long-established tradition. These incurred a strong sense of national pride and restricted the further development of Chinese translation studies. In other words, the distinguished tradition of Chinese translation studies became a stumbling block to the modernization of the research. At the time of Chang (2000), the author considered the then current Chinese translation studies as having lagged behind Western translation research for at least 20 years. The only solution to the problem as seen by Chang was to understand, study, import and learn from Western translation theory, especially the pure theories. Chang concluded the mission of Chinese translation studies as follows:

> 我们不单要向外国介绍中国的翻译现象，还要研究世界各国翻译现象，不单要向外国批评他们的翻译理论，还要向外国介绍经我们改良、发展的外国理论或者由我们自创的理论。(Not only should we introduce the phenomena of Chinese translation abroad, we should also study the phenomena of foreign translations. Not only should we criticize foreign translation theory, we must also introduce the foreign theory that have been improved on and developed by us, or the translation theory created by ourselves.)

(p. 6)

While Chang (2000) explicitly advocated the import of Western translation studies to compensate for the inadequacy of Chinese translation research, Wang and Wang (2004) pointed out a more specific direction where Western and Chinese translation studies can work on a cooperative basis and achieve a much more enhanced translation theory. According to them, the recent trend of translation studies often stops at the declaration of a dichotomy, for example, foreignization or domestication, communicative or semantic translation. Because of a lack of study in the 'middle layer' (that is, making finer distinctions between the two ends of the spectrum), translation theory often fails to explain the function of some micro-techniques in translating, thereby detaching the theory from the practice. A good example is the translation of a Chinese saying 巧妇难为无米之炊, which can be translated into the following three English sentences, among many other possibilities:

1. Even a clever housewife can't cook a meal without rice.
2. One can't make brick without straw.
3. Even a clever housewife can't make bread without flour.

Wang and Wang explained that translation 1 is clearly an example of 'foreignization'. Translation 2 is, on the other hand, a good example of 'domestication'. However, what causes the problem is translation 3, which is also the result of the application of the domestication strategy. However, there is no current translation theory to explain the difference between 2 and 3. That is, according to Wang and Wang, the theory of foreignization and domestication fails to distinguish between translations 2 and 3 on the theoretical level. As a translation theory, the foreignization–domestication distinction is not precise enough and is weak in explanatory capacity. To solve the problem, Wang and Wang pointed out that Chinese translation studies worked well at the applied translation level, and proposed that we should 'organically combine' the Western translation theory and the Chinese micro techniques analysis to break the restriction of dichotomies such as 'foreignization and domestication' and build a translation theory on the basis of systematic continuity. In short,

> 这种宏观微观相结合的研究方法既有利于依托传统翻译技巧来进行细化研究，又有利于依托宏观译论来解释某种微观技巧的启动机制。(This kind of research methodology combines macro perspectives with micro techniques. On one hand, it relies on traditional translation skills to make finer distinctions; on the other hand, it uses a macro perspective to explain the activation of micro techniques.)
>
> (Wang & Wang, 2004, p. 73)

If Wang and Wang (2004) showed a way to combine Western and Chinese translation studies, Lan (2018) seems to provide clearer guidelines and open up more possibilities for integrating the two approaches. In Lan's relatively comprehensive plan for the further development of Chinese translation studies, four future directions are pointed out:

1. 重视学科功能 (to lay more emphasis on the study of disciplinary functions)
2. 拓展理论资源 (to seek out more theoretical resources for translation studies)
3. 革新本体观念 ('to continue reconceptualizing the nature of the discipline')
4. 强化学派意识 (to promote the diversity of scholarly approaches to translation studies)

The first of Lan's (2018) four proposed future directions comes from the fact that translation studies has become an independent discipline in Chinese communities in the past three decades. Lan thinks that the translation theory systems constructed by Holmes in the West and Tan Zaixi in China are rich in explaining what translation studies consists of. What the field needs to do in the future is to enrich the contents of the subject (丰富学科的内涵) and fulfill the social functions of the discipline (发挥翻译学的社会功能). That is, according to Lan, we should 'take the development needs of the country and society as tenets and background for developing the discipline, building service oriented translation theory to serve the nation and other disciplines' (p. 13, my translation). Lan's second direction for the future development of Chinese translation studies focuses on the expansion of resources for the development of translation theory. In this strand, a relatively clear system of methodology for reorganizing the resources of traditional Chinese translation studies is proposed:

1. 从传统译论中汲取思想，用现代理论话语重释原来的理论 (drawing ideas from traditional translation theory, using modern theoretical discourse to reinterpret the original theory);
2. 对传统译论进行类别划分，使之对应不同类别和不同层次的翻译基本问题，整合同类、补充缺项，建构原本隐含的体系 (reclassify traditional discussions on translation theory, allocating them to different categories in different dimensions of basic translation problems; consolidating similar categories, adding in missing items and establishing an explicit system out of the original opaque one);
3. 在传统译论基础上拓展，使之边界延伸向新的领域，扩大其解释范围 (making expansions on the basis of traditional translation theory, pushing the boundary towards the new frontier, augmenting the range of problems that can be explained);
4. 寻求某种框架将传统译论和现代译论融合在一起，以产生新的理论，解释新的翻译现实。(seeking an encompassing analytical framework to integrate traditional and modern translation approaches to generate new theory and explain new translation realities)

(p. 14)

Thus, in Lan's design, as a result of emphasizing traditional translation theory, a new life of translation studies is born in the modern linguistic contexts. Next, Lan (2018) continues to explicate the third direction he proposes for future Chinese translation – reconceptualizing the nature of the discipline. In this regard, Lan refers to Fan's (2006) proposal of a 'one core three peripherals' theory (一体三环论) where the linguistics studies of translation, the interdisciplinary approach and the cultural translation theory are recognized as three supporting elements for the core theory of translation studies. Lan thinks that, importantly, the nature of translation studies constantly evolves as a function of people's conceptualization of translation activities and the development of the discipline. In addition, being interdisciplinary is the most important trait of translation studies. Lan explicitly warns against the nature and enquiry of translation studies being fixed as a frozen system by overly conservative research attitudes. Finally, in his future plan for Chinese translation studies, Lan makes a somewhat surprising proposal He thinks that, in order to explore the branches of translation theory in a highly efficient manner, we need to reinforce the ideology of 'school of thought' (强化学派意识) (p. 15). Lan highly recommends a clear recognition of targeted research areas, further exploration of new research methodology, and the establishment of stable research teams.

We have seen the surprisingly rich discourse from Chinese translation researchers in the past few decades. We have witnessed three strands of Chinese discourse on translation. First, Chinese translation thinkers and researchers are eager to introduce Western thought into the field of Chinese translation studies. Then a second strand of translation research continues to emphasize the importance of traditional Chinese discourse and update its modern meanings and significance. Finally, a third group of Chinese translation scholars concentrates on absorbing both the theoretical thinking on translation in the West and the applied research activities in Chinese translation to produce an ideal translation theory that is at the same time suitable for global studies of translation as well as giving Chinese discourse a rightful place in the world.

Contents of the book

We explore the philosophical foundation of Chinese translation theory in Chapter 1, including how the views of Confucianism, Daoism and Buddhism explicitly or implicitly asserted their influence on Chinese translation. Chapter 1 also offers some initial discussion regarding the introduction of Western translation theory into China, the reception and the debates regarding the current state and the future direction of Chinese translation theory. Chapter 2 introduces various translation theories now prevalent in the Chinese discourses on translation, including the equivalence theory, systemic functional linguistics, functionalist approaches to translation, postcolonial translation theory, deconstructionism, feminism, and relevance theory. Viewed in this light, Chinese translation studies clearly shows the transition from linguistics-based theory to the various cultural approaches brought about by the 'cultural turn' in Western translation studies. In Chapter 3, we scrutinize the history of Chinese translation by remembering its major translation activities during different historical periods such as Buddhist scripture translation, the translation of Chinese classics into ethnic minority languages, and the introduction of Western literature and science into China via translation. Crucially, we also examine a few representative figures in the Chinese history of translating, such as Xuan Zang (玄奘), Yan Fu (严复) and Lu Xun (鲁迅) covering both the characteristics of their works and their views on translation. Chapter 4 turns to explore the relationship between Chinese culture and translation. It discusses the usual problems in translation generated by cultural differences and misconceptions. It also analyses the problems and opportunities involved in the 'Chinese culture going out' initiative. Finally, the chapter illustrates the problems and likely or intermediate solutions in translating a prominent component of Chinese culture – the traditional Chinese medicine – in a very detailed and informative way. Chapter 5 deals with the important genre of literary translation by first looking at the translation of Western literature into China and the ideological issues involved, and then offering a substantial analysis of the translation of a Chinese classic novel Hong Long Meng (*Dream of the Red Mansion*) into foreign languages, and the theoretical discussions surrounding these translation activities. In Chapter 6, we investigate the status quo of Chinese research on the teaching of translation, and explore the concept and theory of translation competence. We boil down to a discussion on Chinese translation programs, curricula, and teaching methods, and conclude with a fresh look at language and translation technology in the 21st century with advanced technology like neural network MT, cloud computing, crowdsourcing translation, and so on. Finally, we conclude the book in Chapter 7.

References

Chinese references

Chang, Nam Fung 张南峰 (2000) 特性与共性—论中国翻译学与翻译学的关系 (Particularity and universality: on the relationship between Chinese translation studies and translation studies). 中国翻译 (*Chinese Translation Journal*). 2000(02): 2–7.

Chen, Dongcheng 陈东成 (2014) 复译原因的大易阐释 (A study of the reasons for retranslation from the perspective of the Great Yi). 广州大学学报(社会科学版) (*Journal of Guangzhou University (Social Science Edition)*). 13(4): 59–63.

Chen, Fukang 陈福康 (1992) 中国译学理论史稿 (*A History of Chinese Translation Theory*). 上海:上海外语教育出版社 (Shanghai: Shanghai Foreign Language Education Press).

Chen, Lin 陈琳 (2004) 近十年加拿大翻译理论研究评介 (A critical introduction to Canadian research on translation studies in the past decade). 中国翻译 (*Chinese Translators Journal*). 25(2): 68–71.

Ding, Zhenqin 丁振琴 (2016) 一位西方学者眼中的中国翻译学 (The Chinese translation studies in the eyes of a Western scholar). 中国翻译 (*Chinese Translation Journal*). 2016(03): 83–86.

Fang, Mengzhi 方梦之 (2006) 译学的"一体三环"—从编纂《译学辞典》谈译学体系 (The 'one body three circles' translation theory – on the system of translation studies from the compilation of 'A Dictionary for translation studies'). 上海翻译 (*Shanghai Journal of Translators*). 2006(01): 1–6.

Gao, Cun 高存 (2016) 国内重译理论研究评述 (A review of studies of retranslation theories in China). 外国语 (*Journal of Foreign Languages*). 39(4): 94–103.

Gu, Zhengkun 辜正坤 (2003) 筛选积淀重译论与人类文化积淀创译 (The filtered translational accumulation theory and the cultural recreation theory on filtered cultural accumulation of mankind). 外语与外语教学 (*Foreign Languages and Their Teaching*). 176: 36–40.

Hu, Dexiang 胡德香 (1998) 论中国翻译理论研究特色 (On the characteristics of Chinese translation theory). 中国翻译 (*Chinese Translation Journal*). 1998(04): 2–6.

Huang, Zhonglian & Li, Mingda 黄忠廉，李明达 (2014) 变译方法对比研究 (A comparative study on translation methods in translation variation). 外语学刊 (*Foreign Language Research*). 2014(06): 88–91.

Jia, Wenbo 贾文波 (2017) 我国译学研究呼唤自己的创新型"子曰"说 (The Chinese translation studies calls for its own creative notions). 上海翻译 (*Shanghai Journal of Translators*). 2017(01): 2–7.

Jia, Yicun and Jia, Wenbo 贾一村，贾文波 (2018) "变译论"立名、立论：回归本源、兼收并蓄 (Establishing the name and foundation for the theory of translation variation). 民族翻译 (*Minority Translators Journal*). 2018(02): 7–12.

Jiang, Haiqing 姜海清 (2002) 浅谈翻译目的论 (On Skopos theory in translation). 盐城师范学院学报(人文社会科学版) (*Journal of Yancheng Teachers College (Humanities & Social Sciences)*). 22(3): 87–89.

Lan, Hongjun 蓝红军 (2018) 从学科自觉到理论建构：中国译学理论研究（1987–2017）(Theoretically oriented translation studies in China: 1987–2017). 中国翻译 (*Chinese Translation Journal*). 2018(01): 7–16.

Li, Hongman 李红满 (2007) 布迪厄与翻译社会学的理论建构 (Bourdieu and the theoretical construct of the sociology of translation). 中国翻译 (*Chinese Translators Journal*). 2007(05): 6–9.

Liu, Fang 刘芳 (2016) 西塞罗翻译思想的历史语境重读 (Rereading the historical context of Cicero's translation thoughts). 中国翻译 (*Chinese Translators Journal*). 2016(02): 22–28.

Pan, Wenguo 潘文国 (2012) 中国译论与中国话语 (Translation theory and discourse of China). 外语教学理论与实践 (*Foreign Language Learning Theory and Practice*). 2012(01): 1–7.

Pan, Wenguo 潘文国 (2016) 大变局下的语言与翻译研究 (The study of language and translation following the big change). 外语界 (*Foreign Language World*). 2016(01): 6–11.

Qiu, Maoru 邱懋如 (1984) 翻译的过程——尤金·奈达的翻译理论简介 (Translation process: a brief introduction to Eugene Nida's translation theory). 外国语 (*Journal of Foreign Languages*). 1984(02):60–62.

Shi, Bingyun 施冰芸 (2017) 康有为翻译思想考 (A probe into Kang Youwei's translation thoughts). 上海翻译 (*Shanghai Journal of Translators*). 2017(02): 63–68.

Sun, Huijun and Zheng, Qingzhu (2000) 译论研究中的文化转向 (On the cultural shift of translation studies). 中国翻译 (*Chinese Translators Journal*). 2000(05): 11–14.

Tan, Zaixi 谭载喜 (2005) 关于西方翻译理论发展史的几点思考 (Investigating translation theory in the West: thoughts on its development and its study). 外国语(上海外国语大学学报) (*Journal of Foreign Languages*). 2005(01): 53–59.

Wang, Dawei and Wang Yuewu 王大伟, 王跃武 (2004) 关于翻译理论现状与发展的思考 (Reflections on the status Quo and development of translation studies). 外国语 (*Journal of Foreign Languages*). 149(1): 69–74.

Wang, Jian 王剑 (2017) 西方翻译史研究理论话语述评 (A review of the meta-discourses on the study of translation history in western academia 1964—2014). 上海翻译 (*Shanghai Journal of Translators*) 2017(02): 43–50.

Wang, Xiangyuan 王向远 (2016) "翻"、"译"的思想—中国古代"翻译"概念的建构 (The thinking behind 'fan' and 'yi' – construction of the concept of 'translation' in ancient China). 中国社会科学 (*Social Sciences in China*). 2016(02): 138–156.

Xie, Tianzhen 谢天振 (2003) 翻译研究新视野 (*New Horizon in Translation Studies*). 青岛：青岛出版社 (Qingdao: Qingdao Publishing Group). 目的论

Other references

Chen, C. (2016) *CiteSpace: A Practical Guide for Mapping Scientific Literature*. New York: Nova Science Publishers.

Chesterman, A. P. C. (2017) Progress in translation studies. *Across Languages and Cultures*. 18(2): 305–316.

Cheung, M. P. Y. (ed.) (2006) *An Anthology of Chinese Discourse on Translation*. Manchester: St Jerome.

Cheung, M. (2017) *An Anthology of Chinese Discourse on Translation (Volume 2): From the Late Twelfth Century to 1800*. In R. Neather (ed.) London and New York: Routledge.

Chomsky, N. (1957) *Syntactic Structures*. The Hague/Paris: Mouton.

Chomsky, N. (1965) *Aspects of the Theory of Syntax*. Cambridge, MA: MIT Press.
Delabastita, D., Sandra, H., José, L. and Kirsten, M. (2017) In Memoriam Gideon Toury (1942–2016). *Target* 29(1): 1–6.
Dong, D. and M. -L. Chen. (2015) Publication trends and co-citation mapping of translation studies between 2000 and 2015. *Scientometrics* 105: 1111–1128.
Halliday, M. A. K. (1994) *Introduction to Functional Grammar*, 2nd edition. London: Edward Arnold.
Holmes, J. S. (1975). *The Name and Nature of Translation Studies*. Amsterdam: University of Amsterdam Press.
Hung, E. (2005) Cultural borderlands in China's translation history. In E. Hung (ed.) *Translation and Cultural Change: Studies in History, Norms, and Image Projection*. Amsterdam and Philadelphia, PA: John Benjamins, pp. 43–64.
Newmark, P. (1988) *A Textbook of Translation*. New York: Prentice Hall.
Pinker, S. (1994) *The Language Instinct*. New York: William Morrow & Co.
Pym, A. (1998) *Method in Translation History*. Manchester: St Jerome Publishing.
Pym, A. (2014) *Exploring Translation Theories*, 2nd edition. London and New York: Routledge.
Shadrin, V. I. (2018) On Eurocentrism in modern translation theory. *Information* 21(3): 937–944.
White, L. (2003) *Second Language Acquisition and Universal Grammar*. Cambridge: Cambridge University Press.

1 The inception of Chinese translation theory

This chapter will start from a look at the influence of Chinese philosophy on the formulation of Chinese translation theory. In particular, we refer to Douglas Robinson's works on the relationship between Chinese philosophy, Western philosophy and translation studies. We examine how Chinese philosophy has influenced the Chinese discourse on translation and how it can be used to interpret traditional thoughts on translation. Then we examine the developmental trajectory of Chinese translation theory by sampling some historical discourse on translation. Thereafter, we investigate the process of introducing modern translation theory into China from the West and its reception. We end with a review and discussion on the outlook of Chinese translation theory.

Philosophical foundation of Chinese translation

Douglas Robinson is an American scholar and translator working at Hong Kong Baptist University at the time of writing. Robinson has published a number of books in translation studies combining Chinese philosophy and Western intellectual thoughts on language with translation (for example, Robinson, 1991, 1997, 2003, 2015), which are enthusiastically received in China. His most recent book on the Dao ('the way') of translation (Robinson, 2015) has caught a lot of attention in Chinese academia since its publication. Ding (2016), for example, conducted an interview with Robinson where Robinson suggested that there are a lot of resources to be drawn from the long tradition of Chinese culture and philosophy for translation research, which the Chinese academics so far had failed to make good use of. This chapter will set out from Robinson's hypothesis and examine the Chinese academic discourse on the implications of Chinese philosophy on translation studies. This will serve as a higher level framework for further discussion on Chinese translation theory based on a review of representative works published by translation scholars from China in recent years. We start from a review of what Robinson (2015) said about the relationship between Chinese philosophy and translation.

In his review of Robinson (2015), J. Wang (2017) explained Robinson's distinction between the big letter 'Dao' and the small letter 'dao'. According to

Wang, for Robinson, *Dao* means the mysterious force that makes everything run smoothly in the Universe; *dao*, on the other hand, refers to the process or pattern by which society functions, or more explicitly, the habitual functioning patterns collectively formed by people living in the same society. Robinson further consolidates the Xin 'heart' of Confucianism and the Dao 'way' of Taoism, using both of them to mean a kind of strong and undefinable, but constantly emerging shaping force unknown to us. Furthermore, Robinson absorbs Mencius' idea that the positive energy of humankind is created by the empathy between persons and among social groups, or through a kind of 'spiritual channelling' as a result of the interactions and mutual influences between various components in the social–ecological system. Robinson created the term 'icosis' (群体趋同) and 'ecosis' (群体趋善) to represent his synthesized view from Chinese and Western philosophies that people in society will think and behave collectively in ways that are considered authentic and legitimate through mass consciousness and generally move toward the direction of the 'good' and 'virtuous'. Both these terms are preconscious driving forces on a par with Dao, which represents the omnipresent mysterious mechanism that 'makes every all right'. In terms of the relevance of Robinson's theory to translation studies, according to Wang, Robinson (2015) proposed six steps to explain 'the way of translation' which guides the translator gradually from collective thinking to individual thinking, or 'collective-becoming-individual functioning' (Wang, 2017, p. 76), making the translation process 'automatic' while at the same time following the established norm of society.

Some Chinese translation scholars also draw ideas from Chinese philosophy to explain the nature and principles of translation or propose guidelines for practicing or researching in translation. Yang (2018) provides a basic tenet to justify the philosophical approach to translation studies:

> 哲学作为人类知识最高层次的理论体系，是一定时代人类文化的结晶，是该时代精神的精华，是一切学科的本源，所有学科均可上升到哲学的层次去研究。(As the highest level of theoretical system in human knowledge, philosophy represents the crystallization of human culture for an era, the essence of human life in that epoch, and the origin of all academic disciplines. The enquiries of any academic discipline can be elevated to the level of philosophy for investigation)
>
> (Yang, 2018, p. 195).

Yang echoes Robinson's concern that, although there are 5000 years' worth of Chinese history, most translation theorists resort to Western philosophy and ignore the essence of our traditional culture and philosophy. Yang insists that the ancient sages' theories and thinking are rich in modern meaning and can serve a 'pan-instructive' function (泛指导性) for all academic disciplines (Yang, 2018, p. 195). Yang makes a cogent distinction between 'translation in the narrow sense' and 'translation in the broad sense'. The former refers to translating between languages; the latter refers to the transfer of meaning between any kinds of symbolic systems. In the West, the founder of modern linguistics Ferdinand de Saussure was also a semiotician, defining language broadly as a kind of symbol. In the Chinese tradition, according to Yang, the study of 'Yi' (易学) is the most representative work of semiotics in Chinese history which also works on the basis of broadly defined symbols. Yang uses the famous saying in Daoism "道生一，一生二，二生三，三生万物" (Dao begets One, One begets Two, Two begets Three, Three begets all things) to interpret 'the way of translation', where the substance of meaning being pursued in translating is One, and the external and the internal worlds carrying the meaning is Two. When the external (objective) world interacts with the internal (subjective) world through the mechanism of symbols (or the world of meanings), the status of Three is reached. As human beings launch an incessant pursuit of knowledge to understand themselves and the world they live in, the ultimate goal is the recognition of the value of objects and things, that is, the substance of meaning. Thus, for Yang, translation can be conceptualized in the following way:

> 翻译其本质就是在保持意义本体不变的原则下，承载意义本体的不同载体之间的相互转换。(Translation is essentially a conversion of the substance of meaning between different carriers of the meaning under the principle that the substance of meaning remains unchanged.)
>
> (Yang, 2018, p. 195)

Importantly, for Yang, translation embodies the pursuit and recognition of meaning by human beings. According to the needs of different times, translation is employed to help people acquire knowledge, culture and ideas through interchangeable and understandable symbolic systems. Therefore, the application of translation can enhance a human's understanding of nature, self and society. The translator is responsible for translating the ST encoded in a symbolic system unknown to the target reader to the TT which they understand, allowing them to absorb required knowledge, culture and ideas, thereby creating the value of social progression. Yang concludes the fairly interesting essay by reminding the reader of the instructional value of translation theory (meaning that generated from Chinese philosophy) to the practice of translation. The ideas and perspectives of Chinese philosophy are worthy of further investigation and application.

A more complicated discussion on the philosophical view of Chinese translation is offered by Zhu (2008), which explores the close relationship between classical Chinese philosophy, Chinese literary concepts and traditional Chinese translation theory. Zhu thought that traditional Chinese translation theory is deeply rooted in Confucianism, Buddhism and Taoism, and that it provided a framework integrating personal experience, practical performance and direct intuitional perception in the analysis of translation. Zhu used a classical Chinese sentence 道释内而儒外 ('Daoism explains the internal and Confucianism, the external') to explain why Chinese literary theory in general adopts a subjective attitude, using internal thought to model the outside world (以己度物 'measuring objects with oneself'). This pattern of thinking is expanded to cover the entire territory of arts and humanities, including the study of translation. More specifically, according to Zhu:

> 在认识论和方法论上，我国传统译论基本上脱胎于古典文论中大而概、偏直 觉重诗性的"心法"内省式人文哲学思辨观。(In respect of epistemology and methodology, the traditional translation theory in our country was born out of the introspective philosophical view for arts and humanities called 'heart method' that resides in the Chinese classical literary theory that is 'big and general' and emphasizes intuitive poetic thoughts.)
>
> (Zhu, 2008, p. 12)

Zhu further explained that Confucianism 'embeds the way in text' (文以载道), which means literature can be used to educate and transform society; Daoism, on the other hand, proposes that 'it is not possible to explain the way' ("道"不可言传) and that people generally forget the words after getting the meaning (得意而忘言). Similar to Daoism, Buddhism also suggests that the goal of theorizing lies in 'having a clear heart and seeing the nature' (明心见性) and 'you are in Buddha land as soon as you understand' (悟即至佛地). This kind of philosophical tradition which takes epiphanic experience as a process of understanding has exerted a lot of influence on the Chinese literary theory, according to Zhu. That is, under the influence of Daoism, Confucianism and Buddhism, Chinese literary theory exhibits the characteristic of metaphysical dialectics and, at the same time, shows a kind of 'poetic wisdom' (诗性智慧) that operates on the principles of instinct and epiphany. As such, the philosophies of Confucianism, Daoism and Buddhism all aim to achieve 'a higher state' (境界) through poetic inspiration and instinctive perception which is characteristic of Chinese literary theory. Incidentally, according to Zhu, Chinese translation theory, which is deeply rooted in the soil of Chinese culture and philosophy, follows the same development trajectory and pattern of expression as Chinese literary theory. In this light, the well-known translation theories in Chinese history, such as the Xin, Da, Ya (信、达、雅) theory of Yan Fu (严复), the Huajing (化境) theory of Qian Zhongshu (钱钟书), and the Xingsi, Yisi, Shensi (形似，意似，神似) theory of Chen Xiying (陈西滢), all manifested the instinctive epiphany approach of the Confucian, Daoist and Buddhist philosophy. Zhu concluded by saying that:

> 我国传统译论明显具有相当大的理论指导意义和思辨启迪，这充分体现了翻译（尤其是文学翻译）的本体特征，体现了人文主体的体认作用之于重现原作美学意义的能动性，因而具有科学理性主义译论所无法替代的作用。(Apparently, our traditional translation approach

is endowed with an ability to guide the development of theory and to inspire dialectical thinking, which manifests the defining characteristic of translation, especially literary translation. This also shows the ability of the epiphanic function in humanities approach to recapture the original aesthetic value in the original work.)

(Zhu, 2008, p. 15)

However, despite all the good points Zhu (2008) raised about the value of traditional Chinese philosophy in fostering Chinese literary theory and Chinese translation theory, Zhu, Y. admitted that there were limitations in the traditional translation studies approach. In particular, its lack of logical analysis, systematic modeling and innovative spirit.

我国传统译论亦不乏自身不可逾越的缺陷，如过分直觉灵动，随机随意点评，缺乏系统形态与创新精神，缺乏西方理性主义译论的逻辑论证的续密思维模式和研究方法论 (Our traditional translation theory has its inherent problems, such as being overreliant on intuitive perception and random criticizing, lacking in systematic outlook and innovative spirit, lacking in the all-round thinking patterns and methodology that exist in Western rationalism)

(p. 15)

Thus, Zhu, Y. ended the discussion by recommending Chinese translation researchers to reflect on the strengths and weaknesses of traditional translation theory in an objective manner; that they should hold a humble attitude and try to surpass themselves, criticize themselves and keep an open mind, and to actively absorb the reasonable parts of Western translation theory in order to generate new life and contemporary meaning for Chinese translation theory.

While Zhu (2008) focused on the essence of Chinese philosophy in general and its influence on Chinese translation theory, Zhu (2018) offers a more detailed view on how a particular strand of philosophical thought on language can guide our way through practical issues in translating. Specifically, Zhu, S. refers to the linguistic view of Zhuangzi who, according to Zhu, explored the value and boundary of language and the relationship between meaning and language in the chapters *Qiwu Lun* (齐物论篇), *Waiwu Pian* (外物篇), *Qiushui Pian* (秋水篇), etc. of his main work *Zhuangzi* (莊子). Basically, Zhu thinks that Zhuangzi's philosophy of language was built on the ontology of 'wu' (无 'void') and the concept of 'dao' (道 'way'); 'dao' exists in the objective world but the essence of 'dao' is 'wu' (i.e. nothing). According to Zhu, Zhuangzi expounded the nature of language by using the phrase 言不尽意 ('language cannot exhaustively express meaning'). That is, he admitted the power of language, but recognized the limitations of language at the same time. Zhu thinks the modeling and recognition of the limitations and boundary of language is an important component of Zhuangzi's philosophy about language. Also, for Zhu, the limitation of language is the limitation of translation, which is a particularly pronounced issue in the translation of Chinese philosophy works. That is, the problem of 'untranslatability' is especially true when translating philosophical works. Zhu used an excerpt from *Zhuangzi* as example:

> 适来，夫子时也；适去，夫子顺也。安时而处顺，哀乐不能入也，古者谓是帝之县解。(When it's time for the saint to come, he comes; when it's time for him to depart, he departs. Be at ease and adapt to the changes; then you will not be overcome with emotion. Ancient sages called this state of emancipation from nature's captivity.)
>
> (Zhu, 2008, p. 95)

From the above extract, the phrase 帝之县解 (literally 'the bondage of emperor being broken', or more communicatively, 'being released from the emotional turmoil imposed by nature') has been variously translated by a succession of Chinese and Western translators, some of them not entirely correct or appropriate:

- 'the loosening of the cord on which God suspended (the life)' – James Legge
- 'the emancipation from bondage' – Lin Yutang
- 'the emancipation of the gods' – Victor H. Mair
- 'God's loosing of the bonds' – A. C. Graham
- 'Liberation from the Lord's Dangle' – Brook Ziporyn

Zhu (2018) uses the above example to illustrate the limitations of language (and therefore of translation) as expounded by Zhuangzi, who also proposed a distinction between 'big language' (大言) and 'small language' (小言); the former being general and accommodative just like 'dao', and the latter being chattering and superfluous. Against this background, Zhu proposes that the translator should follow the wisdom of Zhuangzi by pursuing the 'big language' and forgoing the 'small language'. Specifically, Zhu thinks that the TT is meant to capture the essence of the ST, and so the translator should spend more time explaining the general and the abstract with examples or annotations, rather than being restricted by surface expressions or in pursuit of the splendor of the text. In Zhu's words:

> 在翻译的过程中应追求"大言"、抛弃"小言"，通过谨慎的考据和查证来正确理解和把握"道"或"质"，对抽象的、普遍性的概括或描述进行举例或注解，而不必拘泥于字句或追求文辞的华丽。如此才能摆脱语言的困境，实现"质"的传递和语言的内在超越。(In the process of translation, we should pursue the 'big language' and abandon the 'small language'. We should make sure we correctly understand and grasp the 'dao' or substance of the text through careful research and verification. Thereafter, we use examples or commentary to explicate the general abstraction or description, not being restricted by the surface form or in blind pursuit of the pompousness of the rhetoric. Only in this way can we rid ourselves of the plight

created by language and realize the transfer of 'substance' by transcending the restriction of language.)

(Zhu, 2008, p. 96)

Thus, according to Zhu (2018), Zhuangzi's philosophy of language offers a renewed perspective of language and translation. Against the background of language limitation, the binary opposition of word and meaning in the context of translation studies and practice acquires a new interpretation. For translation scholars, the relationship between text and theme becomes clearer and easier to tackle; for translation practitioners, the translator's subjectivity is further strengthened, and issues like untranslatability or criticisms like 'translation is useless' are no longer sustainable.

A surprisingly illuminating account of how Chinese philosophy can contribute to the theorizing of translation is given by Xi (2017), who explains how the concept of the 'aesthetics of translation' works as inspired by Chinese philosophy. Xi thinks that Chinese aesthetic concepts such as aesthetic psychology, aesthetic orientation and aesthetic experiences are highly influenced by Chinese philosophy. If the Chinese aesthetics of translation are explored from the perspective of the philosophy–aesthetics connection, the characteristics of the subject (i.e. the Chinese aesthetics of translation) will be especially noticeable and the result particularly fruitful. In a cogent manner, Xi (2017) divides the characteristics of the Chinese aesthetics of translation into three categories: the fuzzy kind of beauty (模糊美), the beauty of symmetry in sound, shape and meaning (音形意的对称美) and the holistic perception of beauty (整体感知美), and goes on to explain each of them and their connections to Chinese philosophy, teasing out the relevance to translation studies. For example, in respect of 'fuzzy beauty', Xi suggests there are two kinds: the beauty of fuzziness in structure (结构的模糊美) and the beauty of fuzziness in referring to persons (人称的模糊美). In the former subcategory, Xi notes that many important notions in Chinese philosophy such as kindness (仁), justice (义), politeness (礼) and way (道) are lacking in precise definitions. Chinese philosophy does not resort to dialectical logic or conceptual analysis, but relies instead on the modeling of the heart and repetitive epiphany to grab the idea holistically. Likewise, the Chinese language also does not rely on the surface form to express logical relationships; instead, it allows objects and events to follow a natural order, such as a sequence in time (from previous to current), size (from big to small), distance (from near to far), causality (from cause to effect) and so on. Therefore, the English TT created by a Chinese translator, for one thing, also reflects this kind of fuzziness (i.e. obscure syntax) for example in the spare use of conjunctive and cohesive devices. In terms of the fuzziness in personal reference, Xi usefully points out that Chinese philosophy generally focuses on 'person'. This is manifested by well-known sayings such as 'everything in the world is available to me' (万物皆备于我) and 'Heaven and man follow the same rules' (天人合一). In other words, everything revolves around the person; person is the center of the universe. Importantly, this kind of philosophy translates into a property of language which says 'Hide the subject of a sentence!' especially when the agent of the predicate is the person who utters the sentence, who should be taken for granted and not specifically encoded. Therefore, when translating from Chinese ST into English TT, the subject of a sentence such as *I* or *we* is often missing in the TT, following the Chinese convention. These will have to be added in order to conform to the syntactic requirement of the target language (i.e. English). Such are the implications of Chinese translation aesthetics (generated from Chinese philosophy). The second type of beauty in Chinese translation aesthetics in Xi's typology is the symmetric beauty of sound, structure and meaning. According to Xi (2017):

> 中国美学注重排比、修辞、各种重复等，以达到整齐匀称等美感。因此，中国译者的语篇往往讲究词语文句的整齐匀称，追求声韵节奏的和谐悦耳，善用对偶排比，辞藻华丽，充分体现汉人追求均衡匀称、讲究整齐和谐的心理。(Chinese aesthetics gave the priority to parallelism, rhetoric, repetition and the like in order to achieve the aesthetic sense of orderliness and symmetry. Therefore, Chinese translators often stress the deployment of symmetrical structures, pursued the harmony of rhythm, apply antithesis as well as parallelism to deliver flowery language, which fully echoed the psychology of the Han nationality.)
>
> (Xi, 2017, p. 104)

Thus, at both phonetic and syntactic levels the Chinese translator will seek symmetry in formulating the TT. This is especially true when translating poetic works. For semantic symmetry, the aesthetic sense is realized by rhetorical devices such as 'arguing from both positive and negative sides' (正反两说) and 'piling up synonymic expressions' (同义堆叠). Xi advises that, because Western authors emphasize succinctness and logic in writing, they tend to regard what Chinese authors consider 'beautiful writing' as redundantly lengthy. If this is true, it is certainly a significant aspect in Chinese translation that has not been adequately researched so far. The third and final characteristic of the Chinese aesthetics of translation identified by Xi is a 'holistically perceived beauty'. According to her, the Daoism in Chinese philosophy pursues a holistic epiphany where human and nature form one body. This kind of holistic thinking also affects the Chinese translator's aesthetic perception and dictates their writing style; that is, a TT must be considered 'beautiful' in three ways – sound, structure and meaning, as previously expounded. Many Chinese scholars also formulate their translation theory according to this principle. For example, the theory of Huajing (化境 'perfect state') proposed by Qian Zhongshu (钱钟书) emphasizes the rendering of the original idea, emotion, style and 'shenyun' (神韵 'spiritual charm'). Among them, 'shenyun' is a holistic idea which means the resurfacing of the original holistic beauty in the TT. In a nutshell, Xi (2017) offers an interesting and implicational account of a Chinese translator's writing styles based on Chinese writers' intrinsic sense of textual beauty as a function of their upbringing and socialization under the influence of the supreme existence of Chinese philosophy in Chinese culture and society.

As correctly predicted by Douglas Robinson, we have seen what kind of enlightenment Chinese philosophy can bring to translation theory and practice. From the philosophy of Yi (易), for example, Yang (2018) found that the nature and function of translation – i.e. to transfer the substance of the ST to the TT and enhance the culture and knowledge of civilizations. Zhu (2008) created the term 'poetic wisdom' to show how Chinese literary theory is influenced by the Chinese philosophy shared by Confucianism, Daoism and Buddhism, which all rely on human's intuition and epiphany to understand the way of things; this has direct relevance to the formulation of Chinese translation theory, as all of these philosophies seem to point to an unspeakable state of perfect understanding. Zhu, Y. commended this kind of subjective approach to the humanities, but also deplored its weaknesses in logical analysis and reasoning. A more analytical view, however, is indeed offered by Zhu (2018) regarding the influence of Chinese philosophy on translation theory. In her work, Zhu (2018) builds her theory of translation based on Zhuangzi's view about language, i.e. language is rather limited in the expression of meaning. For the translator, especially that of more advanced work such as books on philosophy, Zhu, S. thinks that they should concentrate on grasping the 'big language' (i.e. the main thesis) and forgo the 'small language' (i.e. the words and expressions) by using examples and footnotes to explain, rather than worrying about the exact wording of the TT. An equally cogent argument is put forward by Xi (2017) about how traditional Chinese philosophy can inspire the study of translation. Xi provides an analytical framework for applying Chinese aesthetic thoughts (generated from the fuzzy concepts residing in Chinese philosophy) to translation theory, namely, the fuzziness, the symmetry and the wholeness of the beauty of the text manifested at the three levels of sound, structure and meaning.

We will conclude this section by looking at a proposal put forward in Yu (2011) regarding the establishment of a subdiscipline in translation studies – Translation Philosophy (翻译哲学) or the Philosophy of Translation. Yu argues that the term itself is uniquely Chinese and is not prevalent in Western translation studies. He googled both the terms 'translation philosophy' and 'the philosophy of translation' but did not find a lot of matches. (This is verified by the current author who received only 41,400 Google hits for the former and 624 for the latter at the time of writing.) Chinese translation scholars, on the other hand, have proposed various definitions for the Chinese term 翻译哲学, as reviewed in Yu (2011, p. 62, my translations):

- Translation philosophy mainly refers to the worldview and epistemology o Maxims and the systematic view and methodology of modern systematic science, which are the guiding principles and the theoretical foundation of translation studies (Zhang Zeqian 张泽乾)
- Translation philosophy is the study of the world view and methodology followed by general translation and literal translation (Zhang Jinye 张今也)

- Translation philosophy is the theoretical system that unites view of translation and translation methodology (Huang Zhonglian 黄忠廉)
- The basic enquiry of translation philosophy is to pursue the relationship between translator's mind and the (target) text; its basic goal is to establish the relationship between translator's thinking and the (target) text and that between the translator and the source text (Liu Bangfan 刘邦凡)
- Translation philosophy is the highest level of theory as a manifestation of a philosophical enquiry into the nature and properties of human translation activities (Yang Zijian 杨自俭)

Yu thinks that many translation researchers confuse 'translation philosophy' with 'translation theory' and neglect the unique contributions that translation philosophy can make to the theorizing of translation. Yu asserts that translation philosophy is a branch of philosophy (rather than one of translation studies) and, as such, it is different from the translation theory derived from empirical research. Thus, Yu defines the philosophy of translation as follows:

> 我们认为，"翻译哲学"同"教育哲学"、"政治哲学"、"艺术哲学"等一样，是哲学的一个分支学科，是论述翻译中出现的哲学问题，从哲学本体论、认识论、方法论、价值论上对翻译及翻译研究进行考察，追问翻译和翻译所涉及的意义与语言的本质。(We propose that translation philosophy, just like 'philosophy of education', 'political philosophy' and 'philosophy of art', is a branch of philosophy designed to expound the philosophical problems arising in translation. Translation philosophy investigates the nature of translation and the meaning and language involved while translating from the perspectives of ontology, epistemology, methodology and axiology in philosophy.)
>
> (Yu, 2011, p. 64)

According to Yu, researchers in translation philosophy are not only interested in the translation activity itself but also consider the translation theory derived from translating experiences. Translation philosophy is a kind of metaphysical thinking which pursues the question of 'how is translation possible?'. This leads us to a reasonable conclusion for this section that, as Douglas Robinson predicted, traditional Chinese culture (which we will investigate in a later chapter) and philosophy have a lot to offer for Chinese translation studies. We have seen that, not only can Chinese philosophy inspire new thoughts and perspectives for reconceptualizing translation theory and practice, the study of Chinese translation can feed back and help form a new branch of Chinese philosophy (i.e. the philosophy of translation), investigating the implication of translating to the understanding of language, communication, cognition and human society, among other things. With that note, we move on next to the consideration of Chinese translation theory, including the developmental trajectory of Chinese translation theory and how different systems of translation theory are conceptualized by Chinese translation researchers and scholars.

The development of Chinese translation theory

The formulation and development of Chinese translation theory is a complex topic and difficult to handle mainly because of the long history of translation practice (> 2000 years) and the relatively short history of the systematic study of translation theory (< 50 years). On one hand, there are some 'occasional discourses' on translation containing elements of translation theory within the 2000 or so periods, which are difficult to organize and 'fit into' modern translation studies paradigms. On the other hand, there are too many 'systematic discourses' on translation theory in the past few decades as a result of China's opening up and the importation of Western translation theory. The old and the new become mixed up and there is no clear rationale to sort out what is Chinese and what is Western or if it is even meaningful to make such a distinction. Chinese translation studies is at a crossroads where many directions are possible allowing all kinds of vehicles (i.e. varieties of translation theory) to take routes.

A very useful summary of the whereabouts of Chinese translation theory is offered by Liu and Mu (2017), which provides a good start for the discussion in this section. Liu and Mu categorize existing Chinese discourse on translation theory into five types:

- The argument between text and substance (文质之争)
- The debate about translation method (方法之辩)
- The dispute about translation criteria (标准之论)
- The contention about the nature of translation (性质之论)
- The speculation about the subject of translation (学科之思)

Each of the five categories represents a stand of discourse on the theory of translation in Liu and Mu's scheme. For example, the argument between text and substance had begun with the translation of Buddhist sutra where people either emphasized the importance of 'language and wording' or that of the 'content of the message' (admitting there were also people advocating for the middle ways). A saying from Zhiqian (支谦) was quoted in Liu and Mu as an example of advocating for the 'substance': 'Follow the main idea; do not add decoration to the text' (因循本旨，不加文饰) (p. 3). The debate about translation method, on the other hand, surrounded the issues of 'literal translation', translation of names, 'conceptual equivalence' and so on. However, according to Liu and Mu, the most heated and fruitful debate must be the one concentrating on the rationale for judging the quality of translation. For example, the Xin, Da, Ya criteria proposed by Yan Fu; the Huajing theory advocated by Qian Zhongshu; or the 'faithful, fluent, beautiful' (忠实、通顺、美) criteria proposed by Lin Yutang (林语堂) all tried to set the norms for characterizing good translation. Equally implicational was the discourse on the nature and function of translation, for example, Jia Gongyan (贾公彦) once said 'Translating means replacement, changing into another language so as to enable understanding'

(译即易，谓换易言语使相解也) and, more recently, Liang Qichao (梁启超) outlined 'the three rationales for translating books' (译书三义) – choosing proper books to translate (择当译之本), setting an official translation paradigm (定公译之例), and fostering translation talents (养能译之才). Finally, the Chinese discourse on translation theory also focused on the issue of how to develop translation studies as an academic subject. Liu and Mu cite many Chinese scholars, including Tan Zaixi (谭载喜), Liu Miqing (刘宓庆), Zhue Chunshen (朱纯深) and Chang Namfung (张南峰), as joining the debates of whether translation studies existed or not in China, and whether there is translation studies 'with Chinese characteristics' as well as the grand issue of how to continue to develop Chinese translation studies.

Apart from offering a typology for Chinese discourse on translation theory, Liu and Mu (2017, p. 4) also put forward a hypothesis regarding the developmental trajectory of Chinese translation theory. They proposed to divide the historical development of Chinese translation theory into three stages:

1. Summarization of translation experiences (翻译经验总结期)
2. Formulation of translation hypotheses (翻译假说形成期)
3. Establishment of the subject of translation studies (翻译学科建设期)

At the first stage, the ample experiences of translating in Chinese history condensed to many rich and versatile translation theories expressed in a number of scholarly works. Liu and Mu cites the examples of Wang (2003), who suggested that traditional Chinese translation theory went through the four stages of 'beginning' (肇始), 'classic' (古典), 'abstruse' (玄思) and 'instinctive' (直觉) thinking; and Wang and Wang (2009), who proposed that the indigenous Chinese thoughts on translation theory were formulated on the basis of Chinese classic literary theory, philosophy and aesthetics, and went through the stages of ancient sutra translation, modern Western technical translation and recent practical translation (p. 4). The second stage of development for Chinese translation theory, for Liu and Mu (2017), came when Western translation studies were introduced into the Chinese regions and started to influence Chinese thinking on translation. At this stage, in addition to learning from the West, the Chinese researchers also attempted to reinterpret the Chinese tradition and came up with many theories and proposed a number of innovative hypotheses, for example, the 'multiple complementary norm of translation' approach (多元互补论) of Gu (1989), the 'culture-centered transfer' theory (文化中心转移论) of Ji (1995), the 'exquisite product' theory (精品论) of Ye (1997) and the 'competition theory' (竞争说) of Xu (2000). Finally, at stage three, as China reforms and opens up to the world, the need for all kinds of translators increases on a daily basis. Therefore, the establishment of translation studies as an academic discipline and the education of a large number of translators are desperately needed.

Another similar but briefer summary of the development of Chinese translation theory up to the present time is given by Lan (2018), who sees the 1980s as the dawning time of Chinese translation studies. From then on, for 30 years, Lan thinks Chinese translation studies has made progress in four areas:

- Theoretical study of translation as an academic discipline
- Research in fundamental theory of translation
- Interdisciplinary translation theory research
- Theory of the subdisciplines of translation studies

Among the achievements in Chinese translation theory mentioned, Lan especially recommends those in the subdiscipline of literary translation, referring to several landmark works in the discussion of literary translation theory, such as the book *Literature and Translation* (文学与翻译) published by Xu Yuanchong (许渊冲) in 2003. The other subdiscipline recommended by Lan is Chinese applied translation studies, which he thinks has made impressive progress in the past three decades. Looking at the future development of Chinese translation theory from the current perspective, Lan suggests four directions: 1. emphasizing subject functionality, 2. expanding theoretical resources, 3. reconceptualizing translation ontology, 4. strengthening school awareness.

> 进入新的发展阶段之后，我们需要走出学习多于创新、演绎多于归纳、批判多于建设的理论发展模式，转变研究范式和创新研究方法，从注重运用西方理论说明中国翻译现实转向关注当前中国社会实践中的翻译理论和实践问题 (Having entered a new developmental stage, we need to shake off the models of 'more learning than innovating', 'more deduction than induction', and 'more criticism than construction' for developing translation theory, changing research paradigms and create new research methodology. We need to switch from applying Western theory to explain Chinese translation realities to focusing on the issues of translation theory and practice in the current situation of Chinese society.)
>
> (Lan, 2018, p. 16)

In another work which attempted to summarize Chinese efforts in developing translation theory, Wen (2010), also proposed some areas for future directions, which he saw as being the weakest links in Chinese translation studies. First and foremost, in terms of the discussions on translation theory, Wen pointed out the regular route in learning from more advanced civilizations: 'import – absorb and digest – critically apply – innovate' and lamented that there had been too few innovative works so far in the theorization of translation. This coincides with Lan's later suggestion in 2018 mentioned above that research in Chinese translation theory needs to become more innovative. This also warns us of the difficulty of creating 'innovative translation theory' since there appears to be little progress in this area between 2010 and 2018 in China. That being said, we do have some innovative ideas in Chinese translation theoretical research such as the 'variations translation theory' (变译理论), which we will discuss later in this book. After the most significant area that required continual attention (i.e. the formulation of innovative translation theory), Wen (2010) went on to suggest more areas for future research. For example, in terms of research on the history of translation, Wen thought there were several areas that required strengthening: the study of foreign translation history, the study of minority translation history in China, and the study of oral translation history. Other future areas that required further research included translation criticism, translator training and machine translation and translation technologies, according to Wen (2010).

Any discussion on the history of Chinese translation theory cannot be complete without a critical look at the importation of translation theory from the West. At the turn of the century, Tu and Xiao (2000) offered a very good summary of how Western translation theory was introduced into China; they analyzed the meaning and significance of the dissemination and reception of Western translation theory in China. Firstly, Tu and Xiao recognized three ways in which Western translation theory was imported into China: by journal articles, by dedicated books and by academic conferences. The three routes each had their own merits and restrictions. The introduction of translation theory into China in the form of journal articles quickly reflects the most recent development of academic research in a rigorous way. Books, however, can offer deeper and more detailed discussion on certain theoretical issues and embody more mature thinking. In symposiums, lastly, researchers can exchange opinions, getting the most recent research results and giving feedback. The three kinds of channels for introducing translation theory into China each reflects their condition of dissemination and reception. In terms of the nature of the introduction, Tu and Xiao distinguished three types: the first kind of work that introduces Western translation theory is simply an introduction, often a translation of English literature with a simple Chinese introduction (i.e. 译介). The second kind of introductory work is the research type that either compares between different translation theories or elucidates the developmental process of a particular theory, in the hopes of providing useful materials for Chinese researchers in translation theory. The third type of work that introduces Western translation theory emphasizes reflection and application, hoping to prove the feasibility of using Western translation theory to solve Chinese translation problems and feeding Western translation theory to existing Chinese translation research. Thus, Tu and Xiao (2000) termed these three types of introductory works: Introduction (引进), Research (研究) and Application (应用), respectively. They suggested that these three modes of introduction are mutually complementary and cannot do well without one another.

Tu and Xiao (2000) also distinguished three stages of introducing Western translation theory into China, roughly corresponding to the three types of introductory works mentioned above. According to them, the first stage happened at the beginning of the 1980s and there was often a time lag between the introductory work and the work originally published. For example, the introduction of Eugene Nida's and J. C. Catford's works in the 1960s did not happen until almost 20 years later. At the second stage identified by Tu and Xiao as being the middle and later period of the 1980s, however, the response of Western translation theory importers was much quicker and the introduction was much more timely and comprehensive. For example, Peter Newmark published his *A Textbook of Translation* in 1988, and its introduction was published in a speedy fashion by the Foreign Language Teaching journal in its 1989 No. 2 volume. At this stage, according to Tu and Xiao, the introductory works began to incorporate some research and reflective elements, with some works even manifesting a critical stance. Thus, at this stage, Chinese researchers gradually achieved a deeper and more comprehensive understanding of Western translation theory and, at the same time, Chinese Translation took major strides ahead. The third stage of Western translation theory introduction began with the 1990s until the present in Tu and Xiao's classification, and can be categorized by the words 'comprehensive, timely, innovative'. At this stage, the Chinese translation researchers are familiar with almost all of the major translation theories in the West. Many publications in translation theory are also published in China in their original language. Academic interactions between the East and the West have become more frequent, in the forms of scholarly visits and participation in international conferences. Most importantly, at this stage, some researchers have begun to propose their own theories by integrating traditional Chinese translation theory with the research results of the West.

In retrospect, Tu and Xiao (2000) thought that Western translation theory had made contributions to Chinese translation studies in two major areas: methodology and 'research practice' (实际研究). In respect of methodology, Tu and Xiao held the interesting view that the familiarity with Western translation theory somehow transformed the view of Chinese researchers who were now able to challenge the authorities and existing paradigms. One example given by Tu and Xiao was Yan Fu's Xin, Da, Ya principle, which had prevailed for one and a half century without being seriously challenged, that is, until Western translation theory was introduced together with its analytical view and method. In terms of the Western contributions to the research practice of Chinese translation studies, Tu and Xiao mentioned the crucial influence of the Western linguistics theories and the independent status of translation studies as an academic discipline. Despite all the accomplishments made possible by the introduction of Western translation theory, however, Tu and Xiao (2000) concluded their discussion by pointing to three weaknesses that still existed in Chinese translation studies: the confusion of disciplinary jargons, the inadequacy at the level of application, and the oversimplification, repetition and lack of systematic research in academic works. In particular, Tu and Xiao bitterly criticized the 'repetition' problem by pointing out that a lot of authors were simply repeating others' works without innovation or progress. For example, Nida's theory had been 'introduced' over and over again (no less than 20–30 times according to Tu and Xiao) without much difference between the works. Tu and Xiao attributed the problem to the lack of a fully dedicated professional organization to consolidate the research and regulate the activities. As a result, researchers and practitioners simply work blindly following their own intuitions without knowing what others are doing. In addition, Tu and Xiao also deplored the incompetence of Chinese journal editors who knowingly published articles that were poor in quality and full of mistakes (Tu and Xiao, 2000, p. 19).

Finally, some authors publish not purely out of scholarly motivations (We can only surmise following Tu and Xiao's logic and academic common sense that these authors publish for promotion or to get funding and other types of reward) and are seriously lacking in quality and innovation. With that caution in mind, we can now look at some of the actual works which introduced Western translation theory into China, especially the second and third type of introductory works in Tu and Xiao's scheme which not only introduce but also criticize and apply the imported theory to domestic practice.

Introducing Western translation theory

As suggested in Tu and Xiao (2000), the introduction of Western translation theory started at the beginning of the 1980s. The first wave would have been those classified by Tu and Xiao as the simplest kind that only introduced or translated Western works (译介) with little personal notes or critical elements. Some works of this type at the initial stage were written in the form of book reviews, which differed dramatically from the book reviews in modern international journals, in that they often included a brief introduction of the book's author and their research background – something that would have been unfamiliar to the then Chinese reader. Moreover, at the beginning of the great enterprise of importing Western translation theory in the 1980s, because of the largely barren ground in the same field in China, it was relatively easy for the introducer of Western theory to find something interesting to say apart from the information relay. It need not be a serious argumentation or a long process of inductive reasoning, but a little paragraph of ingenious-looking thoughts or a few lines of novel suggestions would seem to make the author a more knowledgeable person (i.e. a herald or precursor) in the field and the introductive paper worth reading and publishing, even though the comments were not always well justified.

Mu (1989) is a typical example of a book review with a view to importing Western translation theory to China in the 1980s, which comprised only one page offering a review of J. C. Catford's 1965 work *A Linguistic Theory of Translation*. The paper used the first two paragraphs to introduce Catford as a renowned British linguist and translation theorist born in Edinburgh in 1917, including his educational background, the many languages he spoke and his specialized areas, before going on to introduce the contents and merits of the book itself. Mu praised Catford's effort in applying the scientific research method of linguistics to the study of translation theory, and questioned why the Chinese translation theory, despite its age-old tradition and long lineage, still lingered in the same place without a major break. Lin (1981), on the other hand, offered a more substantial review of eight pages on Nida's 1964 book *Toward a Science of Translating*. The review is more substantial in the sense that more detailed summaries and explanations of the book's contents are offered in the paper. In this case, Lin introduced Nida's life career as a linguist and translator, his educational background, his specialized areas and his theory about language and translation before zooming in on Nida's main thesis in this book: the three steps in the process of translating, analysis → transfer → restructuring. At the end of the paper, Lin made a somewhat surprising and arbitrary conclusion by first vaguely referring to Nida's connecting translation studies to language philosophy, and then by emphasizing the importance of 'model building' for both linguistics and translation studies, and finally by 'predicting' that semantics and discourse analysis (and ultimately stylistics or genre analysis) would be the then future trends for linguistics, which promised great help for translators. This prediction was simply made without much proof or argumentation and demonstrated the style of academic writing in China, at least in the field of translation studies, in that period (i.e. the 1980s). In the same vein, Wang (1982) introduced Newmark's (1978) article and commented on two merits of the paper: 1. It collected a large number of materials and gave a useful review of various schools and translation theories. 2. The author gave some valuable personal opinions, such as why the meaning of the TT 'went astray' and whether the equivalent theory was really workable or not. In addition, Wang criticized the paper by saying that Newmark should have added 'Euro-American' to his translation history and theory as he never mentioned materials from China or Japan, etc. At the end of the paper, Wang suggested five directions for the then future Chinese translation:

1. We should do some translation works of our own.
   (自己动手做些翻译工作)
2. Read, study and comment on current translation works.
3. Compare the similarities and differences between Chinese and foreign languages.
4. Refer to foreign translation theory.
5. Draw from works in philosophy, logic, literature, linguistics and psychology.

As can be seen, the suggestions were quite vague and ungrounded, but they did seem a compulsory module in the book review type of introduction to Western translation theory.

In addition to the review or review-like introductions to Western translation theories, some introductory works were quite substantial and appeared to be the results of more serious research and speculation, which also started to include more organized summaries and detailed comparisons or constructive criticisms in the introductory pieces. Liu Miqing (刘宓庆) was one of the Chinese translation scholars who initiated the first wave of Western translation theory introduction into China. Liu (1989) carried out a representative work which offered a brief look at significant developments in the Western history of translation studies with some critical comments. In that work, Liu followed Steiner (1975) to divide Western history of translation theory into four stages:

Stage 1. from classic translation discourse like that of Cicero (106–43 B.C.) to George Campbell (1719–1796);
Stage 2. from Schleiermacher (1768–1834) to the book *Sous l'invocation de saint Jérôme* ('An Homage to Jerome') published in 1946 by Valéry

Larbaud (However, Liu confused the name with French poet P. Valery);
Stage 3. represented by works from J-P. Vinay and J. Darbelnet and E. Nida in North America to those from G. Mounin and J. Catford in Europe;
Stage 4. from the 1970s to the present (i.e. 1989 when Liu's work was published).

At the time when Liu (1989) was published, according to Tu and Xiao (2000), there was a time lag of around 20 years so that the 1980s works mainly introduced Western translation theory in or before the 1960s. This is true with Liu (1989), which used considerable space introducing classical Western thoughts on translation that were relatively unheard of at the time. In his article, Liu emphasized the pioneering nature of Western translation theory, as translation thinkers routinely held inquisitive minds and critical views about the tradition and their intellectual heritage, which was worth emulating by their Chinese counterparts. For example, Liu noted that the 'natural' and 'harmony' theory proposed by Cicero and Horace must have been influenced by Plato's rationalism. Plato thought that the creation of an artistic state was governed by the rationalist principles. Therefore, Cicero and Horace thought that the imitation carried out in the translation process must follow the rule of rationalism in order for the TT to be natural and smooth and to achieve unity with aesthetics. However, Liu's point is that, even though Cicero inherited Plato's rational aesthetics theory, he was not bound by it but sought to be innovative instead through the stance of relative rationalism. Thus, he claimed a translator 'should not apply a principle of rigid reason in guiding the imitation process in translating lest the style and beauty of the ST be damaged' (Liu, 1989, p. 2, my translation). Another case Liu mentioned as an example of rebelling against tradition was St Jerome's advocacy that 'every translator should be the master of their own language' and that they should not be restricted by the so-called 'stylistic licenses'. Liu thought this was a very courageous movement and an effort to break away from the stagnant feeling associated with translation practice in the 500-year period since Cicero died together with his free and pleasant translation style. Still another example demonstrating the pioneering and innovative nature of Western translation theory, according to Liu (1989), was the 18th century Hermeneutics rebellion against the 'Stupidism' of the Middle Ages, in particular, the German Romanticists who refused to accept the prescriptive interpretation of the Bible given by the Vatican and vigorously pursued the original meanings of the Holy Scripture. By far the most influential pioneering work done for the modern translation studies in the West, however, was from Eugene Nica, according to Liu, who initially used the basic tenets of structuralism and transformational grammar to analyze translation problems and created his 'dynamic equivalence' theory. And then in the latter 1960s, Nida moved on to discourse and information theory and focused on the communicative aspect of language to overcome the restriction of form in translating. In the 1960s, Nida again pioneered in the sociosemiotics-enabled translation models in an attempt to expand the explanatory power of translation theory to tackle the cultural problems often encountered in translation. To Liu (1989), Nida's works represent the pioneering spirit of Western translation theory. In his words:

> 奈达的探索道路是一个为西方翻译理论的科学化而不断户开拓新的疆域的道路，特别能说明西方译论中的语言学派的成就和发展趋势。(The road of Nida is a trajectory of translation theory in the West as a result of continuous scientific input and pioneering of uncharted territory, which is particularly revealing of the achievements and developing trends of the linguistics school in translation studies.)
>
> (Liu, 1989, p. 3)

Being a Chinese translation scholar and prolific author, Liu did not forget to add some critical elements in his introductory work. At the time of writing (i.e. the late 1980s), translation studies was still not a well-established academic discipline. Accordingly, Liu suggested that the Western researchers at that time often neglected the need of translation theory to become an independent enquiry, so for example, they used linguistics to explain interlanguage transfer regularities, and they used stylistics to explain the writing styles in translating. However, translation studies was not a branch of linguistics or stylistics, Liu argued. Research methods can be borrowed from other disciplines, but they should not be transplanted directly; otherwise, translation studies will be delimited by the lending discipline. In addition, Liu also pointed out the respective weaknesses of the then prevalent linguistics and sociosemiotics theories, the former being unable to deal with cultural, communicative and stylistic problems, and the latter failing to provide the ontological principles and mechanisms and systematic methodologies for translation theory. Finally, Liu also noted the Eurocentric nature of Western translation theory and its strong focus on Bible translation, which is worthwhile taking into consideration when Chinese translation theorists tried to learn from the West.

Yin (1998) was a later example of introducing a Western monograph on translation theory, this time concentrating on the book *Théories contemporaines de la traduction* (Contemporary Theories of Translation) published by Robert Larose in 1989. After a decade, however, the introduction became more sophisticated with more complicated organization and presentation of the materials. In that book review, Yin (1998) listed the eight representative works between 1958 and 1982 in translation theory given by Larose:

- *Comparative Stylistics of French and English: A Methodology for Translation* (Vinay and Darbelnet, 1995);
- *Les problèmes théoriques de la traduction* (*The Theoretical Problems of Translation*) (Mounin, 1963);
- *Toward a Science of Translating* (Nida, 1964); *The Theory and Practice of Translation* (Eugene Albert Nida and Charles Russell Taber, 1982 – was listed as a 1964 work in Yin, 1998);
- *A Linguistic Theory of Translation* (Catford, 1965);
- *After Babel: Aspects of Language and Translation* (Steiner, 1975);

- *Traduire: théorèmes pour la traduction* (*Translate: Theorems for Translation*) (Ladmiral, 1979);
- *L'analyse du discours comme méthode de traduction* (*Discourse Analysis as a Method of Translation*) (Delisle and Seleskovitch, 1981);
- *Approaches to Translation* (Newmark, 1988).

Yin then went on to introduce the four points summarized by Larose after studying, comparing and synthesizing the above works:

1. translation studies is a theoretical field targeting translating as a subject of study. translation studies is an accommodative subject as it gains knowledge from other disciplines especially linguistics.
2. There is no such thing as 'perfect translation' or perfect understanding of translation. The success or not of a translation is a relative concept. Although the ST stays the same, each translator understands it differently and the result of translation varies as a function of translator's understanding.
3. 'Textual equivalence' is an unstable concept as there exist differences between two allegedly equivalent languages and cultures.
4. Form and content cannot be separated, and it is wrong to polarize literal translation and liberal translation – the two translation methods should complement each other. Researchers should simulate the actual writing processes and combine both meaning and symbols.

Yin also highly recommended the model for evaluating translation proposed in Larose (1989) which included the following five aspects:

- The accuracy of translation is determined by the match between translation purposes and the result of translation, that is, the so-called 'skopos' theory.
- There are four preconditions of translation which must be fully coordinated: 1. keeping the original narrative objectives, 2. maintaining the carriers of message, 3. respecting the comprising elements of form, and 4. coordinating the relationship between the respective socio-cultural backgrounds of ST and TT receivers.
- The evaluation of the TT can be approached from three layers: 1. surface structure, 2. macro structure and 3. micro structure. The internal structure of the text is conditioned by the surface structure. The more restricted the surface structure, the more influence on the reappearance of macro and micro structures.
- No element of the text can be detached from the integration of all elements in the text which comprises meaning and form.
- The analytical appraisal of the TT is based on the three proposed structures. The higher the structure an element under evaluation is situated, the more influential it is on the quality of the translation.

Yin (1998) summarized her review by recommending Larose's (1989) achievement in proposing a translation evaluation theory which was complete and objective, based on his model of four narrative conditions and three layers of text structure and approached from text analysis research methodology. Yin thought this could a good guideline for translation practice and translator education in China.

In consonance with the book review type of introductory work to Western translation theory, there was also a type of 'second order' introduction, or reviews of Western translation theory based on introductory works written by other authors in the Chinese language. For example, Yu (1985) was a book review based on Tan's (1984) book on Nida's translation theory. Guo (2000) was another example of a book review based on Chan and Chang (2000), which is itself a Chinese book (re)publishing 20 authors' works on Western translation theory (e.g. Dryden, Steiner, Nida, Newmark, Vermeer, Nord, Venuti), with authors' introduction to each. After briefly commenting on the merit of the book, for example, its comprehensive coverage and representative selections, Guo gave some personal observations regarding the development of Western translation theory, presumably to show his familiarity with the field and the credibility of the review. For example, Guo showed his awareness of the two 'turns' of Western translation studies: one was from linguistics-based research to cultural studies; the other was a turn from an author-centered to a reader- (or the TT) centered approach. In addition, Guo criticized that some Western researchers often went from one extreme to another in an effort to accentuate their own theory. Guo gave the example of a deconstructionist approach to translation studies which he thought was wrong to radically deny any distinctions between ST and TT, or those between the author and translator. However, he thought deconstructionism did a good service to the translator and the TT by upgrading their status to that of artistic creation, which was in tune with the Chinese traditional view about translation. Guo also tentatively suggested that issues like translation skopos and readership had already been noted in traditional Chinese translation theory. However, Guo pointed out a critical difference between Chinese and Western research methodologies and made a general recommendation:

> 关于读者对象的问题以及翻译的目的等问题，在我国传统译论中也都有涉及，只不过西方译论家在这方面的论述和分析更系统、更细密，而我们传统的译论大都只是译家随感式的经验之谈。… 只有把这两个方面的研究结合起来，才能进一步推动我国翻译理论的发展。(The issues of targeted readership and translation purposed were already discussed in the traditional translation theory of our nation. The difference is, Western translation theorists are more systematic and more detailed; while our traditional translation discourses were mostly casual talks based on translator's personal experiences. Only by combining the research results of the two are we able to promote the development of the translation theory of our nation.)
> (Guo, 2000, p. 67)

Thus, the heroic endeavor of introducing Western translation theory into China by Chinese thinkers and researchers was launched in the 1980s and pursued well into the 2000s after the millennium. Since then, the introduction of Western translation theory becomes more versatile, specific and detailed. There are also more and more well-grounded arguments and informed opinions in tandem with more sophisticated introductions. Han (2007), for example, reviews Snell-Honby's (2006) book *Turns of Translation Studies* in a relatively compelling way. After giving a substantial introduction to each of the six chapters in the book, Han recommended the author's recognition of the issues of English hegemony in translation studies and the abstruse writing style of translation thinkers. On the other hand, Han also criticized the author of falling into her own trap of Eurocentrism in translation research, by only introducing English and German works in her book. Another author, Wang (2010), introduced Pym's (2010) book *Exploring Translation Theories* in a critically reflective way. He praised Pym's critical introduction method such as pointing out the weakness of descriptive translation studies of focusing on the process of translation exclusively and ignoring the subjectivity and ethics of the translator. Wang emphasized the need for the Chinese translation researcher to develop critical evaluation abilities and to read (Western) translation works on a first-hand basis. Finally and most recently, Zhang and Ma (2018) introduced a less familiar translation scholar, Yves Gambier, summarizing his distinguished works in audio-visual translation and translation policy. In particular, the study of translation policy is a relatively new field of enquiry so the import of the concept and methodology is quite timely and necessary. In their introduction, Zhang and Ma identify three components of translation policy:

- Translation practices: the practices of translation in a certain community
- Translation beliefs: the view of the values of translation held by members of a community
- Translation management: the decision of the authority regarding the use of translation in a certain field

Zhang and Ma (2018) point out that the study of translation policy is all the more important with the increasing globalization of the economy and intercultural communication which implicates policy decisions at the levels of government, non-profit organizations and private companies. They also relay a personal message from Gambier that what he tells is essentially a 'Western story'. As for the questions revolving around the practices of Chinese translation, they can only be solved by Chinese investigators themselves.

Over and above the introduction of an individual author or theory, there are also works which summarize a certain period of history of translation studies in the West or compare between different strands of translation theory. Zhang (1996), for example, explained the development of Western translation theory from Cicero to the 'cultural turn' in the early 1990s based on his own reading and understanding. Song (2018), on the other hand, is a recent work which compares synchronically between three periods of translation theory output: the traditional one, the modern one, and the postmodern one. According to Song, traditional translation theory is primarily prescriptive and emphasizes either faithfulness or stylistic consistency, depending on each translation thinker's theoretical inclination. Modern translation theory is descriptive in nature, which systematically investigates the different norms of translation in different social and cultural contexts. Postmodern translation theory, on the other hand, denies the stability of meaning and objectivity and generalizability claimed by descriptive translation studies. According to Song, Postmodern translation theory carries a predetermined political agenda and represents the benefits and position of the oppressed group (for example, in studying the function of translation in the expansion and invasion of Eurocentrism). Song recognizes that the three strands of translation theory are not mutually exclusive or one replacing another, but each provides a meaningful perspective in understanding the history, practice and conceptualization of translation.

An iconic person whose works deserve extra attention in this intellectual effort of importing Western translation theory is Tan Zaixi (谭载喜). There are nearly 50 works output by Tan as a result of searching author name in the CNKI database, which include a significant number of papers introducing Western translation theory or discussing its implications for Chinese translation studies. For example, Tan (1982, 1983, 1989, 1995) introduced and explained the significance of Nida's translation theory. Tan (1985, 1988, 1998, 2000, 2005) continued to explore and explain the history of Western translation theory and started to compare it with Chinese translation theory. From then on, Tan began to output specific translation theory presumably as a result of integrating thoughts and learning from both Chinese and Western translation theories. For example, Tan (2006) discussed the meaning and application of 'metaphors of translation' and Tan (2008) investigated the idea of 'third form' – a kind of translation product whose identity is both the ST and the TT, but at the same time it is neither ST or TT. The concept of 'third form' is used to highlight the relativity in applying and judging the effect of equivalence when translating from ST to TT and to ultimately tease out the nature of translating. More recently, Tan (2010) explained the generation and application of the 'fuzziness principle' when doing literary translation. Tan (2011), on the other hand, pondered the possibility of breaking away from the binary oppositions in translation studies such as form vs. meaning, domestication vs. foreignization and so on by adopting the concept of a 'prototype' in cognitive linguistics to explain the nature and norm of translation, etc. In 2014, Tan output a paper on the 'taboos on translation' which works on a dialectical basis and discusses how cultural and political systems in different nations create specific ideologies that naturally impose restrictions (i.e. creating taboos) on what can be translated and how. As a leading advocate for translation studies to become an independent discipline in China, Tan (2017) concluded the achievements of Chinese translation studies in the past three decades:

1. Massive import of foreign (especially Western) translation theory modernized Chinese translation studies within a short time
2. Comprehensive development of translation research and large numbers of publication pushed the field forward in a steady and vigorous fashion
3. Tremendous progress has been made in the teaching of translation and the translation establishment's education degrees.

Through his own works of importing Western translation theory and conducting well-informed and original research in translation studies, Tan personally illustrated the trajectory of the development of Chinese translation theory, especially regarding the significant role played by the importation of translation studies from the West.

Reconceptualizing Chinese translation theory

The incubation of modern Chinese translation theory has been a long and continual process that accelerated rapidly after receiving significant input from the West in the 1980s. The initial input of Western translation theory had inspired many academic talents to reconsider the meaning and significance of translation practice in China who then started to put out their own translation theory based on their understanding of the imported theory and the domestic experience of translation practice and research. In this long and persistent process of absorbing (Western), integrating (Western and Chinese) and reconceptualizing (Chinese) translation theory, many creative ideas in the formulation and modification of Chinese translation theory were put forward, which became the foundation for the next generation of Chinese translation theory. At this point in time, some Chinese thinkers were quick to respond to the need of reconfiguring the field of translation studies in China, taking responsibility to summarize the current findings and offer alternative perspectives and insightful maps for conceptualizing the current status and future directions for Chinese translation theory. Some of the works that strived to do this are considered below.

The first type of work which attempts to summarize the current situation and point to a future direction for Chinese translation theory mainly functions at the conceptual level, providing well-meant but not necessarily cogently argued guidelines for directions of future research in translation theory. Han (1997), for example, noted that ever since China's opening up policy from 1978, translation has become a hot topic, especially the need to establish a system of Chinese translation theory. However, even though some improvements had been made in putting together Chinese traditional theory and learning from Western theory, Han thought the progress of establishing a Chinese translation theory system was still slow due to 'conceptual differences', 'methodological flaws' and that it was far from being able to meet the requirements of a fast-developing society. Han recommended three actions at the then current stage: firstly, to introduce Western translation theory (further), not to blindly follow but not to casually dismiss either; secondly, to build translation theory in accordance with China's historical background, practical reality and cultural heritage; and thirdly, to build translation theory strictly on the basis of translation practice. Han believed that only by personally participating in a substantial number of translation projects and having accumulated enough practical experience can a person start to produce really useful theory. This kind of three-page essay aiming to summarize the existing state of things and provide general guidance for future action, in my view, is far too abstract and vague to be useful to future translation researchers looking to be enlightened. Zhang and Xin (2008), on the other hand, advised that, as researchers on translation theory in the third world, we should insist on the 'mobility' of our own intellectual thoughts, strengthening our own subjective consciousness, identify the differences between China and the West in respect of history, culture and politics, and avoid following the Western steps too closely and blindly while concentrating on their theoretical findings. Zhang and Xin found postcolonial translation theory particularly to their liking, praising it as a worthwhile endeavor to overthrow the ideology hidden behind the practice of translation; the hegemony of Eurocentrism. They recommended that, when importing translation theory from the West, we should systematically reflect on the implications in the areas of culture, scholarship and theorization. By drawing from a constructive and positive theory like postcolonial translation theory, according to Zhang and Xin (2008), we will get enough nutrition to broaden the perspective of Chinese translation theory, which will also become more open and inclusive. In the same vein, Wang (2017) reviewed Zhang and Xin (2016) and reiterated their blueprint for establishing Chinese translation theory, which consists of three broad directions: 1. the modern transformation of traditional Chinese translation theory; 2. the mutual complementation and integration of the Chinese and Western translation theories; and 3. establishment of new territory of Chinese translation theory in the new digital and big data era.

Another type of work produced as a result of the import of Western translation theory is the one that attempts to reinstate the value of traditional Chinese theory by finding similarities between Chinese and Western translation theories, thereby showing that the Chinese translation theory is not that far behind. Cheng (2017), as an example, examined four historical figures' discourse on translation and highlighted their similarities to elements of modern translation theory. Firstly, Cheng explained Liang Qichao's (梁启超) ideas about translation based on his work *Translated Literature and Buddhist Sutra* (翻译文学与佛典). According to Cheng, Liang's discussion on the translation of the sutra was fairly mature and systematic, looking at issues like the language ability and professionalism of the translator, the comparison between different TT versions, the influence of translated sutra on Chinese literature, and his definition for 'immature literal translation' and 'immature free translation'. Secondly, Cheng called attention to a questionnaire survey conducted by Ai Wei (艾伟) in the 1920s regarding issues like the boundary between literal and liberal translation, different advocacies of translation theory, comparisons of text difficulties, translator's proficiency, relationship with text, stylistic problems involving classic and vernacular Chinese, proper noun translation and reader reaction. Subjects investigated included both experts (for the first six items) and students (for the last item). Cheng commented that the questionnaire survey was a very advanced research method in that period of time. Also, based on his survey results, Ai Wei distinguished five categories between literal translation and free translation. Cheng pointed out that this was similar to Newmark's model of translation methods involving semantic translation and communication translation, although Ai Wei invented his model 50 years earlier than Newmark. The third person Cheng (2017) referred to was Qu Qiubai

(瞿秋白) who advocated the literal translation method with TT fully expressed in vernacular Chinese. In particular, according to Cheng, Qu looked upon translation as a component of 'revolutionary literature' and thought that it was loaded with two missions: to introduce the revolutionary literature of the proletariat and to introduce the language of the new culture in order to shape the modern Chinese language. For Cheng, Qu's view of translation aimed to break the old order and establish a new order, and is representative of pioneering work in modern translation theory. The fourth and last person Cheng mentioned was Lu Xun (魯迅) who advocated a kind of 'tolerant literal translation' and is regarded by Cheng as a precursor of the foreignization view of translation, in the same camp as Venuti and Benjamin.

In the face of the importation of the Western translation theory, the most assertive kind of reaction would be that striving to unearth new and innovative translation theories as uniquely Chinese contributions to global translation studies. Lan (2018), for example, makes a good attempt at digging up innovative translation theories output by Chinese researchers when the so-called new era of Chinese translation studies began as a reaction to the stimulation of Western translation theory. According to Lan, a new page of Chinese translation studies was turned with the opening of China's first postgraduate conference in translation theory and China's national conference in translation theory in Nanjing and Qingdao, China, respectively, in 1987. According to Lan, the past 30 years' research coincided with China's opening up policy and has taken giant steps forward with the prompt of globalization and digitalization at the background. Now translation studies is an established academic discipline in China and the achievement in translator education is remarkable. Chinese translation scholars are gaining influence on the global stage, in Lan's opinion. Meticulously, Lan (2018) maps out the achievements of Chinese translation theory research in the past 30 years:

1. Research in the nature, target, structure, methodology of translation studies as an academic discipline including its relationship with other disciplines.
2. Research in the basic questions of translation theory such as translatability and the philosophy of translation.
3. Interdisciplinary research in translation studies.
4. Research on the branching of subdisciplines within Chinese translation studies.

Lan painstakingly showed that many original works of Chinese translation scholars exist among those categories. For the first category, Lan thinks that Chinese translation scholars have collectively verified the status of translation studies in China through persistent teamwork over the past 30 years. This is similar, but also in stark contrast, to Holmes (1988) establishing the status of translation studies in the West with a single article. Next, Lan recommended the Chinese achievements in defining principles and norms of translation, especially the work of Gu Zhengkun (辜正坤) (1989). The book proposed a system of translation norms consisting of 'absolute norm' (绝对标准), 'highest norm' (最高标准) and 'specific norm' (具体标准), breaking away from the traditional concept of defining a single norm for all kinds of genres and contexts. In the interdisciplinary research thread, Lan gives high regards to the 'translating and introducing theory' (译介学) initiated by Xie Tianzhen (谢天振), describing it as an intersection between and a combination of translation studies and comparative literature, a major accomplishment in the expansion of translation studies as an interdisciplinary subject, which currently has no Western counterpart. Likewise, the Chinese invention of Eco-translatology (生态翻译学) is regarded by Lan as an original theory and a critical exploration in creating China's own discourse of translation theory. Finally, regarding research in the subdisciplines of translation studies, Lan mentions two areas where Chinese scholars have made spectacular advances: literary translation and applied translation. For the former, Lan commended Xu Yuanchong (许渊冲) as not only an award-winning creative writer but also a great theorist of literary translation. Xu's literary translation theory, for Lan, inherits the Chinese traditional thought of aesthetics and expresses ideas of translation theory in contemporary, colorful terms, following a subjective epiphanic convention. This breaks away from the ST-focused convention and enhances the status of the translator as creative writer. As regards applied translation, Lan (2018) refers to the increasingly prosperous non-literary translation practice in areas like law, travel, business and technology. As to future directions for the further development of Chinese translation theory, Lan suggests we should move from 'applying Western translation theory to Chinese practice' to focus on the theoretical and practical concerns of current social practice; how translation can help further construction of China in the globalized linguistic context; and how to use translation to promote the 'spiritual reform' of human beings and deepen research in truth and universal regularities.

If Lan's (2018) ultimate goals for Chinese translation theory as stated above seem a far cry to researchers in translation studies, Luo's (2009) caution at the end of his discussion on the fundamental questions of Chinese translation is decisively more achievable and down to earth. In his paper, after presenting his view on four areas of Chinese translation theory (theoretical exploration, translation methods, related disciplines, history of translation studies), Luo advised that translation theory should not be emphasized at the expense of translation practice. According to Luo, the reason why translation theory is currently a hotly pursued topic in China is, firstly, we have absorbed a lot of the essence from the West and secondly, academics do research in order to get promotions (and funding, to which we can add). However, nothing like that can be gained by actually doing the translation. There are currently too many translation theorists in our country and too few translation practitioners. If we had some gallant translators to translate great literary works like those existing in the West, not only will our translation business prosper, but our translation studies will also make spectacular advances. With that caution in mind, we turn to the next chapter to understand more about the current branches of Chinese translation theory, some of which may have more to do with translation practice than others.

References

Chinese references

Chan, Tak hung and Chang, Nam-fung 陈德鸿, 张南峰 (2000) 西方翻译理论精选 (*Selected Western Translation Theories*). Hong Kong: City of Hong Kong University Press.

Cheng, Yongsheng 程永生 (2017) 我国传统译论中的现代元素——以直译意译研究为例 (The modern elements in our traditional translation theory: using semantic translation as an example). 外语研究 (*Foreign Languages Research*). 2017(02): 84–88.

Delisle, J. and Seleskovitch, D. (1982) *L'Analyse du discours comme méthode de traduction.* Ottawa: Éditions de l'Université d'Ottawa.

Ding, Zhenqin 丁振琴 (2016) 一位西方学者眼中的中国翻译学 (The Chinese translation studies in the eyes of a Western scholar). 中国翻译 (*Chinese Translation Journal*). 2016 (03): 83–86.

Gu, Zhengkun 辜正坤 (1989) 翻译标准多元互补论 (Multiple complementary theory of the translation norm). 中国翻译 (*Chinese Translators Journal*). 1989(01): 100–105.

Guo, Jianzhong 郭建中 (2000) 简评《西方翻译理论精选》 (A brief comment on *Selected Western Translation Theories*). 中国翻译 (*Chinese Translators Journal*). 2000(05): 66–67.

Han, Zhen 韩珍 (1997) 我国翻译理论建设之思考 (Thinking about the construction of our translation theory). 语言与翻译 (*Language and Translation*). 1997(04): 40–42.

Han, Ziman 韩子满 (2007) 西方翻译研究的转向与进展——评《翻译研究的多重转向》 (The turns and progress of Western translation studies: on *Turns of translation studies*). 中国翻译 (*Chinese Translators Journal*). 2007(05): 42–45.

Ji, Xianlin 季羡林 (1995) 西方不亮东方亮 (The west is dark and the east is lightened). 中国文化研究 (*Chinese Culture Research*). 1995(04): 1–6.

Ladmiral, J-R (1979) *Traduire Théorèmes Pour la Traduction.* Paris: Payot.

Lan, Hongjun 蓝红军 (2018) 从学科自觉到理论建构：中国译学理论研究（1987–2017）(Theoretically oriented translation studies in China: 1987–2017). 中国翻译 (*Chinese Translators Journal*). 2018(01): 7–16.

Lin, Shuwu 林书武 (1981) 奈达的翻译理论简介 (A brief introduction to Nida's translation theory). 国外语言学 (*Foreign Linguistics*). 1981(02): 1–7+14.

Liu, Jianzhu and Mu, Lei 刘建珠, 穆雷 (2017) 中国翻译理论话语体系的构建及其划界 (On the construction and demarcation of discourse system for China's translation theory). 上海翻译 (*Shanghai Journal of Translators*). 2017(2): 1–5.

Liu, Miqing 刘宓庆 (1989) 西方翻译理论概评 (A critical overview of the Western translation theory). 中国翻译 (*Chinese Translators Journal*). 10(2): 2–21.

Luo, Xuanmin 罗选民 (2009) 谈我国翻译理论研究的几个基本问题 (On a few fundamental questions in the research of translation theory in our nation). 中国外语 (*Foreign Languages in China*). 2009(06): 101–105.

Mu, Lei 穆雷 (1989) 卡特福德及其《翻译的语言学理论》 (Catford and his *A Linguistic Theory of Translation*). 上海科技翻译 (*Shanghai Journal of Translators for Science and Technology*). 1989(02): 42.

Song, Meihua 宋美华 (2018) 西方翻译研究的传统、现代与后现代：区别、对立、共存 (Three distinct historico-cultural formations of TS and their contentious yet mutually supportive coexistence). 中国翻译 (*Chinese Translators Journal*). 2018(2): 17–24.

Tan, Zaixi 谭载喜 (1982) 翻译是一门科学——评介奈达著《翻译科学探索》 (Translation is a science: on Nida's toward a science of translating). 中国翻译 (*Chinese Translators Journal*). 1982(04): 4–11.

Tan, Zaixi 谭载喜 (1983) 奈达论翻译的性质 (Nida on the nature of translation theory). 中国翻译 (*Chinese Translators Journal*). 1983(02): 11–15.
Tan, Zaixi 谭载喜 (1984) 奈达论翻译 (*Nida on Translation*). 北京: 中国对外翻译出版公司 (Beijing: China Translation Corporation).
Tan, Zaixi 谭载喜 (1985) 西方翻译史浅谈 (About the history of Western translation history). 中国翻译 (*Chinese Translators Journal*). 1985(07): 36–39.
Tan, Zaixi 谭载喜 (1988) 现代西方翻译发展概述 (An overview of modern development of translation in the West). 湖南大学学报(社会科学版) (*Journal of Hunan University*). 15(02): 94–101.
Tan, Zaixi 谭载喜 (1989) 奈达和他的翻译理论 (Nida and his translation theory). 外国语(上海外国语大学学报) (*Journal of Foreign Languages*). 1989(05): 30–37+51.
Tan, Zaixi 谭载喜 (1995) 中西现代翻译学概评 (Comments on the modern Chinese and Western translation studies). 外国语(上海外国语大学学报) (*Journal of Foreign Languages*). 1995(03): 12–16.
Tan, Zaixi 谭载喜 (1998) 翻译学必须重视中西译论比较研究 (Comparative study of translation theory between China and the West must be emphasized). 中国翻译 (*Chinese Translators Journal*). 1998(02): 11–15.
Tan, Zaixi 谭载喜 (2000) 中西翻译传统的社会文化烙印 (The social cultural brand of the Western and Chinese traditions of translation). 中国翻译 (*Chinese Translators Journal*). 2000(02): 14–18.
Tan, Zaixi 谭载喜 (2005) 关于西方翻译理论发展史的几点思考 (A few thoughts on the development of translation theory in the West). 外国语(上海外国语大学学报) (*Journal of Foreign Languages*). 2005(01): 53–59.
Tan, Zaixi 谭载喜 (2006) 翻译比喻中西探幽 (The exploration of metaphors of translation in China and the West). 外国语(上海外国语大学学报) (*Journal of Foreign Languages*). 2006(04): 73–80.
Tan, Zaixi 谭载喜 (2008) 翻译的"第三形态"特质 (The 'third form' in translation). 外语与外语教学 (*Foreign Languages and Their Teaching*). 2008(01): 39–43.
Tan, Zaixi 谭载喜 (2010) 翻译·模糊法则·信息熵 (Translation, fuzzy principle, information entropy). 中国翻译 (*Chinese Translators Journal*). 2010(04): 11–14+94.
Tan, Zaixi 谭载喜 (2011) 翻译与翻译原型 (Translation and translation prototype). 中国翻译 (*Chinese Translators Journal*). 2011(04): 14–17+96.
Tan, Zaixi 谭载喜 (2017) 翻译学:作为独立学科的发展回望与本质坚持 (Reflection on translation studies as an independent discipline and the insistence on intrinsic quality). 中国翻译 (*Chinese Translators Journal*). 2017(01): 5–10+126.
Tu, Guo yuan and Xiao, Jinyin 屠国元, 肖锦银 (2000) 西方现代翻译理论在中国的传播与接受 (The dissemination and reception of Western translation theory in China). 中国翻译 (*Chinese Translators Journal*). 2000(05): 15–19.
Wang, Bihui 汪璧辉 (2017) 中国译论建设新图景——《译学研究叩问录——对当下译论研究的新观察与新思考》评介 (A new blueprint for building Chinese translation theory: a critical review of *Questions and Answers in Translation Studies: New Perspectives and New Thoughts on the Study of Contemporary Translation Theory*). 外语研究 (*Foreign Languages Research*). 162(2): 109–111.
Wang, Bingqin and Wang, Jie 王秉钦, 王颉 (2009) 20 世纪中国翻译思想史(第二版) (*20th Century History of Chinese Translation Thoughts*, 2nd edition). 天津: 南开大学出版社 (Tianjin: Nankai University Press).
Wang, Hongyin 王宏印 (2003) 中国传统译论经典诠释——从道安到傅雷 (*Reinterpretation of Traditional Chinese Translation Theories – From Dao'an to Fulei*). 武汉: 湖北教育出版社 (Wuhan: Hubei Educational Press).

Wang, Jun 王军 (2017) 翻译中的儒道哲学 --《翻译之道》 (The Dao of Translation) 评介 (Confucianism and Taoism in translation: review of *The Dao of Translation*). 中国翻译 (*Chinese Translators Journal*). 2017(01): 74–78.

Wang, Peng 王鹏 (2010)《翻译理论探讨》——对当代西方翻译理论的批判性认识 (*Exploring Translation Theories* – a critical exploration of contemporary Western translation theory). 中国翻译 (*Chinese Translators Journal*). 2010(03): 33–37.

Wang, Zongyan 王宗炎 (1982) 纽马克论翻译理论和翻译技巧 (Newmark's translation theory and translation techniques). 中国翻译 (*Chinese Translators Journal*). 1982(01): 11–17.

Wen, Jun 文军 (2010) 建国以来中国翻译理论著作出版评述 (A critical summary of the publications on translation theory since the establishment of the nation). 中国翻译 (*Chinese Translators Journal*). 2010(01): 33–37.

Xi, Rui 席蕊 (2017) 论中国哲学思想下的特色翻译美学 (Translation aesthetics with characteristics under the influence of Chinese philosophical thoughts). 西华大学学报(哲学社会科学版) (*Journal of Xihua University (Philosophy & Social Sciences)*). 36(6): 102–105.

Xu, Yuanchong 许渊冲 (2000) 新世纪的新译论 (New translation theory for the new century). 中国翻译 (*Chinese Translators Journal*). 2000(03): 2–6.

Yang, Qing 杨青 (2018) 以中国哲学视角看翻译 (A look at translation from the perspective of Chinese philosophy). 才智 (*Ability and Wisdom*). 2017(02): 195.

Ye, Junjian 叶君健 (1997) 翻译也要出精品 (Exquisite products are also needed in translation). 中国翻译 (*Chinese Translators Journal*). 1997(05): 95–96.

Yin, Lingxia 尹玲夏 (1998) 当代西方译学研究的梳理与分析—《当代翻译理论》评介 (The organization and analysis of contemporary translation studies in the West: A critical introduction of *Théories contemporaines de la traduction*). 中国翻译 (*Chinese Translators Journal*). 1998(04): 56–58.

Yu, Fengping 喻锋平 (2011) 翻译哲学：哲学的分支学科 — 从中西哲学和翻译研究史出发 (Translation philosophy: a subdiscipline of philosophy – from the study of Chinese and Western philosophy and the history of translation studies). 江西社会科学 (*Jiangxi Social Sciences*). 2011(02): 61–65.

Yu, Pei 于沛 (1985) 翻译的新概念 (New concept about translation). 读书 (*Dushu*). 1985(10): 27–28.

Zhang, Boran and Xin, Hongjuan 张柏然, 辛红娟 (2008) 翻译理论研究的新课题 (New agenda in the research on translation theory). 中国外语 (*Foreign Languages in China*). 2008(03): 79–82+94.

Zhang, Boran and Xin, Hongjuan 张柏然, 辛红娟 (2016)《译学研究叩问录——对当下译论研究的新观察与新思考》(*Questions and Answers in Translation Studies: New Perspectives and New Thoughts on the Study of Contemporary Translation Theory*). 南京: 南京大学出版社 (Nanjing: Nanjing University Press).

Zhang, Hesheng 章和升 (1996) 西方翻译理论研究发展纵横谈 (An overview of the development of research on translation theory in the West). 外语教学 (*Foreign Language Education*). 1996(04): 44–48.

Zhang, Yingying and Ma, Huijuan 张迎迎, 马会娟 (2018) 当代西方翻译研究的新趋势 (Recent trends in contemporary Western translation studies). 上海翻译 (*Shanghai Journal of Translators*). 2018(4): 17–23.

Zhu, Shuran 朱舒然 (2018) 庄子语言哲学的翻译学意义 (The significance of Zhuangzi's philosophy of language on translation studies). 河南社会科学 (*Henan Social Sciences*). 26(5): 93–97.

Zhu, Yu 朱瑜 (2008) 中国传统译论的哲学思辨 (A philosophical interpretation of traditional Chinese translation theory). 中国翻译 (*Chinese Translators Journal*). 2008(1): 12–15.

Other references

Catford, J.C. (1965) *A Linguistic Theory of Translation*. Oxford: Oxford University Press.
Holmes, J. S. (1988) The name and nature of translation studies. In J. S. Holmes (ed.) *Translated! Papers on Literary Translation and Translation Studies*. Amsterdam: Rodopi, pp. 67–80.
Larose, R. (1989) *Théories contemporaines de la traduction*, 2e édition. Sillery, QC: Presses de l'Université du Québec.
Mounin, G. (1963) *Les problèmes théoriques de la traduction*. Paris: Gallimard.
Newmark, P. (1978) The theory and the craft of translation. In V. Kinsella (ed.) *Language Teaching and Linguistics: Surveys*. Cambridge and New York: Cambridge University Press.
Newmark, P. (1988) *A Textbook of Translation*. New York: Prentice-Hall International.
Nida, E.A. (1964) *Toward a Science of Translating: With Special Reference to Principles and Procedures Involved in Bible Translating*. Leiden: Brill.
Pym, A. (2010) *Exploring Translation Theories*. London and New York: Routledge.
Robinson, D. (1991) *The Translator' Turn*. Baltimore, MD and London: The John Hopkins University Press.
Robinson, D. (1997) *Translation and Empire: Postcolonial Theories Explained*. Manchester: St. Jerome Publishing Company.
Robinson, D. (2003) *Performative Linguistics: Speaking and Translating as Doing Things with Words*. New York and London: Routledge.
Robinson, D. (2015) *The Dao of Translation*. New York: Routledge.
Snell-Hornby, M. (2006) *The Turns of Translation Studies: New Paradigm or Shifting Viewpoints*. Amsterdam: John Benjamins Publishing Co.
Steiner, G. (1975) *After Babel*. London: Oxford University Press.
Vinay, J-P. and Darbelnet, J. (1995) *Comparative Stylistics of French and English: A Methodology for Translation*. Amsterdam: John Benjamins.

2 The blossoming of Chinese translation theory

This chapter picks up from the ending of the previous chapter and investigates the current state of Chinese translation theory in as many different forms as possible. We divide our topics on the theory of translation into sections mainly based on the bibliographic corpora collected from CNKI (China National Knowledge Infrastructure), here presented as Figure 2.1 and Table 2.1 in respective visualization and word list forms. The search words used to generate the results were 翻译理论 (translation theory) specified in the 'Topic' area of search functions. On the basis of the keywords identified by the scientometric tool *CiteSpace* (Chen, 2016), several 'concept groups' were identified to form the infrastructure of the chapter. For example, from the keywords 对等 ('equivalence'), 动态对等 ('dynamic equivalence'), 奈达 (Nida) we can identify a section named 'equivalent theory' in this chapter; from the keywords 解构主义 (deconstructionism), 结构主义 (structuralism), 后殖民翻译理论 (postcolonial translation theory) a section called 'postcolonial translation theory' can be formed, and so on and so forth. Other concept groups we can identify from Figure 2.1 and Table 2.1 are: functional theory, feminism, norm and principle, applied translation and so on, which will all be discussed in the course of the chapter.

As shown in the previous chapter, the introduction of Western translation theory from the 1980s onward plays a decisive role in the incubation of Chinese translation theory. The blossoming of Chinese translation theory gives rise to a wide range of academic works spread on a continuum, with Western translation theory on one end and original Chinese theory on the other end. On the 'Western end', the simplest kind of work is adopting ideas from the imported theory (e.g. principles of dynamic equivalence) and examining Chinese translation data to reveal new light brought about by new theory. On the 'Chinese end', conversely, some academic output concentrates on 'rediscovering' the merits of traditional Chinese translation discourse as a reaction to stimulation from the West. Others gradually come up with their own ideas about translation and claim to have formed new theories that are both original and 'Chinese' in nature. Most works, however, can be seen to fall within a certain band between these two ends and contain elements of theory and practice from both China and the West. Each of the strands of

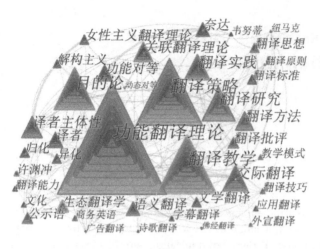

Figure 2.1 Visualization of bibliographic corpus collected from CNKI with 翻译理论 (translation theory) as search phrase in the topic domain (see this image in color at www.routledge.com/9780367209872)

Table 2.1 100 keywords with higher frequency from CNKI research on the topic of 翻译理论 (translation theory)

Frequency	Keyword	Frequency	Keyword
385	功能翻译理论（functional translation theory）	21	实践 (practice)
224	翻译策略 (translation strategies)	20	诗歌翻译 (poetry translation)
219	翻译教学 (translation teaching)	20	生态翻译 (ecological translation)
164	目的论 (skopos theory)	19	纽马克 (Newmark)
125	翻译研究 (translation studies)	18	西方翻译理论 (western translation theory)
108	翻译实践 (translation practice)	17	应用 (application)
104	交际翻译 (communicative translation)	17	文本类型 (text type)
89	关联理论 (relevance theory)	17	英汉翻译 (English-Chinese translation)
88	译者主体性 (translator subjectivity)	17	直译 (Literal translation)
88	关联翻译理论 (relevance translation theory)	16	广告翻译 (advertisement translation)
84	英译 (English translation)	16	研讨会 (conference)
74	翻译方法 (translation methods)	14	女性主义翻译 (feminist translation)
71	功能翻译 (functional translation)	14	功能对等理论 (functional equivalence theory)
70	功能对等 (equivalence theory)	13	旅游翻译 (tourism translation)
68	女性主义 (feminism)	13	翻译学科 (translation studies subject)

65	语义翻译 (semantic translation)	13	翻译过程 (translation process)
62	翻译学 (translatology)	12	功能派翻译理论 (functional translation theory)
60	译者 (translator)	12	动态对等 (dynamic equivalence)
59	女性主义翻译理论 (feminist translation theory)	12	意识形态 (ideology)
56	奈达 (Nida)	11	翻译史 (translation history)
55	翻译批评 (translation criticism)	11	对等 (equivalence)
55	文学翻译 (literary translation)	10	启示 (enlightenment)
53	公示语 (public notices and signs)	10	局限性 (limitation)
52	翻译思想 (translation thoughts)	10	中国 (China)
51	生态翻译学 (Eco-translatology)	10	影响 (influence)
50	归化 (domestication)	10	佛经翻译 (Buddhist scripture translation)
50	异化 (foreignization)	10	鲁迅 (Lu Xun)
49	解构主义 (deconstructivism)	9	教学 (pedagogy)
47	英语翻译 (English translation)	9	翻译伦理 (translation ethics)
42	翻译标准 (translation norm)	9	中国传统译论 (Chinese traditional translation theory)
39	许渊冲 (Xu Yuanchong)	9	异化翻译 (foreignized translation)
36	大学英语 (college English)	9	综述 (review)
35	字幕翻译 (subtitle translation)	8	隐喻 (metaphor)
35	文化 (culture)	8	文化差异 (cultural difference)
34	交际翻译理论 (communicative translation theory)	8	翻译专业 (English major)
32	翻译技巧 (translation skill)	8	功能理论 (functional theory)
31	理论 (theory)	8	《红楼梦》 (Hong Lou Meng)
30	应用翻译 (applied translation)	8	文化负载词 (culture-loaded word)
30	外宣翻译 (publicity translation)	8	主体性 (subjectivity)
29	最佳关联 (optimal relevance)	8	功能主义翻译理论 (functionalist translation theory)
29	理论与实践 (theory and practice)	8	忠实 (fidelity)
27	教学模式 (teaching model)	8	意译 (free translation)
27	翻译能力 (translation competence)	8	对策 (countermeasure)
25	策略 (strategy)	7	文化学派 (the cultural school)
25	问题 (problem)	7	功能 (function)
24	译文 (target text)	7	翻译目的 (translation purpose)
24	商务英语 (business English)	7	创新 (innovation)
24	生态翻译理论 (ecological translation theory)	7	研究 (study)
23	翻译原则 (translation principle)	7	文化转向 (cultural turn)
22	韦努蒂 (Venuti)	7	阐释学 (hermeneutics)

translation theory presented below examine where the theories fall on the different parts of the spectrum (i.e. between the imported Western theory and the claimed original Chinese theory).

Equivalence theory

The concept of equivalency in Chinese translation theory can be traced back to Nida, whose innovative idea of 'dynamic equivalence' (later replaced by 'functional equivalence') was first introduced to China in the 1980s. For more than 30 years, Nida's theory has been extensively studied and applied to actual translations in a wide variety of contexts (for example, the principle of 'functional equivalence' has been applied to the translation of medical terms in Gong, 2018; TV documentary subtitles in Pan, 2018; care product manuals in Lin and Wang, 2018; Chinese dish names in Yu and Lu, 2018 and so on). A large amount of research and discussion has been generated, ranging from verifying the theory's insights with Chinese examples to contrasting Nida's ideas with other Western or domestic discourses on translation, or adding personal thoughts to expand or complement his theory.

Early on, Tan (1989) and his other works on Nida gave fairly comprehensive and thorough introductions to Nida's translation theory. Among them, the concept of 'dynamic equivalence' was understood by Tan to be:

> 所谓动态对等翻译，是指从语义到文体，在接受语中用最切近的自然对等语再现源发语的信息。在动态对等翻译中，译者着眼于原文的意义和精神，而不必拘泥原文的语言结构，即不必拘泥于形式对应。(So-called dynamically equivalent translation means reinstating the message of the source language with the most natural equivalent expressions in the receptive language. In dynamically equivalent translation, the translator focuses on the meaning and essence of the source text and does not worry about the linguistic structure of the source text or the equivalence in form.)
>
> (Tan, 1989, p. 32)

Tan was thoughtful to add that 'dynamic equivalence' was not equal to the traditional concept of 'free translation', as the former imposes strict requirements on the target text, which must relay the intended meaning of the source text in different linguistic structures, while the latter does not introduce such restrictions.

Since Waard and Nida (1986), the term 'dynamic equivalence' has rarely been used in the Chinese translation theory field, and it has largely been replaced by the term 'functional equivalence' adopted in that book. This is both a fortunate and an unfortunate turn of events that produces both positive and adverse effects in the Chinese translation literature. For one thing, the word 'function' now has three affiliated translation/linguistic theories – Nida's functional equivalence, the German functional approach to translation, and Halliday's systemic functional grammar – and when the term 功能翻译理论 (functional translation theory) is vaguely used, there is no way of telling which one (or which combination of the three) is being referred to. Indeed, this is perhaps why the exact same phrase has occupied the most prominent place in Figure 2.1, that is, the most frequently used keyword found when searching a Chinese database for 'translation theory'. The positive effect is, however, that a subset of these three theories (e.g. the 'functional equivalence' concept and the 'functionalist approach' or the 'systemic functional grammar') are sometimes discussed together in an integrated fashion and produce novel results. We will come back to this point later on in this chapter.

Picking up from Tan's initial introduction of Nida's 'dynamic equivalence' or 'functional equivalence', many subsequent academic works have tried to test and expand the concept in both theoretical and applied domains. Liu et al. (2015) did a scientometric study using *CiteSpace* to reveal the crucial role played by Nida's equivalence theory in generating a vast body of research in China centering around the concept of equivalence. The high-frequency keywords they found related to 'equivalence' (对等) are 'Nida' (奈达), 'dynamic equivalence' (动态对等), 'functional equivalence' (功能对等), 'equivalent value' (等值), 'correspondence' (对应) and so on. After providing a meta-analysis of Chinese translation theory literature from 1979 to 2013 extracted from the CNKI database, however, Liu et al. concluded that Chinese research on 'equivalence' was mostly based on Western literature, especially on Nida's works, and that very little connection existed between the concept of equivalence and the traditional Chinese translation theory in academic research. They suggested that more should be done on extracting terminology from Chinese traditional resources while developing contemporary Chinese translation theory systems.

The idea of 'functional equivalence' was considered innovative and a major breakthrough from the traditional, rigid paradigms of formal or semantic equivalence in Chinese translation studies circles from the 1980s onward. Intelligent Chinese translation theorists started to apply the principle of functional equivalence to a wide variety of domains, generating new norms and strategies for translation practice in those fields. Many related terms were also invented or borrowed from other translation theories to be integrated into the general principle of functional equivalence. In this process, there has been chaos and confusion (in terms of the 'correct interpretation' of the term) as well as an expansion of the original theory to subsume more related concepts and theories. Lu and Liu (2012), for one, applied the idea of functional equivalence to the translation of Chinese poetry into English. They proposed that there were common stylistic features between Chinese and English poems, notably the artistic mood (意境), music disposition (音乐性) and laconic style (凝练), which could serve as a basis of functional equivalence and the translator's strategies accordingly. This is in stark contrast to Cai (2018), however, who also professed to work under Nida's dynamic equivalence principle, but advocated presenting the meaning or connotation of the poem in its entirety while taking care of the rhymes expediently. Cai thought this was what 'equivalent effect' meant (i.e. meaning rather than stylistic features).

Lu and Liu's (2012) and Cai's (2018) different interpretations of Nida's functional equivalence theory show us how the term can inspire various intellectual thoughts and fruitful findings on the part of Chinese researchers even though it does not come with a very strict definition. Creative applications of the principle of functional equivalence to translating include, for example, Wu and Zheng (2014) who came up with a theory of achieving functional equivalence while translating TV and movie subtitles consisting of 1. reduction (concise and colloquial rendering of dialogues), 2. meaning-based translation (disregarding forms), 3. domestication (using domestic cultural terms to achieve the same effect). H. Liu (2008), on the other hand, applied the notion of 'equivalent effect' to the translating of Chinese antithetic couplets (对联) which, according to Liu, is an 'organic (a word often used by Chinese researchers to refer to linguistic units or mechanisms) body' consisting of sound, shape and meaning and incorporating a lot of cultural information. Liu thought that the 'highest level' of translation for antithetic couplets was to faithfully render the content of thought and to reproduce the style and artistic concept of the original work. In order to do that, it is essential that the translator be fully acquainted with the linguistic context of the couplets, and that they take full control. In other words, the translator should carefully consider the intention of the author and pursue the same effect as the original as much as possible. In doing so, the reader's ideas, perception and reaction should also be taken into consideration. H. Liu called this 'pragmatic translation' (语用翻译), which not only emphasizes faithfulness to the original meaning but also focuses on the inferences that can be derived from the discourse connotations. This is one way to achieve the 'equivalent effect' by which the cultural communication purpose of antithetic couplets is fulfilled, as proposed in Liu (2008).

Other creative applications of the principle of functional equivalence can still be seen to this day. For example, Zhan (2018) applied the concept of functional equivalence to the translation of a scientific text on climate change; Zhou (2018) and Gong (2018) claimed to apply the same principle to medical text; Yu (2018) on financial reports; Liu and Wang (2019) on tourism promotion text; and Yu and Lu (2018) on the translation of Chinese dishes. A more systematic account on how to apply the concept of functional equivalence to practical domains (other than literal translation including Bible translation originally discussed in Nida's works), however, can be found in Zhai and Hu (2017), who developed a possible scheme for applying the principles of functional equivalence to the translating of political news text from Chinese to English. Zhai and Hu first recognized the three areas where Nida's functional equivalence should be considered: text type, author or translator's purpose and kind of readership. In particular, they thought that Chinese newspapers such as *China Daily* should assume the responsibility of abiding by the government's political principles and stance, such as establishing a positive national image for China internationally. From the three perspectives of text type, translation purposes and readership, Zhai and Hu (2017) explored translation strategies from cultural, linguistic structural and communicative functions seeking equivalent effects. For example, they thought that the translation of

打断骨头还连着筋 by *China Daily* into 'connected by our flesh even if our bones are broken' (p. 88) was quite good, where 筋 (a Chinese term rich in cultural and traditional medical meanings) was not literally translated for fear of confusing the reader but was rendered into 'flesh' to achieve the same cultural effect. Another example noticed by Zhai and Hu was the translation of Xi Jinping's 我提出要对世界经济把准脉、开好方 by *China Daily* into 'I proposed that we make an accurate assessment of the health of the world economy and give right prescriptions', which used the methods of literal translation and free translation for 开好方 (give right prescriptions) and 把准脉 (make an accurate assessment), respectively (p. 89), and made the TT comprehensible to the readership. Zhai and Hu concluded by saying that the translator needs to adjust the ST by adding, changing or removing text in order for the TT to meet the linguistic and cultural habits, the thinking patterns and the ideology of the Western countries and to achieve communicative functions.

Su (2008) discussed the idea of equivalence using the framework of Systemic Functional Grammar (SFG) and, by doing so, integrating the concept of equivalence in translation studies into a major linguistics theory in some ways. Specifically, Su remapped the three metafunctions of SFG into translational terms of 'ideational equivalence', 'interpersonal equivalence' and 'textual equivalence', and claimed that the translator must fulfill equivalence in all three domains in order to accurately capture the meaning of the ST and the 'attitude' of the original author. To further integrate the three kinds of equivalence, Su borrowed the term 'attitude' from Martin and White's (2005) appraisal theory, which includes three components: affect, judgment and appreciation. Among them, affect is the stance that the speaker takes toward something and plays a central role in determining the speaker's attitude aside from the consideration of social norms (judgment) and social values (appreciation). Furthermore, Su ingeniously used the terms 'overtranslation' and 'undertranslation' to represent cases where equivalence was not achieved in translation. For Su, only when the functions of the ST and the TT are equivalent in the same context can we be sure that the TT truthfully expressed the author's attitude. Thus, when the phrase 很听话的孩子 was literally translated into 'such an obedient boy' in Lu Xun's work *Zhu Fu* (祝福), Su cogently argued that this failed to achieve equivalence due to a misjudgment of the author's attitude, who simply wanted to express the meaning of 'a good boy'. By resorting to the appraisal theory, which was supposed to be an updated component added to SFG, according to Su (2008), the translator could accurately grasp the 'attitude' of the author and achieve equivalence in ideational, interpersonal and textual domains, or the intended meaning of the ST.

As discovered by Liu et al. (2015), a keyword which figures prominently in a search of literature for 'equivalence' (对等) is 'equivalent value' (等值). Both terms are used in the Chinese translation literature in a more or less synonymous fashion. However, when the word 等值 is used, it seems other equivalent theories than Nida's are more likely to appear (possibly because 对等 has been so strongly associated with Nida's dynamic/functional equivalence theory). Lin and Zhao

(2017), for example, adopted Koller's (1989) idea about equivalence in translation, and focused especially on the joint work of formal equivalence, connotative equivalence and pragmatic equivalence, the last of which was thought by them to be most subtle and changeable and required extra treatment. Xu (2015), on the other hand, referred to Pym's (2010) idea that equivalence between two languages means the values between the two languages are the same as manifested in syntax, semantics and pragmatics. Translating, accordingly to Xu, means to reproduce in the TT the values of the ST as manifested in the process of communicating, notably the semantic and the pragmatic values. Subsequently, Xu illustrated how to analyze the semantic values of the ST and seek semantic equivalence between the ST and the TT. According to her, the norms for judging the quality of translation are whether or not the semantic values of the TT are the same with those of the ST, and whether the pragmatic effects are the same in both versions. After mainly using Halliday and Hasan (1976) as an analytical framework to examine various examples of collocation, lexical fields, lexical chains and cohesion between ST and TT, Xu (2015, p. 18) proposed a model for evaluating the quality of the TT based on semantic equivalence, which seems quite interesting despite its vagueness in some respects:

1. Equivalence in number of semantic features: If a translation unit (TU) in ST and its corresponding TU in TT both have the same number of semantic features, then they have the same semantic value.
2. Equivalence in semantic relations: Have the semantic relations like antonyms, synonyms, hyponyms, meronyms and so on from the ST been fully or mostly represented in the TT? If so, we have a case of equivalence in semantic relations.
3. Equivalence in co-occurrence: Co-occurrence relationship includes collocations within sentence and cohesion across sentences. If co-occurrence relationship in TT follows the general semantic rules just like the ST, then both texts should be equally reasonable, clear and fluent.
4. Equivalence in lexical chains: Lexical chains are made up of semantically related words falling within the same topic. If both ST and TT are equivalent in the representation of lexical chains, they have reached semantic equivalence in topic and effect, a substantial component of textual equivalence.

Xu noted that 'semantic translation' (语义翻译) is done by reproducing in the TT various semantic features and relationships from the ST using the target language's syntactic rules. In that sense, conducting semantic analysis is the primary way for achieving (and for examining) semantic equivalence in translating. Xu's (2015) systematic account of equivalence at the level of meaning seems to assume there is an explicit 'grading system' among different translations of an ST. In sharp contrast, He (2016) offered a fuzzy view of functional equivalence based on the porotype theory from cognitive linguistics. He claimed that there was not such a thing as 'absolute equivalence' but that there were only 'prototypical equivalents' and 'non-typical equivalents', which were distinguished by the degree of 'family resemblance' shared among them (a member is the most prototypical of the category if it has the most family resemblance traits). He (2016) used eight Chinese translations of (four lines of) the same poem *The Princess* by Tennyson to illustrate the family resemblance effect, as well as the fact that there were more prototypical translations and non-prototypical translations, all of which constituted a 'translation equivalent cluster'. He claimed that the existing model of translation equivalence had 'walked into a dead alley' (p. 108) since its expansion from word equivalence and sentence equivalence etc., to pragmatic equivalence, where it found no room for further development. The translation prototype theory, He claimed, first created a translation equivalent cluster and then distinguished between the prototype and the variants, thereby making it reasonable for multiple translations to coexist with a prototypical translation standing out. In that way, we are able to break the dead end of an absolute translation equivalent.

The Chinese discourses revolving around the concept of equivalence, especially those inspired by Nida's dynamic equivalence (and later on functional equivalence), marked the beginning of a new era of Chinese translation theory research from the 1980s onward. This important role played by the concept of equivalence in Chinese translation studies is beyond question. As previously mentioned, due to the novelty and significance of the word *function* (功能) when it first appeared in the field of translation research in China, which was initially associated with Nida's theory of 'functional equivalence' (功能对等) but later gained its own life in the increasingly popular term of 'functional translation theory' (功能翻译理论), two other theories are now affiliated with the term: the linguistic theory of systemic functional grammar and the translation theory of functionalism, which will be discussed in the next two sections.

Application of Systemic Functional Linguistics in translation

Halliday's systemic functional linguistics/grammar (SFL/SFG) seems to have received more attention in the field of translation studies in China than it has in the West, probably due to its overlap with Nida's functional equivalence in the word *function*, as previously mentioned, the latter having provided great momentum for contemporary Chinese research on translation theory. Many works in this strand also tried to integrate Nida's thought of functional equivalence with the analytical framework conveniently provided by the SFL. A good example is Si (2005), which ingeniously extracted useful components and methodology from SFL and matched these with the functional equivalence paradigm of translation theory. The first thing Si did was to identify three levels of function for a piece of linguistic communication: the conceptual function (概念功能), the interpersonal function (人际功能) and the textual function (语篇功能), which were presumably engendered from Holliday's *field*, *tenor* and *mode* in SFL's register analysis. Si also drew from House's (1977) idea of assessing translation by evaluating the semantic and pragmatic equivalence achieved by the TT. Si made a distinction between 'language function' (语言功能) and 'textual function' (文本功能), and suggested that the fulfillment of the former was dependent on the latter. However, here the notion of 'text types' as proposed in Bühler (1990) or Reiss (1989) must come into play, where texts were distinguished into three types: representation/informative, expression/expressive, and appeal/appellative. For the first kind of text, there is a convenient parallelism between language function and textual function. That is, when translating representative text, so long as the conceptual function and interpersonal function embedded in text are successfully translated, the textual function can be said to fulfill the language function of the text. For the second and third type, however, extra translation strategies must be applied. That is, for the expressive type of text (e.g. poetry), a transformation in form must take place in order to fulfill the original language function of the ST. For the appellative type of text (e.g. an advertisement), the translator must seek an equivalent effect in TT. In a nutshell, Si (2005) proposed a two-level equivalent model based on systemic functional linguistics and text types. First and foremost, the translator must seek equivalence at the level of 'language function' for all three types of texts, which is mostly manifested in semantics and pragmatics. This goal is the easiest to achieve for the informative text, for which the content is most important and easy to reproduce in the target language. For the other two types of text, the second level of equivalence, textual equivalence, must involve adjustment in the form and the effect created by the TT in order to fulfill the first level of equivalence – the 'language function' of the ST.

Si (2005) and his other works on the relationships between SFL and translation are not the only works in Chinese translation studies that attempt to make a connection between the two. In fact, the same connection between various linguistics and translation theories at the interaction of 'function' had also been noticed by Zhang and Qian (2007), who made a bold attempt to associate and clarify between four schools of thought they believed were connected through the keyword of 'function' in translation theory: Nida's functional equivalence, Holmes's functionally oriented translation research, Halliday's systemic functional linguistics (SFL), and the German school of functionalism. They claimed that all four schools emphasized the importance of context to the understanding and interpretation of a text; the differences between them being that, firstly, Nida's functional equivalence was restricted by the influence of its structuralism ancestor and still tied to the concept of 'equivalence'; Halliday's SFL, on the other hand, was able to break through the look of equivalence and combine the micro aspects of language with the macro aspect of context and explain the phenomenon of translation in a more discerning way. As for the German school of functionalism, Zhang and Qian (2007) indicated that it had surpassed the considerations of language and moved into the realms of translation's purposes and interpersonal functions.

Many works along the line of SFL and translation theory also proposed analytical frameworks for understanding and resolving translation problems. Wang (2008), for example, demonstrated how detailed analysis at the level of thematic structure and cohesion, based on SFL methodology, can help translators understand how a speaker or writer organizes messages and structures information in order to express meaning and achieve interpersonal goals. What is more, Wang claimed, systemic functional analysis based on theme and cohesion can also help understand how the listener or reader is likely to notice, understand and react to the message. However, like Si (2005), Wang advised that textual equivalence would not guarantee a most satisfactory TT; it was also crucial to pay attention to equivalence at the level of idea and pragmatics. Another example of textual analysis for translating under the general guidance of SFL is Yang (2016), who believed that translating as a process of regeneration demands complete understanding and accurate control of all of the information contained in the ST on the part of the translator. Furthermore, to achieve textual equivalence between the ST and the TT, the translator must consider the factors of text, language system, context and co-text and cultural background in a holistic fashion. As a reader–analyzer of ST, an author of TT and a mediator of cultural differences, according to Yang, the translator must play multiple roles and fulfill multiple functions in the process of translating, including:

1. correctly inferring the connotations of the ST
2. precisely identifying the text type of ST and analyze it in terms of field, tenor and mode, as well as the rhetoric devices
3. reproducing the textual meaning of ST in the process of constructing TT
4. mediating between cultural differences in regenerating the text

Yang's (2016) position is essentially the same as that of Si (2005), emphasizing the usefulness of the SFL analysis and the importance of maintaining a balance in the three parameters of semantic, interpersonal and textual functions. For Yang, it is essential for the translator to generate an equivalent text very close to the ST in communicative purpose, text type, semantic coherence, language style and so on. In order to achieve that aim, Yang maintained, the translator must assume the multiple roles of ST reader, text analyzer, TT writer and cultural mediator. Text analysis is apparently a crucial part in Yang's model and demands a lot of skills and efforts. Huang (2004) was one of the first works to offer detailed steps in conducting textual analysis within the SFL framework. For Huang, the six steps of Observation, Interpretation, Description, Analysis, Explanation and Evaluation constitute a method not only for analyzing text, but also for studying translation problems and translated works.

Thus, we saw how SFL provided a useful analytical framework for Chinese translation researchers, where the mapping of *field*, *tenor* and *mode* into various related terms such as semantic, pragmatic and textual functions, created ample opportunities for researchers to introduce pragmatic concerns and interpersonal relationships into the equation while discussing the functional aspects of translation. Another functional school in translation theory is the functionalist approach to translation, to which we now turn.

Functionalist approaches to translation

In Chinese translation discourse, the functionalist approaches to translation, or the 'German school' represented by Reiss, Vermeer, Nord and so on, are collectively known as the 目的论 (literally 'purpose theory', originally translated from 'skopos theory'). This has been a highly regarded translation theory, but it has not exerted as great an impact as Nida's 'dynamic' or 'functional equivalence theory'. Although the skopos theory has stimulated some innovative thinking in the field of Chinese translation studies, there have been only a handful of works seriously discussing its theoretical implications. Wang (2010), in his commemorative paper written for Vermeer as his former PhD supervisor, commented that the skopos theory broke through the limits of the equivalence model and raised the researcher's and the translator's consciousness on the purposes of translation, 'liberating their thoughts' (Wang, 2010, p. 82); he claimed that it had brought about 'revolutionary effect' on translation criticism and translation teaching (ibid.). Wang mentioned how Vermeer saw the weaknesses of the previous approaches to translation criticism, which were often entangled in faithfulness or not at the word level. Wang recommended a translation criticism model developed by Vermeer together with his student Ammann (1990), which seems to work in the same way as a translation assessment model:

1. Identify the function of the ST.
2. Confirm the intratextual coherence of the ST.
3. Identify the function of the TT.
4. Confirm the intratextual coherence of the TT.
5. Verify the intertextual coherence between the ST and the TT.

According to Wang (2010), Vermeer's work provided a good model for translation criticism that is scientific, dialectal and constructive in nature.

Other Chinese works in translation studies focusing on the skopos theory are mostly introductory in nature, signifying the first stage of importing a new translation theory from the West into China according to Tu and Xiao's (2000) classification (the next two stages are 'research' and 'application'). Recall that Zhang and Qian (2007) pooled four translation theories together, all of which made use of the word *function* in some ways: Holmes's *function*-oriented translation studies, Nida's *functional* equivalence theory, Halliday's systematic *functional* grammar, and the *functionalism* of the German school. Zhang and Qian's treatment of the four theories in the paper was mostly introductive in nature. In the section on functionalism, they first introduced the work of Reiss and Vermeer (1984) focusing on the 'skopos rule', the principle of 'the end justifies the means', the fact that readership was one of the important factors deciding translation purposes and that the status of the ST was now apparently lower than that of the TT. Zhang and Qian (2007) next introduced Holz-Mänttäri's 'translational action theory' as the second thread of the functionalist approaches to translation, which again diminished the importance of the ST and focused on the communicative function in the process of translating, with client and translator and many other roles jointly carrying out an instance of cultural communication. The third and last strand Zhang and Qian mentioned in their introduction to the functionalistic approaches was Christiane Nord's concept of 'function plus loyalty' as a repercussion and caution against radical functionalism. According to Zhang and Qian, Nord's notion of loyalty is an interpersonal relationship between the translator, the author, the reader and the translation commissioner.

Ma and Lin (2007) was a work fully dedicated to the introduction of functionalist translation theory, which they claimed had transformed translation theory from the static linguistic–translational symbolism to the dynamic methods of functional translational analysis. They summarized the thesis of the functionalistic translation theory proposed by Reiss, Vermeer and Nord first, by saying that translation was a purposeful communicative behavior involving the consideration of the readership and the client's requests. Then they offered a reasonable account of the motivation and the principle of the functionalist theory, as follows:

> 由于语言种类、文化背景、思维方式、表达习惯上的差异,原语作者的意图和采 用的语篇形式与译文读者的接受 能力存在着一定差异…。因此,译者在翻译过程中有必要从译语读者角度出发,根据译文的预期目的决定自己的翻译策略与方法。(Due to the differences in types of language, cultural background, thinking patterns and methods of expression, the intention of the original author and the form of text adopted differ to a certain degree from the acceptability of the readership. Therefore, the translation needs to think from the perspective of the translation reader and decide the translation strategies and methods based on the expected aim of the target text.)
>
> (p. 118)

Like Zhang and Qian (2007), Ma and Lin (2007) then went on to introduce the skopos theory and the theory of translational action as the main components of the functionalist approaches. They continue to emphasize that the translator must decide on the translation strategies or methods based on the purpose of translation under the skopos theory. Specifically, four main points of view are proposed in skopos theory. Firstly, translation is an action that involves intentionality, which is not necessarily the intentionality of the original author, but the intentionality held by the various participants of the activity. Secondly, the basic rules for translation are skopos rule, intratextual (coherence) rule and intertextual (fidelity) rule – recall Vermeer's translation criticism model mentioned by Wang (2010) in the previous text. Thirdly, the initiator of translation identifies translation's purpose and sets the translation brief, including the function of the text (informative, expressive or operative), projected aim of the TT, the receiver of translation and receiving time, venue and occasion. The translator adopts translation strategies based on the translation brief and produces text in the target culture to express the communicative intention received by the ST reader in the source culture. Fourthly, the norm of translation should be 'adequacy' instead of 'equivalence', meaning the TT must meet the requirements of the translation brief. Like Zhang and Qian (2007), Ma and Lin (2007) also mentioned Nord's addition of loyalty to overcome the perceived inadequacy of the skopos theory (i.e. the undesirable, unlimited disparity between the ST and the TT as a result of differences in translation's purpose.) That is, the principle of loyalty dictated that, when there was a clash among the initiator of translation, the readership of the TT and the ST author, the translation must take the responsibility to negotiate between the parties and seek a resolution. Ma and Lin (2007) concluded that the functionalist approach to translation is a top-down theory (in contrast to the traditional bottom-up theory), which largely shortened the distance between translation theory and practice, as it explicitly considered the intention of the initiator and the requirements of translation, making the research method more purpose-oriented and easily executable.

A consensus among the Chinese researchers about Nord's functionalistic view on translation is its application to a translator's education. Both Zhang (2005) and Hu (2008), for example, noticed that Nord's 'function plus loyalty' approach is particularly useful for translator training, especially her contributions in three aspects of a translation didactic model: 1. the translation brief, 2. the model of translation-oriented text analysis, and 3. a typology of translation problems. Zhang explained that the translation brief is a request submitted by a translation commissioner, which should ideally include (explicitly or implicitly) the following information: the projected function, readership, media, publication time and venue of the TT and the purpose or motivation of the commission. As for the translation-oriented text analysis, Zhang thought that such an analysis was very helpful in guiding the translator through the translation processes. In particular, it can help the translator decide whether the translation commission is achievable, what information in the ST is related to the proposed function of the TT, and what translation strategies to adopt in order for the TT to fulfill the specifications of the translation brief. As for Nord's treatment of translation problems, Zhang (2005) made a useful distinction between 'translation difficulty' and 'translation problem', the former being engendered by the translator's own inadequacies or the lack of resources; the latter being entirely objective and existent in all circumstances. Zhang then pointed out that translation problems exist at the level of pragmatics, culture, language and text. Like Ma and Lin (2007), Zhang recognized functionalism as a top-down approach and the first step in problem-solving should occur at the level of pragmatics. First, the translator decides on the targeted function of the TT, then a distinction is made between the contents in the ST that need to be reproduced and those that need to be adjusted based on the receiver's background knowledge, mental expectations, communicative needs and various media and instruction factors. Thereafter, the translator took different measures in response to different translation problems.

Xiao (2010) went one step further than Zhang (2005) and Hu (2008) and proposed a didactic model based on functionalistic approaches for teaching translation in China's foreign language programs. After repeating the same guidelines offered in Zhang (2005) regarding Nord's top-down approach for translator training, Xiao especially noted that a clear understanding of the prospective usage and the purpose of the TT was very important in helping to produce high-quality translations. This point was reiterated in Zhu and Ma (2010), who thought that functionalistic approaches helped ensure a sound external environment to regulate the quality of translation and reduce the number of poor translations. Xiao then went on to suggest a pedagogical model for teaching university translation courses in China based on functionalistic approaches. The model consists of six steps:

1. The teacher chooses material for translation practice.
2. The teacher creates a translation brief.
3. Teacher and students jointly do a translation-oriented text analysis.
4. Students conduct a translation problem analysis.
5. Students independently do the translation.
6. Teacher and students jointly evaluate and comment on the translation product.

In her detailed description of the model, Xiao (2010) usefully pointed out that under the functionalistic approach, the teacher of translation has changed their role from knowledge distributor to translation initiator. She also suggested that, at the crucial text analysis stage, the teacher could use modern technology products like movies, TV programs and video clips to make a background introduction to the ST. Also, at the final stage of the discussion, when students are evaluating the TT, the teacher should lead the students to integrate theory with practice and notice the translation techniques applied in the production of the TT.

Apart from the merits discussed in various works, Chinese translation researchers are also quick to notice some weaknesses of the functionalistic approaches to translation theory. Zhang (2005), for example, criticized that Nord's 'function plus loyalty' method is quite difficult to achieve in practice; that is, it is not a trivial matter to show loyalty to the commissioner, the ST author and the reader all at the same time. The same criticism was echoed in Hu (2008), who thought it was an idealism to be loyal to all three parties simultaneously. Also, Zhang (2005) considered it pointless to do a detailed analysis of the ST if the main determining factor is the function of the TT. She contended that it might be more feasible to conduct an analysis of the prospective function of the TT, and then extract the required information from the ST.

Tian and Zhao (2018) recorded a recent interview with Christiane Nord which may well serve as a proper ending to this section. During the interview, Tian and Zhao brought up the issue of the similarity between Halliday's SFG and the functionalistic approaches. Nord commented that the word 'function' is the only similarity between them, and that SFG is a bottom-up approach and that functionalism is a top-down one. Moreover, Nord was eager to detach the functionalism from Applied Linguistics and claimed that it should be subsumed under the discipline of Applied Cultural Studies. That is, under functionalism, translation is seen as an interpersonal communicative activity, which should first be studied from the pragmatic aspect of language and then approached from the cultural perspective, with different cultural norms and regularities taken into consideration before contemplating the actual wording of the TT. Nord mentioned a very interesting personal experience to illustrate the possible benefits brought about by the consideration of a given translation's purposes as seen in two different English translations of the Chinese masterpiece 紅樓夢 ('Dream of the Red Chamber'). Nord said that when she first read the English version translated by Yang Xianyi (杨宪益) and Dai Naidie (戴乃迭), she could not continue after the first dozen or so pages because there were simply too many exotic cultural elements and the footnotes introduced even more complicated background information that was strange to a foreign reader. Later on, however, when she read the version translated by David Hawkes, she found the book much more comprehensible and enjoyable. Nord thought that when Hawkes was translating the book, he must have had the purpose in mind to introduce this great Chinese work to English-speaking people, rather than to create reading difficulties for them.

Postcolonial translation theory

According to Munday (2016), the research scope of postcolonialism is not always well defined, although it broadly refers to 'studies of the effect of the imbalance of power relations between colonized and colonizer' (p. 209). Also, Munday believes that 'postcolonial translation studies take many forms' (p. 213) and goes on to use the translation of Indian literature in colonial times to illustrate how the theory works. The Chinese translation thinkers also provided interesting ideas regarding how postcolonial translation theory should be understood and conceptualized in China. In his introductive paper to postcolonial translation theory, Wang (2003) gave the background information and motivation as follows:

> 由于我国的后殖民翻译研究才刚刚起步，而我国昔日的帝国辉煌和半殖民地的屈辱又给我们的后殖民翻译研究留下了太多的历史疑问和空间，因此引进后殖民翻译研究范式对于我们反思中国的文化和翻译史，有着深远的借鉴意义。(Since China's post-colonial translation studies have just begun, and the glory of our past empire and the humiliation of semi-colonialism have left too much historical doubts and space for our post-colonial translation studies, the introduction of post-colonialism translation research paradigm has far-reaching implications for us to reflect on Chinese culture and translation history.)
>
> (Wang, 2003, p. 3)

Wang's words seem to endorse Munday's view that postcolonial translation theory takes many forms. For each country, the cultural backgrounds and its interactions with the colonizing countries will be different from other countries having been colonized. The factors to be taken into consideration and the research results will therefore be different as a function. In the case of China, as Wang indicated above, the rich culture and history of the country form a strong contrast with its recent humiliating experience of being subject to semi-colonialism. China's translation theorists should seize this opportunity to reexamine the translation history of the country with the postcolonial paradigm, as suggested by Wang. Like Munday, Wang also assumed that postcolonial translation theory worked on the basis of power differences (or an 'imbalance of power relations' in Munday's terms) and adopted the methodology of New Historicism to observe, study and explain the conscious and unconscious value orientation of the translator in the context of power differences. Wang pointed out that postcolonial translation theory departed from the traditional structural approach by focusing on external conditions that controlled the production of the TT and the subversion it brought to the target culture. It queried the relations between the TT and its historical conditions; questioned the metaphorical existence of 'the violence of translation'; carried out anthropological study on the diversions of the TT, and unveiled the power relations embedded in the historical conditions of the TT.

For Wang (2003), the previous linguistics-based translation research was an experiment conducted in the vacuum environment of a laboratory, taking slices of the TT for examination one at a time. Postcolonial translation theory, on the other hand, was able to uncover a crucial factor that influenced the practice of translation by using empirically based, cultural anthropological methods – power differences. This proved that the so-called 'culture equivalence' and 'language equivalence' assumed by the 'language laboratory' approach was unsustainable, according to Wang. With that awareness and caution in mind, Wang continued to argue, translation research had walked out of the closed and static system of the structural approach of linguistics, and refocused its attention from text internal to text external, asking questions about the cultural and historical sources of the TT and discovering many unanswered questions under the previous structural research paradigm. However, when China's researchers were reexamining the domestic translation problems from the postcolonial perspective, Wang advised, they should neither condone the patronizing attitudes of the First World discourses nor focus narrowly on the complaints of the Third World speakers and become entrapped by radical nationalism. Instead, Wang endorsed the 'hybridization' approach, suggesting that intercultural communication is necessary to encourage development and innovation. Translation is an essential means to help create a contemporary Chinese language.

Wang's (2003) advice for Chinese postcolonial translation researchers to take a balanced view between the awareness of power differences in colonial times and the resultant translation products, which probably reflected language hegemony *and* the recognition that intercultural communication is still necessary to promote cultural and linguistic innovation, was reiterated in Zhang and Qin (2004). Zhang and Qin first explained that postcolonialism revealed how the First World had controlled the process of cultural export, giving their own ideology an absolute advantage and imposing it upon Third World countries. However, like Wang, Zhang and Qin advocated that the Chinese should break away from the binary confrontation between the East and the West and face up to the cultural differences with an open mind while upholding the idea of multiple coexistence

76 *The blossoming of Chinese translation theory*

and symbiotic complementarity. It is alright, according to Zhang and Qin, for a 'weaker literature' in a vulnerable position to model on the 'strong literature' of foreign countries. Under such circumstances, translation assumes the mission of introducing advanced literary forms into the country, bringing opportunities for reforms to the language and literature of the country and providing a source of alternative choices. On one hand, Zhang and Qin thought that the 'aphasia' (or 'the loss of discourse right') encountered by Chinese scholars on the global stage was not entirely due to the discourse hegemony of the West, but partly due to their inability to make effective use of traditional Chinese thought. On the other hand, Zhang and Qin also disapproved of some researchers' proposal to 'establish translation theory with Chinese characteristics', warning that this would make Chinese translation studies 'fall into the trap of narrow nationalism and unable to free itself' (陷入狭隘的民族主义泥沼而难以自拔) (p. 116).

The above discussion shows how Chinese translation thinkers have not followed the steps of, say, Susan Bassnett and Harish Trivedi (1999) in condemning the role played out by translation in the colonial contexts as purely 'a shameful history' (p. 5). Chinese thinkers, in general, take a balanced view toward the so-called language hegemony of the West in colonial times. A more detailed look at postcolonial translation theory with some reflective elements is offered in Qu (2016) after a decade of its initial introduction into China. Qu observed that, since the 'cultural turn' of translation studies, researchers' perspectives had expanded from the 'imprisonment of language' to various factors such as the relationships between the translator, the text, the author and the reader, translation and social power, the relationship between source culture and target culture and so on. When it came to postcolonial translation theory, Qu initially followed the usual criticisms of colonialism and flagged the issues of discourse hegemony, pointing out that translation was only a unidirectional tool, which unilaterally served the purposes of the colonists to impose their language, culture and ideology on the colonized. Qu shared Venuti's (2008) observation that from the selection of the ST to the application of translation strategies, editing, commentary writing and reading, almost every step and decision was closely related to political aims and steered by source culture values. Qu also reported a technique of translating in a colonialist style, quoting from Tymoczko (1999); that is, when translators introduced an ST from the hegemonic culture, they never added any explanatory notes, thereby signaling the unquestionable status of myths, historical events and customs of the cultural hegemony.

Despite his clear introduction and cogent analysis of postcolonialism and its influence on Chinese translation studies, Qu does not condone all of the tenets put forward by postcolonial translation theorists. For example, Qu points out that 'double standards' was applied in postcolonialism when it comes to who colonizes whom. That is, the theorists only treated the case of non-Western countries being conquered as colonization. In the case of colonization occurring in the West, such as the Germanic tribes who migrated to England from continental Europe to form the Anglo-Saxons cultural group with the indigenous British groups, accused Qu, the postcolonialism scholars would not analyze them from the postcolonial point of view. In the same vein, Qu (2016) does not accept all criticisms voiced by postcolonial translation theorists. In an insightful way, he alludes that the postcolonial theorists have unwisely (or unwittingly?) deemed all contacts between Western and non-Western cultures a colonial relationship, thereby expanding a historical event tied to particular regions into a pan-global phenomenon across all times. To Qu, opposing the cultural hegemony of the West is opposing the hegemony and not the culture itself. Western culture is created by people and not by the hegemony. Western civilization is a result of the interactions between different people and belongs to all humankind. Qu especially questions the instrumental view of translation in postcolonial theory. He opposes the view that translation only serves the West and the cultural hegemony, and the assumption that translating the non-Western culture necessarily implies vilification and suppression. Qu thinks that the development and reality of cultures are much more complicated than that depicted by postcolonial theory, whose view of translation is therefore distorted and unsuitable. For Qu, the function of translation is never unidirectional. No matter Western or non-Western, the development of culture cannot occur without the interaction and communication between people, and any interaction and communication between cultures cannot happen without the help of translation.

On the practical side, some Chinese works were able to apply the principles of postcolonial translation theory to literary translations which introduced classic Chinese literature to the world. Liang and Hu (2017), for example, highly recommended Lin Yutang's English translation of *Six Chapters of a Floating Life* (浮生六记). They thought that Lin (inadvertently) adopted translation norms and strategies that were in line with the postcolonial view of translation, keeping Chinese culture at the central position and maintaining the 'heterogeneity' of translation. The choice of the ST itself, for one, was Lin's tactic to introduce a work representative of ancient Chinese intellectual life and aesthetic aptitudes when exporting Chinese culture to the West. In the actual translating, Lin kept the original Chinese cultural elements to the maximum extent, for example, by translating culturally loaded words such as 马褂 with 'makua', 亩 with 'mow' and 馄饨 with 'wonton'. Liang and Hu thought that Lin Yutang's translation of the book was capable of correcting foreigners' misunderstanding of Chinese society, enabling a fair and objective scrutiny of Chinese culture and society, and helping them to appreciate the profoundness and depth of the Chinese culture. A similar applied study based on postcolonial translation theory was presented in Zhang (2010), this time on Pearl S. Buck's Translation of *Shui Hu Zhuan* (水浒传). While Liang and Hu (2017) praised Lin Yutang's ability to promote Chinese culture in his translation, Zhang recommended that Buck was able to apply the concept of 'hybridity' in her work, flagging the differences between Western and Chinese language, culture and literature while keeping qualities from both in the translation, thereby promoting the communication and integration between both cultures.

Overall, since its introduction to China in the latter half of the 1990s, like the functionalistic approaches to translation, postcolonial translation theory has brought about some innovative ideas to the field of Chinese translation studies and expanded the scope of external consideration for translation beyond the smaller circle of initiator, author, translator and reader and into the wider historical and geographical realms. Postcolonial translation theory has made people think about the historical circumstances of China, especially during the semi-colonial times, the role translation played during those times, how Chinese cultures have been affected and how such new perspectives and findings can guide future translation research. After two decades of delving into postcolonial translation theory, Hu (2014) still noted several problems in the Chinese acceptance of the theory: 1. lack of introductory materials written in Chinese, 2. varying degrees of acceptance, 3. misunderstanding of the theory (exaggerated Western influence on Chinese culture), and 4. detachment of theory from reality. Despite the many different voices and debates, a likely consensus of the implications of postcolonialism to Chinese translation theory is expressed in Zhang and Zhai's (2018) conclusion, who said:

> 在中国译论建设上，既注重本土挖掘，又重视外部借鉴；在重视宏观理论的同时，也不应该忽视微观现实的分析以及译者的地位；在反对文化霸权时，反对褊狭的民族主义需要逐渐成为共识，要以共同对话取代话语对抗，以多元阐释取代话语霸权，用兼容并包取代话语独断。(In the construction of Chinese translation theory, we need to pay attention not only to local cultivation but also to external borrowing. While attaching importance to macro theory, we should not neglect the analysis of microscopic reality and the status of translator. When opposing cultural hegemony, we need to form a consensus to oppose narrow nationalism. We must replace discourse confrontation with common dialogue, replace discourse hegemony with multiple interpretations, and replace discourse dogmatism with reconciliation and accommodation.)
>
> (p. 105)

With that note in mind, we move on to the next section to consider, deconstructionism, which created a very similar impact to postcolonialism in the Chinese translation circles at around the same time (i.e. from the latter half of the 1990s).

Deconstruction

While postcolonial translation theory was seen as a 'cultural and ideological turn' in Munday (2016), deconstruction was treated as one of the 'philosophical approaches' by him. Such being the case, Munday did not go into extended discussion on the theoretical side of the term, other than pointing out that Jacques Derrida was the person initiating the approach and that the main idea was to question the linguistics convention established by Saussure and the premise that meaning can be defined, captured and stabilized. The Chinese discourse on deconstruction mostly followed this line of reasoning with some serious pondering about the significance of the theory and its implications for Chinese translation studies.

A typical introductory work, this time to introduce the deconstructionist approach or philosophy, was offered in Xu (2008), which discussed the main ideas of Derrida such as 'difference' (差异), 'différance' (延异), 'trace' (印迹), 'iterability' (再制), 'survival' (重生) and so on. Xu explained that Derrida's theory was not designed for translation specifically; however, it happened that we could use translation studies to illustrate his point pertinently. According to Xu, Derrida's theory broke all the binary oppositions distinguished by conventional translation theory such as stability and instability, singularity and universality, translatability and untranslatability, original work and translation, and argued that these concepts at different polarities actually were reliant on and supplementary to each other. In particular, the idea that the ST came with a fixed meaning was totally shattered. Instead, under the deconstructionist approach, meaning was unsure and recreated through the act of translation. Zhang (2006) further explained that the deconstructionist approach dictated that the translator was the main creator of the text and that the translation was more decisive than the original in the whole process of translating. Due to a change of language, the cultural environment that generated the ST was reconstructed and the translation opened up a brand-new history for the text in the new culture.

Not all Chinese translation thinkers agreed to the main ideas of the deconstructionist approach. Zhou (2006), for example, suggested that the deconstruction research paradigm had offered a new way to contemplate translation, enhanced the status of translator and TT, and broadened the horizon of translation studies. However, she also criticized that merely emphasizing the differences between texts and focusing entirely on external factors of translation is not a good way forward. After all, Zhou thought, studying the regularities of language would always be an indispensable part of translation research. She advised that translation studies should eventually return to rational thinking and proper order. Huang and Ma (2008) also cautioned that, although deconstructionist translation theory broke away from the closed binary opposition system and extended into an open and diversified research paradigm, it is after all not the ultimate truth. Deconstruction did not represent a full ideological system; instead, it was only an inquisitive and reflective method. Eventually, a compromised position is often proposed, like what happened in the debate of postcolonial translation theory. Ma and Luo (2006), for example, pointed out that although structuralism (结构主义) and deconstructionism (解构主义) – note the two terms only differ in the first Chinese character, making them seem intimately related and closely comparable – appeared to be contradictory and oppositional to each other in philosophical principles, the two views are however compatible and complementary in forming a translation methodology. They advised that Chinese translation researchers should correctly apply both 'loyal' and 'fluent' principles and unify the structural and deconstructive approaches in effective and reasonable ways.

Lü (2002) seemed to offer a cogent solution to how the deconstruction approach should be conceptualized in Chinese translation theory. He suggested that there were three things the Chinese researchers could do when learning from deconstruction. Firstly, they should contemplate on the creative or the 'reconstructive' side of the theory rather than the negative, destructive aspect of the theory. Secondly, Lü advised Chinese translation researchers to adopt the phenomenology paradigm rather than the logic–mathematics paradigm when doing non-traditional transcendent thinking. That is, they should study the more interesting hidden phenomena rather than pursuing the abstract nature of things. Thirdly, they should learn from the open-ended thinking patterns of deconstructionism. In a parallel fashion, Lü also advised two things that Chinese researchers should avoid when considering the deconstructive approach. Firstly, they should avoid treating 'subconsciousness' as 'consciousness' in the process of deconstructing. For example, for deconstructionists, 'translation as rewriting' meant rewriting was a subconscious process which occurred when the translator was trying to accomplish a certain aim with the new text, and not a purposeful activity to change the nature of the text. Secondly, Lü advised against treating deconstruction as an objective itself (rather, the reconstruction process after deconstruction is). Finally, we should not take irrationality as rationality. Even though pointing out irrationality was an important procedure in deconstruction, Lü emphasized, in the subsequent reconstruction process, rationality is still an important guiding factor. A similar overview was offered by Cai and Gong (2011) almost a decade later, who, after reviewing the then past ten years' research on deconstruction, suggested some areas that were still inadequately addressed: 1. the study of the contents and nature of deconstructive translation theory, 2. argumentation and reflection from an interdisciplinary perspective, taking in views from both functionalist and cognitive linguistics etc., 3. participating in internationally based applied and comparative translation research, 4. investigating the meaning and significance of deconstruction to translation studies as a whole.

Cai and Gong's (2011) advice for translation researchers to investigate deconstruction from an interdisciplinary perspective and to integrate it into the overall picture of translation studies was partially accomplished by such works as Guo (2000) and Pang and Zhu (2009). In Guo (2000), the deconstructive theory was related to postcolonialism through an examination of Venuti's (1995) work. According to Guo, Venuti generated his translation strategies from a deconstructive point of view. Meaning was thought to be different and deferred and not residing in the ST alone. The meaning of a literary work was multidimensional and unstable. Its translation was also a temporarily fixed form of meaning. In the process of translating, Venuti advocated, the translator should no longer remain invisible and consider it a priority to create a smooth translation with no trace of the translator or translation. Instead, the translation should now be an independent work by itself. Guo used the translating of Shakespeare into Chinese as an example to illustrate the idea that each generation needed a new translation for great literary works, and that the 'foreignization' strategy becomes more conspicuous with each new translation. Pang and Zhu (2009), on the other hand, associated deconstructionism with the functionalist approaches to translation. Specifically, they thought that traces of deconstructionism could be found in the functionalistic approaches, for example, in the latter's overturn of the central position of the ST and its deconstruction of the original author's status. For both functionalistic and deconstructive views, the ST was only a 'source of information' in the context of translating; its sole function was to provide information. Moreover, Pang and Zhu explained that the word *deconstruction* consists of two meanings: 'destruction' and 'construction'. That is, deconstruction did not mean destroying everything, but emphasized reconstruction after destruction. Again, this was in line with the functionalistic approaches that aimed to create the TT based on a reconceptualized goal and function of the text. Another deconstructive measure of the functionalistic approaches could be seen in its treatment of the author. Traditionally, there had been three participants in the process of translation: the ST author at the center, the 'invisible' translator and the TT reader (who was rarely ever taken into consideration). The functionalistic approaches, however, deconstructed the author-centered paradigm and rebuilt a multidimensional model involving the author, translator, readership, translation initiator and the TT user. In Pang and Zhu's words, whether it was the 'function plus loyalty' view or the 'author is dead' deconstructionist view, both camps were consistent in the goal they pursued.

Thus, all three theories or approaches – the functionalists, the postcolonialists and the deconstructionists – seem to have performed the same functions of broadening the concerns of translation, adding many contextual factors and extra players into the equation, highlighting the importance of the translator, the status of the TT and the very goal and purpose of translation and fundamentally changed the philosophy and practice of translation. Last but not least in this thread, we will consider feminist translation theory in the Chinese context, which bears many resemblances to the theory and approaches mentioned above.

Feminism

As expected, in introducing feminist approaches to translation, Chinese thinkers logically mentioned Western feminism in literary, cultural or political domains first before discussing their implications for translation studies and noting their similarities to deconstructionism, postcolonialism and so on. Jiang (2004), for example, noted that the main aim of feminism was to overturn the patriarchal social system, and that the whole process was very similar to the deconstructionist approach. Since the 1980s, according to Jiang, the targets of feminism had expanded (under the influence of postcolonialism) to include any form of cultural hegemony. For Jiang, however, the impact of feminism on Chinese translation studies was still indecisive, even with all the innovative ideas it brought forward to the field.

In her brief introductory piece, Wang (2009) noted that feminist translation theory had subverted the traditional view of translation and recalibrated the relationships between ST and TT, author and translator, translation and ideology, translation and gender and so on, and adopted various translation strategies to interfere with the ST and to take back the control of and rewrite the text. Wang also said that the feminists had assumed a strong political stance and distinct translation attitudes, emphasizing the manipulation of the ST through a translator's subjectivity and gender experience to reexamine society's ideology and conception under a certain historical background. However, Wang also noted that the then current awareness of feminist translation theory was relatively weak and underdeveloped, although female Chinese translators often left some traces of female consciousness, women's dignity, female ego and so on in their works, which were absent in male's translations. Wang called for more attention to be paid to the 'forgotten', 'inundated' and 'ignored' women translators and to help establish the subject status (主体地位) of female translators.

Liu (2004) proposed that thinking about the author, text, translator and readership from the perspective of feminism would bring about an all-new enlightenment to translation studies. In the multicultural and multilinguistic context of postmodernism and postcolonialism, according to Liu, women, diversity and otherness would create infinite possibilities for rebuilding the subjectivity of the translator. Liu mentioned many positive traits of female translators, such as females being better at empathy and replacement and therefore more capable of reproducing the mood of female actors. Women, said Liu, were also more understanding and intuitive, more sensitive to reality, their soul and spirits 'more perfect' than men, more in the state of 'self sufficiency' to better coordinate and balance themselves, so much so that the energy of nature can flow easily through women's bodies. In addition, the sexual desire and experience, which cannot be penetrated by males, would have to be subtly rendered by female translators. Liu used the example of Bing Xin's (冰心) translation of Tagore's poems to show the mindfulness of the female translator, her empathy of the author and her scholarly foundation of Chinese language, which all contributed to her fluent and everlasting translation of the poems, fully conveying Tagore's love for his country, sympathy for women and fondness of children. Liu ended his paper with the following conclusion:

> 女性不是单一的自我,不是等待定义然后被这个定义僵化的本质。相反,女性是自由精神和创造精神的体现。在跨文化交际中,女性、差异性、他者性将继续成为翻译研究的话语主题, 并且还会为建立译者主体性、女性译者主体性以及其它翻译模式提供无限的可能性。(Femininity is not a singular self and is not something waiting to be defined and be frozen by this definition. On the contrary, femininity is the representation of freedom and creation. In cross-cultural communication, femininity, diversity, and otherness will continue to be the subjects of translation research. Moreover, femininity will provide infinite possibilities for establishing translator's subjectivity, women-translator subjectivity and other translation models.)
>
> (p. 9)

Liu's (2004) optimism about feminism in Chinese translation studies was not shared by all Chinese authors. Zhang (2004), for example, admitted that feminism did help us understand translation as a venue of interaction for various factors like history, culture and ideology, diverted our attention to minority culture and marginal culture, and made us realize the value orientation and ideological tendencies in translating while recognizing the meaning and value of translation. However, Zhang also insisted that the overemphasis of the feminist translation theory on the diversity and the political nature of language had inadvertently exaggerated the importance of the translator's subjectivity. In Zhang's opinion, we should avoid the tendency to overstress the concept of subjectivity in our efforts to downplay linguistic regularities and upgrade the translator's status. Liu (2008) also observed that the feminist translation theory advocated 'rebellious translation' or rewriting, using supplement, prefacing and footnoting and 'hijacking' methods to manipulate text and to subvert men's control of female translation. However, Liu thought the feminist translation approaches suffered from major weaknesses, such as a relatively thin philosophical basis, biased and radical argumentations, the tendency to create new 'discourse hegemony' and a monolithic experimental method. Finally, Hu et al. (2013) pointed out three reasons why feminist translation theory was not so prevalent in China. Firstly, the traditional Chinese value system of harmony and friendliness prompted Chinese feminists to take milder measures in promoting feminism. Secondly, the traditional 'loyalty' principle of translation prevented the feminists from diverting from this highest norm. Third and finally, feminism had been entangled in campaigns against feudalism, therefore lacking a strong concentrated force to promote the movement.

As in other works regarding recently imported translation theories, Chinese authors also proposed compromised approaches to feminist translation theory. Ou and Wu (2010), for example, suggested that the concept and strategy of 'androgyny' can be used to eliminate gender discrimination in translation and help achieve unification and harmony between the ST and the TT. Chen (2008), on the other hand, suggested that in order to correct the problems of the feminist approaches in overemphasizing the translator's subjectivity and diminishing the importance of the ST, feminist translators should adopt the functionalist approaches in strengthening the acceptability of the TT in the target culture, by considering the differences in culture, world knowledge, social background and value systems. Also, the feminist translation theory will be more acceptable to the field if it can offer a combined strategy of loyalty and subjectivity in translating.

Relevance theory

In their recent scientometric analysis of the Chinese research on relevance theory, Zhao and Xiang (2018) found that between 1986 and 2015, although relatively speaking there had been more research in this area in China than internationally, there were however no significant concentrated points in the Chinese research on relevance theory. There had been plenty of research topics that came in all varieties, but there was no systematic concentration. Zhao and Xiang discovered that relevance theory had developed into interdisciplinary explorations with complicated scientific research methodologies in the West but, in China, progress is still limited to its application in translation studies and other areas of applied studies. In fact, in Munday (2016), relevance theory also gets very little mention, amounting to fewer than two pages of discussion in total. Thus, it is most likely that relevance theory has not become a major research trend in global translation studies (despite its claimed potential to become the 'universal theory' in translation as discussed in the next paragraph) and in China, most research done in this strand is applied in nature.

Munday's (2006) introduction to relevance theory is almost solely based on Gutt's (2000) work, again confirming the fact that there is not a large body of research on the application of this theory to translation studies in the West, despite Gutt's ambitious claim that 'there is no need for developing a separate theory of translation' (Gutt, 2000, p. 25) since translation as a form of human communication can be readily explained by relevance theory, which uses concepts like 'informative intention', inferencing and interpretation, contextual effects and minimal effort to account for human communicative behaviors. At the Chinese front, it seems relatively more attention has been paid to relevance theory in translation studies in comparison with the West. Wang (2005), for one, noted that relevance theory was scarcely mentioned in works such as Baker (1998) and Munday (2001), and went on to introduce Gutt's relevance-based translation theory extensively. For Gutt's claim that relevance theory can explain all phenomena in translation, Wang revealed that most Chinese scholars expressed doubt about it, but they all felt positively about the explanatory power of relevance to translation, especially in the problem of cultural mediation during translating.

An analytical framework based on relevance theory was offered in Wu and Wu (2017) consisting of three levels of relevance-based analysis: phonetics, vocabulary and syntax. Wu and Wu first explained their understanding of the relevance theory and its implications on the analysis of translation problems. Namely, for relevance theory, language communication is a cognitive process based on an ostensive-inferential mechanism where success is dependent on 'relevance', which is in turn determined by the interaction between two factors: cognitive effect and processing effort. The greater the cognitive effect achieved and the lesser the processing effort required, the stronger the relevance of the text. In communication, optimal relevance is sought rather than maximal relevance, as the latter may require greater processing effort, which is undesirable. Wu and Wu used an example to illustrate how translation is assessed using the concept of relevance at the word level of consideration. The ST in question was 王若飞在狱中, concerning a highly regarded revolutionary hero in the Chinese Communist Party literature who was wrongfully imprisoned by the rival party-controlled government for five years. This title phrase was translated into 'Iron

Bars But Not a Cage' which was considered excellent by Wu and Wu as it nicely maintained the contextual effect to help the TT reader derive the same relevance available to the ST reader. This was because the phrase 'iron bars but not a cage' was derived from the verse *Nor iron bars a cage* written by the 17th century British poet Richard Lovelace, which easily connected the English reader of the TT to the contextual effect (a great martyr in prison) experienced by the ST readership. If the ST had been literally translated to 'Wang Ruofei in Prison', then the communicative intention of the ST can no longer be recovered due to the loss of contextual effect and relevance, as 'Wang Ruofei' did not ring any bells to the English reader. Wu and Wu also showed how phonetic and syntactic cues should be regenerated in the TT to help the reader obtain optimal relevance and achieve successful communication.

In the same vein, Duan (2010) gave another demonstration of how the communicative intention of the ST can be understood through a successful manipulation of the TT based on the principle of relevance. Duan explained that communication, from the speaker's point of view, is an ostensive process clearly showing the speaker's 'informative intention'. From the listener's perspective, on the other hand, communication is an inferential process in which the listener makes inferences based on the ostensive behavior of the speaker and the contextual effect to derive the communicative intention of the speaker. Duan used the poet Du Fu's (杜甫) work Chun Wang (春望 'spring-watch') as an example and examined five different translations of the poem. Firstly, she noted that 'A Spring View' was a good translation, while 'The Hope of Spring' was not. She reasoned that 望 had been used by the poet to mean 'looking into the distance' (although the character could also mean 'hoping'). Translating the title of the poem into 'The Hope of Spring' would have lost the communicative intention of the original author. Likewise, as analyzed by Duan, translating the character 国 in 国破山河在 into 'country', 'nation' or 'kingdom' was also inappropriate, as it meant the capital of the nation, 长安 (Chang An), in the poem rather than the entire country. Duan thought one of the translations of the word into 'land' was more acceptable, as it better relayed the author's communicative intention.

Some specific areas of translation where relevance theory could offer analytical advantages were mentioned in Wang (2000), which were translatability, faithfulness vs. validity, and retranslation. On the issue of translatability, Wang reasoned that the communicative function of translation could be fulfilled if the cognitive schema formed by the TT reader was comparable with those of the ST reader. As long as the TT could correctly pass on the schematic information, it did not matter what language symbols were used. Translatability was no longer an issue under the relevance theory. In terms of faithfulness and validity, relevance theory dictated that the translator's main responsibility was to correctly construct the cognitive schema of the ST and create the necessary contextual effects in the TT so the original communicative intention of the author can be grasped by the reader. Faithfulness was not an important concern then, but the schema and communicative intention were. As regards the phenomenon of retranslation, Wang suggested that, under relevance theory, language communication is an inferential activity based on the dynamic development of contexts. In translating, the dynamic aspect of communication is expressed in the relationships between the author and translator, the translator and reader, the original author and the translation's reader, the ST and ST's culture, the TT and TT's culture, respectively. Any of the above-mentioned relationships would create new contextual cues in the process of translating, which in turn would engender new inferencing patterns; otherwise, the communication would break down. This was, according to Wang (2000), the reason why major literary works such as *Pride and Prejudice*, *Emma*, etc. had been translated again and again. However, Wang also mentioned one aspect of translation which cannot be explained away by relevance theory. This was the so-called 'cultural default' (文化缺省) which received a lot of attention among Chinese translation researchers. 'Cultural default' referred to aspects of culture which are necessary to understanding messages communicated among people of the same culture which are nevertheless often assumed and omitted from the message, easily retrievable by people sharing cognitive schemas of the same culture. Wang thought that relevance theory failed to explain how the cultural default could be reconstructed from the ST and transferred to the equivalent of the TT, since it was often difficult to find even in the ST.

We have seen how relevance theory has enlightened the field of Chinese translation theory, especially in the area of applied research, where the concepts of communicative intention, contextual effects and inferencing have been used to scrutinize examples of literary translation. Despite the lack of theoretical construction, the applied translation research based on relevance theory in China has brought about some unexpected results and innovative thinking, which are certainly helpful to further the development of Chinese translation theory.

Conclusion

Eugene Nida's view on translation has created an unprecedented impact on Chinese translation theory, especially his innovative idea of 'dynamic equivalence', or the term 'functional equivalence' he later used, which translated into 功能对等 in Chinese. The word 功能 then caught on in the Chinese translation field, giving birth to many thoughts, studies and theories in translation which are not necessarily related to Nida's original theory. However, be it accidental or intentional, the word 'function' has generated a mass of research at the beginning of the modern era of Chinese translation theory. As seen in the previous discussion, Nida's equivalence theory was closely followed by research on the application of Halliday's systemic functional linguistics in translation and functionalist approaches to translation. Even the notion of communicative intention brought up by Chinese researchers on relevance theory is reminiscent of Nida's emphasis on 'equivalent effect' under functional equivalence. The post-Nida translation theory, easily identifiable in the Chinese context, started in the 1990s when postcolonial translation theory, deconstruction, feminism, etc. took the floor, not in the sense of replacing the equivalence theory but in diverting the attention of some of the researchers to the external factors of translation. Thereafter, Chinese translation theory is 'ready to go', having been equipped with knowledge and experience in both linguistics theory and cultural studies. All that Chinese researchers have to do now is look back with new light to the history of Chinese translation, create new Chinese translation discourse in the 21st century, and reinvent Chinese translation theory to reflect the accumulated Chinese wisdom and experiences in translation over 1000s years on the global stage.

References

Chinese references

Cai, Lijian 蔡力坚 (2018) 翻译效果对等 (Equivalent translation effect). 中国翻译 (*Chinese Translators Journal*). 2018(05): 122–124.
Cai, Longwen and Gong, Qi 蔡尤文, 宫齐 (2011) 回顾与展望：我国解构主义翻译研究 (2000–2010) (Retrospect and prospect: China's deconstructive translation research (2000–2010)). 兰州大学学报(社会科学版) (*Journal of Lanzhou University (Social Sciences)*). 39(4): 143–148.
Chen, Meixia 陈梅霞 (2008) 功能翻译理论在女性主义翻译批评中的应用 (The application of functionalist translation theory in feministic translation criticism). 宁夏大学学报(人文社会科学版) (*Journal of Ningxia University (Humanities and Social Sciences Edition)*). 30(3): 171–175.
Duan, Haohui 段昊卉 (2010) 关联理论视角下汉诗英译的认知推理过程探析——以唐诗《春望》五种译文为例 (Analyzing the cognitive inferencing process of translating Chinese poetry into English in perspective of the relevance theory: using the five translations of Tang poem Chung Wang as example). 外语教学 (*Foreign Language Education*). 31(4): 96–100.
Gong, Xuan 贡璇 (2018) 功能对等理论指导下的医学英语翻译的句法研究 (A study on the syntax of medical English translation under the guidance of functional equivalence theory). 继续医学教育 (*Continuing Medical Education*). 2018(12): 58–59.
Guo, Jianzhong 郭建中 (2000) 韦努蒂及其解构主义的翻译策略 (Venuti and his deconstructive translation strategy). 中国翻译 (*Chinese Translators Journal*). 2000(01): 49–52.
He, Aijun 贺爱军 (2016) 翻译对等的原型范畴理论识解 (Understanding the prototype category theory for translation equivalence). 外语教学 (*Foreign Language Education*). 37(5): 107–110.
Hu, Zuoyou 胡作友 (2008) 德国功能派翻译理论述评 (A critical introduction to the German functionalistic translation theory). 学术界 (*Academics in China*). 133: 249–255.
Hu, Zuoyou 胡作友 (2014) 后殖民主义翻译理论在中国的接受 (Reception of postcolonial translation theory in China). 学术界 (*Academics in China*). 193: 121–130.
Hu, Zuoyou, Hu, Xiaojuan and Li, Erwen 胡作友，胡晓娟，李而闻 (2013) 女性主义翻译理论在中国的接受 (Reception of feminist translation theory in China). 学术界 (*Academics in China*). 178: 152–160.
Huang, Guowen 黄国文 (2004) 翻译研究的功能语言学途径 (Functional linguistics as a research pathway in studying translation). 中国翻译 (*Chinese Translators Journal*). 2004(05): 15–19.

Huang, Haijun and Ma, Keyun 黄海军, 马可云 (2008) 解构主义翻译: 影响与局限 (Deconstructionist translation: influence and limitation). 外语教学 (*Foreign Language Education*). 29(1): 88–92.

Jiang, Xiaohua 蒋晓华 (2004) 女性主义对翻译理论的影响 (Influences of feminism upon translation theory). 中国翻译 (*Chinese Translators Journal*). 25(4): 10–15.

Liang, Manling and Hu, Weihua 梁满玲, 胡伟华 (2017) 林语堂"解殖民化"的话语翻译策略: 后殖民视阈 (Lin Yutang's discourse translation strategy under 'decolonization': postcolonial perspective). 外语教学 (*Foreign Language Education*). 38(4): 78–82.

Lin, Tiantian and Wang, Jinxiang 林甜甜, 王进祥 (2018) 从功能对等理论看洗护产品说明书汉英翻译的语言特征 (On the linguistic features of Chinese-English translation for care product manuals from the perspective of functional equivalence theory). 英语广场 (*English Square*). 2018(12): 28–31.

Lin, Wei and Zhao, Youbin 林巍, 赵友斌 (2017) 微妙之处寻等值 (Looking for equivalent value in subtle places). 中国翻译 (*Chinese Translators Journal*). 2017(05): 121–125.

Liu, Hongmei 刘红梅 (2008a) 对联的语用翻译 (Pragmatic approach to the translation of antithetic couplets). 中国翻译 (*Chinese Translators Journal*). 2008(02): 60–63+96.

Liu, Jinyu 刘瑾玉 (2008b) 后现代主义框架中女性主义翻译理论及其局限性 (Feminist translation studies and its limitations in postmodernism). 内蒙古大学学报(人文社会科学版) (*Journal of Inner Mongolia University (Humanities and Social Sciences)*). 40(1): 104–109.

Liu, Junping 刘军平 (2004) 女性主义翻译理论研究的中西话语 (Towards an east-west discourse on feminist translation studies). 中国翻译 (*Chinese Translators Journal*). 25(4): 3–9.

Liu, Runze, Wei, Xiangqing and Zhao, Wenjing 刘润泽, 魏向清, 赵文菁 (2015) "对等"术语的谱系化发展与中国当代译学知识体系建构 (Equivalence as a key term and its impact on the organization of knowledge in contemporary translation studies in China: a genealogical study). 中国翻译 (*Chinese Translators Journal*). 2015(05): 18–24.

Liu, Xin and Wang, Lin 刘欣, 王林 (2019) 功能对等视角下的旅游外宣翻译研究 (Translating tourism promotion text in perspective of functional equivalence). 英语广场 (*English Square*). 2019(01): 37–39.

Lu, Gan and Liu, Xiaohui 陆干, 刘晓辉 (2012) 基于文体特征的功能翻译方法——以古汉语格律诗英译为例 (Functional translation method based on stylistic features: using the translation of classic Chinese poems into English as examples). 外语教学 (*Foreign Language Education*). 33(6): 109–113.

Lü, Jun 吕俊 (2002) 翻译学应从解构主义那里学些什么——对九十年代中期以来我国译学研究的反思 (What could we learn from deconstructive theories in translation studies). 外国语 (*Journal of Foreign Languages*). 141: 48–54.

Ma, Hong and Lin, Jianqiang 马红, 林建强 (2007) 功能翻译理论与其翻译原则和方法 (Translation principles and methods of functionalist translation theory). 外语学刊 (*Foreign Language Research*). 138: 118–120.

Ma, Keyun and Luo, Siming 马可云, 罗思明 (2006) "解构'忠实'"之解构——与王东风教授商榷 (A deconstruction of the deconstruction of 'loyalty': challenging professor Wang Dongfeng). 外语教学 (*Foreign Language Education*). 27(4): 55–59.

Ou, Yamei and Wu, Yang 欧亚美, 吴阳 (2010) 女权主义翻译理论与"雌雄同体"说 (Feminist translation theory and the theory of androgyny). 深圳大学学报(人文社会科学版) (*Journal of Shenzhen University (Humanities and Social Sciences)*). 27(4): 126–129.

Pan, Haiou 潘海鸥 (2018) 功能对等理论下英语纪录片字幕翻译探究——以《文明》为例 (Exploring the translation of TV documentary subtitles under functional equivalence theory: using *Civilisation* as example). 齐齐哈尔师范高等专科学校学报 (*Journal of Qiqihar Junior Teachers' College*). 2018(06): 49–51.

Pang, Yuehui and Zhu, Jianping 庞月慧 朱健平 (2009) 功能学派翻译理论的解构主义印记 (*Trace of Deconstruction on Functionalist Translation Theory*). 中国外语 (FLC). 6(1): 95–99.

Qu, Weiguo 曲卫国 (2016) 剪不断、理还乱的西方中心主义情结——论后殖民翻译理论的局限 (Complexity towards West-centered emotion: on the limitation of postcolonial translation theory). 山东社会科学 (*Shandong Social Sciences*). 254: 33–38.

Si, Xianshu 司显柱 (2005) 从功能语言学的语言功能观论翻译实质、翻译策略与翻译标准——兼与朱志瑜博士商榷 (On translation quality, translation strategies and translation norm from the perspective of the function of language from the systemic functional linguistics: also including a discussion with Dr Zhu Zhiyu). 中国翻译 (*Chinese Translators Journal*). 26(3): 61–64.

Su, Yihua 苏奕华 (2008) 翻译中的意义对等与态度差异 (The equivalence of meaning and differences in attitudes within translation). 外语学刊 (*Foreign Language Research*). 2008(5): 100–102.

Tan, Zaixi 谭载喜 (1989) 奈达和他的翻译理论 (Nida and his translation theory). 外国语(上海外国语大学学报) (*Journal of Foreign Languages*). 1989(05): 30–37+51.

Tian, Lu and Zhao, Junfeng 田璐 赵军峰 (2018) 新世纪的功能翻译理论——克里斯蒂安·诺德教授访谈录 (A translation theory for the new century: interviewing professor Christiane Nord). 中国翻译 (*Chinese Translators Journal*). 2018(04): 86–90.

Tu, Guo yuan and Xiao, Jinyin 屠国元, 肖锦银 (2000) 西方现代翻译理论在中国的传播与接受 (The dissemination and reception of Western translation theory in China). 中国翻译 (*Chinese Translators Journal*). 2000(05): 15–19.

Wang, Bin 王斌 (2000) 关联理论对翻译解释的局限性 (The limitation of relevance theory in explaining translation). 中国翻译 (*Chinese Translators Journal*). 2000(04): 13–16.

Wang, Dongfeng 王东风 (2003) 翻译研究的后殖民视角 (Postcolonial perspective of translation studies). 中国翻译 (*Chinese Translators Journal*). 24(4): 3–8.

Wang, Hongyang 王紅陽 (2008) 翻译中的语篇功能对等研究 (Equivalence of textual function in translation). 中国翻译 (*Chinese Translators Journal*). 2008(03): 55–59.

Wang, Jianbin 王建斌 (2010) 泰山北斗一代通儒——缅怀德国功能派翻译理论创始人汉斯·费梅尔教授 (Taishan Beidou, an outstanding scholar: commemorating professor Hans Vermeer, founder of German Functionalist Translation Theory). 中国翻译 (*Chinese Translators Journal*). 2010(03): 80–83.

Wang, Jianguo 王建国 (2005) 关联翻译理论研究的回顾与展望 (Relevance theoretically informed translation studies: retrospect and prospect). 中国翻译 (*Chinese Translators Journal*). 26(4): 21–26.

Wang, Jing 王静 (2009) 女性主义翻译观照下的译者性别意识显现 (On visualization of gender awareness under feminist translation). 外语与外语教学 (*Foreign Languages and Their Teaching*). 248: 43–45.

Wu, Dilong and Wu, Junhui 吴迪龙, 武俊辉 (2017) 关联翻译理论可适性范围与关联重构策略研究 (Scope of applicability and reconstruction of relevance of the relevance translation theory). 广西民族大学学报（哲学社会科学版） (*Journal of Guangxi University for Nationalities (Philosophy and Social Science Edition)*). 39(4): 185–190.

Wu, Yimin and Zheng, Weihong 吴益民, 郑伟红 (2014) 论功能对等理论视域下的字幕翻译 (On subtitles translation from the perspective of functional equivalence). 河南师范大学学报(哲学社会科学版) (*Journal of Henan Normal University (Philosophy and Social Sciences Edition)*). 2014(01): 165–166.

Xiao, Meng 肖萌 (2010) 功能翻译理论指导下的我国高校外语专业翻译教学模式探究 (On China's college translation teaching models for foreign language majors in the perspective of functionalist approaches). 云南大学学报(社会科学版) (*Journal of Yunnan University (Social Sciences Edition)*). 2010(04): 85–89+96.

Xu, Lina 徐莉娜 (2015) 析翻译等值的语义路径 (Semantic approaches to equivalence in translation). 中国翻译 (*Chinese Translators Journal*). 2015(02): 11–18.

Xu, Minhui 徐敏慧 (2008) 浅说意义—— 解构与翻译关键词解读 (Toward an in-depth understanding key Derridean concepts in translation theories). 中国翻译 (*Chinese Translators Journal*). 2008(05): 19–24.

Yang, Zhong 杨忠 (2016) 功能语言学视域的语篇翻译对等——以《谏太宗十思疏》英译为例 (Textual equivalence in translation from the perspective of functional linguistics: taking *A Memorial to Tai Zong on Ten Aspects of Self-discipline* as example). 山东社会科学 (*Shandong Social Sciences*). 2016(10): 51–56.

Yu, Jianjun 余建军 (2018) 功能对等理论下的财务报表词汇特点及翻译 (Translating strategy of financial report's vocabulary under functional equivalence theory). 佳木斯职业学院学报 (*Journal of Jiamusi Vocational Institute*). 2018(01): 339–340.

Yu, Linjiao and Lu, Pengxu 于凌蛟, 卢鹏旭 (2018) 功能对等理论下的中式菜名翻译探究 (Exploration of Chinese dish translation under the functional equivalence theory). 英语广场 (*English Square*). 2018(11): 28–29.

Zhai, Fang and Hu, Chuanhua 翟芳，胡伟华 (2017) 功能对等视角下汉英国际新闻编译探析——以《中国日报》中的政治语篇为例 (Chinese-English international news translation in perspective of functional equivalence: using political text of China Daily as example). 西安外国语大学学报 (*Journal of Xi'an International Studies University*). 25(4): 87–91.

Zhan, Wangshu 展望姝 (2018) 功能对等理论下气象类文本的翻译 (Translating meteorological text under functional equivalence theory). 安徽文学 (*An Hui Literature*). 418: 55–57.

Zhang, Boran and Qin, Wenhua 张柏然, 秦文华 (2004) 后殖民之后: 翻译研究再思—— 后殖民主义理论对翻译研究的启示 (Rethinking translation studies enlightened by postcolonial theory). 南京大学学报 (*Journal of Nanjing University*). 2004(1): 111–117.

Zhang, Jinghua 张景华 (2004) 女性主义对传统译论的颠覆及其局限性 (On the contributions and limitations of feminist translation theory). 中国翻译 (*Chinese Translators Journal*). 25(4): 20–25.

Zhang, Meifang 张美芳 (2005) 功能加忠诚——介评克里丝汀·诺德的功能翻译理论 (Function plus loyalty: a critical introduction to Christiane Nord's functionalistic translation theory). 外国语 (*Journal of Foreign Languages*). 155: 60–65.

Zhang, Meifang and Qian, Hong 张美芳, 钱宏 (2007) 翻译研究领域的"功能"概念 (Concepts of 'function' in translation studies). 中国翻译 (*Chinese Translators Journal*). 2007(03): 10–16.

Zhang, Wanfang and Zhai, Changhong 张万防, 翟长红 (2018) 接纳与诘难之后: 中国语境下的后殖民主义翻译 (After acceptance and criticism: post-colonial translation in Chinese context). 成都理工大学学报(社会科学版) (*Journal of Chengdu University of Technology (Social Sciences)*). 26(6): 100–105.

Zhang, Yongxi 张永喜 (2006) 解构主义翻译观之再思 (Rethinking the deconstructionist approach to translation studies). 外语研究 (*Foreign Languages Research*). 100: 55–58.

Zhang, Zhiqiang 张志强 (2010) 后殖民翻译理论观照下的赛珍珠《水浒传》译本 (All men are brothers: a postcolonial approach to Pearl S. Buck's translation of *Shui Hu Zhuan*). 中国翻译 (*Chinese Translators Journal*). 2010(02): 44–48.

Zhao, Yi and Xiang, Mingyou 赵毅, 向明友 (2018) 关联理论研究前沿探析 (Emerging trends in relevance theory research). 现代外语(双月刊) (*Modern Foreign Languages (Bimonthly)*). 41(1): 130–140.

Zhou, Xiaomei 周晓梅 (2006) 翻译研究的"解构"之后 (Translation studies after 'deconstruction'). 外语研究 (*Foreign Languages Research*). 100: 62–65.

Zhou, Xingyu 周星煜 (2018) 功能对等理论指导下的医学翻译 (Medical translation under the guidance of functional equivalence). 海外英语 (*Overseas English*). 2018(08): 172–173.

Zhu, Yiping and Ma, Caimei 朱益平, 马彩梅 (2010) "译"在言外——翻译研究的视角转变 (Translating outside the words: a change of perspective in translation research). 外语教学 (*Foreign Language Education*). 31(1): 109–112.

Other references

Ammann, M. (1990) *Grundlagen der modernen Translationstheorie – Ein Leitfaden für Studierende*. Heidelberg: Translatorisches Handeln.

Baker, M. (1998) *Routledge Encyclopaedia of Translation Studies*. London and New York: Routledge.

Bassnett, S. and Trivedi, H. (eds) (1999) *Post-colonial Translation: Theory and Practice*. London and New York: Routledge.

Bühler, K. (1990) *Theory of Language: The Representational Function of Language*. Amsterdam: John Benjamins Publishing Company.

Chen, C. (2016) *CiteSpace: A Practical Guide for Mapping Scientific Literature*. New York: Nova Science Publishers.

Gutt, E. (2000) *Translation and Relevance: Cognition and Context*, 2nd edition. Manchester: St Jerome.

Halliday, M. A. K. and Hasan, R. (1976) *Cohesion in English*. London: Longman.

House, J. (1977). *A Model for Translation Quality Assessment*. Tübingen: TBL-Verlag Narr.

Koller, W. (1989) Equivalence in translation theory. Translated from German by A. Chesterman. In A. Chesterman (ed.). *Readings in Translation Theory*. Helsinki: Oy Finn Lectura Ab.

Martin, J. R. and White, P. R. R. (2005) *The Language of Evaluation: Appraisal in English*. Houndmills, Basingstoke, Hampshire and New York: Palgrave Macmillan.

Munday, J. (2001) *Introducing Translation Studies: Theories and Applications*. Oxon: Routledge.

Munday, J. (2016) *Introducing Translation Studies: Theories and Applications*, 4th edition. London and New York: Routledge.

Pym, A. (2010) *Exploring Translation Theories*. London and New York: Routledge.

Reiss, K. (1989). Text types, translation types and translation assessment, translated by A. Chesterman. In A. Chesterman (ed.) *Readings in Translation Theory*. Helsinki: Finn Lectura, pp. 105–115.

Reiss, K. and Vermeer, H. J. (1984) *Grundlegung einer allgemeinen Translationstheorie*. Tubingen: Niemeyer.

Tymoczko, M. (1999) Post-colonial writing and literary translation. In S. Bassnett and H. Trivedi (eds) *Post-Colonial Translation: Theory and Practice*. London and New York: Routledge, pp. 19–40.

Venuti, L. (1995) *The Translator's Invisibility*. London and New York: Routledge.

Venuti, L. (2008) *The Translator's Invisibility: A History of Translation*. London: Routledge.

Waard, Jan de and Nida, Eugene A. (1986) *From One Language to Another: Functional Equivalence in Bible Translating*. Nashville: Nelson.

3 Chinese translation activities, translators and translation theory

In this chapter, we will retrace the beginning of Chinese translation activities and try to uncover the many faces of Chinese translation practice during the long history of China. We will then focus on some major periods where translation has played a significant role in reshaping the Chinese culture and history. We discover how translation was done in these periods, including a description of the translator, institution, the readership and the functions of translation in society. We then consider some of the great translators in the history of Chinese translation, finding out the nature of their work, the concepts they embraced toward translation and the preeminent positions they held in the history of Chinese translation. After considering the practical side of Chinese translation and having focused on some renowned translators in Chinese history, we move on to discuss how Chinese translation theory is regenerated in these contexts, inheriting the traditional Chinese wisdom and learning from the experiences of translating, while combining these with recently introduced Western translation theory. Finally, we explore some innovative Chinese translation theory as a result of a long history of accumulation, fermentation and integration.

The history of Chinese translation

Although discourse and theory about Chinese translation have been presented abundantly throughout Chinese history, there is not a long record of study on the Chinese translation activity itself. According to Zou (2014), despite an uninterrupted 3000 years of translation history, it was relatively late that translation itself as an activity started to be investigated as an independent topic – not until the beginning of the 20th century. However, Zou also noted that the onset of Chinese translation activities was marked by the participation of many famous Chinese literary scholars such as Liang Qichao and Hu Shih. Studying translation activities is important because this is where Chinese translation theory is rooted and by doing so we can examine whether models and theories proposed are valid.

According to Han (2008), there have been five major 'surges of translation' in Chinese history. The first intensive translation activities in China started in the Eastern Han (东汉) dynasty and lasted until Wei Jin Nan Bei Chao (or the Northern and Southern dynasties 魏晋南北朝). These were the times when political situations in the country were chaotic and the 'barbarous' tribes from the northwest of China constantly disturbed the borders and looted the common households. Civilians were quite helpless in the face of these situations; therefore, they turned their attentions to literature imported from exotic countries as a form of withdrawal from society and reality. The translation of Buddhist Sutras led to the introduction of Buddhism into the country, along with its philosophy and ideology. The concept of tolerance in Buddhism, the thoughts of the afterlife and the idea of Se Kong (色空 'All things will expire') had somehow produced a 'calming effect' on the part of the common people and weakened their mind for rebellious thoughts. Therefore, in those eras (approximately between 20 and 600 CE) a primary function of the translating of Buddhist Sutras was to help maintain social order and strengthen the control of the feudal rulers. As a result, the rulers of those dynasties kept sending official messengers to get sutras from the West established dedicated venues for translating, resulting in thousands of Buddhist Scriptures being translated into the Chinese language. This was the first climax of translation activities in Chinese history, mostly officially initiated and probably politically motivated.

According to Han (2008), the second surge of translation activities occurred at the beginning of the 17th century, when European countries have largely transformed from feudal society to capitalism with unprecedented accomplishments in science and technology. In contrast, China at this time was relatively weak under the rule of conservative feudal systems by the end of the Ming dynasty when the low-productivity of small-scale peasant economy had seriously hindered the progress of science and technology. At this juncture, the missionaries of the Jesuits came to China to engage in religious activities, taking science and technology translation as an important part of their mission. By coincidence, they brought a wider range of European culture than religion itself. Their translations of science and technology also exerted a more powerful influence on Chinese society than their preaching activities. Some Chinese officials began to work with the missionaries to translate scientific literature imported from the West. Technical translation at this stage, as it were, helped Chinese intellectuals divert their attentions from highly abstract literary thinking to concrete scientific learning. This was the second climax of translation activities in Chinese history.

The third 'climax' of translation activity, in Han's opinion, consisted of three sub-stages: late Qing dynasty and early Republic of China, the May Fourth Movement, and the post-May Fourth Movement period. Translation activities in the late Qing dynasty was a concerted and somewhat desperate attempt to save the country initiated by intellectuals like Liang Qichao, Kang Youwei and Yan Fu. The books translated by Yan Fu, for example, Huxley's *Evolution and Ethics* and Adam Smith's *An Inquiry into the Nature and Causes of the Wealth of Nations*, strongly promoted the development of the reform movement and created a profound impact on society. According to Han, the translation of this period gradually awakened the sleeping masses, and to some extent broke the feudal ideology of the people, so that the Chinese began to understand the West and comprehend the world. During and after the May Fourth Movement (4 May, 1919), Han thought that most translation activities (or at least the most useful of them) were related to the introduction of Marxism into China, giving birth to the Chinese Communist Party and bringing about the integration of Marxism with the Chinese revolution, helping to realize great changes in Chinese society.

The fourth concentrated efforts of Chinese translation according to Han (2008) started after the founding of the People's Republic of China in 1949, when the government established a Central Compilation and Translation Bureau to introduce the Marxism and Leninism literature in large quantities. The importance of translation activities to the newly established PRC in this period is claimed by Han in his words below:

> 在建国不到十年的时间里，社会主义民主制度的确立，经济获得的飞速发展，是得益于翻译事业的。 (In this period of less than ten years' time since the founding of the nation, the democratic system of socialism was established, and the economy flourished in an unstoppable fashion. All these were due to the business of translation.)
>
> (Han, 2008, p. 62)

The fifth and final surge of translation activities in China, according to Han, also occurred during the reign of the current PRC administration. This started from the completion of the 3rd Plenary Session of the 11th Central Committee of the Communist Party in 1978 and the beginning of the opening up policy. Han commented that a lot of scholarly works in the West were imported into China via translation in this period to help establish the socialist economy marketing system. These new thoughts and methodologies also constituted a reference framework to inspire Chinese people and guide them toward new ways of feeling and thinking about the world. Series after series of translated books were published with grand titles like *Twentieth Century Western Philosophy Translation Series* (二十世纪西方哲学译丛), *Contemporary Academic Thinking Trend Translation Series* (当代学术思潮译丛), *Western Scholarship Translation Series* (西方学术译丛) and so on. Han believed that these translated books exerted their influences intensively on the culture and thinking of society, and fundamentally helped the implementation of the opening up policy. Han (2008) concluded his introduction to the five major translation surges in Chinese history by suggesting that, despite the different social backgrounds of the times for each translation climax, the impacts of the translations on society at that time were equally enormous and far-reaching. In particular, the translation activities have greatly promoted the development of China's culture, economy, politics, and science and technology. They have also helped carry out the transformation of Chinese society at turbulent times.

Han's (2008) summary of five major concentrations of Chinese translation activity is useful but somewhat oversimplified. Some details or even other significant translation activities were understandably left out in a paper of this length. One important kind of translation activity that was not mentioned by Han was that between Chinese and other minority languages, which can be collectively called 'ethnic translations' (民族翻译). Xia's (2017) work is an example of giving particular emphasis on this translation activity, which had not received adequate attention in the main trend of studying translation between Chinese and foreign languages. Instead, Xia drew attention to the important role played by ethnic translation in the process of nation building and regime legitimation in China's history. According to Xia, the activity of ethnic translation lasted for more than 2000 years in China without any gaps. Xia's ethnic translation referred to the translation of Han literature (汉语典籍) or Chinese classics, including historical documents, sutras, novels, poetry, scriptures and so on, into minority languages such as Mongolian and Manchu. This kind of translation activity (or 'big tide' 大潮 in Xia's words) occurred in the Liao (辽), Jin (金), Yuan (元) and Qing dynasties, when ethnic minorities ruled China for more than 700 years. The ethnic translation activities Xia had in mind were initiated by the emperors of these dynasties who, after having conquered China, considered it a top priority to introduce Chinese culture into the minority communities and promote national integration. Xia noted that 'ethnic fusion' (民族融合) was an important process to build China as a nation integrating multiple ethnicities under the common Han language (汉语). In particular, when the frontier tribes were strong enough to conquer China and dominate the mainstream Chinese people, the making of a melting pot initially through translation is key to eventual success, as cogently remarked by Xia:

> 民族接触和混居固然是推动民族融合的前提条件，但更重要的推动力来自文化融合，而翻译则是文化融合过程中不可替代的关键环节。(Ethnic contact and mixed living are admittedly prerequisites for promoting ethnic fusion, but the more important driving force comes from cultural integration, and translation is an irreplaceable key link in the process of cultural integration.)
>
> (Xia, 2017a, p. 89)

Xia also compared ethnic translation with Buddhist Sutra translation and the technical translation initiated by Jesuit missionaries. He noted that, after sutra translation had declined in the Song dynasty, ethnic translation took over and became even more prosperous. Also, Xia pointed out the important fact that translation as an officially recognized activity was more so in the four dynasties of Liao, Jin, Yuan, Qing (when China was ruled by frontier tribes) than in late Ming and early Qing dynasties, when missionary translation occurred. This is evidenced by there being a lot more translation-related records, according to Xia, in the Chinese historiography of the four dynasties regarding translation institutions, translators, translated works and records of translation activities, than that of the missionary translation in the late Ming and Qing dynasties. Because of its cultural meaning and political implication, translating was assumed to be an important activity in the mainstream ideology during those times. The minority ethnic regimes established a large number of translation bureaus and translator positions in order to endure the correct interpretation of the orders by lower rank officials passed down from the court. Therefore, translation became an essential part of political life. Xia gave a very telling example to illustrate the heightened status of translation at that time. That is, in Liao History (辽史) and Yuan History (元史), the descriptions of prominent figures like Chen Zhaogun (陈昭衮) and Yelü Xuegu (耶律学古) include clauses like 'good at translating and poetry' (工译及诗) and 'good at translating and language and riding and shooting' (通译语，善骑射), where the skills of translation were placed before the ability to make poetry and to perform 'riding and shooting'. In contrary, Xia thought that the technical translation brought about by missionaries was far less meaningful than ethnic translation in terms of its influence on how translation was conceptualized in mainstream culture and common ideology. This was because, according to Xia, the missionaries had not fundamentally changed the status of translating as an activity in the minds of the upper echelons or its role in the political-cultural systems, despite their contributions in the area of science and technology.

At the end of his paper, Xia lamented that researchers studying the history of Chinese translation had paid too little attention to ethnic translation. Xia attributed this negligence to the fact that translation, being a subject usually associated with foreign language disciplines, normally focused solely on the interactions between China and the West. He advised that when we set out to explore the ancient wisdom of translation, we should not only limit our attention to sutra translation and technical translation. Ethnic translation is equally important, where many hidden translators and translation activities facilitating communication between Han and the minority languages are also worthy of our attention. One important fact about ethnic translation of the kind discussed in Xia (2017) is that such activities of translating Chinese classics into minority languages like Mongolian and Manchu are no longer a live practice. As Xia so cogently argued, the activities have their historical significance, in helping with the ethnic fusion and regime legitimation after conquests of mainstream Chinese culture made by frontier peoples. Being no longer a contemporary practice, ethnic translation of the historical kind can however still be investigated out of scholarly interest and with some practical implications.

Another important kind of ethnic translation was discussed in Mu (2015), which investigated the current situation of minority language translation policies in China. Mu commented that there were currently seven minority languages officially listed as frequently used working languages in China: Mongolian, Tibetan, Uighur, Kazakh, Korean, Yi (彝语) and Vahcuengh (壮语). Mu noted that in China's National People's Congress meetings, documents were translated into these seven languages, so that the country's minorities could understand major policies of the government and the party. To Mu, ethnic translation in this sense is as important as foreign language translation and is intimately related to the security and the development of the economy and culture of the nation. However, even though the government continued to strengthen the service of minority nationality language translation, the study and the practice of ethnic translation are still in danger. Mu investigated doctoral dissertations, journal papers, national social

98 *Chinese translation activities*

science projects, etc. for the past two decades, and found four problems in minority language translation:

1. There is a paucity in minority language translating and research talents.
2. The scientific construction and theoretical studies of minority language translation is relatively backward.
3. The problem with research on minority language translation may be getting worse due to increasing loss of speakers of these languages.
4. There is a lack of integration between minority language translation and general translation studies.

Thus Mu (2015) reiterated the importance of minority language translation services, recommending the work as key to forging interracial relationships, implementing minority policies, promoting the economic, political, cultural and social construction of the minority regions and ensuring national security. While the status and functions of minority language translation were affirmed by national policies, according to Mu, the work of ethnic translation had been politically guaranteed. The only thing left to be done was to strengthen both the practice and the research of minority language translation. Only when there is protection from the policy level and there exists a continuous supply of talents, can the minority nationality language translation jobs be successfully accomplished.

A more comprehensive review of translation activities involving the Chinese classics was given in Wang (2017), which included the two types of ethnic translation discussed in Xia (2017) and Mu (2015), respectively, plus some other categories. Overall, Wang identified three stages of translating Chinese classics into other languages (including minority languages and foreign languages): 1. initiation, 2. expansion, 3. internationalization. In addition, the three stages are characterized by 'self-centred classicalism, ethnically related communalism and cosmopolitanism' (Wang, 2017, p. 128), respectively. At the first stage (Initiation), Chinese classics such as Tao Te Ching (道德经), Analects (论语), The Twenty-Four Histories (二十四史) and so on were disseminated via translation from the capital of China to the frontier, and from China to foreign countries, creating a huge and lasting impact. According to Wang, the translation task at this stage was based on the principles of philology, in this case, the exegesis and annotation methods conventionally used to interpret Chinese Confucian classics, such as textual proofs, textual screenings, annotations, interpretations, etc. Two modes of translation were involved: translating from classic Chinese to vernacular Chinese, and translating from classic Chinese into foreign languages such as English, Russian, French and German. At this stage, the purpose of translation was mainly to reinterpret and re-evaluate the Chinese classics and eventually to modernize the Han canons (汉语典籍).

The second stage of Han canon translation in Wang's scheme (Expansion) was characterized by an initial movement of Chinese classics from the center to the peripheral, that is, translating from Han to minority languages in the manner described by Xia (2017) in previous discussions. In those times, however, the translation task was accompanied by the gradual formation of the Chinese Empire, so to speak, through repeated national integration and separation, war and peace in history which generated a complex and slow process of the migration of national capital from the north to the south, and the political and economic center moving eastward. Moreover, this process of cultural integration demanded bidirectional translations – not only from Chinese to minority languages (for Han canons) but also from the minority languages to Chinese (for the ethnic literatures). In other words, the 'multi-symbiosis' kind of ethnic relations and the grand vision of integrated national culture broke through the conventional Central Plains (中原) Han culture and created bidirectional cultural exchanges. According to Wang, there are three paths through which the minority literatures are circulated to the Han culture:

1. The original literary work was passed down through oral communication, such as King Gesar (格萨尔王), the Tibetan and Mongolian epic.
2. The literature was first translated into foreign languages and then translated back into Chinese, such as Kutadgu Bilig (福乐智慧), a long poem written in Uyghur.
3. The minority literature was translated into Chinese, nourished by Chinese culture, and then disseminated abroad, such as Ashima (阿诗玛), the narrative poem originally written in Nuosu (撒尼语), a variety of Yi (彝语).

There are more types of ethnic translation works than alluded to in the above paths though. For example, minority literature can also be translated directly into another minority language without being mediated by a foreign language or Chinese. Overall, however, Wang noted that the translation and dissemination of Han canons had started quite late and both the quality and quantity of translations needed upgrading. For example, the important work written by an unknown Mongolian author living in the Qing dynasty nicknamed Hasibao (哈斯宝), annotating and commenting on *Dream of the Red Chamber* (红楼梦), so far has not been fully translated into Chinese. A lot of minority literary works have not been translated into foreign languages either. Wang's observation here largely coincides with Xia's (2017) opinion that there is generally not enough attention paid to ethnic translation in the field of Chinese translation studies.

The third stage of translating and disseminating Han classics, termed 'Internationalization' by Wang (2017), is characterized by the idea of cosmopolitanism (世界主义) and the translation activity involves three text types: travel notes, biographies and literary works. Wang explains that the kind of cosmopolitanism advanced by China is different from the one advocated by the West, which largely means a modernization process dictated by cultural hegemony that is characterized by global westernization. Instead, Wang proposes a cosmopolitanism defined by the Chinese approach:

中华民族需要文化自信，但不应自诩为东方主义名义下、西方人眼中的"他者"，更不是某些西方霸权所预设的作为欧美文明对立面而崛起的经济军事强国，而是世界范围内大国崛起语境下的大国关系和国际关系，是"一带一路"发展目标下的人类共同发展和共同繁荣。(The Chinese nation needs self-confidence in culture, but it should not be regarded as the 'other' in the eyes of the Westerners in the name of Orientalism, or the economic and military power that emerged as the rival of the European and American civilization assumed by some Western hegemonic views. On the contrary, (the Chinese cosmopolitanism) is the relationship between the major powers and international relations in the context of the rise of great powers within the scope of the world. It is the common development and common prosperity of mankind under the development goal of the 'Belt and Road'.)

(Wang, 2017, p. 27)

As regards translation activities, Wang thinks that under this context, there are three current trends which dictate the further development of Chinese classics translation. Firstly, the ancient religious, philosophical and historical works have declined, and the era of contemporary literature creation, especially fiction writing, has become more prosperous and presumably the likely target for translating into foreign languages. Secondly, with the deconstruction of traditional society, Chinese culture has become more diversified. As pieces of information about these classic works are easily broadcast and disseminated on the Internet, the monolithic nature of Han canons and their integrity have been challenged. Thirdly, literary tasks including creative writing and translating are now easily performed by individuals at home or in work. There is increasingly no distinction between language internal vs. language external or domestic vs. international disseminations of Chinese classics. All in all, Wang thinks that Chinese people should continue to enhance their communicative and translation competencies and improve their national quality and cultural taste, until the ideal of 'world commonwealth' (世界大同) is reached. Wang's (2017) works seem to offer a good summary of the history of Chinese translation activities and their cultural connections as well as their current status and a Chinese intellectual's expectation of future directions.

Representative Chinese translators

From the previous section, we understand that a late beginning of the study of Chinese translation history in the 20th century (Zou, 2014) has distinguished China's translation activities in the past into three or more kinds or stages. In retrospect, three types of translation activities in the history of China are worthy of our attention:

- Sutra translation: Chinese emperors initiated these translation activities as they imported Buddhism for various political and cultural reasons
- Ethnic translation: Conquerors of China from the frontier initiated translation of Chinese classics into minority languages for racial integration and political harmony

- Technical translation: Officials and intellectuals translated science and technology books into China to absorb knowledge and skills from the West

A good way to gain more understanding of these translation activities is through an examination of the translators who carried out these jobs of translation, which may shed light on the understanding of the complicated relationships between the author, the commissioner, the translator, the texts and the contextual factors. Ji (1988), for example, pitched on the introduction of a few translators at the times of sutra translation and technical translation, respectively, to offer a more comprehensive view of the ancient and modern history of Chinese translation and to make the narrative more informative and interesting. That is, at the time of Buddhist Scripture translation, he introduced well-known Buddhist monk translators like Zhi Qian (支谦), Dao An (道安), Kumārajīva (鸠摩罗什), Xuan Zang (玄奘); and famous Ming, Qing dynasty translators such as Xu Guangqi (徐光启), Li Zhizao (李之藻) and Zhang Cheng (张诚) as representative translating figures of their times, along with their works and contributions. More recently, Zhang and Wen (2014) did a rare meta-analysis of research on scholarly translators in China's history. They collected bibliographic data of 467 papers published between 1980 and 2013 from China's leading journals on foreign language and translation studies, which focused on the study of scholarly translators (翻译家). They analyzed the trend of research on this topic from the perspectives of numbers of papers published, research themes, research topics and content and research angles. The research themes Zhang and Wen discovered were introduction to scholarly translators, their views on translation, contrasting different views of translators and so on. The topics of research, on the other hand, included research on a certain type of translator, research on the influence of scholarly translators, (critical) introduction to the texts translated by these translators, and studies on their translation strategies or styles. Most usefully, Zhang and Wen (2014) listed the ten most referred-to translators in their work (in order of number of mention, from the most mentioned to the least): Yan Fu (严复), Lu Xun (鲁迅), Fu Lei (傅雷), Wang Zuoliang (王佐良), Lin Yutang (林语堂), Yang Xianyi (杨宪益), Zhu Shenghao (朱生豪), Qian Zhongshu (钱锺书), Hu Shih (胡适) and Lin Shu (林纾). It seems then that current Chinese researchers on translation are predominantly concerned with modern translators rather than those from distant history. This is not to say that sutra translators like Kumārajīva and Xuan Zang are not important in the history of Chinese translation. It simply means that they generate fewer topics on the part of contemporary translation researchers than the translators from later periods such as the Ming and Qing dynasties. Another point worth noting in Zhang and Wen's work is that research on Chinese translators often includes exploring their views on translation. In fact, this is often how traditional Chinese translation theory was represented – not as a body of literature consisting of systematic thoughts and dedicated discussions, but as intermittent discourses offered by renowned translators and the responses they brought forth.

Zhang and Wen's (2014) list of ten most frequently mentioned Chinese translators in China's academic journals did not include well-known names in the Buddhist Sutra translation periods such as Dao An, Kumārajīva and Xuan Zang.

This does not mean they are unimportant – it simply means they are less well researched. The lack of research on these ancient translators is partly due to the limited availability of second-hand materials (a point ruefully noted in Xia, 2017) and the relative inaccessibility of first-hand materials (because of the rarity of the materials and the difficulty in understanding the classic Chinese they are written in). We will have a closer look at two prominent ancient translators here, Kumārajīva and Xuan Zang, based on the few academic papers found dwelling on them. But first, we can benefit from some background information of the Buddhist Scripture translation activities in the ancient history of China. According to Yuan (1982), the translation of Buddhist Scriptures in China began in Dong Han (东汉) and terminated in Northern Song (北宋), lasting for approximately 1000 years (i.e. from 58–1063). In the initial period, the translation was mainly carried out or led by foreign monks. Due to their inadequate mastery of the Chinese language, translation in that period was often inaccurate. Also, the translation activities at the beginning were not well planned, and the translation methods were quite random, sometimes literal, sometimes based on meaning, but overall of an exploratory nature. From the very beginning, sutra translation was a kind of teamwork and the process of translation was divided into three rudimentary phases: first, the scripture was recited by one of the foreigner monks (from memory). Then, each verse was interpreted into Chinese by another person. Finally, one or more people transcribed the interpreted Chinese and further organized and modified the text (Ma, 1982). At some point, Chinese emperors started to officialize the Buddhist Scripture translation activities and set up dedicated venues and official positions to carry out the functions. According to Yuan (1982), the first well-recorded venue of translation was Guanzhong Yi Chang (关中译场) established in the Former Qin (符秦351–394) period. This was a translation bureau with a fixed position and a clear division of labor consisting of five components:

1. Oral broadcast (口宣): sounding out the original Sanskrit sutra.
2. Verifying text meaning (证文义): understanding the meaning of the sutra.
3. Oral interpretation (译语): orally interpreting the sutra.
4. Transcribing (笔录): recording the sutra in written Chinese.
5. Proofreading (校订): verifying the meaning of Chinese sutra.

Thereafter, working under this or similar procedures, there were four monk translators who have been regarded as the four greatest Buddhist Scripture translators in Chinese history: Kumārajīva (鸠摩罗什), Zhen Di (真谛), Xuan Zang (玄奘), Bu Kong (不空), who largely followed the same model described above (which were later expanded into as many as ten sectors to accommodate finer divisions of labor) and in similar translation bureaus. For example, Kumārajīva worked at Ximing Temple Yi Chang (西明寺译场) sometime between 401 and 409, and Xuan Zang at Hongfu Temple (弘福寺) for nearly two decades between 645 and 664. Both these monk translators not only translated a large number of Buddhist Scriptures but also demonstrated translation methods, provided translation thoughts and left fragments of translation discourse for academic research and discussion to this date.

Kumārajīva (344–413) was born into an elite family of Kucha (龟兹), an ancient Buddhist kingdom located at present-day Aksu Prefecture, Xinjiang, China. He went with his mother to Tianzhu (天竺), the ancient Chinese name for India, as a nine-year-old to learn the Buddhist Scriptures for three years. After returning to Kucha, he started lecturing on Buddhism and also continued to learn from other well-established monks. He endured some hardship when Chinese emperors sent military forces to his country and collected him when he was 40 years old. However, he later started working on the translation of Buddhist Scriptures in Chang'an (长安) from 401 until his death in 413. According to Ma (1982), Kumārajīva was very proficient in Buddhism and understood Chinese. He was also ably assisted by a group of well-learned monks. Therefore, with his consummate skills and unprecedented translation quality, Kumārajīva opened up a new era in the history of Chinese translation. Ma also noted that, before the Former Qin (前秦, 350–394) period, the translation method for Buddhist Sutra was mainly 'direct translation'. It was Kumārajīva who started the trend of translating based on meaning. Another researcher on Kumārajīva, after closely studying and interpreting historical books written in classic Chinese by successive Buddhist monk translators, identified six important contributions made by Kumārajīva to the field of Chinese translation in Wang (2018):

1. The theory of untranslatability.
2. The 'Wen' literary translation approach.
3. The translator's honesty oath, the simplicity of TT.
4. The abandonment of the '*geyi*' translation method,
5. The striving for excellence and the procedure of explaining while translating.
6. The Chinese-foreigner translator cooperation mode at the translation venue.

According to Wang, Kumārajīva's idea of untranslatability was reflected in his claim that translating Sanskrit Sutras into Chinese could be compared to 'chewing the food and feeding it to another person'. Specifically, Wang read the biography of Kumārajīva included in a highly regarded historical book entitled *Compilation of Notes on the Translation of the Tripitaka* (出三藏记集) written by a monk called Shi Sengyou (释僧祐). This book recorded some ideas expressed by Kumārajīva about a translation issue that later became known as the problem of translatability.

改梵为秦，失其藻蔚，虽得大意，殊隔文体。有似嚼饭与人，非徒失味，乃令呕哕也。(Translating from Sanskrit to Chinese causes the feel of the text to be lost. Even though the substance is obtained, the difference in style is profound. It is like chewing the food and feeding it to another person. Not only is the taste lost, it is also disgusting.)

(from Wang, 2018, p. 169)

104 *Chinese translation activities*

Indeed, the doubt so eloquently expressed by Kumārajīva about the possibility of translating Sanskrit Sutras into Chinese in a satisfactory manner, especially in terms of 'flavor' and style, made him a representative figure of the untranslatability issue in Chinese translation discourse, according to Wang. The second good quality that Wang attributes to Kumārajīva's translation is his objection to a 'dull' writing style and his preference for a pompous writing style of the TT (反对语言质朴，主张译文文丽) (Wang, 2018, p. 169). Again, this made Kumārajīva a representative figure of the Wen advocator (文派) in contrast to the opposite idea of emphasizing the essence in translating, or the advocator of the substance (质派). The third point Wang mentions about Kumārajīva's translating career is his last words as recorded in *Compilation of Notes on the Translation of the Tripitaka* subtitled 'Farewell words to fellow monks at death bed' (临终与众僧告别辞). The original words recorded in the book go as follows:

> 愿凡所宣译，传流后世，咸共弘通。今于众前发诚实誓，若所传无谬者，当使焚身之后，舌不焦烂。(I pray that all the translations I have worked on will be passed on to the future generations and broadly disseminated and understood. Today I would like to take an honesty oath in front of all of you. If all that I have passed down prove flowless, then after I have been cremated, my tongue will stay intact.)
>
> (from Wang, 2018, p. 170)

History has it that Kumārajīva's tongue was intact after his body was cremated. Wang also confirmed that the Buddhist Sutras translated by Kumārajīva had been widely circulated, more so than Xuan Zang's translations. However, Wang observed that an intriguing comment followed Kumārajīva's deathbed announcement, made by a visiting Sramana, saying that Kumārajīva's translation did not even count toward one tenth of the ST (罗什所译，十不出一). Wang thought that this was due to the fact that Kumārajīva often omitted the complicated and duplicated parts of the ST, and were not bound to the original text's organization. This could be an inadequacy of Kumārajīva's translation. However, that being said, pompous and concise TT could be a significant feature of Kumārajīva's translations.

By far the most significant contribution of Kumārajīva to sutra translation up to his dates, was his discarding the existing *geyi* (格义) method and directly translating the original meaning of the Sanskrit ST. *Geyi* was a somewhat peculiar translation method where ancient monk translators replaced terms in Buddhist Sutras with Confucian or Daoist terms in the process of translating, which could be seen as a kind of 'radical domesticating' translation method. Wang defined it as follows:

> 简单地说，格义就是用原本中国典籍的概念解释外来佛学，让弟子们以熟悉的中国固有的概念理解外来佛学的一种方法。(To put it simply, Geyi is to explain foreign Buddhism with the concept of the original Chinese

classics, and let the disciples understand foreign Buddhism with the familiar concept of China.)

(Wang, 2018, p. 171)

Two examples Wang gave to illustrate how *geyi* worked were Zhiqian's (支谦) translating Prajñā (般若 'wisdom') to *Ming* (明 'bright') following the Daoist convention, and Siddhārtha Gautama (释迦牟尼 'Buddha') into *Neng Ru* (能儒 'a Confucian master') for obvious reasons. Kumārajīva, however, was against the *geyi* translation method and insisted that Sanskrit Sutras should be directly translated into Chinese with annotations explaining the Buddhist terms – resembling the 'foreignization' method as formally introduced in Venuti (1995) some 1600 years later! Since Kumārajīva, Buddhism was able to rid itself of the influence of Confucianism and Daoism and develop on its own course.

But these are not all the contributions Kumārajīva made to the field of Chinese translation as recognized by Wang (2018), who also highly commended Kumārajīva's process of translation. According to Wang, Kumārajīva was never satisfied with the intermediate results of his translation. Instead, he kept on refining his translation through many stages of reinterpretation and revision so that the TT could capture as much essence of the ST as possible, both in terms of denotation and connotation. Wang said Kumārajīva's translations were able to spread widely due to this spirit of 'pursuing excellence after excellence' (精益求精) and aiming for perfection. In addition, Wang explained the innovative model of team translation directed by Kumārajīva, which divided the process of translation into three steps. First, Kumārajīva orally translated sutras from Sanskrit to Chinese and, in the meantime, explained the meaning of the sutra in question (边译边讲 'lecturing while translating'). Next, some talented persons well-versed in Chinese transcribed Kumārajīva's words into Chinese texts took advantage of their superiority in the Chinese language. Finally, at the third step, the next group of translators scrutinized the text produced in the previous stage and refined it, generating the final TT. In this team effort, Chinese and foreign translators worked seamlessly together, giving full play to both Kumārajīva's knowledge in sutras and Chinese authors' superior writing ability. The quality of translation was improved to an unprecedented level.

Kumārajīva's achievements were to be emulated some 250 years later by another great monk translator – Xuan Zang (玄奘), more widely known as Sanzang Fashi (三藏法师) or Tang Sanzang (唐三藏), born in 602 in Henan, China. Like Kumārajīva, Xuan Zang also became a monk at a very early age – for him, at 13 years old in Luoyang (洛阳) according to Ma (1980). He set out in 629 all the way to India to study Buddhism with a high monk in a Buddhist monastery called Nalanda (那烂陀寺) and toured the country for 17 years before returning to China, bringing hundreds of volumes of Sanskrit hymns with him. He was heartily welcomed by Chinese officials and civilians alike and was set up in a temple by emperor Taizong of Tang (唐太宗) to start translating the scriptures. Before his death in 664, Xuan Zang had translated 75 sutras divided into

1335 chapters in total – in comparison, Kumārajīva had translated 74 sutras with only 384 chapters, which means Xuan Zang generally translated much longer sutras. In addition, the Chinese Sutras produced under Xuan Zang's new translation methodology were generally regarded as 'new translation' (新译). This is because previously, in Kumārajīva's times, the translation had been produced in three phases: the ST was first translated into Chinese using Sanskrit grammar; it was then modified according to Chinese grammar, before finally being refined and revised into a good Chinese TT by a different team. In the 'new translation' attributed to Xuan Zang, because he was a well-learned Buddhist monk and good at both Sanskrit and Chinese, the first two stages in the older translation method were combined into one. That is, the Chinese text produced by Xuan Zang no longer needed revision as he 'made utterances into verse' (出语成章) (from Ma, 1980, p. 18). According to Ma, Xuan Zang used a 'direct translation' method coupled with 'semantic translation'. He is also said to have set the 'five categories of untranslated terms' principle ('五不翻'原则): the cryptic terms, polysemic items, things absent in domestic culture, existing Sanskrit transliterations, and original terms which had Buddhist implications. These were said to be largely followed by later monk translators.

Ma (1980) commented that the Tang dynasty was the heyday of the translation of Buddhist Scriptures in China, and the translation of sutras was concentrated in the period from Zhenguan (贞观) to Zhenyuan (贞元), that is, from 627 to 805. In these 79 years, although the work of Xuan Zang constituted only 19 years, his influence was considerable. In addition, during the period when Xuan Zang was in charge of the translation venues, a lot of talents were discovered and developed who then went on to play a vital role in the subsequent translation endeavors of Buddhist Scriptures. Despite Xuan Zang's achievements as a great sutra translator, however, his contributions to Chinese translation was somewhat controversial. Fu (2012), for example, attributed the 'anti-*geyi*' translation method to Xuan Zang, which we earlier explained on the basis of Wang's (2018) discussion of Kumārajīva's thoughts on translation. In fact, to Fu (2012), Kumārajīva himself still followed the *geyi* approach in his translation of the sutra, which was entirely different from Wang's (2018) view. This is then a moot point, requiring further research on Chinese translation history to make clarification. Another controversial point surrounding Xuan Zang is the origin of the sentence 'You must be both faithful and idiomatic (in translating)' (既须求真，又须喻俗) as a translation norm. Ma (1980) and many others attributed the phrase to Xuan Zang. However, scholars like Yuan (1993) took pains to prove that it was instead a sentence coined by Liang Qichao (梁启超), not Xuan Zang. In fact, Yang (2010) went so far as to prove many false attributions of Chinese translation discourse to Xuan Zang and argued that Xuan Zang was a great translator, but not necessarily a theorist due to his heavy workload or lack of interest or talent in developing translation theory. In any case, we have now concluded our discussion on the more ancient history of Chinese translation by looking at two outstanding sutra translators in China's history. As can be seen, even as far back as more than 1500 years ago, China's translators had already invented the concepts of foreignization vs. domestication, and recognized many fundamental ideas about translating such as untranslatability, norms of translation and so on. As the eras of sutra translation drew to an end by the year 800, Chinese translation history would be waiting another 1000 years for the next significant event to happen. We will now look at one representative figure in the translation of Western science and philosophy in the Qing dynasty: Yan Fu (严复).

Yan Fu (1854–1921) was a famous modern translator and educator. He graduated from the Fujian Shipping Administration School and the Royal Naval College, Greenwich in 1871 and 1879, respectively. He had served as the General Office of the Translation Department of the Jingshi University, the President of Shanghai Fudan University, the President of the Anqing Higher Normal School, and the Editor-in-Chief of the Qing dynasty Academic Department. But by far the most significant and remembered work he had done was in the area of translation. During his service period at the Beiyang Naval Academy (北洋水师学堂) founded by Li Hongzhang (李鸿章), not only did Yan Fu train the first batch of naval talents in modern China but, more significantly, he translated the book *Evolution and Ethics* (天演论), founded the Kuo Wen Pao (国闻报 'National News') as an avenue for publishing his translations, and systematically introduced Western democracy and science into the country while publicizing the ideas of reform and transformation. While he successfully introduced Western sociology, political science, political economy, philosophy and natural science into China, the translation norm of *xin, da, ya* (信、达、雅 or 'faithfulness, expressiveness, elegance') he proposed had exerted far-reaching influence on the translation work of later generations. In short, Yan Fu, being a bourgeois enlightenment thinker, translator and educator and a very influential person in the late Qing dynasty, was among the 'advanced Chinese' (先进的中国人) who sought truth from the Western countries in modern Chinese history.

Keying in 信、达、雅 as a topic in the Chinese database CNKI generated around 700 results and searching the same words in Google returned 39,900,000 hits at the time of writing. This set of translation assessment criteria proposed by Yan Fu 12 decades ago is still enthusiastically talked about to this day. Chinese discourses centering around *xin, da, ya* can be roughly distinguished into two kinds: theoretical discussion and applied research. Despite the somewhat vague nature of these criteria, Chinese investigators still manage to generate applied research based on their own interpretation and elaboration of the tenets. A lot of researchers used the three criteria to examine literary translations from Chinese to English or vice versa. For example, Yuan and Zheng (2018) did a comparative analysis of two different English translations of *Three Character Cannon* (三字经) using *xin, da, ya* as the evaluation guideline. Lin (2018) examined the nicknames in an English translation of a classic Chinese novel *Outlaws of the marsh* (水浒传), using the three criteria to verify whether the artistic concept and charm had been adequately translated. Zhang (2018) used the principle to analyze his own translation of an English novel with a view to demonstrating how the criteria were applicable to real translation work. Literary translation, however, is not the only genre which makes use of this overarching principle invented by

Yan Fu. Luo and Zheng (2018), for example, explained how the translation of traditional Chinese medicine can benefit from the concept of *xin, da, ya*. They argued that the instructions for Chinese medicine are related to people's life and health; therefore their English translations must first be 'faithful' to the original text, and be loyal to the readers and other participants of the translation project. The name of the medicine and the effect, on the other hand, should be translated in elegant and expressive ways, respectively. On the more theoretical side, Yang (2018) connected the principle of *xin, da, ya* to the concept of intercultural communication and advocated the understanding of background information in the ST of different domains so that, for words, vocabulary and sentences in different language families, we could ensure the accuracy of the meaning of expression and the gracefulness of the language and eventually the readability, audibility and intelligibility of the translation.

The theory of *xin, da, ya* as the norm of translation has also been seriously discussed, debated, elaborated, contrasted and even refuted. Zhang (1995) compared Yan Fu's principle with Nida's translation theory and explained their seminaries and differences. That is, firstly, Zhang thought that Nida's translation thoughts did not really surmount the traditional contrast between form-based and meaning-based translation. To Zhang, the so-called dynamic translation was still based on meaning. This coincided with Yan Fu's translation strategies of modifying form to preserve meaning and to make the TT as natural as possible. Both approaches were similar on this account. Secondly, Zhang noted that Yan Fu focused on faithfulness; while Nida put emphasis on the reader's response. He thought that Yan's principle was more capable of drawing out the aesthetic value of the original work, so it was more suitable for use in literary translation. Nida's readership centered approach, on the other hand, was suitable for the multidimensional communicative use of different kinds of ST. Another work, Huang (2016), attempted to build a more systematic model of Yan Fu's translation theory on the basis of *xin, da, ya* and his other ideas and approaches. Specifically, Huang thought there were three levels of Yan Fu's thoughts on translation, which he subsumed under the umbrella term of *bian yi* (变译 'translation variation', Huang's own translation in the English abstract of his Chinese paper): Translation Variation Concept (变译思想, TVC), Translation Variation Strategy (变译策略, TVS) and Translation Variation Techniques (变译方法, TVT). In Huang's scheme, the TVC was represented by Yan Fu's overarching principle of *xin, da, ya* and the TVS was the phrase *da zhi shu* (达旨术 'method to achieve understanding') used by Yan Fu as a methodological guidance to all his translation tasks. The TVT level subsumes various translation techniques that could be observed to function in Yan Fu's translations in fulfilling the concept of 'translation variation', including *zhaiyi* (摘译 'selected translation'), *bianyi* (编译 'edited translation'), *shuyi* (述译 'narrated translation'), *suoyi* (缩译 'condensed translation'), *zongshu* (综述 'summarized translation'), *shuping* (述评 'summarized translation plus comment'), *yiping* (译评 'translation plus comment'), *chanshi* (阐释 'translation plus explanation'), *gaiyi* (改译 'translation plus rewriting'), *yixie* (译写 'translation plus writing') and *canyi* (参译 'translation plus quotation'). Huang's model successfully extended Yan Fu's rudimentary concepts of *xin, da, ya* to the levels of translation strategies and techniques, forming a hierarchy from the top concept of 'translation variation' to the bottom of hands-on translating techniques.

There are also works which explored the history and authenticity of Yan Fu's *xin, da, ya* theory. Yan and Zhu (2017), for example, argued that *xin, da, ya* was not Yan Fu's sole invention. Instead, they found that it was through three stages of evolution that *xin, da, ya* was generated as an integrated concept. They argued that, at the first stage, Yan Fu himself proposed the view of *qiu da* (求达 'pursuing expressiveness') in his commentary to the translation of *Evolution and Ethics*. Subsequently, another scholar named Wu Rulun (吴汝纶) helped draw Yan Fu's attention to the issue of 'faithfulness' (*xin*) in the preface he wrote for Yan Fu's translation. Wu also encouraged Yan Fu to emulate the accumulated wisdom of great translators in the previous dynasties. A third scholar named Lü Zengxiang (吕增祥) also helped proofread Yan Fu's translation and suggested ways of refinement (*ya*). Finally, the three concepts of *xin, da, ya* were combined to form an overarching principle for future translators to follow. For Yan and Zhu, the formulation of this important concept was a joint effort between three eminent Chinese intellectuals at the time. In addition, it was also the outcome of an evolutionary process as a result of scholarly interactions among Yan, Wu and Lü, the combined wisdom of intellectuals at late Qing dynasty and the summarization of all the knowledge and experiences of sutra translation from Han to Tang dynasty (Yan & Zhu, 2017, p. 130). According to Yan and Zhu, a timely investigation into the contributing factors for the formulation of *xin, da, ya* could help us clarify the historical background and see the real essence of Chinese traditional culture which, in turn, would help generate a better understanding of the historical development of Chinese translation discourse. The last point made by Yan and Zhu was echoed by Lü (2017), who also attempted to put Yan Fu's achievements in translation theory and practice in a historical context. Lü's argument was based on Yan Fu's controversial claim that his own translation was 'non-mainstream' (非正法 'not regular'), which seemed to contradict the perfect criteria of *xin, da, ya* he set for high-quality translations. Lü, however, explained that this seemingly incongruent positioning by Yan Fu of his own translation actually showed his profound thinking and integrity as an intellectual translator in that turbulent time. Lü showed from Yan Fu's commentary on *Evolution and Ethics* that he had recognized the huge gap between the then Western science and philosophy and the Chinese culture and society, and had adopted various 'non-mainstream' translation strategies in order to make his translations understandable to the Chinese readers at that time, including omitting large parts of the book on sophisticated physics, mathematics, logics and sociology. Lü commended that Yan Fu's approach had been a rational choice for circumventing the limitations imposed by socio-historical conditions. For Lü, Yan Fu's 'non-mainstream' translation method offered a 'historical unification' (历史统一) between translation ideal and translation reality. This was highly implicational, according to Lü, to China's recent campaign of 'Chinese culture going out' (中国文化'走出去'), which also faced a large gap between ideal and reality in its translation initiations.

We have seen three prominent translators and the translation activities they carried out (as well as the translation theory or philosophy associated with their practice) during the two critical periods of the Chinese translation history – the Buddhist Scriptures imported from India between the 7th and the 9th centuries, and the translation of science and technology from the West several hundred years later. A new era began since the death of the Qing dynasty in 1911 and the establishment of the Republic of China in 1912 after the Xinhai Revolution (辛亥革命 'the 1911 revolution'). As China faced an uncertain future after the termination of feudal society and was still lagging behind in science and technology, it was vitally important to introduce various aspects of Western culture and society into China via translation. Many Chinese intellectuals were involved in this collective endeavor, such as Liang Qichao (梁启超 1873–1929), Lu Xun (鲁迅 1881–1936), Hu Shih (胡适 1891–1962), Lin Yutang (林语堂 1895–1976), Liang Shih-chiu (梁实秋 1903–1987) and so on. All these were well-learned Chinese intellectuals who not only published in Chinese but were capable of translating from foreign languages or commenting on translation issues. As current affair commentators and well-respected scholars, their discourses on translation were important in shaping the practice of translation and the further development of translation theory. Due to the limits of space, we will only look at Lu Xun as a representative figure in this period of Chinese translation.

Lu Xun was both a creative writer and a translator. He was well known for having written such novels as *A Madman's Diary* (狂人日记) and *The True Story of Ah Q* (阿Q正传). According to Zhou et al. (1981), however, Lu Xun also translated three million words' (which normally means 'characters' in the Chinese context) worth of literary works from foreign languages into Chinese, among which, translations from Russian accounted for more than half (i.e. 160 million 'words') of the word counts. They praised Lu Xun's contributions to the Chinese culture in the following way:

> 鲁迅光辉的一生, 给我们留下了极其丰富和宝贵的精神财富。他在从事新文学活动的同时, 还对我国近代翻译事业作出了卓越的贡献。他的瑰丽多采的译著以及他在翻译理论所发表的精辟卓见, 成了我国文化宝库中珍贵的历史遗产。(Lu Xun's glorious life has left us with an extremely rich and precious spiritual wealth. While engaging in new literary activities, he also made outstanding contributions to China's modern translation career. His magnificent translation and his brilliant insights in translation theory have become precious historical heritage in China's cultural treasure house.)
>
> (Zhou et al., 1992, p. 47)

Thus, it is for certain that not only was Lu Xun a creative writer and a prolific translator, he was also a commentator on the theory of translation. Moreover, according to Liu (1992), the reason why Lu Xun attached so much importance to translation was he believed that the function of translation fit into his overall goal of transforming society with new literature so as to 'awaken' the Chinese people. Therefore, the literary works he chose to translate were invariably those he thought to be beneficial to the country, which included a wide range of genres like novels, plays, fairy tales, prose, poetry, science fiction and literary theory. The overall goal for Lu Xun in translating all of these materials was, according to Liu, to transform society and enhance the national character. With that ideal in mind, Lu Xun did not only translate by himself but also encouraged other people to translate, so much so that he produced a well-quoted sentence '我要求中国有许多好的翻译家, 倘不能就支持着"硬译"' (I ask that there be many good translators in China; if not, then I support 'hard translation') (see Zhou et al., 1981, p. 48). The 'hard translation' concept advocated at some point by Lu Xun in the three decades of his translation career then became symbolic of his position on the general method of translation. The impression was further strengthened by his maintenance of the '宁信而不顺' ('I would rather go for disfluency in order to be faithful') principle. However, Zhou et al. argued that it was a general misunderstanding that Lu Xun was regarded as a fervent believer in 'hard translation'. They explained that the reason why Lu Xun emphasized 'faithfulness' (信) was because he was eager to introduce new thoughts and new culture from abroad by translating the foreign literature; therefore it was mandatory that the translation be completely faithful. On the other hand, Lu Xun also considered it important for translators to introduce new words and new structure to the home language in order to enrich the language for the people. This was indeed a timely suggestion after the May Fourth Movement (五四运动) in 1919, when written vernacular Chinese (白话文) gradually became the norm to replace classical Chinese but was still lacking in vocabulary and structure to resurface as a fully functional modern language.

Liu (1992) wrote about Lu Xun's open recognition of the difficulty in translating literary works and his humble attitude about the quality of his own translation. For example, despite his eagerness to introduce children's literature into China for the benefits of parents, educationists and fairy tale writers, and his determination to use easier words for child readers around ten years old, Lu Xun still 'hit a snag' when the project started and considered himself having done a poor job, in his own words:

> 一开译, 可就立刻碰到了钉子了, 孩子的话, 我知道得太少, 不够达出原文的意思来, 因此仍然译得不三不四。 (As soon as I started translating, I immediately encountered a problem. I knew too little about children's language, not enough to fully express the meaning of the original text, so my translation is still far from satisfactory.)
>
> (from Liu, 1992, p. 5.)

A related point to Lu Xun's constant feeling of inadequacy of his own and others' translations was his insistence on the advantages of retranslation (重译 or 复译). At a time when copyright and other forms of intellectual property were not an issue, people seemed to decide to translate a literary or scientific work 'at will'. The easiness and randomness of self-initiating a translation project without having to ask the copyright owner's permission can be gathered from Liu's (1992) remarks that '对于重译, 鲁迅先生是一贯热情地呼唤着的' (Regarding retranslation, Mr Lu Xun consistently and passionately advocated) (p. 5) and Lu Xun's condemnation of people advertising in newspapers announcing their 'right' to a certain translation like so: '已在开译, 请万勿重译为幸' (The work is being translated; please do not retranslate) (ibid.). In the present day, any translator would have to obtain 'translation rights' from the copyright owner, usually the publisher, in order to carry out the translating job. Since it was presumably easy for translators to work on original works without asking for permission, on one hand, more than one person might contemplate on translating the same work and, on the other hand, someone who was already doing the translation might try to prevent others from offering alternative versions for credential or monetary reasons. Lu Xun's position on the issue of retranslating was, according to Liu, extremely open and persistent in stressing the necessity and benefits of it, so much so that he was highly critical of people who placed those 'anti-retranslation' advertisements in newspapers (Liu, 1992). There were at least three reasons why Lu Xun highly recommended the practice of retranslating, according to Liu:

1. Retranslating is a measure to defeat 'erratic translation' (乱译).
2. Works having been translated into classical Chinese need to be retranslated into vernacular Chinese.
3. Anyone thinking they can offer a better translation than existing one(s) should be encouraged to do so.

According to Liu (1992), Lu Xun was often dissatisfied with his own translations, regarding them as something between 'none' (无有) and 'better' (较好); therefore, he eagerly anticipated better translations to come up though other people's retranslating. Lu Xun also emphasized the importance of translation criticism as a way to enhance the overall quality of translation. He thought that, apart from the translator, the readership, the publishers and the critics in particular were responsible for the weaker performance of the translation profession. Lu Xun thought that 'correct criticism' of translation should: 1. point out bad translations, 2. applaud good translations, and 3. encourage acceptable translations (if there were no good translations). Interestingly (and somewhat desperately), Lu Xun also indicated that if there were not even acceptable translations, then critics should mention the strengths of poor translations which were still useful to the readership. In a nutshell, Lu Xun had been a humble and dedicated translator, an advocate for literary translation and its social functions, and an applied translation theorist who left a wealth of translation materials and thought for further studies.

Lu Xun's death in 1936 occurred in the midst of the Chinese Civil War between 1927 and 1950. The establishment of the People's Republic of China in 1949 marked the beginning of a new era. After three decades of relatively turbulent times, and with the advent of the opening up policy in 1979, China gradually became an important pillar of the world economy. In the overall trend of globalization, Chinese culture had ushered in the historical opportunity of 'going out'. With the implementation of the Chinese culture going global strategy, people began to pay more attention to the study of Chinese–English translation. Therefore, the translation theory and works of Xu Yuanchong (许渊冲), who is known as 'the only person in English and French translations of poetry' (诗译英法唯一人), has become the focus of attention. Xu Yuanchong was born in Nanchang, Jiangxi in 1921. He studied at the Department of Foreign Languages of National Southwest Associated University and was a graduate from the Institute of Tsinghua University. He later pursued French language and literature at Sorbonne University and returned to China to teach at Beijing Foreign Studies University in 1951. He began to publish translations subsequently but, due to the interference of the political events in this period, he only published four books in the next 30 years. In 1983 he was made professor of international culture at Peking University and his translation career entered a golden age.

A brief examination of Xu's translation history shows his concentration on two main strands: one is translating works from Western countries, mainly representative classic literary works of Britain and France such as *Madame Bovary* and *The Red And The Black*. The other is translating the classic works of China that reflect the essence of Chinese traditional culture, involving more than 3,000 poems and words, such as *The Book of Songs* (诗经), *Songs of the Chu* (楚辞), *The Romance of West Chamber* (西厢记), *300 Tang Poems: A New Translation* (唐诗三百首新译), *Song of the Immortals: An Anthology of Classical Chinese Poetry* (中国古诗词六百首) and so on. 30 of his translated poems were selected into textbooks by foreign universities. In 1999, he was nominated for The Nobel Prize in Literature. In 2010, he was awarded the 'Lifetime Achievement Award in Translation' (中国翻译文化终身成就奖) by the China Translation Association (中国翻译协会). In 2014, he was awarded the 'Arctic Light' translator award by the International Federation of Translators. He was the first Asian translator to receive this honor. In 2016, Xu Yuanchong Institute of Translation and Comparative Culture was established in Datong University, Shanxi Province, and became an academic platform for studying Xu Yuanchong's translation theory and practice, providing an opportunity for Chinese translation studies to go global.

Xu Yuanchong is a renowned translator rarely seen in the history of Chinese translation who has both practical experience in translating between Chinese, English and French, and has presented a systematic translation theory. Xu summed up his literary translation theory as 'The Art of Beautification' (美化之艺术). He selected the first word of the name of his translation theory 美 (beauty) from the 'three beauty' (三美) linguistic theory pioneered by Lu Xun, the second word 化 (sublimity) from Qian Zhongshu's (钱钟书) 'theory of sublime condition' (化境说), and the third word 之 *zhi* from Confucius's saying 知之者不如好之者，好之者不如乐之者 (Those who know are not as good as those who are good, those who are good are not as good as those who are happy) and the final word 艺术 (art) from Zhu Guangqian's (朱光潜) motto that "从心所欲，不逾矩"是一切艺术的成熟境界 (Doing whatever you want without going beyond the rules is the mature realm of all art). In addition, Xu coined the phrase 创优似竞赛 (creating the best as if in a competition) to be a tenet of his theory. He took the word 创 (create) from Guo Moruo's (郭沫若) 'transcreation theory' (创译论), the word 似 (alike) from Fu Lei's (傅雷) 'spirit alikeness theory' (神似说), and the word 优 (excellent) from his own 'theory of advantage' (优势论) plus the word 竞赛 (competition) to represent his literary translation approached from a new perspective. For Xu, the ontology of literary translation is the 'optimization theory' (优化论) and the Three Beauty Theory (三美论) – the first character of the name of each theory can be put together to form the word 优美 (excellent and beautiful). The methodology for literary translation is the 'creative translation theory' (创译论), the 'principle of three transformations' (三化论) and the 'optimization theory'. The purpose of literary translation is subsumed in the 'three *zhi* theory' (三之论); whereas the epistemology for literary translation is the 'competition theory' (竞赛论). In a nutshell, in Xu's scheme, literary translation is the art of manipulating the 'three beauty' (三美), 'three transformation' (三化), 'three *zhi*' (三之) and other useful concepts that can be divided into three ways. Pan (2017), for one, held very high regards for the translation theory put together by Xu, as expressed in the paragraph below:

> 许老的理论，是严复以来，第一个由中国人自己提出的理论。有自己的哲学思想，有自己的学术资源，有自己的话语系统。他的翻译理论是中国第一个成熟的文学翻译理论，也是第一个成熟的中译外理论。
> (Xu's theory is the first theory put forward by the Chinese themselves since Yan Fu. It has its own philosophical thinking, its own academic resources, and its own discourse system. His translation theory is not only China's first mature literary translation theory but also the first mature translation theory for translating Chinese into foreign languages.)
> (Pan, 2017, p. 5.)

Qin and Xu (2018) analyze the thinking patterns and theoretical tendency of Xu's translation theory and believe that a three-way thinking mode is an important tool for the construction of his three-stratum theory. This method of thinking subsumes, but also transcends, the dichotomy of existing analytical frameworks, embodying the wisdom of traditional Chinese philosophy. For example, Daoist cosmology believes that *dao* produces one, one produces two, two produces three, and three produces all things (道生一，一生二，二生三，三生万物). Qin and Xu highly regard Xu Yuanchong's three-stratum concept in translating as the best embodiment of the three-way thinking model in general, for example, the 'three beauty' distinction (意美 音美 形美 'beauty in sense, sound and form'), the 'three force' theory (三势论: 优势、劣势、均势 'advantages, disadvantages, balance of power', also named as the 'competition theory'), the 'three transformation' methodology (深化、等化、浅化 'deepening, equalization, shallowness'), and the 'three *zhi*' ideology (知之、好之、乐之 'Make people understand, like and happy') and so on.

In terms of the usefulness of his translation theory to practical work, according to Qin and Xu (2018), Xu Yuanchong is very skillful in the application of his three-way thinking style to translating. The inner logic is that any language that touches the heart should include three aspects: beauty in meaning, sound and form (意美、音美、形美). The beauty of meaning touches the heart, the beauty of sound moves the ears, and the beauty of the form pleases the eyes. Translation is the unity of two languages, but the vocabulary and grammar of the two languages are different and present challenges. Sometimes, the expressive powers of the two are in a balanced state; but in many cases, one is at an advantage over the other. Therefore, in order to achieve the unification of the two languages, it is necessary to offset the disadvantages, strike a balance of power and press home the advantages. The corresponding translation methods are 'making shallow' (浅化), equalizing (等化) and deepening (深化) (i.e. the 'principle of three transformations' to be discussed in the next paragraph). The purpose of translation is to make the target readers understand, like and be happy with the translation. Xu believes that '乐之' (making happy) is the greatest achievement of translation, the reader's highest evaluation of the translator and the laurel in the field of translation.

A generally recognized strategy in translating ancient Chinese poems into English is to 'preserve the beauty' of the original poems to the greatest extent. An equally important task for the translator is to deliver the 'lifelike spirit' of the original poem (or the 'beauty of the meaning' in Xu Yuanchong's term). An example from Wang (2002) illustrates how Xu applies the 'principle of three transformations' to reproduce the original 'beauty of the meaning' in his translation of Li Bai's (李白) poem:

> 故人西辞黄鹤楼,
> My friend has left the west where the Yellow Crane towers,
> 烟花三月下扬州。
> For Yangzhou in spring green with willows and red with flowers.
> 孤帆远影碧空尽,
> His lessening sail is lost in the boundless blue sky,
> 唯见长江天际流。
> Where I see but the endless River rolling by.

Xu translates the word 烟花 ('fireworks') into 'green with willows and red with flowers', from more abstract to more concrete objects, which is a manifestation of the 'deepening' strategy. The translation of 三月 ('March') into 'spring' is the result of 'making shallow', on the other hand; whereas the translation of 扬州 into 'Yangzhou' is a case of transliteration and the result of 'equalization'. The phrase 孤帆远影 ('lone sail, distant shadow') being translated into 'his lessening sail' is a kind of 'deepening' strategy. Thus, the sentiment of the poet when seeing his friend off is preserved and conveyed in the translation, reaching the realm of 'beauty in meaning'. As Zhang (2017) put it, if a keyword is to be chosen from Xu's translation theory, it is none other than 'beauty', which seems to manifest itself in the examples of translation discussed above. To Zhang, the word 'beauty' is indeed at the core of Xu's translation theory represented by the slogan 美化之

艺术，创优似竞赛 (literally 'the art of beautifying; creating excellence as if in competition').

Although more and more people seem to find Xu's translation theory of interest, Zhang (2017) points out some important aspects of the theory which have not been adequately addressed in current research. Firstly, regarding the distinction between literal translation and free translation. Zhang commends Xu's definition that literal translation is a method which puts the faithfulness of *content* to the ST first, faithfulness of the *form* to the ST second and *fluency* of the TT last. Free translation, on the other hand, is also putting *content* faithfulness in the first place, but the *fluency* of the TT comes second, while the *form* of the ST is the final concern. Xu also explains, according to Zhang, when the original expression is 'higher than' (高于) the target language, it is necessary to take advantage of the original language and adopt a literal translation method to enrich the language of the target culture. Conversely, when the TT is 'higher than' the ST, the translator can develop the strengths and hide the weaknesses, that is, adopt the free translation method and press home the advantages of the target language. The discourse on literal translation has reflected the dialectical view of Xu Yuanchong's translation. However, his other theories such as 'chemistry theory' (化学论), 'superconductivity theory' (超导论), 'cloning theory' (克隆论), 'translation literature theory' (翻译文学论), etc., have not been seriously discussed.

Secondly, current studies of Xu Yuanchong mainly concentrate on his translation theory and his translation of Chinese poetry. According to Zhang (2017), there is plenty of space remaining to be explored in Xu's practical works, including his English translations of non-poetry Chinese classics, such as the *Analects of Confucius* (论语), the *Tao Te Ching* (道德经), *The Romance of West Chamber* (西厢记), *The Peony Pavilion* (牡丹亭), and *The Peach Blossom Fan* (桃花扇); his French translations of Chinese poetry; his Chinese translations of French novels; and his Shakespeare translations. Any translations in these four categories can form a large research topic in translation studies. These contents that need to be further explored are highly implicational for Chinese–English translation under the national strategy of 'Chinese culture going global'. Zhang thought that a serious study of Xu Yuanchong's literary translation theory and practice is vitally important for solving the problem of shortage in translators for Chinese Classics.

Revisiting Chinese translation theory

We have looked into some prominent trends and activities of translation in the history of China. We have also examined some representative figures in the history of Chinese translation, including a look at their contexts of translating and, where available, their translation theory and philosophy. The same idea of extracting a lineage of Chinese translation theory out of prominent translators in China's history was independently arrived at in the three-book series entitled *Translators through Chinese History* edited by Fang and Zhuang (2016) and reviewed in Huang and Meng (2017), who usefully pointed out that five aspects of distinguished translators were relevant to Chinese translation studies: 1. translator's biography, 2. their translation activities, 3. their ideas about translation, 4. analysis of their translations, and 5. the influence of their translations. Most of these aspects have been covered in our previous introduction and analysis of some distinguished translators in Chinese history. Thus, equipped with this extra dimension of knowledge, we are now able to reconsider the meaning and contents of Chinese translation theory, and investigate the thoughts and discourses engendered through a combination of the history and heritage of Chinese translation and the new input from Western translation theory.

Xia (2017b) provided a useful connection between the role played by translators and the mainstream culture's view on translation as a social practice in the history of China. This is highly implicational for the formation of Chinese translation theory in the historical sense. Xia distinguished between three kinds of 'translation ideology' (Xia, 2017, p. 191) as a result of his examination of the 25 volumes of historical records such as *Shi Ji* (史记) and *Qing Shi Gao* (清史稿). The three views of translation (under the influence of mainstream ideology) are said to correspond to three kinds of translation activity in the history of China: 'the dynastic diplomatic translation' (政事外交翻译) before Song dynasty, the translation of Buddhist Sutras (佛经翻译) and the translation between Han Chinese and minority languages (民族翻译) from the Liao to the Qing dynasty. Xia used the concept of a translator's visibility from Venuti as the main parameter or benchmark to draw out the differences between the three lines of translation. The first kind of Chinese translation activity consisted mainly of translations of diplomatic documents from China's royal court to neighboring countries. Because there were plenty of countries involved and not all of them came with translators who understood Chinese, a process called 重译 ('repeated translation', or more precisely in this context, 'indirect translation') frequently occurred, where the Chinese ST was first translated into TT1 before being translated into TT2 and even TT3 or beyond. Xia said this type of translation was conducted in the view that the Chinese culture was dominant, and the translation readers were subordinates of the royal court. This ideology, according to Xia, had not changed even with the coming of the sutra translation, when China was supposedly learning from a foreign culture. Xia argued that the Chinese mainstream culture in the diplomatic translation strand consistently considered translation a symbol of power over the neighboring weaker countries. The more times a document was translated (e.g. the fourth or fifth translation of an ST was not rare), the stronger the Chinese royal court deemed itself to be. Translators were relatively 'invisible' and unimportant under that political ideology. In the sutra translation phase, translator's status was slightly heightened, but overall translating as a social practice was still not treated decently, since it was the mainstream culture (China) condescending to learn a small aspect of culture (i.e. religion) from a smaller neighboring country. Xia reasoned, however, that the minority language translation stage from the Liao to the Qing dynasty substantially changed the status of the translator and the overall impression of translation as a social practice. As previously mentioned, minority language translation was prevalent when China was conquered by frontier people who subsequently used translation as a means for assimilating into the mainstream culture and achieving cultural integration. After examining the official history of China, Xia found that the status of translators, translated works and translation activities was largely enhanced in the formal records of China's history at this stage. Xia therefore thought that minority language translation should be called the third translation surge in China's history. More importantly, Xia's work showed how Chinese translation theory can be generated from a sociological and political perspective and how translators' visibility and other variables can reflect the contexts and ideologies of their times.

Given the strong influence of mainstream ideology and sociocultural contexts to translation activities and the pivotal role played by eminent Chinese translators in China's history, we may well surmise that the relationship and interaction between translators and their sociopolitical environments will generate very interesting results and implications for theoretical and applied translation studies. Indeed, we have seen how Yan Fu's translation discourse has been compared with Nida's translation theory in Zhang (1995) and how it has been redeveloped into a 'translation variation' theory in Huang (2016). In fact, the 'translation variation' theory developed in many of Huang's works has been hailed as a highly promising theory with strong character and stamina to become the first great 'Chinese translation theory' in history. Wu, for example, said that

变译理论是在全方位发掘本土翻译学术资源基础之上建构的具有普适性的翻译理论中国学派，对中国译学理论的-演进有重大推动作用。(The 'varied translation' theory is a universal Chinese school of translation theory based on the exploration of domestic academic translation resources. It offers a significant impetus to the evolution of Chinese translation theory.)

(Wu, 2018, p. 75)

The term 变译 *bianyi* (literally 'changed translation') has been variously translated in the Chinese translation literature. Wu (2018) used 'adaptative translation strategies' to translate 变译理论 *bianyi lilun* ('theory of varied translation') in the English abstract for his Chinese paper (possibly unwittingly degrading the theoretical status of the approach in doing so). Zhang (2018) translated *bianyi* narrowly to 'shortened translation' in his English abstract for the Chinese paper. Huang himself seemed to have settled down for the phrase 'translation variation' for *bianyi* and 'translation variation theory' for *bianyi lilun* (e.g. see the English abstract of Huang, 2016) in his recent works. Mu and Fu (2018) noted other English translations for the term 变译 such as 'variation translation' (i.e. in reversed word order from 'translation variation') and 'alternative translation' and suggested the former as their preferred translation. Based on the review of literature to be presented in the next paragraphs, however, the author of this book suggests that 'variable translation' or 'adaptive translation' may be a more appropriate and informative translation for the term *bianyi*, and that 'theory of variable (or adaptive) translation' may be a better term for *bianyi lilun* than a term using the word 'variation'.

Huang (2002) offered a good review of his existing works on the 'variation view of translation' by first tracing the theory back to Yan Fu's translation practice. He reminded the reader that Yan was a renowned scholar proficient in both Chinese and English; therefore, his variously manipulated translations in words and structures should not be treated as 'erroneous translations'. (Recall our previous discussion on Lü's (2017) defense of Yan Fu's 'non-mainstream' translation methods, which made the same point of justifying Yan's approach, although on slightly different grounds.) Huang cautioned that Yan's adaptive translation method changed the meaning, form and style of the ST and these should not be seen (merely) as alterations carried out at the micro-level. Instead, these changes were macro-level phenomena that have theoretical implications. According to Huang, Yan's translations were done as a response to the demand of time, that is, the necessity to import cultural resources from abroad for the targeted readers of Chinese society. In that sense, it was never his intention to import complete, unaltered books. His translations were obviously different from the usual micro-translation techniques but were the result of a macroscopic ideology. Although what Yan Fu implemented was a 'nonorthodox' translation method, it was nevertheless the most effective method to a certain extent under the circumstances. Thus, Huang defined *bianyi* in the following way:

> 变译(翻译变体)指的是译者据读者的特殊需求采用扩充、取舍、浓缩、阐释、合并、改造等变通手段摄取原作的中心内容或部分内容的翻译活动。('Variable translation' (translation variant) refers to the translator's translation activities of expansion, trade-off, condensation, interpretation, merging, transformation and other means of extracting the central content or part of the content of the original work based on the reader's specific requirement.)
>
> (Huang, 2002, p. 47)

In this sense, Huang's variable translation method is somewhat similar to Lefevere's (1992) translation as 'rewriting' theory, although the *bianyi* theory seems to be more complicated, and includes both an ideological domain and an accurately defined technical domain (in the form of various translation strategies as described below). Huang and Li (2014), for example, listed 12 adaptive translation strategies (all translations from the English abstract in their original Chinese paper): selected translation (摘译), edited translation (编译), narrated translation (译述), condensed translation (缩译), summarized translation (综述), summarized translation plus comment (述评), translation plus comment (译评), translation plus writing (译写), translation plus explanation (阐译), translation plus rewriting (改译), translation plus quotation (参译) and translation plus imitation (仿作). At the conceptual level, Huang apparently tried to raise the theory to the macro-level of sociocultural concerns and make *bianyi lilun* a more general and serious translation theory. He argued that *bianyi* or *fanyibianti* (翻译变体 'varied form of translation') was a more general method than microscopic techniques often associated with full translation. The *bianyi* method was conceived as a 'broad-form' translation (宽式翻译) where the translator converted the original cultural information into target language to meet the specific needs of the reader. This is in contrast to the 'narrow-form' translation (窄式翻译) where ST information was converted into a TT of similar style. The latter is translation in the traditional sense, sometimes called *quanyi* (全译 'full translation'). Huang (2011) clarified that the adaptive translation theory (or, in his own term, 'translation variation theory') was an entirely new kind of theory distinct from the traditional translation theory which was built on the study of full translation. He considered it '[a set of] scientific principles and an ideological system that reflect the nature and laws of adapted translations generalized from the practice of variable translation' (从变译实践中概括出来的反映变译的本质和规律的科学原理和思想体系) (Huang 2011, p. 101, my translation). Thus, Huang was eager to establish 'variable translation' as a subcategory of translation on an equal footing with 'full translation'. Additionally, Huang believed that the study of the nature of adaptive translating would change the understanding of the nature of translation as a whole, which in turn would bring new insights to other problems of translation. Huang (2011) went so far as to propose ten pairs of research types in variable translation theory, that is, phenomenon study vs. essence study, process research vs. product research, historical vs. contemporary research, applied vs. theoretical research, inductive vs. deductive research, topic-centered vs. subject-centered research, general vs. problem-centered approach, sub-disciplinary vs. disciplinary research, general vs. genre-specific research and translation-based vs. original research. Huang hoped that researchers in variable translation could adopt one or more of the proposed types of research and collectively build toward a dedicated research methodology and carve out a new path of research in the broad area of translation studies.

The variable translation theory has brought in some new insights for practical translation activities. Zhang (2018), for example, notes that the adaptive translation method is especially useful for the 'Chinese culture going-out' initiative. He says that the full translation method usually dictates a full reproduction of the ST information in the TT. The length of the TT and the production time are therefore likely to be larger and longer than those of the variable translation version. In the era of informationization and 'culture as fast food' trend, variable translation has the advantage of short-and-fast communication. Therefore, Zhang argued:

> 在中国文化与西方文化相比还处于弱势状态的时期，在西方读者休闲娱乐形式多样化的当下，对外传播的中国文化文学作品在内容上可首先采用摘译、编译、缩译、译述等变译方法进行传播，在西方读者对变译的精彩内容熟悉后，再以全译这种大篇幅的形式进入海外市场，这种战术能达到好的传播效果。(In the period when Chinese culture is still in a weak state compared with Western culture, in the current situation of Western readers' entertainment and entertainment forms, Chinese cultural literature works that are widely disseminated can be firstly translated, compiled, translated, translated, etc. The translation method is spread. After the Western readers are familiar with the wonderful content of the translation,

they will enter the overseas market in the form of full translation. This tactic can achieve good communication effects.)

(Zhang, 2018, p. 80)

That is to say, the variable translation method is useful not only in English-to-Chinese translation as was the case for Yan Fu's introduction of Western literature, it is also helpful for Chinese-to-English translation as in translating Chinese classics for Western readers.

The variable translation theory does not come without criticism, however, in its 20 years of life since its official proposal made by Huang Zhonglian (黄忠廉) in 1998. Chen (2018), for example, makes two observations about the variable translation theory. Firstly, he thinks that there is a lack of collaborative research surrounding this topic. Chen alludes that the variable translation theory has not undergone a desirable expansion beyond its original advocator. He advises that a school should be formed out of a group of participating scholars to establish and reinforce the theory. Secondly, Chen thinks that the research area covered by variable translation theory is ambiguous. He finds some fundamental problems in the theory which need to be clarified. For example, Chen is critical about the clear division between 'full translation' and 'variable translation'. He thinks that there is a continuum between the two extremes and a lot of methods and target texts existing in-between. He suggests that the theory should go deeper into the concrete description of each varied translation method. Externally, changeable reality and practice should be constantly monitored. Internally, a dialectical system of self-criticism, others-initiated criticism and repeated criticisms should be formed to support the healthy growth of the theory. Lan (2018) expresses the same doubt about some fundamental concepts revolving around variable translation theory. For example, he asks whether *bianyi* is a variety of translation (subsumed under full translation), or a different type of translation (parallel with full translation). Lan suggests that the theory should further develop and perfect the definitions of its core concepts and clarify its exact theoretical position and research objectives.

Another translation theory originating in China and claimed to have attracted international attention is the 'Eco-translatology' (生态翻译学) proposed by Hu Gengshen (胡庚申) in 2001 (see, e.g. Tao & Hu, 2016). According to Hu's various works, so-called 'Eco-translatology' was born out of a combination of recent global trends to apply the concept of ecology to arts and humanities, traditional Chinese eco-friendly thoughts and the inadequacy of existing translation studies to address problems in a holistic fashion. Hu (2010), for example, explained that as ecology became a scientific way of thinking, the word *ecology* had acquired a new and deeper meaning. In academia, environmentalism has transcended the boundaries of science, geography and social sciences and entered the field of arts and humanities.

As researchers worked hard to shift their study of culture to a broader research framework of living environment, many social science disciplines started to adopt the ecological approach in their research. In addition, Hu thought that traditional Chinese philosophy represented by such phrases as *tian ren he yi* (天人合一

'heaven and human in one body'), *zhongyong zhi dao* (中庸之道 'the middle way'), *yi ren wei ben* (以人为本 'based on human') offered inherently holistic, general and organic views of traditional Chinese cultural values, which are very congenial and facilitative to ecology-based translation studies. In addition, Hu thought that current translation studies failed to catch up with the ecology-based research trend, was inadequate in addressing some problems in the 'cultural turn' such as the translator's interaction with their ecological system and the influence of translation to the evolution of human cognition, and lacked integration in common basic research across the discipline. All the above recognitions and inadequacies gave rise to the creation of the Eco-translatology theory or paradigm, based on Hu's reasoning.

Hu (2011) gave nine research foci of the Eco-translatology research paradigm which help us conceptualize what the theory is about:

1. The ecology paradigm (生态范式): Hu explained that Eco-translatology research was guided by the basic principles of Darwin's 'adaptation/selection' doctrine, with the theme of 'translation is adaptation and choice' as the keynote, and the translator at the center as the core concept. All these contribute to the formation of a new translation research paradigm that helps provide new perspectives and solutions to existing translation problems.
2. The sequence chain (关联序链): Translation is the transformation of language, and language is a part of culture; culture is the accumulation of human activities, and human beings are part of nature. From these relations we can see a meaningful internal connection: Translation → Language → Culture Human Nature. This sequence chain gives Eco-translatology the necessary theoretical premise and foundations.
3. Ecological rationality (生态理性): This appears to translate into rationales that guide the research of Eco-translatology according to Hu's explanation, to include five aspects:
    a. focusing on the whole and the relations
    b. stressing the dynamics and the balance
    c. realizing the ecological aesthetics
    d. attending to 'translation communities'
    e. promoting diversity and unification
4. 'doing things with translation' (译有所为): This research strands include two aspects. First, studying the translator's motivations for translating, including survival, ambition, interest, empathy and competition. Second, studying the functions of the TT, for example, promoting intercultural communication, initiating language innovation, increasing cultural vitality, triggering social reform and promoting the advancement of translation theory.
5. Eco-environment for translation (翻译生态环境): This seemed an all-inclusive term in Hu's design. It originally referred to 'the world comprising ST, SL and TL' (原文、源语和译语所构成的世界) (Hu, 2011, p. 7) but later on was expanded to mean 'everything apart from the translator' (译者以外的一切)

(ibid). This idea was to investigate the environmental factors that conditioned the content, style and the vocabulary and syntax of the TT.
6. Translator at the center (译者中心): The translator is the meeting point of all the 'contradictions' in the process of translation. The 'translator-centered' concept and approach push the living, emotional and creative translator to the forefront of translation theory and formulate a real and concrete base for translation studies.
7. Translation as adaptation and selection (适应/选择): Translation is described as an alternating cycle of translator's adaptation and selection. The purpose of adaptation is to survive and produce results, and the means of adaptation is to optimize the choices. The rule of making choices is to 'eliminate weaknesses and keep the strengths' (汰弱留强). The best translation is one that makes the best integration of adaptation and selection.
8. Three-dimensional transformation (三维转换): The basic tenet of Eco-translatology expresses the translation method in the form of a 'three-dimensional' transformation, that is, under the principle of 'multi-dimensional adaptation and adaptive selection', the translation process is concentrated on the adaptive selection of the language, culture and communicative dimension respectively.
9. 'Post-event penalty' (事后追惩): After the selection of each stage, or after the "after the fact" (that is, after the translation), the choice of the translator. In particular, the final translation is judged and processed. Specifically, after the translation, the translator's choice is made according to the rules of "survival of the fittest" and "the weak and strong" followed by the translational ecological environment. Choose and arbitrate again.

Among the nine research foci or perspectives, Hu commented that items 1, 3, 4, 5 and 6 touch more on the macroscopic views of translation; while items 2, 7, 8 and 9 are relatively more 'microscopic' in nature. He also noted that 1, 4, 5, 6, 7 and 8 appeared to be more popular research topics among the Chinese translation studies circle and generated more applied studies; while 2, 3 and 9 seemed to attract less attention. In addition to these nine research foci, Hu (2014a) also suggested seven areas where the Eco-translatology approach 'differed' from other translation theory and methodologies. Hu thought that the 'differences' were exactly the innovative ideas brought about by the theory.

- Research perspective (立论视角): Hu found previous translation approaches and theories all too narrowly conceived, be it the linguistic, cultural, feministic or the functional approach. Only the Eco-translatology was able to provide an overall perspective to examine translation holistically.
- Philosophical background (哲学理据): Hu noted that ecology is a competitive, symbiotic, regenerative, and spontaneous development mechanism. Eco-translatology systematically explored translation issues using ecological principles as a guide.

- Research foci (关注焦点): Hu advocated the 'three life' (三生) approach to translation studies: 翻译生态 (translation ecology), 文本生命 (life of text) and 译者生存 (survival of translator). He thought that a reliance on ecology would break through the limited view of linguistic context, an orientation towards the life of text would unveil the ecological principles of 'translatability', and a focus on translator's survival would reinforce the importance of 'doing things with translation' (译有所为), signaling a 'return' (to mother nature) (Hu, 2014a, p. 108).
- Research methodology (研究方法): According to Hu, the study of Eco-translatology emphasized a general holistic view because the theory of Eco-translatology was created on the basis of ecological holism. In addition, the "analogous transplantation" research method formed by the cross-referencing between translation and ecology is also an important indicator of the difference between Eco-translatology and other translation research approaches. The reason is that there is a certain degree of association, similarity and isomorphism between the ecology of translation and the ecology of nature, which provides opportunities for transplantation of concepts and comparison of analogous phenomena.
- Unique terminology (配套术语): Hu pointed out that each theory has specific terms as basic constituents that make up the theory, and serves as an important sign that distinguishes it from other theoretical systems. Hu claimed that a series of interrelated terms and concepts like 'translation ecology', 'adaptation and selection', 'ecological rationality', 'translation community', 'symbiotic interaction' and so on, having been tested by continuous theoretical research and applied research and with the accumulation of research findings, made Eco-translatology 'unique' in the multiplicity of translation theories.
- Discourse construction (话语体系): In the discourse domain, Hu appeared to claim that Eco-translatology had presented three levels of discourse structure: the meta discourse of 'translation studies' (译学), the discourse of 'translation theory' (译论) and the study of 'written text' (译本), forming a 'three in one' development pattern. Hu argued that the same macro architecture of discourse system was not seen in other translation theories.
- Translation ethics (翻译伦理): Hu proposed four 'principles' as ethical guidelines for the Eco-translatology approach which he considered unique in translation studies: the 'balance and harmony' principle, the 'multidimensional integration' principle, the 'multiplicity symbiotic' principle and the 'translator responsibility' principle.

In addition to the seven claimed innovations of the Eco-translatology approach, Song and Hu (2016) also proposed some 'eco-translational explanations' to some notable existing translation problems. For example, according to Song and Hu, the problem of translatability can now be resolved using the eco-translation theory and concepts. That is, the 'degree of translatability' (可译性) can now be understood as the 'ecology of the source language' (原语生态) divided by the 'differences between the source language and the target language' (原语生态与译语生态的差异度). They claimed, for example, that the translatability between classic Chinese and vernacular Chinese is higher than that between

Chinese and Japanese. The translatability between Chinese and Japanese, in turn, is higher than that between Chinese and English. However abstract the manipulation may be and however lacking it is in experimental support, this kind of higher level reasoning seems readily acceptable to China's translation researchers and congenial to their research styles. In fact, the Eco-translatology approach proposed in Hu's various works have largely been welcome by translation researchers in China and widely followed as guiding principles for investigation various translation problems. Tao (2012) was one of the many examples that seek to introduce new perspectives from Eco-translatology into existing Chinese translation domains, in this case, translator's education. Tao thought that under the guidance of Eco-translatology, translation textbooks were no longer static materials, but multi-dimensional and in the process of continuous evolution. Translation textbooks should serve as a 'point' and a 'chain' in the entire translation ecosystem, linking the translation subject, object, ontology and national translation policy, translation education concept, translation market demand and other factors. For Tao, the construction of translation textbooks is a systematic project which can be based on Eco-translatology while making macroscopic controls and universal connections. Eventually, translation materials can be produced in line with natural ecology in a harmonious translation ecological environment (Tao, 2012, p. 87). In the same vein, Qi (2017) developed an interpreting training model using the theory and concept of Eco-translatology as the guideline where the interpreter's awareness of the echo-environment was enhanced, followed by the release of full self-ability, the actualization of self-value and the upgrading of interpreting skills. Hu (2017) himself also proposed some applied research domains of his Eco-translatology 'paradigm': translation teaching, the history of translation (theory), translation criticism, translation ethics and translation schools.

The Eco-translatology approach did not come without criticism or questioning. Its name created some confusion or at least ambiguity in the first place. Liu (2011), for example, traced the term 'translation ecology' (翻译生态学) back to Cronin (2003) and consistently used the term throughout his paper to refer to the 'Eco-translatology' (生态翻译学) approach proposed by Hu Gengshen. More recently, Zeng and Huang (2018) also argued that 'translation ecology' is a more logical term to use rather than the 'Eco-translatology'. Guo (2015), on a different note, alluded that both 'translation ecology' and 'Eco-translatology' are proper academic terms, each presenting a slightly different subject. For Guo, 'translational ecology' focused on the mechanism and law of interaction between translation and its surrounding ecological environment, and 'Eco-translatology' emphasized the translational ecology as a whole and the ontology of translation theory from an ecological perspective. More severe criticisms about Hu's Eco-translatology are also present, though rare. Chen (2014), for example, pointed out three major weaknesses of the Eco-translatology approach in its then current form:

- The translational ecological environment is regarded as the overall living and surviving environment of the translator and the TT, ignoring the 'cross-regional' characteristics of translation activities, which is contrary to the heterogeneous nature of translation.

- The approach overemphasizes the translator's central position in the translation process, showing a one-sided, narrow anthropocentrism value orientation, which is contrary to ecological ethics.
- The adaptation and selection strategy is regarded as the 'backbone' of the approach, ignoring other factors in the broader research space and impeding the further development of the discipline.

Although Hu (2014b) offered immediate feedback to Chen's (2014) criticism, the reply was quite emotional and based on a clarification of terms and the introduction of more abstract notions and logical reasoning. Miao and Wang (2014) seemed to provide an appropriate summary to the Eco-translatology approach so far advanced:

> "生态"早就成为了一种日常话语体系:人文生态、城市生态、大学生态、电影生态等等… 就目前可见，建构生态翻译学学科若无深厚的哲学底蕴，仅仅借用生态之"名"恐难形成厚实、久远的学科思想体系；难免让人怀疑"旧酒新瓶"而流于肤浅。('Ecology' has long been a daily usage forming a discourse system: human ecology, urban ecology, university ecology, film ecology, etc.... As far as we can see, if there is no deep philosophical foundation for the construction of Eco-translatology, it is difficult to create a substantial and sustainable theoretical system by simply borrowing the 'name' of ecology; it is inevitable that people will doubt the 'old wine in new bottle' approach and consider it superficial.)
>
> (Miao & Wang, 2014, p. 81)

Despite these doubts and criticisms, more and more translation researchers in China are adopting Eco-translatology as a high-level framework to help conceptualize various factors in existing translation problems. For example, Li (2018) relied on the conceptual guidelines of Eco-translatology to direct the translation of tourist information. Cao and Huang (2017) and Liu and Zhu (2017) used the so-called 'three-dimensional transformation' (三维转换) model of Eco-translatology to deal with the linguistic, cultural and communicative transformation of ST's in the Chinese cuisine and the movie subtitling domains, respectively. Zhang (2019), in the same vein, suggests using the concept of adaptation and selection in Eco-translatology to formulate strategies for translating Chinese cultural classics such as *Shijing* (诗经 'classic of poetry'), as well as the idea of translator's subjectivity and the 'skilful transformation' of the three dimensions (i.e. language, culture and communication). It does seem the Eco-translatology trend will continue to thrive at least for some time in the Chinese translation studies circles in China.

Conclusion

Chinese translation practice and theory have come a long way and a satisfactory conclusion to the cumulative experiences and achievements so far is far from being reached. However, we have now had a clearer understanding of the nature of Chinese translation activities, the trajectory of the role played by translation and translators in China's history, as well as some significant concepts and discourses developed by prominent Chinese translators in history. Last but not least, we have also seen some recent attempts made by enthusiastic Chinese translation researchers to generate translation theory 'of Chinese characteristics' and to acquire the 'rights of discourse' (话语权) in global translation studies. This can be seen by the passionate embrace of the Eco-translatology 'paradigm', as claimed by its original proposer Hu Gengshen, by many researchers in Chinese translation studies. In effect, however, just as it was pointed out by Miao and Wang (2014), the Eco-translatology approach may end up being a superficial transplantation of ecological terms to translation studies if no viable philosophical foundation is offered. To this author and to many readers of this book, the Eco-translatology approach may seem like a renewed set of *xin, da, ya* that have been acting as conceptual principles in formulating Chinese translation strategies and criticism, only more complicated and awe-inspiring due to its proposed connection with the science of ecology. However, whether it can stand the test of time depends on further elaboration of the theory (if any), and the proof of its usefulness in generating practical applications and evidence-based research. That being said, the Eco-translatology approach and the variable translation theory as discussed above both illustrate the desire, need for and timeliness of the appearance of a Chinese translation theory that can lead the way forward for the great undertaking of Chinese translation studies.

References

Chinese references

Cao, Wanzhong and Huang, Yinxia 曹万忠、黄银霞 (2017) 生态翻译学视角下的中式菜肴英译研究 (Investigating the English translation of Chinese cuisines from the perspective of eco-translatology). 龙岩学院学报 (*Journal of Longyan University*). 2017(06): 38–41.

Chen, Shuiping 陈水平 (2014) 生态翻译学的悖论——兼与胡庚申教授商榷 (The paradox of eco-translatology: also deliberating with professor Hu Gengshen). 中国翻译 (*Chinese Translators Journal*). 2014(02): 68–73.

Chen, Yuanfei 陈元飞 (2018) 变译理论批判与反思 (Criticizing and reflecting on variable translation theory). 解放军外国语学院学报 (*Journal of PLA University of Foreign Languages*). 41(4): 21–24+33.

Fang, Mengzhi and Zhuang, Zhixiang 方梦之、庄智象 (eds) (2016) 中国翻译家研究 (*Translators through Chinese History*). 上海外语教育出版社 (Shanghai Foreign Language Education Press).

Fu, Huisheng 傅惠生 (2012) 玄奘《道德经》梵译思想研究 (Xuanzang's conception of translation as seen in his Sanskrit rendition of *Dao De Jing*). 中国翻译 (*Chinese Translators Journal*). 2012(04): 31–35+127.

Guo, Xiaofei 果笑非 (2015) 论翻译生态学与生态翻译学: 研究对象、方法和走向 (On translation ecology and eco-translatology: research targets, methods and directions). 外语学刊 (*Foreign Language Research*). 182: 105–108.

Han, Zhenyu 韩振宇 (2008) 试论翻译在中国社会文化发展进程中的作用 (On the function of translation in the development of Chinese society and culture). 国外理论动态 (*Foreign Theoretical Trends*). 2008(10): 60–62.

Hu, Gengshen 胡庚申 (2010) 生态翻译学:产生的背景与发展的基础 (Eco-translatology: backgrounds and bases for its development). 外语学刊 (*Foreign Language Research*). 122: 62–67.

Hu, Gengshen 胡庚申 (2011) 生态翻译学的研究焦点与理论视角 (Eco-translatology: research foci and theoretical tenets). 中国翻译 (*Chinese Translators Journal*). 2011(02): 5–9.

Hu, Gengshen 胡庚申 (2014a) 生态翻译学的"异"和"新"—不同翻译研究途径的比较研究并兼答相关疑问 (Eco-translatology: a new paradigm of Eco-translation: a comparative study on approaches to translation studies and a brief response to some related questions/doubts). 中国外语 (*Foreign Languages in China*). 11(5): 104–111.

Hu, Gengshen 胡庚申 (2014b) 对生态翻译学几个问题"商榷"的回应与建议 (Response and suggestions to the 'deliberation' on eco-translatology). 中国翻译 (*Chinese Translators Journal*). 2014(06): 86–89.

Hu, Gengshen 胡庚申 (2017) 若干生态翻译学视角的应用翻译研究 (Different dimensions of applied research inspired by eco-translatology). 上海翻译 (*Shanghai Journal of Translators*). 2017(05): 1–5.

Huang, Zhonglian 黄忠廉 (2002) 变译观的演进 (The evolution of the variation translation view). 外语与外语教学 (*Foreign Languages and Their Teaching*). 2002(08): 46–48.

Huang, Zhonglian 黄忠廉 (2011) 变译理论研究类型考 (A study of research types in variation translation theory). 外语学刊 (*Foreign Language Research*). 2011(06): 101–104.

Huang, Zhonglian 黄忠廉 (2016) 达:严复翻译思想体系的灵魂—严复变译思想考之一 (Da: the soul of Yan Fu's translation thought system – one of the investigations on Yan Fu's Translation Variation theory). 中国翻译 (*Chinese Translators Journal*). 2016(01): 34–39.

Huang, Xinyan and Meng, Xiangchun 黄新炎, 孟祥春 (2017) 中国翻译学派的译道传承——评《中国翻译家研究》 (The lineage of Chinese translation school: Commenting on *Translators through Chinese History*). 出版广角 (*View on Publishing*). 2017(24): 85–87.

Ji, Jiayou 吉家友 (1988) 谈中国古代翻译事业的发展概况 (An overview of the development of China's ancient translation enterprise). 信阳师范学院学报(哲学社会科学版) (*Journal of Xinyang Teachers College* (*Philosophy and Social Sciences Edition*)). 1988(02): 40–43+107.

Lan, Hongjun 蓝红军 (2018) 变译论之辨与思:理论类属、学科贡献与概念界定 (Category, contribution and definition of the translation variation theory). 解放军外国语学院学报 (*Journal of PLA University of Foreign Languages*). 41(4): 7–10.

Li, Ping 厉平 (2014) 变译理论研究: 回顾与反思 (Research on variable translation theory: retrospection and reflection). 外语学刊 (*Foreign Language Research*). 176: 94–98.

Li, Yuanyuan 李媛媛 (2018) 生态翻译学视角下的旅游宣传语翻译的研究 (Research on translation of tourism propaganda language from the perspective of eco-translatology). 湖北开放职业学院学报 (*Journal of Hubei Open Vocational College*). 2018(23): 166–172.

Lin, Sisi 林思思 (2018) 从严复的"信、达、雅"看沙博理英译《水浒传》人物绰号的翻译 (From Yan Fu's *xin, da, ya* to the translation of nicknames in the English translation of the Outlaws of the marsh by Shapiro). 佳木斯职业学院学报 (*Journal of Jiamusi Vocational Institute*). 2018(10): 368.

Liu, Chaoxian 刘超先 (1992) 温故而知今:鲁迅翻译思想的教益 (Reviewing the old to know the new: the benefits of Lu Xun's translation thoughts). 中国翻译 (*Chinese Translators Journal*). 1992(01): 2–6.

Liu, Guobing 刘国兵 (2011) 翻译生态学视角下的译者主体性研究 (A study of translator subjectivity under the perspective of eco-translatology). 外语教学 (*Foreign Language Education*). 32(3): 97–100.

Liu, Yao and Zhu, Chenguang 刘瑶，朱晨光 (2017) 生态翻译学下的《奇幻森林》字幕翻译研究 (A study of the subtitles translation of *The Jungle Book* under the eco-translatology approach). 海外英语 (*Overseas English*). 2017(21): 111–112.

Luo, Haiyan and Zheng, Haijing 罗海燕，邓海静 (2018) 浅谈中药说明书英译中的"信达雅" (On the application of xin, da, ya to the English translation of Chinese traditional medicine manuals). 英语广场 (*English Square*). 2018(07): 3–5.

Lü, Shisheng 吕世生 (2017) 严复"信达雅"与"非正法"翻译的社会历史统一性解读 (Socio-historical interpretation of Yan Fu's three-character translation principle and his 'abnormal translation' strategy). 外国语(上海外国语大学学报) (*Journal of Foreign Languages*). 2017(03): 72–77.

Ma, Zuyi 马祖毅 (1980) 伟大的佛经翻译家玄奘 (The great Buddhist scripture translator Xuan Zang). 中国翻译 (*Chinese Translators Journal*). 1980(02): 18–19.

Ma, Zuyi 马祖毅 (1982) 佛经翻译家鸠摩罗什 (The Buddhist scripture translator Kumārajīva). 中国翻译 (*Chinese Translators Journal*). 1982(03): 24–25.

Miao, Fuguang and Wang, Lina 苗福光，王莉娜 (2014) 建构、质疑与未来: 生态翻译学之生态 (Eco-translatology: construction, doubts and future possibilities). 上海翻译 (*Shanghai Journal of Translators*). 2014(4): 77–82.

Mu, Lei 穆雷 (2015) 我国少数民族语言翻译研究现状分析 (An analysis of current translation studies on China's minority nationality languages). 外语教学与研 (*Foreign Language Teaching and Research*). 2015(01): 130–140.

Mu, Lei and Fu, Linling 穆雷 傅琳凌 (2018) 翻译理论建构的原则与途径 (Constructing translation theory in the Chinese context: principles and approaches). 中国翻译 (*Chinese Translators Journal*). 2018(03): 9–18.

Pan, Wenguo 潘文国 (2017) 许老,译之时者也 (Xu Lao, the translator of the time). 山西大同大学学报(社会科学版) (*Journal of Shanxi Datong University* (*Social Science Edition*)). 2017(2): 3–7.

Qi, Yuanyuan 齐媛媛 (2017) 生态翻译学视域下的口译训练模式研究 (A study of the training model of interpreting from the perspective of eco-translatology). 黑龙江科学 (*Heilongjiang Science*). 2017(23): 126–127.

Qin, Jianghua and Xu, Jun 覃江华，许钧 (2018) 许渊冲翻译理论思维的特征与倾向 (The characteristics and tendency of Xu Yuanchong's translation theory thinking). 外语研究 (*Foreign Languages Research*). 2018(05): 51–56+67.

Song, Zhiping and Hu, Gengshen 宋志平，胡庚申 (2016) 翻译研究若干关键问题的生态翻译学解释 (Explaining some key translation problems from the perspective of eco-translatology). 外语教学 (*Foreign Language Education*). 37(1): 107–110.

Tao, Lichun and Hu, Gengshen 陶李春，胡庚申 (2016) 贯中西、适者存: 生态翻译学的兴起与国际化 (Going global: eco-translatology in bridging the oriental and the west: an interview with professor Hu Gengshen). 中国外语 (*Foreign Languages in China*). 2016(05): 92–97.

Tao, Youlan 陶友兰 (2012) 我国翻译专业教材建设: 生态翻译学视角 (The construction of teaching materials for our translation profession: from the perspective of eco-translatology). 外语界 (*Foreign Language World*). 150: 81–88.

Wang, Dongping 王东平 (2018) 回归翻译本质：解读鸠摩罗什的翻译思想 (Return to translation essence: Interpret Kumarajiva's translation thought). 学术研究 (*Academic Research*). 2018(12): 168–173+178.

Wang, Hongyin 王宏印 (2017) 典籍翻译：三大阶段、三重境界——兼论汉语典籍、民族典籍与海外汉学的总体关系 (From Han canons, ethnic canons to texts of Sinological interests: the shifting foci of the three stages in the translation of Chinese classics). 中国翻译 (*Chinese Translators Journal*). 2017(05): 19–27+128.

Wang, Xiqiang 王西强 (2002) 浅议许渊冲古诗英译"三美"论在翻译实践中的得失 (A brief discussion on the gains and losses of Xu Yuanchong's translation of the 'three beauties' in the translation of ancient poems). 陕西师范大学学报(哲学社会科学版) (*Journal of Shaanxi Normal University* (*Social Science*)). 31: 328–333.

Wu, Zixuan 吴自选 (2018) 变译理论与中国翻译理论学派的建构 (Adaptative strategies can contribute to the construction of Chinese translation theory). 上海翻译 (*Shanghai Journal of Translators*). 2018(04): 75–77+62.

Xia, Dengshan 夏登山 (2017a) 对中国古代翻译大潮的重新认识 (A reconsideration on the views of ancient translation movements). 中国外语 (*Foreign Languages in China*). 2017(05): 87–92.

Xia, Dengshan 夏登山 (2017b) 中国翻译史上的三种翻译观 (Three translation ideologies in Chinese history of translation). 中南大学学报(社会科学版) (*Journal of Central South University* (*Social Science*)). 2017(06): 182–191.

Yan, Liangliang and Zhu, Jianping 闫亮亮, 朱健平 (2017) 从"求达"到"信达雅"——严复"信达雅"成因钩沉 (Evolving from *da* to *xin, da, ya*: on formation of Yan Fu's *xin, da, ya*). 外语与外语教学 (*Foreign Languages and Their Teaching*). 2017(05): 122–131+151.

Yang, Qisi 杨淇斯 (2018) "信达雅"翻译原则在跨文化交际中的应用 (The application of 'xin, da, ya' principle to intercultural communication). 郑州铁路职业技术学院学报 (*Journal of Zhengzhou Railway Vocational and Technical College*). 2018(03): 64–66.

Yang, Quanhong 杨全红 (2010) 玄奘翻译思想辨伪 (Xuan Zang's translation thoughts: clarification of true or false). 解放军外国语学院学报 (*Journal of PLA University of Foreign Languages*). 33(6): 61–65+80.

Yuan, Jing and Zheng, Haicui 袁婧, 郑海翠 (2018) "信、达、雅"视角下《三字经》两个英译本对比分析 (Contrastive analysis of two English translations of three character classic under the perspective of xin, da, ya). 海外英语 (*Overseas English*). 2018(03): 121–122.

Yuan, Jinxiang 袁锦翔 (1993) 玄奘译言考辨 (The authenticity debate of Xuan Zang's translation discourse). 中国翻译 (*Chinese Translators Journal*). 1993(02): 24–26.

Yuan, Yi 苑艺 (1982) 中国古代的佛经翻译与译场 (Ancient sutra translation and translating venues in China). 天津师院学报 (*Journal of Tianjin Normal University*). 1982(02): 74–78+84.

Zeng, Ting and Huang, Zhonglian 曾婷, 黄忠廉 (2018). 翻译研究创新术语逻辑化问题——以"翻译生态学"VS"生态翻译学"为例 (The problem of logicalization of terminology in innovative translation research: using the example of 'translation ecology' vs. 'eco-translatology'). 外语教学 (*Foreign Language Education*). 39(4): 75–79.

Zhang, Gu and Wen, Jun 张汨, 文军 (2014) 国内翻译家研究现状与流变趋势 (On the current characteristics and trends of the research on translators in China). 中国外语 (*Foreign Languages in China*). 60: 97–104.

Zhang, Minglin 张明林 (1995) 奈达与严复的翻译原则比较 (Comparison between the translation principles of Eugene A. Nida and Yan Fu). 外语与外语教学 (*Foreign Languages and Their Teaching*). 1995(05): 38–42.

Zhang, Wei 张薇 (2019) 生态翻译学视角下中国文化典籍英译研究的现状和对策 (The situation and countermeasures of the study of translation of Chinese cultural classics from the perspective of ecological translation theory). 广西科技师范学院学报 (*Journal of Guangxi Science & Technology Normal University*). 34(1): 95–97.

Zhang, Wenlong 张文龙 (2018) "信达雅"翻译三原则在小说翻译中的运用 (The application of 'xin, da, ya' translation principles to the translation of novel). 海外英语 (*Overseas English*). 2018(16): 162–163.

Zhang, Yongzhong 张永中 (2018) 变译和全译在文化对外传播中的不同效度 (Remarks on shortened translation vs. full translation). 上海翻译 (*Shanghai Journal of Translators*). 2018(04): 78–82.

Zhang, Zhizhong 张智中 (2017) 误几回天际识归舟？—论国内许渊冲翻译研究的误区与不足 (Misunderstandings, limitations, and future efforts in domestic research on professor Xu Yuanchong and his translation). 中国文化研究 (*Chinese Culture Research*). 97: 146–153.

Zou, Zhenhuan 邹振环 (2014) 20世纪早期中国翻译史研究的发轫和演进 (The beginning and evolution of the research on Chinese translation history in early 20th century). 东方翻译 (*East Journal of Translation*). 2014(01): 41–47.

Other references

Cronin, M. (2003) *Translation and Globalization*. London: Routledge.

Lefevere, A. (1992) *Translation, Rewriting, and the Manipulation of Literary Fame*. London/New York: Routledge.

Venuti, L. (1995) *The Translator's Invisibility*. London and New York: Routledge.

4 The translation of Chinese culture and the culturalization of Chinese translation

In this chapter, we explore the relationship between Chinese culture and Chinese translation. In particular, we focus on three aspects of this relationship:

- How Chinese culture has created problems for Chinese translation and what are the strategies for tackling them?
- What can translation do to disseminate or further shape Chinese culture?
- What are the vital components of Chinese culture that have been actively translated?

Recall that we have seen a visualization image in the introduction chapter based on a CNKI database search using the word 翻译 ('translation'), which showed a set of keywords being actively discussed among the Chinese translation researchers revolving around the topic of 'translation'. Now, if we narrow the topic down to not only 翻译 ('translation') but also 文化 ('culture'), then we can get a set of keywords more specifically related to the intersection between translation and culture. These are shown in Figure 4.1 and Table 4.1 in visualization and tabular form, respectively.

We can condense the 50 keywords in Table 4.1 into four conceptual groups as follows:

- Translation theory and studies: e.g. 'skopos theory', 'relevance theory', 'cultural turn', 'ecological translation studies.'
- Translation problem and strategy (culture related): e.g. 'culturally loaded words', 'cultural default', 'functional equivalence', 'cultural imagery'.
- Culture dissemination through translation: e.g. 'globalization', 'Intercultural translation', 'intercultural communication'.
- Specific cultural asset: e.g. 'tea culture', 'Dream of the Red Mansion', 'subtitles translation', 'folk Culture'.

The above four conceptual categories seem to largely coincide with the three research questions posited at the beginning of this chapter in a useful fashion. We will accordingly divide the main content of this chapter into three sections. Firstly, we explore the problems presented by cultural factors in translation and

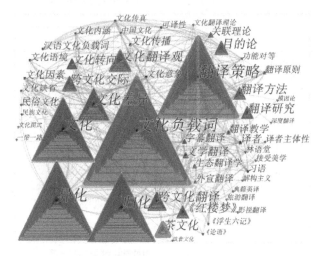

Figure 4.1 Keywords in Chinese culture and translation (see this image in color at www.routledge.com/9780367209872)

the strategies developed by Chinese researchers in dealing with them. Secondly, we discuss the problem of cultural dissemination via translation in China's context. Finally, we introduce some elements of Chinese cultural translation using the translation of traditional Chinese medicine (TCM) as the prime example.

Cultural problems and strategies in translation

Culturally loaded words constitute a great challenge for translators working on intercultural communication. In her linguistic approach to translation problems and strategies, Baker (2011) prioritized issues caused by cultural differences when discussing word level non-equivalence problems and common strategies for handling them. According to Baker, there are 'culture-specific concepts' where '[t]he source-language word may express a concept which is totally unknown in the target culture' (p. 18) and there are instances where '[t]he source-language concept is not lexicalized in the target language' (ibid.). In the first category, we can easily think of something unique to the Chinese or the English culture which is unfamiliar to the other culture. For example, *xiaoshun* (孝顺 'being caring for and obedient to parents') although commonly translated as 'filial piety' in English, is nevertheless a concept unknown to the Western culture which fosters parental relationships in different ways. In British culture, the 'Speaker of the House of Commons' cannot be easily understood by a person from China because such a concept and the supporting concepts such as the House of Commons, the presiding officer and parliamentary debates, etc. do not exist in the Chinese culture. In the second category, we have Chinese words like *baibai* (拜拜 'to pray with incense clasped in hands') which can be understood by someone from the English

Table 4.1 50 top keywords from scientometric analysis of 翻译 'translation' and 文化 'culture'

Frequency	Keyword	Frequency	Keyword
556	文化负载词 (culturally loaded words)	47	关联理论 (relevance theory)
490	文化翻译 (cultural translation)	41	翻译技巧 (translation skill)
438	翻译策略 (translation strategy)	41	生态翻译学 (ecological translation studies)
419	异化 (foreignization)	39	外宣翻译 (publicity translation)
372	归化 (domestication)	38	全球化 (globalization)
347	文化 (culture)	37	汉语文化负载词 (Chinese culturally loaded words)
208	文化差异 (cultural differences)	37	民俗文化 (folk Culture)
146	跨文化翻译 (Intercultural translation)	36	英语翻译 (English translation)
141	文化翻译观 (cultural translation view)	36	文化语境 (cultural linguistic context)
112	英译 (English translation)	34	翻译理论 (translation theory)
107	跨文化 (intercultural)	34	直译 (direct translation)
107	跨文化交际 (intercultural communication)	32	文化意象 (cultural imagery)
107	翻译方法 (translation method)	31	译者主体性 (translator's subjectivity)
100	《红楼梦》 (*Dream of the Red Mansion*)	31	习语 (idiom)
99	翻译研究 (translation studies)	30	翻译原则 (translation principle)
97	目的论 (skopos theory)	29	红楼梦 (*Dream of the Red Mansion*)
92	茶文化 (tea culture)	28	文化缺省 (cultural default)
84	策略 (strategy)	28	翻译特性 (translation features)
81	文化转向 (cultural turn)	27	文化内涵 (cultural connotation)
62	译者 (translator)	26	英译策略 (English translation strategy)
61	文学翻译 (literary translation)	26	影响 (influence)
61	语言 (language)	25	异化翻译 (foreignization translation)
52	翻译教学 (translation teaching)	23	林语堂 (Lin Yutang)
52	文化因素 (cultural factor)	22	功能对等 (functional equivalence)
51	字幕翻译 (subtitles translation)	22	汉英翻译 (Chinese to English translation)

culture, but the concept is nevertheless not lexicalized in English. The reverse is true with the English word *savory* when used to mean something salty or spicy rather than sweet. Although the word is understandable to a Chinese person when explained, the Chinese culture nevertheless has not found it necessary to put the concept into words. Baker's solutions for these culturally related problems are to translate by 'cultural substitution', to translate using a load word plus an explanation, to translate by paraphrasing and so on.

Acquiring a better understanding of the notion of 'culture' and analyzing it systematically may help us better conceptualize the problems and work out the solutions. As a translation practitioner and educator, Newmark (1988) defined culture as 'the way of life and its manifestations that are peculiar to a community that uses a particular language as its means of expression' (p. 94). Furthermore, Newmark classified culture into five broad categories: Ecology, Material culture (artifacts), Social culture, Organizations/customs/ideas, Gestures and habits. There are general problems for translating culture, but each subcategory of culture as classified by Newmark may create its own problems for translation. At the general level of consideration, Newmark offered two translation procedures for culture words 'at opposite ends of the scale': 'transference' and 'componential analysis' (Newmark, 1988, p. 96). By 'transference' Newmark meant the conversion of different alphabets into English (For Chinese, this would mean expressing the word in Pinyin only), which then became a 'loan word' in English. As for 'componential analysis', Newmark said that the procedure was 'based on a component common to the SL and the TL' plus some 'extra contextual distinguishing components' (ibid.). Whereas transference 'emphasises the culture and excludes the message'; componential analysis 'excludes the culture and highlights the message' (ibid.). Applying Newmark's thinking, the word 孝顺 would be translated into *xiaoshun* with the transference procedure, and into 'filial duty (performed with genuine care and great respect)' or something similar. Ke (1999) offered a different way to exploit cultural problems by first distinguishing culture into four conceptual subcategories: Techno-economic System, Social System, Ideational System, and Linguistic System. Ke highlighted a problem that could potentially cause a misreading in intercultural communication if the cultural presupposition behind the culture-loaded word was not made explicit for the reader. In the ideational domain, Ke used the example of *santou liubi* (三头六臂 literally 'three hands and six arms') to illustrate how the background knowledge in the role played by Buddhism in Chinese culture was required to understand the meaning of the phrase, which referred to the supreme wisdom and power possessed by a Buddhist god.

Researchers in China working on translation and culture, as previously mentioned, generally focused on four areas of research: theoretical discussion, problems and strategies, cultural dissemination and specific areas of Chinese culture translation. On the theoretical side, some researchers considered it a priority to do some ontology research on the cultural issues of translation, clarifying what 'culture' means to translation studies. Xiong (2018) rightly argues that, due to the multidisciplinary and interdisciplinary nature of translation studies and the multiplicity of translation theories, the concept of 'culture' has not been consistently understood and applied, creating a state of confusion. Xiong proposes to clarify the concept of 'culture' in translation studies by approaching it from three angles: anthropology, cultural studies and philosophy. For Xiong, the conceptualization of the cultural in anthropology generally revolves around a basic idea that culture is a systemic thought and emotion that unites a group and gives it a social identity, which in turn affects or restricts people's behavior. However, according to Xiong, anthropology originated in the West and was initially created with a focus on Western ethnocentrism, as it paid more attention to primitive and interracial cultures. Regrettably, this feature was used by colonialism as a tool for conquest and colonization. Thus, anthropology seems to provide a link between translation studies and the cultural turn, especially postcolonial thinking and translation theory. The second perspective from which Xiong approaches the meaning of culture in translation is the discipline of cultural studies. In particular, Xiong highlights the polysystem theory pioneered by Even-Zohar as an important achievement in the cultural turn of translation studies. According to the polysystem theory, literature in a particular society is a collection of multiple systems, or 'a system of systems'. In this system, various genres, schools, groups, etc. compete with each other to win readers or to gain status and power. This broad look at translation and other contextual factors has helped translation studies to focus on culture instead of text alone. However, Xiong also notes that although cultural studies is by nature interdisciplinary and multidisciplinary, the main research object of 'culture' should still refer more to the non-elite and marginal mass culture, rather than to the general meaning of various cultures. If cultural concepts from different disciplines and theoretical systems were to be incorporated into cultural studies indiscriminately, the discipline would become all-encompassing and ambiguous. This is probably a caveat of approaching translation from the perspective of cultural studies. A third perspective Xiong takes in trying to figure out the meaning of culture in translation studies is that of philosophy. According to Xiong, the history of human cross-cultural communication proved that there was no clearly visible boundary or 'fault line' between cultures, but there were indeed overlapping gray areas. The translator (or translation) standing in the middle of different cultures is considered to possess 'interculturality' or a certain degree of cultural interactivity. The concept of the 'hybrid' in postcolonial theory is a manifestation of cultural interactivity. When cultural boundaries become blurred from the perspective of philosophy, Xiong looked to Pym (1998) for guidance, who proposed that no definition of culture be given in order to leave more room for new discoveries. A history of translation based on cross-cultural investigations will tell us what culture is, not the other way around. Although Xiong's research has not clarified what culture is for translation studies, it has provided some ideas as to how to conceptualize culture and to approach cultural issues in translation research via different routes.

In an attempt to clarify the cultural identity of translation in society, Jiang (2016) suggested that translation is a 'cultural factor', a kind of cultural activity. To Jiang, translation is, on the one hand, an important medium for cross-cultural communication and thus has the linguistic identity of being a communicative tool.

On the other hand, translation is a cultural activity itself and has the social and cultural identity of being the subject (i.e. performer) of cultural behavior. Sun (2016) went one step further to combine both words (i.e. *culture* and *translation*) in the phrase 'cultural translation' (文化翻译) and derived a new subcategory in translation studies. Sun contended that cultural translation that transmitted cultural information must cross the boundary of cultures at the same time it crossed the barrier of languages. Furthermore, cultural translation is the venue where hybridity of meaning is created. Hybridity is the cultural effect of globalization. It causes cultures to be reformed, which means cultures change in the process of cross-cultural communication and as a result of cultural integration. For Sun, translating transferred a text from a cultural context to another, which not only represented a textual transformation but was also a complicated process of continuous negotiation between two cultures. Sun advised that we should continue to enhance our abilities to negotiate, integrate and improvise so that cultural translation could truly become a highly effective means for cross-cultural communication. Yang (2017) offered yet another way to conceptualize 'cultural translation'. To him, cultural translation is but a subsystem of the overall system of TRANSLATION, which consists of 'language transfer subsystem', 'message transmission subsystem', 'aesthetics reproduction subsystem', 'cultural translation subsystem' and other subsystems. These subsystems work together to produce the best translation. In terms of language transfer, culture facilitates the accurate understanding and proper transformation of the structure of the source language. In respect of message transmission, culture (directly or indirectly, explicitly or implicitly) participates in the formation of messages from sentence to larger speech units. From the perspective of aesthetic reproduction, whether it is a single cultural image or an entire literary text, without the help of cultural interpretation, it is difficult to obtain a true understanding of the ST or to achieve the goal of aesthetic reproduction.

Many translation problems and strategies that involve the workings of culture have been identified and proposed by Chinese researchers. From a top-down perspective, Hu and Guo (2018) contrive a model of 'political strategies for cultural translation' which consists of five key components:

- Establishing the guiding principles for political strategies of cultural translation (确立文化翻译政治策略的指导原则).
- Developing translator's literacy for the political strategies of cultural translation (译者文化翻译政治策略素养的建构).
- Confirmation of texts and recognition, reorganization and reinterpretation of original content (翻译文本的确定及原语内容的认知、重组和再阐释).
- Choice of translation strategies (翻译策略的选择).
- Selection of target language forms and compliance with national language planning and language policy (目标语言形式的甄选及顺应国家语言规划和语言政策).

According to Hu and Guo, adopting the right political strategy of translation in the process of cultural translation plays a substantial role in respecting the traditional culture and mainstream ideology of the TL country, and in consciously resisting and weakening the negative impact of cultural hegemony on the national security and social stability of the TL country. In addition, Hu and Guo think that China's traditional culture is comprehensive and profound. On the basis of the translator's cross-cultural awareness and identification of national culture with the correct translation strategy as the means to achieve the organic combination of 'soft translation' (柔性翻译) and 'soft dissemination' (柔性传播) while resisting cultural hegemony, this kind of cultural translation can greatly improve the extraterritorial acceptance and dissemination effect of Chinese academic translation works, Hu and Guo claim.

Fan (2008) analyzed an English translation of the Chinese classic *wen xin diao long* (文心雕龙, otherwise translated as 'The Literary Mind and the Carving of Dragons') in an attempt to discover how the culturally specific terms in the book were dealt with by the translator. Fan classified the culturally specific items he could find from six out of 50 chapters of the book into six categories: person names, geographic names, dynasty names, titles of the classic work, literary jargons and philosophical jargons. Furthermore, Fan used a modified analytical framework based on Aixela (1996) consisting of 12 translation strategies to analyze the 504 culturally specific items he found from the book. The analytical framework consisted of twelve translation procedures: 1. transliteration (音译), 2. 'referential translation' (指称翻译), 3. extratextual gloss (文外解释), 4. intratextual gloss (文内解释), 5. synonymy (使用同义词), 6. limited universalization (有限泛化), 7. absolute universalization (绝对泛化), 8. naturalization (移植), 9. deletion (删除), 10. autonomous creation (自创), 11. 'fixed translation' (定译) and 12. other procedures (其他). For example, Fan said that translating 《骚》 into 'a work of rhyme prose' was a case of 'absolute universalization'; and translating '经理玄宗' into 'Daoist', a case of 'limited universalization'. Fan did not find any meaningful concentration of translation strategies against culturally specific items in a general sense. However, he did mention that intratextual gloss and extratextual annotation (in the form of endnotes) were two primary ways for dealing with the problem of historical allusions, myths and legends. In addition, Fan also recognized six 'controlling factors' (or constraints) that allegedly offered rational explanations as to why a certain translation strategy was selected for a given culturally specific item. These controlling factors were: constraints imposed by the process of translation itself, the historical context, the purpose of translation, the nature and characteristics of the commissioner and the translator, the expectation of the TT's readership, the coherence of the TT, existing versions of translated work and the fixed translations of culturally specific items.

Chinese buzzwords on social media have become a popular trend since the beginning of the millennium. To translate these Chinese neologisms requires a lot of knowledge about conventional and contemporary Chinese culture. Wu (2017) examined two recent Chinese–English dictionaries, *A Dictionary of New Chinese Phrases in English* (最新汉英特色词汇词典) and *A Chinese-English Dictionary of New Words and Expressions* (汉英新词新语词典), in the hope of extracting translation strategies used by the compilers of the dictionaries. Wu claimed that most English translations listed in both dictionaries were the results of 'free translation' (意译) based on the meaning of the source word, for example, 钓鱼执法 → 'entrapment', 鹊桥网 → 'match-making website', 裸婚 → 'bare-handed marriage', 留守儿童 → 'child left behind' and so on, where the original 'cultural flavor' was generally lost while the meaning was largely conveyed. Wu urged the field to consider two questions in translating Chinese cultural buzzwords: firstly, is the English word a correct and full translation of the original? Wu used the case of translating 精神支柱 into 'spiritual pillar' as an example of a possible mistake since 'spiritual' has religious connotations which were absent from the original Chinese phrase. Secondly, Wu would like translators to ask whether or not their translations could correctly or fully reproduce the cultural content of the original Chinese words. Wu referred to a survey conducted by her in 2015 of 100 English native speakers on English translations of 20 Chinese culture words based on 35 common translation strategies identified by the investigator, of which only five were thought appropriate by over half of the subjects. Some translations were considered 'derogatory' by the subjects surveyed, for example, 剩女 → 'leftover lady'. Some were thought to be 'offensive', for example, 房奴 → 'house slave'. Wu noted that when interpreting the vocabulary of Chinese social and cultural content, the higher-acceptance translations tend to retain the original expressions first, and then offer explanation and supplementary information when encountering cultural problems. She suggested that when translating Chinese social and cultural words into English, translators should insist on retaining Chinese social and cultural elements in the translation. At the linguistic level, we should consider the reader's ability to accept the translation and flexibly adopt the strategies of non-translation (transliteration), interpretation, description, free translation and replacement to convert the culture words. The translation of the same word need not be static but be in keeping with the times. To Wu, the ultimate goal of cultural translation is to convey the true image of China.

At the beginning of this section, we mentioned Baker's (2011) reference to 'culture-specific concepts' when discussing non-equivalence at the word level in translating. In Chinese translation studies, this is commonly referred to as 文化缺省 (commonly translated as 'cultural default') understood as referring to the lack of common cultural background knowledge shared by the writer/translator and the intended readership. Wang (2018b) uses reception theory (接受理论, a kind of reader response literary theory, also known as reception aesthetics) to argue that readers of literary works no longer assume a passive position, but are actively interacting with the author and the work to derive their own interrelations. With the cultural turn of translation studies, Wang reminds us that translation problems are no longer approached from a linguistic view alone but are considered within a bigger, cultural context. Under these circumstances, Wang suggests that there are two main strategies for handling translation problems generated by the cultural default phenomenon from the perspective of reception theory. Firstly, the translator can use 'cultural substitution' (文化置换) to allow the TT reader to feel the same effect as that achieved by the original. Conversely, the translator can try to keep the exotic feelings (保持异国情调) so the reader can enjoy a roaming experience in exotic countries. These are of course equivalent to the 'domestication' and 'foreignization' translation methods put forward in Venuti (1998) for example, only looked at from a different angle. Liu and Xiao (2016) commented that cultural differences inevitably caused the problem of cultural default, which was often dealt with by translators using explanatory translation as a way of compensation. However, they noted that interpretive translation as a common method used by translators to process cultural information in translation had its inherent advantages, but the interpretation inevitably highlighted the identity of the translator and altered the original text in some ways. Excessive use of the method would inevitably lead to the destruction of the original's content, expression and style. A good translation should always be as close as possible to the original text. Therefore, the translator should always pay attention to the restrictions of the interpretive method in translating and exert some kind of control in their long-term translation practice. For Liu and Xiao, the explanatory notes to compensate for cultural default in translation should abide by two rules. First, they should be fluently written and, secondly, the length of a note is best limited to a sentence only. Finally, in tackling cultural problems in translation, Wang and Wang (2016) recognized two kinds of cultural gaps: complete cultural blank (完全空缺) and partial cultural blank (部分空缺). For the complete cultural gap, Wang and Wang thought transliteration should be adopted in priority, supplemented by explanation when it first appeared in the work. For the partial blank, however, various translation strategies can be flexibly used, determined by many textual and extratextual factors.

Translating the Chinese culture

Nowhere is translation and culture more relevant or their relationship more intimate than the current 'Chinese culture going out' (中国文化走出去) initiative where translation is one of the important means for implementing China's strategy of Chinese culture going global. Xin (2011) highlighted some important theories and concerns of the Sixth Plenary Session of the Seventeenth Central Committee (十七届六中全会, referred to as 'the committee' below) among which 'Chinese culture going out' was a key issue. Chinascope (2019) summarized the content of the culture 'going out' initiative as proposed in the committee in three components.

- External cultural exchanges: to encourage cultures to learn from each other and to enhance the appeal and influence of Chinese culture around the world.
- External publicity about Chinese culture: to explain China to the world by introducing its basic national conditions, values, development path and internal and external policies.
- External cultural trade: to export to the world large numbers of modern cultural products with Chinese characteristics and high technological content.

In the same document, Chinascope also analyzed the three factors for creating the good conditions for China's cultural going global policy at present. Firstly, the rapid development of China's economy has moved Chinese culture gradually out of its previously weak position. Secondly, China's modern culture is constantly evolving and progressing and now it has a strong global appeal. Thirdly, China has a large overseas community which has a high demand for Chinese cultural products. Also, according to Chinascope, the methods for implementing culture going out policy proposed by the committee include strengthening the establishment of Chinese cultural centers and Confucius Institutes abroad, encouraging national-level academic groups and art organizations to play a constructive role in appropriate international organizations, and sponsoring the translation of outstanding academic achievements and cultural products into foreign languages.

If the Sixth Plenary Session of the Seventeenth Central Committee had laid out a clear 'physical plan' for Chinese culture going global in 2011, then Wang (2016) added an all-important ideological touch. According to Wang, there are two layers of meaning in Chinese culture going out. One is the direct or common sense understanding of the initiative, associated with the superficial activities of promoting Chinese language and culture to the world through translation, Confucius Institutes, etc. The other meaning of Chinese culture going out is deeper and involves value, having to do with making people all around the globe sympathize with Chinese culture. The second kind of culture going out must build on the success of the first kind, according to Wang, since anyone needs to know and become familiar with a culture before being able to comprehend and accept it. Wang proposed the interesting contrast between 价值认同 ('identifying with similar value') and 价值认异 ('sympathizing with different value') and said that China did not expect the former from people around the world. Rather, it was good enough for people from other countries to respect and tolerate China's concept of value (i.e. recognizing and respecting the differences). In addition, Wang made a very interesting and somewhat unexpected clarification that the so-called culture going out did not mean (only) the traditional Chinese culture, but mainly the contemporary Chinese culture, which, according to Wang, meant the modernized, global-facing, futuristic, nationalistic, scientific and socialistic culture for the general public. For Wang, the current effort in promoting Chinese culture inevitably stays at the first level, which is far from enough. More work needs to be done to realize the true value of Chinese culture going out, which, just like the need to upgrade the 'Made in China' reputation, is an endeavor to produce a large number of cultural exquisites representing the contemporary Chinese value system and to disseminate them worldwide. From the perspective of translation, Wang's insistence on the modernized value of culture is echoed by Li's (2018) work on the value of translation. According to Li, translation inevitably involves value. This is not only reflected in the value of the translation itself, but also in the value system prevailing in a particular society. Modern translation values have become inconsistent with traditional translation values in some respects. It is of great theoretical and practical significance to explore the translation value that conforms to the characteristics of the times. Thus, Wang (2016) and Li (2018) inadvertently concur in reexamining the values of culture and translation and giving them revitalized meaning to fulfill the current purpose of disseminating

Chinese culture with translation (its value reconceptualized in this light) as one of the means.

Zhou and Xu (2015) discussed the cultural values of Chinese classics and the work that had been carried out thus far in disseminating these cultural assets via translation. They thought that, in addition to classic Chinese literature, China's medical, military and legal classics, as well as representative classics of Chinese ethnic minorities, should also be 'going out' as essential parts of Chinese culture. The reason for promoting these cultural exports, according to Zhou and Xu, was to seek common development of the world, enrich the world culture, turn conflicts into understanding, and realize the diversification and harmonious coexistence of world literature and culture. Zhou and Xu introduced the Library of Chinese Classics (大中华文库) series as a major publishing project planned at the national level and supported by state finance. This project was officially regarded as the first major cultural project in China's history for the compilation and translation of Chinese ancient books systematically and comprehensively to be introduced to the world. It is also the basic project for carrying forward the excellent traditional culture of the Chinese nation. The project has selected more than 100 classic works in China's literature, history, philosophy, economy, military, science and technology, including *The Analects of Confucius*, *Mencius*, *Laozi*, *Zhuangzi* and so on. As for the kind of translation research to be done against this background of Chinese culture going out, Zhou and Xu suggested that, first of all, researchers can examine the status of translation activities in the history of social change from the nature and function of translation, and clarify the role and mission of translation activities. Secondly, we can conduct research on translator patterns and explore the effectiveness of different models in translation practice. Thirdly, it is also helpful to analyze the styles of the TT and consider the impact of different forms of TT on the acceptance factor of the readership. Finally, Zhou and Xu advised that researchers could also conduct research on the transmission mechanism of translation works. According to them, in the field of Chinese translation, there have been few studies on the transmission mechanism of translation works in the past. It is vitally important to study how we can fully and effectively use foreign publishing institutions and mainstream media in helping to publish and promote Chinese classics so that their growing acceptance by foreign readers can be achieved. Jia (2017) also pondered the Chinese culture going out issue from the policy level. According to Jia, a number of subjective and objective factors such as the unclear definition of 'Chinese cultural classics', insufficient research on translating into foreign languages, inaccurate perception about audience taste, lack of understanding of translation work and a shortage of translation talents, potentially compromised the quality of translated Chinese cultural classics. He suggested that a good solution was to use a diversification of carrying media and flexible means of presentation and cooperation methods. Also, it would be useful to reflect on the shortcomings of talent training in Chinese translation and to adopt the goal of market-oriented training, multi-disciplinary integration, as well as a 'workshop training mode' conducted between government institutions and colleges, between enterprises and colleges, and between colleges.

At the level of translation strategy in the Chinese culture going out initiative, Zhu (2016) pointed out that, in the past 30 years, Chinese translation scholars have made outstanding contributions to the literary and cultural undertakings of China's academic fields. But at the same time, people are beginning to realize that the Chinese translation researchers seem to be lost in the discourse of Western literary and cultural criticism. Zhu strongly advised Chinese translation workers to improve self-awareness, strengthen cultural consciousness and criticism, and boldly follow their own path of translation practice, translation criticism, translation studies and translation teaching. Only then can Chinese literature and culture truly go out and be better positioned in the global arena of literature. One 'bold' way Zhu recommended in translating Chinese culture was to faithfully reproduce the Chinese classics in English with the direct translation method (忠实地原汁原味地把中国经典"直译"成英文), thereby manifesting a strong cultural confidence and cultural consciousness currently lacking in China's translation products. Chang (2015), however, offered a different opinion. He thought that the Chinese literature going out initiative had been carried out for 60 years without significant results. He observed that, from the perspective of the polysystem theory, a translation initiated by the source culture was intrinsically difficult to accept for the target culture. Moreover, the Chinese translators were increasingly adopting foreignization strategies (i.e. using the 'direct translation' method recommended by Zhu above) without considering the norm and attitude of the target culture, making the effect of exporting culture even less ideal. Chang thought that cultural introspection was desirable, and it is imperative to realize that the increase of economic strength and the improvement of literary and cultural reputation are not a synchronized matter. China should not rush in exporting culture or overemphasize the autonomy of cultural output.

Wang (2018a) offers a very good example of how to conceptualize and solve the intricate problem caused by cultural connotations in translating culturally loaded words. Wang recognizes that language is an inseparable part of culture; therefore the meaning of a word is often related to its cultural connotation, structural composition and the context of use. Wang cautions that if there is a lack of serious research on the cultural contrasts and correlations between these culturally conspicuous words; if analysis is carried out only at the surface transformation level with the translator being led into believing in the superficial culturally equivalent terms, then this will not only cause misunderstanding on the part of the readership, but also may obscure the important ideological and cultural characteristics behind the words. Wang uses the Chinese word 龙 ('Chinese dragon') being customarily translated into 'dragon' as an example of inappropriate translation. According to Wang, certain animals in traditional Chinese culture and the meaning behind them are mostly imaginary fables created in a certain historical period. Their image and meaning as cultural symbols gradually accumulated in the progress of national culture. In fact, the legends of various cultural regions in the world have different forms of 'dragon'. These repeatedly mentioned animals originate from different historical and cultural traditions and contexts, each with its different connotations, shapes and cultural orientations. However, as soon as a word specific to a certain word is mentioned, its cultural connotation and accompanying image will enter the dimension of discourse comprehension. The Chinese word 龙 is commonly translated to *dragon* in English, where the cultural differences in meaning will no doubt produce comprehension problems in the cross-cultural context. This is because, in English, the word *dragon* originally refers to a certain kind of giant snake. In *A Dictionary of Literary Symbols* published by Cambridge University, the dragon entry directly refers to serpent (snake). Therefore, this solidified shape and the image described in the Western myths and legends continue while retaining its 'evil' property. In Chinese culture, on the other hand, 'dragon' is the most symbolic cultural imaginative totem, and also the most 'spiritually strong' symbol. Different from the Western concept, the Chinese dragon is an auspicious creation: symbolizing positive power and richness. From the Han dynasty (206BC–AD220), the dragon also symbolizes the emperor. In a nutshell, although the English dragon and the Chinese 'dragon' may carry similar shapes, their symbolic values are derived from specific cultures and are dramatically different from each other. Wang insists that only by knowing a certain culture in depth will it be possible to avoid misunderstandings in intercultural communication. When China's 'dragon' is repeatedly converted into *dragon* in English discourse without necessary explanation, the occurrence of cultural misreading is inevitable. Wang advises that this kind of culturally specific word be introduced in Pinyin in the first instance to let it enter the cross-cultural context in the form of phonetic symbols. On this basis, contextual interpretation can be made and gradually the word and the concept behind it can be understood and accepted.

Translating traditional Chinese medicine

We saw earlier how researchers like Newmark (1988) and Ke (1999) have divided culture into subsystems in order to understand the issue at a conceptual level. When it comes to analyzing the practical work of translating culture, we are looking at different forms or genres of culture such as art, literature (fiction, poetry, drama), media, science and technology. In fact, the two books first authored by Valerie Pellatt organized their chapters mainly based on the particular theory and practice associated with the translation of different genres of Chinese culture (see Pellatt & Liu, 2010, Pellatt et al., 2014). That is to say, each aspect of culture presents a different set of problems to the translator and requires the development of different approaches and translation strategies. From Figure 4.1, we can see a few keywords at the intersection of translation and culture which represent this line of research (i.e. specific genres in cultural translation), for example, 民俗文化 (folk culture), 饮食文化 (food culture), 茶文化 (tea culture), 文学翻译 (literary translation), 典籍英译 (translating the classics), 红楼梦 (Dream of the Red Mansion), 影视翻译 (film translation), 字幕翻译 (subtitles translation) and so on and so forth. We will discuss literary translation, in particular, the translation of the great Chinese classic novel, *Dream of the Red Mansion*, in a separate chapter. In this section, we will introduce the translating of Chinese medicine as an important branch of Chinese culture. The reason that 中医 (Chinese medicine) does not occupy a discernible place in the keyword list of Chinese 'culture + translation' literature in Table 4.1 is presumably because Chinese medicine is not often subsumed under the umbrella term of 'culture' but instead has gained its own hierarchical place directly under the notion of 'Chinese'. As is done in Pellatt and Liu (2010), however, we will take up the translating Chinese medicine as a key aspect of Chinese culture, just as we treat Chinese literary text, media text, legal text, scientific text, and business text in translating.

Traditional Chinese medicine (TCM) is an important part of Chinese culture. It integrates not only Chinese traditional medical knowledge but all philosophy, such as Taoism, Confucianism, Buddhism and the Hundred Schools of Thought (诸子百家), showing a splendid 5,000-year Chinese civilization. The Chinese medicine culture touches on the traditional Chinese scientific and human culture and humanistic spirit and embodies the Chinese people's unique concept of harmony between man and nature, the whole system of health and disease prevention, and unique healthcare treatment methods. All cultural elements mentioned above reflect the essence and characteristics of traditional Chinese culture.

The guiding ideology of TCM is mainly derived from the *Book of Changes* (易经), which represents a significant development in ancient Chinese philosophy. The changes in the natural world are consistent with the changes in the human body itself, so the Chinese medicine advocates 'correspondence between man and universe' (天人相应), 'man is an integral part of nature' (天人合一) and so on. As a result, Chinese medicine language has expressions closely related to the nature of heaven and earth, such as 'eliminating dampness by cooling (清热化湿), 'clearing heart fire' (清心泻火), etc. The Vitality Theory (元气论), an ancient philosophy regarding the basic material that constitutes human and nature, has made a huge impact on Chinese medicine by claiming that the world is filled with recurring, continuous, and endless vitality. If this vitality is unimpeded, the human body will be healthy and disease-free. If the reverse is true, that is, in the case of 'stagnation of vital energy' (元气壅塞停滞), then frequent natural disasters and human diseases will occur.

The translation history of Chinese medicine is more than 300 years old. In 1683, the Dutch doctor William ten Rhyme in his book *On Arthritis* has a chapter devoted to acupuncture therapy, which served as a precedent for the translation of Chinese medicine into English. TCM classics are a combination of medicine and culture, and their production and development are integrated into history, society and culture. Accurate translation of these books not only promotes the development of Chinese medicine, but also enables more people in the world to understand Chinese medicine and benefit from it. The clinically synergistic treatment of difficult diseases such as SARS has been globally recognized. Other contributions such as assisting astronauts to adjust their bodies between the earth and space, inspiring scientific research and development, helping to discover the Nobel Prize-winning artemisinin and so on, have shown the value and wisdom of traditional Chinese culture.

Dong et al. (2017) reviewed the current status of research on Chinese medicine terminology translation by searching 613 articles published from 1991 to

2015 from the CNKI database and the Periodicals Charged by Chinese Medical Association in Wanfang (万方) database. With the help of CiteSpace, they analyzed the general status, major authors and institutions, high-frequency keywords, and research highlights of these TCM-related publications. Among the 613 articles, around 54% (or 330 papers) were published on China's prestigious 'core journals' and among these 330 articles, only 4.4% (that is, 27 papers) were published on dedicated translation journals. This shows how dispersed research outputs were in China's TCM translation studies. Dong and colleagues' research also revealed five groups of keywords within the domain of TCM terminology translation:

- TCM terminology: e.g. 中医方剂 (TCM prescription), 中医病名 (TCM disease name).
- Linguistics or translation theory: e.g. 语言学 (linguistics), 目的论 (scopos theory).
- Translation method: e.g. 音译法 (transliteration), 解释性翻译 (explanatory translation).
- Normalization: e.g. 规范化 (normalization), 标准化 (standardization).
- Culture and tradition: e.g. 黄帝内经 (Yellow Emperor's Canon of Internal Medication), 中国传统 (Chinese tradition).

In particular, Dong et al. noted that researchers in China increasingly concern themselves with the cultural connotations behind TCM. This can be evidenced from the recently popularized, culture-related keywords (between 2001 and 2015) like 词汇空缺 (lexical gap), 文化负载词 (culturally loaded word), 跨文化交际 (intercultural communication), 中医药文化 (TCM culture) and so on. Dong et al. (2017) concluded their paper by suggesting more cooperation between researchers to form great research teams, innovation in research perspectives and working towards evidence-based research, and further standardization of TCM terminology translation as well as systemization of theory construction.

Dong et al. (2017) correctly recognized the importance of standardization of terminology translation in future TCM translation research. In fact, terminology management is arguably the most difficult aspect of TCM translation, including disease and prescription names, terms related to TCM theory of causes and remedies of disease and so on. The allegedly first bilingual TCM dictionary, the *Chinese-English Glossary of Common Terms in Traditional Chinese Medicine* (汉英常用中医词汇), was published in 1980. Subsequently in 1991, *A Proposed Standard International Acupuncture Nomenclature: Report of a WHO Scientific Group* (针灸命名国际标准化方案: WHO专家小组报告) was promulgated as the first English term standard for Chinese medicine. However, attempts like this to standardize TCM terminology were not always successful. Li (1993) and Wiseman (2004), for example, each challenged these attempts at standardization of TCM terminology translation, with the latter also challenging the former's position.

Li (1993) was correct in believing that the quality of translation of TCM terminology was the key to Chinese medicine going global. He thought that the study of the structure of TCM terminology was pivotal, and summarized the following structural patterns of terminology based on his long-term experience in TCM translation and intercultural communication practice:

1. Subject-predicate structure: The first part of these terms is the core object of the statement and the second part is the description of the previous part. For example, the entry 'earth has a desire for warmth and dryness' (土喜温燥) as listed in the *Chinese-English Dictionary of Traditional Chinese Medicine* (Ou, 1999) manifests such a syntactic structure.
2. Verb-object construction: The first part is the verb and the second part is the object implicated in the action. This structure accounts for a large proportion of TCM terms. They are two-syllable words or four-syllable words regarding the pathological changes or treatments of the human body. For example, 'diarrhea with indigested food in the stool' (下利清谷) (ibid.) means the excrement is clear and thin, with indigestible food.
3. Combined structure: The relationship between the various components of this structure is equal. For example, the phrase 金寒水冷 (literally 'gold, chilly, water, cold') means 'deficiency in lung and kidney' (肺肾虚寒). But in *Terminology of Traditional Chinese Medicine* (Shuai, 2006), the phrase was translated into 'chilly metal and cold water' which did not make any sense.
4. Modifying construction: The first part of this structure has a modification effect on the second, indicating a relationship between the attributive modifier and the central word. For example, 'qi-stagnated celialgia' (气结腹痛) is translated into a pattern 'A due to B' in Ou (1999), which is awkward in practice.
5. Cause and effect: The first part of this structure represents the cause and the second part the result. These terms fully reflect the characteristics of TCM thinking in syndrome differentiation, and each term is a theory itself. For instance, 'overexertion consuming qi' (劳则气耗) means overwork wears and consumes energy.
6. Overlapping structure: The first and the second part of this term overlap in meaning or have the same or similar meaning which constitute the 'cadence in voice, parallel prose in form' (抑扬顿挫，四六成句), a highly regarded form of Chinese text. For this construction, Li recommended direct translation such as using 'relieving dyspepsia' for 消食化滞 (literally 'resolve food and eliminate stagnancy').

According to Li, the translation of 土喜温燥 (literally 'earth, like, warm, day') into 'earth has a desire for warmth and dryness' is tantamount to talking Greek to foreign readers who do not know much about Chinese medicine. *Tu* (土 'earth') here actually refers to the spleen. This phrase explains the physiological characteristics of the spleen and the condition for maintaining its normal function. In that light, Li proposed a translation using a neologism based on Latin and Greek: *thermoxerophil* of spleen. However, it seems nothing much was gained by borrowing such ingredients from Western medicine and Li's terminology has never appeared in textbooks or clinical literature available in the West. As a result, Li has apparently reduced the number of Greco-Latin derivations in his terminology in recent publications on Chinese medical translation (Wiseman, 2004, p. 8). According to Wiseman, since Li listed as many structures and translation methods as he deemed acceptable and placed no limits on their applicability, he effectively made no contribution to the problem of TCM term selection.

Nigel Wiseman, a British TCM translator, noted the lack of a standardized English terminology of Chinese medicine despite its rising popularity in the West (Wiseman, 2004). He claimed that TCM had an immense vocabulary of around 30,000 terms and, according to him, numerous term lists proposing English equivalents had been published which generally differed in the translation methods applied and lacked a systematic approach. In view of this, he proposed a set of four methods for creating TCM bilingual terminology: a) using existing terms; b) using loans (i.e. transliteration); c) loan-translations; or d) creating neologisms based on the definition of the term. English cannot borrow from Chinese on a large scale and, as such, loan-translation can be used to avoid imposing on the foreign reader interpretations of these concepts that might not be unanimously approved. Terms created principally by loan-translation have a high degree of transparency, which is helpful to translators. Unschuld (1989), Western historian of Chinese medicine, also pointed out that loan-translation was in fact easily applicable to Chinese medical term translation because Chinese medicine largely dealt with the gross objects and phenomena of the body and natural world, and its terminology was built around images from the natural and human world that could easily be translated. Moreover, an English terminology in which specialist terms are created by loan-translation meets the approval not only of the modern terminologist, but also that of the philologist. Meanwhile, Wiseman suggested that if loan translation failed to produce an adequate term, a new term could be devised on the basis of the definition or Pinyin transcription could be used. Put simply, Wiseman's idea followed the reasoning that 'strictly specialist terms be translated primarily by loan translation' was the first measure, 'non-literal translation based on definition be used where loan-translation does not produce satisfactory terms' came as the second, and 'the use of Western medical terms be limited to terms where they do not obscure Chinese medical meaning and do not introduce Western medical concepts into Chinese medical discourse' was the final solution if all failed.

Dong et al. (2017) noted that *The Inner Canon of Huangdi* (黄帝内经) was sometimes translated into *Huangdi Neijing* using Pinyin (i.e. transliteration). This practice began as early as the beginning of the 1990s and aroused concern in the next two decades about the translation of culturally loaded terms in TCM. Since 2001, there was a sharp increase in the research on cultural connotations of TCM terminology in translation. In fact, the research on TCM-related culture has become a hot topic in the new century. Surprisingly, the classic Chinese novel *Dream of Red Mansions* (红楼梦) as a non-Chinese medical vocabulary item, appeared to be a high-frequency keyword in the current English translation of TCM terminology, indicating that the research on Chinese medicine culture-related phenomena and vocabulary in Chinese classical literature has also been included in the field of TCM terminology translation.

Sun (2016) thought that TCM terminology was characterized in terms of semantic connotation, cultural imagery and cognitive background. These characteristics caused certain translation difficulties and also generated different translations for the same items. *Huangdi Neijing* (黄帝内经) is often considered the theoretical and ideological basis of Chinese classical medicine. It is also one of the earliest and most complete Chinese medical classics. As one of the four classic works of Chinese classical medicine, *Huangdi Neijing* comprehensively summarizes the medical experience since Three Sovereigns and Five Emperors to the Qin and Han dynasties, and developed Chinese medicine from the practical field up to the theoretical level. The traditional viewpoints of TCM, such as holistic view (整体观), meridian study (经络学) and pathology (病理学), play a decisive role in the development of traditional Chinese medicine and consolidate the theoretical basis for it. *Huangdi Neijing* includes Su Wen (素问) and Ling Shu (灵枢) and has spread abroad since the Han and Tang dynasties and had a great impact on foreign cultures. In the early 20th century, some chapters of *Huangdi Neijing* were translated into English. After the 1980s, various complete translations began to appear in the Western medical community. However, because the translation of *Huangdi Neijing* involved hundreds of literature and history scholars with dramatically different translating styles and rhetoric on top of the language barriers, it is difficult to produce a completely satisfactory translation, which largely hindered the spread of the book and, by extension, the TCM itself. The situation can be illustrated with the following examples.

In a sentence where the subject must be present in the TT where it was only implied in the ST, the reselection of the subject is important. The translation of Luo using the third person 'doctor' as the subject is more objective and consistent with the characteristics of the original medical book (Luo, 2009)

《脉要精微论篇第十七》：诊法常以平旦，阴气未动，阳气未散。

In diagnosing the pulse that represents the pathological condition, the doctor should feel the pulse in the morning before the patient has taken his breakfast when the Yang Vital Essence is not moving, and the Yang Vital Energy is not evanescent.

On a different note, cultural considerations are also important in translating TCM as the latter is intimately related to Chinese culture and philosophy.

《阴阳应象大论篇第五》：阴阳者，天地之道也，万物之纲纪，变化之父母，生杀之本始，神明之府也。

Yin and Yang are the Tao between the Heaven and the Earth, the dominating force of all creatures, the origin of all changes, the root of germination and killing, the housing of spirit and consciousness.

In the above example, Luo highlighted the medical function of *Huangdi Neijing* while not losing its literary character. Here 'all creatures' translates *wan wu* (万物 'all things') and refers to the vitality and dynamics of TCM theory; 'the origin' delivers the meaning of the original text but more objectively; and 'housing' nicely embodies the metaphor of the word *fu* (府 'residence') in the translation.

《四气调神大论篇第二》：逆之则伤肝，夏为寒变，奉长者少。

> To run counter to this, Kidney Vital Energy will be damaged, bringing with it diseases in cold nature in summer, as the germination and growth of spring has been damaged.

The translator's detailed choices in the translation process may be related to his own cultural background and domain knowledge. Luo's translation in the introduction of Chinese medicine theory and TCM terminology is very specific and describes the operation mode of TCM theory in detail by enriching the content of the translation, as illustrated by the above example. Here, *gan* (肝) translates to the more elaborated phrase of Kidney Vital Energy rather than the lexical equivalent of 'liver'. On the one hand, it is out of the necessity to repair the original text; on the other hand, it explains that the injury is the kidney gas, not the 'kidney' itself, which is linguistically meticulous and pathologically accurate.

Lan (2003) pointed out that many of the problems in the translation of Chinese medicine were caused by the lack of both the knowledge of traditional Chinese medicine and the appreciation of ancient Chinese culture. In other words, the connotation of Chinese medicine culture plays a vital role in properly understanding the literature and expressions of TCM. Take *Dream of Red Mansions* as an example, which represents the highest achievement of novels in the Ming and Qing dynasties and is the pinnacle of ancient Chinese novels. In addition to describing a character's appearance and talent to shape their personality, the author also took plenty of trouble going into the details of any patient's condition and diagnosis. Hu (2006) has counted in this novel more than 290 pieces of medical and health knowledge including more than 50,000 words, 161 medical terms, 114 cases of description, 13 Chinese medicine cases, 45 prescriptions and 125 Chinese medicines. The knowledge of Chinese medicine in the book plays an important part in promoting the development of the plot, revealing the situation and destiny of the characters and reflecting the background of the times. Many Chinese medicine ingredients mentioned in the book are still used today: Ginseng Tonic Pills (人参养荣丸), Eight-treasure-leonurus pills (八珍益母丸), Left restorative (左归丸), Right restorative (右归丸), to name just a few. This requires translators to not only have good language and translation skills, but also to have profound knowledge of Chinese medicine culture, in order to better translate and spread Chinese TCM literature abroad.

Bao et al. (2014) took the Chinese medicine culture in *Dream of Red Mansions* as the research object by selecting some sentences or paragraphs from three translated versions: *The Story of the Stone* by David Hawkes (Cao, 1973), *The Dream* of the Red Chamber* by H. Bencraft Joly (Cao, 2010a), and *A Dream of Red Mansions* by Xianyi Yang and Gladys Yang (Cao, 2010b). They tried to compare and analyze the translations of TCM culture based on its concepts and principles, diseases and symptoms, diagnosis and treatment and to point out the existence of any cultural misunderstanding. For example, there appears to be a very common cultural misunderstanding of certain TCM vocabulary:

…每日早起，拿上等燕窝一两，冰糖五钱，用银吊子熬出粥来，要吃惯了，比药还强，<u>最是滋阴补气的</u>…

David Hawkes: …First thing every morning you ought to take an ounce of the best quality bird's nest and five drams of sugar candy and heat them up in a silver skillet until they make a sort of syrup. If you were to take that regularly, it would do you more good than medicine. There's nothing like it for building you up if you have low vitality…

(Cao, 2012, p. 495)

Yang and Yang: …When you get up each morning, you should take an ounce of the best quality bird's nest boiled into a gruel with half an ounce of crystal sugar in a silver pot. Taken regularly, <u>this is a better tonic than any medicine</u>…

(Cao, 2010b, p. 69)

H. Bencraft Joly: …As soon as you get out of bed, every morning, take one ounce of birds' nests, of superior quality, and five mace of sugar candy and prepare congee with them in a silver kettle. When once you get into the way of taking this decoction, you will find it far more efficacious than medicines; <u>for it possesses the highest virtue for invigorating the vagina and bracing up the physique</u>…

(Cao, 2010a, p. 753)

During the conversion, Bao-chai (宝钗) persuades Dai-yu (黛玉) to take bird's nest porridge to nourish her body and attain mental tranquility. Because bird's nest is thought to have the function of nourishing *yin* ('darkness') and moistening dryness, supplementing *qi* ('energy') and replenishing the body, it is commonly used to cure a physical deficiency – hemoptysis. The phrase *zi yin bu qi* (滋阴补气 'nourish *yang*, supplement *qi*') indicates that the bird's nest is medicinal in the text. Yang and Yang and Hawkes both chose a free translation method based on their correct understanding of the medical connotation of the text, and fully conveyed the efficacy of bird's nest and the cultural information of Chinese medicine. On the other hand, Bencraft Joly made a mistake of rendering *zi yin* (滋阴) as 'invigorating the vagina', which is a typical mistake generated by a misreading of cultural information, causing the translation to deviate from the original intention of the text.

Wang and Yang (2014) offered another example to show that in the cross-cultural communication between Chinese medicine and Western medicine, there are many items and expressions that cannot be translated in an easily achieved equivalent fashion. The reason is that there are significant differences in the cognitive patterns that conceptualize Chinese and Western medicines, respectively. Having an intimate knowledge of Chinese medicine when translating diseases is the basis for success. A direct comparison with Western medicine and the application of foreign ready-made terminology often does not work.

……进来诊脉看了，说是经水不调，全要大补。胡太医道：'不是胎气，只是淤血凝结。'

David Hawkes: her trouble was 'irregularity of the menses caused by anaemia'... 'It is not pregnancy,' said the doctor. 'There is some clotted blood which is holding back the natural discharge.'

(Cao, 2012, pp. 1369–1370)

Yang and Yang: His diagnosis was that her menstruation was irregular and some tonic would set her right... Asked what the trouble was he said: 'It is not pregnancy, just congestion of the blood, To make her periods normal, we must get rid of the congestion.'

(Cao, 2010b, p. 2081)

In the above example, Hawkes rendered 经水不调 ('Irregular menstruation') in the original as 'irregularity of the menses caused by anaemia' based on his understanding of the content with extra information added without much firm ground. This was presumably due to the influence of the next phrase 全要大补 ('all require full supplement') which the translator believed had to do with anemia. Such inferences were neither in line with the original text nor in the relevant theories of Chinese medicine. In this regard, Yang and Yang fully followed the original meaning and produced a simple and correct translation – 'her menstruation was irregular'.

Another phrase in the same text, 淤血凝结 ('blood coagulation'), was acceptably translated by Yang and Yang into 'congestion of the blood'. According to the Longman Dictionary of Contemporary English (LDCE), if a part of the body is congested, it means the part is full of liquid, usually blood or mucus. Wang and Yang thought that 淤血凝结 means stagnant blood or blood stagnation. Since *stagnant* means 'water or air does not move or flow and often smells bad' according to the LDCE, 淤血凝结 in the original can be taken to mean 'blood not flowing' without emphasizing the congestion aspect. However, Hawkes translated the phrase into 'clotted blood' presumably through an attempt to introduce the Western medical concept 'blood clot' into Chinese medical discourse, obscuring the Chinese medical understanding of the disease instead. In order for westerners to gain a full understanding of Chinese medicine, it is important to preserve Chinese medical concepts in the translation of terms. With the purpose of spreading Chinese culture, Yang and Yang emphasized integrity and independence of Chinese medical concepts, and their translation was closer to the original.

This shows that some TCM terms seem to have corresponding terms in English in a superficial sense but, in effect, there are subtle differences between the two (i.e. a case of 'false friends').

We have seen in this section how difficult it is to translate and standardize the terminology of traditional Chinese medicine due to its structural opacity, cultural connotation and embedded medical knowledge. TCM, however, is only a part of Chinese culture, albeit a significant one. There are many other parts of Chinese culture, each of which has their unique characteristics, dedicated vocabulary and background knowledge, which require special treatment and extensive research to produce satisfactory translations.

Conclusion

We have explored the possible meaning and composites of culture and some unique traits of Chinese culture that may cause problems in translation and their corresponding strategies. In addition, we have expounded the Chinese culture 'going out' initiative by looking at its motivation, policy, challenges and possible solutions. Finally, we examined in some detail the complicated situation of translating a particular area of Chinese culture – traditional Chinese medicine – into English, including the problem of standardizing the terminology and the important role played by background knowledge in trying to produce the correct translation. Despite the interesting and fruitful consideration offered by culture in the process of translation, however, translation studies is still a distinct discipline and an overreliance on culture runs the risk of ignoring other aspects in the process of translation, such as linguistics, psychology, politics, sociology and technology. Yi (2014) had a point when he said that too much emphasis on the decisive significance of cultural factors in the translation process, or claiming that translation *is* the transformation of culture or even that the unit of translation is culture, is bound to blur the fundamental fact that translation is a bilingual transformation, an exchange between languages. While the cultural translation view emphasizes the macroscopic level of translation on one side, it ignores the same important micro-language treatment to a certain extent – language is the carrier of culture, and the so-called cultural transformation in translation ultimately has to be implemented in language. Translation studies is not the same as cultural studies, and translation studies is not subordinate to cultural studies. All in all, Yi emphasized that translation studies and cultural studies are inherently different, and thought that the cultural school's one-sided emphasis on the core role of culture in translation is seriously biased. The fact is, on the one hand, social and cultural background has a profound influence on translation. On the other hand, translation also fundamentally influences the development of language and the formation of culture. Translation is not only passively influenced by culture, it also plays a role in the building of new cultural forms. At the end of his paper, Yi offered some cogent concluding remarks which also serve as a good conclusion to this chapter. First, cultural studies offers an indispensable perspective for translation studies. The two studies can learn from each other and promote each other.

Secondly, there are differences in the subjects investigated by translation studies and those by cultural studies, and the two cannot be equated. Thirdly, translation studies is an independent discipline; it is not subordinate to cultural studies.

References

Chinese references

Bao, Yuhui, Fang, Tingyu and Chen, Shaohong 包玉慧, 方廷钰, 陈绍红 (2014) 论《红楼梦》英译本中的中医文化误读 (Misinterpretation of TCM culture in the English translation of A Dream of Red Mansions). 中国翻译 (*Chinese Translator Journal*). 2014(5): 87–90.

Chang, Nam Fung 张南峰 (2015) 文化输出与文化自省 — 从中国文学外推工作说起 (Cultural export and cultural retrospection: from the job of Chinese literature going out). 中国翻译 (*Chinese Translator Journal*). 2015(04): 88–93.

Dong, Jian, Wang, Tianfang, Du, Lilan and Wu, Qing 董俭, 王天芳, 都立澜, 吴青 (2017) 1991年–2015年国内中医术语英译研究现状的计量学与可视化分析 (Bibliometric and visualization analysis of Chinese research articles on Chinese medicine terminology translation (1991–2015)). 中华中医药杂志 (*China Journal of Traditional Chinese Medicine and Pharmacy*). 32(9): 4277–4281.

Fan, Xiangtao 范祥涛 (2008) 文化专有项的翻译策略及其制约因素—以汉语典籍《文心雕龙》的英译为例 (Translation strategies for culture specific items and the controlling factors: using the English translation of the Chinese classic *wen xin diao long* as example). 外语与外语教学 (*Foreign Languages and Their Teaching*). 231: 61–64.

Hu, Weihua and Guo, Jirong 胡伟华, 郭继荣 (2018) 文化翻译政治策略的理据及模型构建 (The theoretical foundation and model construction for political strategy of cultural translation). 外语教学理论与实践 (*FLLTP*). 2018(02): 78–83.

Hu, Xianguo, Hu, Aiping and Sun, Zhihai 胡献国, 胡爱萍, 孙志海 (2006) 看红楼说中医 (*Traditional Chinese Medicine in A Dream of Red Mansions*). 山东画报出版社济南 (Shandong Pictorial Publishing House) Jinan.

Jia, Hongwei 贾洪伟 (2017) 中华文化典籍外译的推进路径研究 (Exploring the progressive path of Chinese cultural classics going out). 外语学刊 (*Foreign Language Research*). 197: 110–114.

Jiang, Qiuxia 姜秋霞 (2016) 翻译在社会系统中的文化身份 (Cultural identity of translation in social system). 中国翻译 (*Chinese Translator Journal*). 2016(05): 7–9.

Lan, Fengli 兰凤利 (2003) 论中医文化内涵对中医英译的影响—中医药古籍善本书目译余谈 (Cultural connotations and the translation of traditional Chinese medical texts: with the titles of some ancient rare books as a case in point). 中国翻译 (*Chinese Translator Journal*). 24(4): 70–73.

Li, Linna 李琳娜 (2018) 我国新时代翻译价值探析 (Exploring the value of translation in the new times of our nation). 上海翻译 (*Shanghai Journal of Translators*). 2018(03): 12–14.

Li, Zhaoguo 李照国 (1993) 中医名词术语的结构及英译 (Structure and English translation of TCM terms). 中国翻译 (*Chinese Translator Journal*). 1993(6): 28–30.

Liu, Guilan and Xiao, Yonghe 刘桂兰, 肖永贺 (2016) 浅谈补偿文化缺省的解释性翻译限度 (On the limitation of the explanatory translation in compensating for cultural default). 上海翻译 (*Shanghai Journal of Translators*). 2016(02): 61–63.

Ou, Ming 欧明 (1999) 汉英中医辞典 (*Chinese-English Dictionary of Traditional Chinese Medicine*). Hong Kong: 三联 (Joint Publishing). 外语与外语教学 (*Foreign Languages and Their Teaching*). 231: 61–64.

Shuai, Xuezhong 帅学忠 (2006) 汉英双解常用中医名词术语 (*Terminology of Traditional Chinese Medicine*). Hunan: 湖南科学技术出版社 (Hunan Science & Technology Press Co., Ltd.)

Sun, Fenglan 孙凤兰 (2016a) 识解理论视角下的《黄帝内经》医学术语翻译 (Translation of medical terms of Huangdi Neijing under the construal theory). 外语学刊 (*Foreign Language Reach*). 2016(3): 107–111.

Sun, Yifeng 孙艺风 (2016b) 文化翻译的困惑与挑战 (Cultural translation as a puzzle and a challenge). 中国翻译 (*Chinese Translator Journal*). 2016(03): 5–14.

Wang, Kefei and Wang, Yingchong 王克非, 王颖冲 (2016) 论中国特色文化词汇的翻译 (On translation of Chinese culture-specific items). 外语与外语教学 (*Foreign Languages and Their Teaching*). 291: 87–93.

Wang, Xiaolu 王晓路 (2018a) "中国文化走出去"语境下跨文化传播的基本问题——以"龙"和"Dragon"为例的词语文化轨迹探讨 (Basic questions of intercultural dissemination in the context of 'Chinese culture gong out': using the cultural trajectory of the translation of 'dragon' as basis for investigation). 四川大学学报(哲学社会科学版) (*Journal of Sichuan University (Philosophy and Social Science Edition)*). 219: 116–124.

Wang, Xinyan 汪信砚 (2016) 中国文化走出去的两种意涵 (Two connotations of Chinese culture going out). 学习时报 (*Study Times*). 10 October. Viewed 9 April 2019 http://theory.people.com.cn/n1/2016/1010/c49157-28764806.html.

Wang, Yanxia 王艳霞 (2018b) 接受理论关照下看文学作品中文化缺省的翻译——以《名利场》两个翻译版本为例 (On the translation of cultural default in literary works under Reception Aesthetics: using the two translated versions of Vanity Fair as example). 海外英语 (*Overseas English*). 2018(24): 62–63.

Wang, Yinquan and Yang Le 王银泉, 杨乐 (2014) 《红楼梦》英译与中医文化西传 (A dream of red mansions and Chinese medicine culture spreading to the West). 中国翻译 (*Chinese Translator Journal*). 2014(4): 108–111.

Wiseman, Nigel 魏迺杰 (2004) 中医名词英译：应用系统化原则的翻译模式 (English translation of Chinese medical terms: a scheme based on integrated principles). 科技术语研 (*Chinese Terminology*). 2004(4): 30–34.

Wu, Bo 吴波 (2017) 中国社会文化热词英译的立场和方法 (On the strategy and methods of translating Chinese social and cultural words into English). 外语教学理论与实践 (*FLLTP*). 2017(01): 85–91.

Xin, Ming 辛鸣 (2011) 十七届六中全会后党政干部关注的重大理论与现实问题解读 (*Interpretation of the Major Theoretical and Pragmatic Issues Concerned by Party and Government Cadres after the Sixth Plenary Session of the Seventeenth Central Committee*). 北京 (Beijing): 中共中央党校出版社 (Central Party School of the Communist Party of China Press).

Xiong, Wei 熊伟 (2018) 翻译研究的文化概念问题 (On the concept of culture in translation studies). 理论月刊 (*Theory Monthly*). 2018(01): 92–96.

Yang, Shizhang 杨仕章 (2017) 文化翻译功能说 (The functional aspect of cultural translation). 解放军外国语学院学报 (*Journal of PLA University of Foreign Languages*). 40(4): 108–115.

Yi, Jing 易经 (2014) 文化研究派对翻译学定位的反思 (Reflecting on the position of the cultural school regarding the status of translation). 外语教学 (*Foreign Language Education*). 35(4): 109–112.

Zhou, Xinkai and Xu, Jun 周新凯, 许钧 (2015) 中国文化价值观与中华文化典籍外译 (Chinese cultural value and the translation of Chinese culture classics). 外语与外语教学 (*Foreign Languages and Their Teaching*). 284: 70–74.

Zhu, Zhenwu 朱振武 (2016) 翻译活动就是要有文化自觉—从赵彦春译《三字经》谈起 (Translation must come with cultural awareness: from the translation of the *Three Word Primer* by Zhao Yanchun). 外语教学 (*Foreign Language Education*). 37(5): 83–85.

Other references

Aixela, J. F. (1996) Culture-specific items in translation. In R. Alvarez and M. CarmenAfrica Vidal (eds) *Translation, Power, Subversion* (pp. 52–78). Clevedon: Multilingual Matters.

Baker, M. (2011) *In Other Words: A Coursebook on Translation*, 2nd edition. London and New York: Routledge.

Cao, X. (1973/2012) *The Story of the Stone*. Translated by David Hawkes. Shanghai: Shanghai Foreign Language Education Press.

Cao, X. (2010a) *The Dream of the Red Chamber*. Translated by H. Bencraft Joly. Singapore: Tuttle Publishing.

Cao, X. (2010b) *A Dream of Red Mansions*. Translated by Xianyi Yang and Gladys Yang. Beijing: Foreign Languages Press.

Chinascope. (2019) *The Strategy of Chinese Culture Going Global, Part I*. Viewed 9 April 2019. http://chinascope.org/archives/18017.

Ke, P. (1999) Cultural presuppositions and misreadings. *Meta* XLIV: 133–143.

Luo, X. (2009) *Introductory Study of Huangdi Neijing*. Beijing: China Press of Traditional Chinese Medicine Beijing.

Newmark, P. (1988) *A Textbook of Translation*. New York: Prentice Hall.

Pellatt, V. and Liu, E. T. (2010). *Thinking Chinese. Translation: A Course in Translation Method: Chinese to English*. London and New York: Routledge.

Pellatt, V., Liu, E. T. and Chen, Y. Y. -Y. (2014) *Translating Chinese Culture: The Process of Chinese-English Translation*. London and New York: Routledge.

Pym, A. (1998). *Method in Translation History*. Manchester: St. Jerome.

Unschuld, P. U. (1989) Terminological problems encountered and experiences gained in the process of editing a commentated Nan-Ching edition. In P. U. Unschuld (ed.) *Approaches to Traditional Chinese Medical Literature* (pp. 97–108). Dordrecht: Kluwer.

Venuti, L. (1998) *The Scandals of Translation: Towards an Ethics of Difference*. London and New York: Routledge.

5 Translating Chinese literature

This chapter dwells on 'Chinese literary translation', as the name suggests, as a genre of research in translation studies. However, if we look to the West for a definition of 'literary translation', it is somewhat difficult to find a popular definition or a set of established features or tenets associated with the concept. The five volumes of *The Oxford History of Literary Translation in English*, for example, assume it is already clear (or that it need not be entirely clear) what 'literary translation' is, and go on to divide the English literary translation into five periods (beginning–1550, 1550–1660, 1660–1790, 1790–1900, 1900–2000). Within each period, issues like contexts of translation, renowned translators and particular lines of literary works (e.g. romance or sacred texts) are discussed without much clarification or debate as to what 'literary translation' really is. (In fact, volume one of the above series also includes a chapter entitled *Scientific and Medical Writing*). Notwithstanding, the general editors of the series did try to define the concept of what 'literary' in literary translation means, albeit in a somewhat obscure fashion:

> While we emphasize the value of such high artistic achievements as Pope's Homer or FitzGerald's *Rubáiyát*, we use the word 'literary'" in the broad old sense which it has still not completely lost, to encompass something like the full range of non-technical work which has made up the reading of the literate public.
>
> (France & Gillespie, 2008, p. vii)

Notably, there does not seem to be a concentrated effort within the above series in defining what 'literary translation theory' is, either. Among the 38 sections included in the four published volumes of *The Oxford History of Literary Translation in English* series, there are only two sections entitled *Theories of Translation* (in volume one and volume three, respectively) with only three chapters between them, which largely dwell on 'one-off' issues and observations of particular persons and trends within a given period (e.g., 'the medieval translator'); the thoughts of some individual thinkers on translation (e.g. Dryden); the resources available for investigation (e.g. Oxford English Dictionary or OED); or the translation of certain high-profile works (e.g. the Bible). There appears to be no systematic account of translation theory for the translating of literature in this English literary translation series. Instead, the concerns of literary translation seem to fall within the combined set of problems regarding time periods, literary works and translators with widely scattered outputs.

If the literary translation camp (in the West and obviously also in China) has not emphasized the output of consolidated theories as those seen in linguistics and culture-based translation studies discussed in the previous chapters, the latter kind of study has little to say about the practice of literary translation either. Munday (2016), for example, has not offered a dedicated chapter on literary translation in his popular introductory book. Instead, the majority of the 53 instances of 'literary translation' appearing in the book (minus at least 20 of them found in bibliography, summary and discussion or further reading sections) get a mention in passing when a variety of topics are under discussion, such as the genesis of translation studies, 'stylistic shifts' in translation, text analysis, various approaches (e.g. Mary Snell-Hornby's 'integrated approach') and theories (e.g. Even-Zohar's polysystem) to translation studies, the ethics of translation and so on. In a nutshell, we do not expect to cover in this chapter a lot of universal or comprehensive theories for Chinese literary translation as we saw in previous chapters. Instead, we focus on various issues regarding the translation of Chinese literature, revolving around the translation of a great classic Chinese novel – Hong Lou Meng (红楼梦, often translated as *'Dream of the Red Chamber'* or *'The Story of the Stone'*), hoping to give some comprehensive and in-depth ideas as to the nature of literary translation activities and its research in China. Before that, however, we shall have a look at how translated literature has entered the culture and society of China and how this phenomenon has been studied.

Translated foreign literature in China

With surprising insights, the Belgian translation theorist André Lefevere conveyed an impression of how translated literature was created and treated in China in an article entitled *Chinese and Western Thinking on Translation*. Lefevere boldly claimed that China developed translational strategies only three times in its history: while translating the Buddhist scriptures, the Christian scriptures, and the various texts of Western thought and literature, respectively. Furthermore, Lefevere inferred from this impression that the image of 'the Other' was not very important in China. Lefevere said that China was much like Classical Greece, which hardly translated anything at all as it 'showed no interest in the Other' and 'did not develop any thinking about translation' (Lefevere, 1998, p. 13). There were several reasons why a culture such as that of China did not pay attention to the Other, according to Lefevere. First of all, it must be a culture that sees itself as central in the world it inhabits. (This is obviously true for China as indicated by the name 中国 'the middle country'). Such a culture had no interest in dealing with the Other unless it was forced to. Lefevere thought China was 'forced to deal with the Other by the spread of Buddhism', although in Chapter 3 we saw how the emperors of the Tang and Song dynasties, etc. were voluntarily and actively introducing Buddhism at least partly for political reasons. In any case,

Lefevere was correct in pointing out that (at least initially) Taoist concepts were used to acculturate Buddhist concepts into China in translating, thereby lessening the impact of the Other. Secondly, Lefevere suggested that cultures that did not pay attention to the Other were also relatively homogeneous. This, again, applied to China where Han culture was generally dominant, into which ethnic minority cultures were often seamlessly integrated. Moreover, homogeneous culture has its own way of doing things and it sees things from its own perspective. Lefevere describes how translation worked in such a culture:

> When Chinese translates texts produced by Others outside its boundaries, it translates these texts in order to replace them, pure and simple. The translations take the place of the originals. They function as the originals in the culture to the extent that the originals disappear behind the translations.
> (Lefevere, 1998, p. 14)

What Lefevere meant was that the Chinese generally used the 'domestication' method when introducing foreign literatures into China, so to speak, leaving no trace of foreign elements in the translation, making the translation look like an original work, being absorbed naturally into the Chinese culture. Along this line, Lefevere also correctly pointed out that Chinese translators like Yan Fu had a strong readership in mind when carrying out their translation activities and rhetorically adapted their translations to their intended audience. This was different from the concurrent Wester practice which normally concentrated on faithful linguistic transcoding without paying attention to the particular readership. Another related aspect, which Lefevere noted about Chinese translation, or its difference from Western translation, was that the former had traditionally 'stay[ed] closer to the interpreting situation' (meaning Chinese translators had worked on the basis of spoken ST, which was true in the case of Buddhist translation as discussed in Chapter 3). Therefore, due to the less well-organized nature of the spoken language, the Chinese tradition had attached comparatively less importance to the 'faithfulness' criterion, which had been a central notion of translation theory in the West. Thus, Lefevere concluded his discussion by saying that cultural factors such as power, self-image and homogeneity were much more critical than linguistic factors in deciding how a culture defines translation for itself. In addition, contingency was also an important factor for Lefevere, who wanted the reader to imagine the different paths that Chinese translation would have taken if the translators of Buddhist sutras had had written Sanskrit texts to work with rather than the spoken forms.

Lefevere's 'prediction' that translated literatures will not occupy an important place in the Chinese literary field (except perhaps through a naturalization process where they become similar to original works in the Chinese culture) is borne out by our scientometric investigation where we looked up the CNKI database with the search words 翻译 ('translation') and 文学 ('literature') and compiled a list of the top 50 keywords as Table 5.1 shows, which should indicate the interests and concerns of Chinese translation researchers on the translation of literature into and

Table 5.1 50 top keywords from scientometric analysis of 翻译 'translation' and 文学 'literature'

Frequency	Keyword	Frequency	Keyword
2127	文学翻译 (literary translation)	107	主体性 (subjectivity)
1365	翻译 (translation)	107	文化差异 (cultural difference)
412	翻译策略 (translation strategy)	98	译介 (introductory translation)
388	译者 (translator)	98	读者 (readership)
287	异化 (foreignization)	94	翻译教学 (translation teaching)
275	翻译文学 (translated literature)	93	比较文学 (comparative literature)
255	归化 (domestication)	88	葛浩文 (Howard Goldblatt)
237	文学 (literature)	84	作家 (author)
231	意识形态 (ideology)	81	外国文学 (foreign literature)
215	创造性叛逆 (creative rebellion)	78	翻译标准 (translation norm)
215	翻译研究 (translation research)	71	诗学 (poetry translation)
202	儿童文学 (children's literature)	71	翻译学 (translation studies)
173	文学作品 (literary works)	68	林纾 (Lin Shu)
172	译者主体性 (translator subjectivity)	65	忠实 (faithfulness)
168	翻译理论 (translation theory)	63	中国文学 (Chinese literature)
164	鲁迅 (Lu Xun)	62	风格 (style)
160	接受美学 (acceptance aesthetics)	62	译介学 (Medio translatology)
159	翻译家 (scholarly translator)	59	影响 (influence)
135	儿童文学翻译 (translation of children's literature)	59	翻译实践 (translation practice)
127	翻译批评 (translation criticism)	53	译本 (translated text)
126	中华人民共和国 (People's Republic of China)	51	英美文学 (Anglo-American literature)
117	翻译思想 (translation thought)	51	文化转向 (culture turn)
117	目的论 (skopos theory)	49	多元系统理论 (polysystem theory)
114	文化 (culture)	49	直译 (direct translation)
113	诗歌翻译 (translation of poetry)	47	莫言 (Mo Yan)

out of Chinese culture. As a result, the most important piece of information shown in Table 5.1 is the absence of keywords in the translated names of foreign authors (e.g. Shakespeare) or literary works (e.g. *Pride and Prejudice*). This seems to echo Lefevere's observation that, as a self-centered and homogeneous culture, the Chinese indeed have relatively little interest in exploring the theory and practice of translated literature from abroad. This is not to say, however, that there is entirely no interest or discussion in this area. In what follows we will review some of the works output by Chinese researchers on the translation of foreign literature into the Chinese culture.

There is relatively little discussion on the power relations between cultures or ideological concerns when attention is indeed paid to the import of foreign literature to China via translation, which falls largely in line with Lefevere's argument that a self-centered and homogeneous culture such as China and classic Greece cares very little about the Other. Thus, most of the papers we find published in China's journals dwell on the language issues, translation strategies and qualities, translation activities or other practical aspects of literary translation. Sun and Zheng (2010), for example, reviewed the literary translation activities in China between 1976–2008, focusing on Anglo-American literature (英美文学). Since Sun and Zheng held the opinion that, in the process of examining Chinese history of literary translation, politics was always a factor that could not be ignored, it was logical for them to divide this span of time into three periods, with each given a politically implicated name:

1. Thawing period (解冻时期) Oct 1976–Nov 1978
2. Renaissance period (复兴时期) Nov 1978–June 1989
3. Active development period (活跃发展时期) 1990—2008

According to Sun and Zheng, the date of October 1976 marked the end of the Cultural Revolution and the beginning of a new era for China. Prior to this date, foreign literature had been banned by the Chinese government, but with the crushing and prosecution of the Gang of Four (四人帮) in October 1976, the 'thawing period' of foreign literature began. In 1977, translated literary works such as *Myths and Legends of Greece* (希腊的神话和传说), *One Thousand and One Nights* (一千零一夜), *Venice Merchants* (威尼斯商人), *Hamlet* (哈姆雷特) were published by People's Literature Publishing House. Translation activities in this period, according to Sun and Zheng, manifested three traits. Firstly, the foreign literary and translation circles were the forerunners in the liberation and opening up of China's ideological domain after the Cultural Revolution. Secondly, the translations output by publishers in this period were all reprints of older translations. Thirdly, some foreign literary journals started to be published or reissued in this period. Then, the second period of the new foreign literature translation movement started in 1978, according to Sun and Zheng, with the publication of the article 'Prudently Adjusting the Party's Literary and Art Policy' (认真调整党的文艺政策) on the People's Daily in June and the Eight-Year Planning Meeting of National Foreign Literature Research Work

(全国外国文学研究工作八年规划会议) held in Guangzhou in November. The policy adjusting article marked a political watershed between the literary works purely serving the Communist Party's purposes in the past and its future use for the benefits of the general public. Thereafter, the ban on foreign literature during the Cultural Revolution was revised, and the western modern and contemporary literary works were reevaluated. Meanwhile, translation policies suitable for the new historical period were formulated; the important mission of studying and introducing new achievements and new trends in contemporary and contemporary foreign literature was launched. Sun and Zheng characterized this period of China's literary translation activities with four traits. Firstly, they observed a surge in periodicals and journals specializing in foreign literary translation and literary studies, such as World Literature (世界文学) which had started in 1953 as Translated Text (译文) but changed to its current name in 1978, Foreign Literature and Art (外国文艺), which started in 1978. Secondly, Sun and Zheng noted that many publishers in this period published literary translations, and special foreign literature publishing institutions were also established. Thirdly, they observed that Anglo-American modernist and postmodernist literary works had been systematically translated into Chinese, and become the mainstream and focus of foreign literature translation. Finally, Sun and Zheng claimed that the publications of translated English literature and American literature were generally on the rise in this period. Sun and Zheng's survey ended with an optimistic assessment of the period between 1990 and their time of writing. According to them, since the 1990s, China's society had gradually entered an era of relative stability, pluralism, openness and democracy. The degree of political relaxation was unprecedented, which had created favorable conditions for the translation of English and American literature. In addition, the development of translated criticism, the rewards for excellent translation books, and the recognition of translators with special achievements had gradually improved the quality of Anglo-American literary translations. The translation of British and American literature in China had embarked on a healthy development path.

Despite the recent thriving of the introduction of English literature into China via translation, some Chinese researchers had been worried about the quality of the Chinese translation of English literature and flagged the problem. A well-respected foreign language and translation scholar in China, Ji Mulin (季慕林), for example, wrote an article entitled 'The Crisis of Translation' (翻译的危机) pointing out that China was not No. 1 in the quantity, coverage or timeliness of translation (he thought that Japan was ahead of China in all these respects). Moreover, he was worried about the quality of the then current translations, complaining about some translators having a low level of foreign language proficiency and unwilling to work hard to improve it. Instead, they were eagerly after quick profit and relied solely on dictionaries to translate (Ji, 1998). In addition, Ji lamented that the crisis had so far not caused widespread concerns in society, especially in the literary and art circles and academia. Ji's grave concerns were revisited in Sun (2008) ten years later, who claimed that it was a consensus of the profession that China was 'a big nation of translation' (翻译大国) but not 'a strong nation of translation' (翻译强国). Sun estimated that only a quarter of the translations of English literature produced during the new period (presumably referring to the post-Cultural Revolution era) were of higher quality, half of which were produced by translators of an older generation. Younger translators' performance, then, was more unpredictable based on Sun's observation. Overall, Sun thought that recent achievements in the translation of English and American literature in China should be recognized with a substantial number of well-known translations having emerged. In the meantime, a large quantity of inferior works also existed. Sun called for China's literary, publishing and foreign language teaching communities to join hands and build a high-level translation team to improve the level of literary translation in China in the long run.

What remains to be said in this section is, notably, the attention paid by Chinese researchers to the challenges and solutions faced by translators translating English literature into Chinese. Most problems raised by researchers in this thread are caused by cultural differences between China and the West. Chen (2018) uses Edward T. Hall's concept (without giving a specific reference) of 'high-context culture' vs. 'low-context culture' in anthropology to explain the influence of cultural context on literary translation. Chen explains that China is a high-context culture because land and family are important concepts in that culture, where people are also familiar with each other and have a common historical background and shared customs. Britain and the United States, on the other hand, are countries with low- to medium-context cultures, because English-speaking countries are mostly industrial countries with highly mobile populations, where 'individual' and 'freedom' are also emphasized and 'spiritual communication' between people is less common. These cultures rely on language heavily to express meaning clearly in communication. Chen infers that there are four areas where these two kinds of culture differ:

1. Differences in customs and values
2. Difference in language and thinking
3. Differences in environment and belief
4. Differences in etiquette and habits

In view of these contextual differences between the Anglo-American and the Chinese cultures, Chen proposes that the domestication and foreignization methods should be skillfully synthesized and flexibly applied (complementing each other) in order to cancel out the cultural differences between the ST's author and the TT's readership so that a balanced state can be reached. Using foreignization while not interfering with a reader's understanding, and using domestication while not losing the connotation of the ST, is a way to reach the 'middle point' where the two strategies are 'organically combined'. The other two translation strategies Chen proposed for solving cultural problems in literary translation are the 'elasticity method' (伸缩法) and the 'split-combine method' (分合法), the former referring to the common method of replacing a culturally unknown word with its superordinate (i.e. a more abstract or common word) or hyponym (i.e. a more specific word); the latter being the frequently applied technique of splitting a long sentence in the ST or combining several short ones.

Liang (2018) proposes another set of cultural parameters causing problems in literary translation and some of the strategies for managing them. For Liang, cultural differences between China and the West may arise in four areas: 1. customs and habits, 2. religion and beliefs, 3. symbolic meanings, 4. thinking patterns and value systems. In the area of symbolic meaning, Liang gives the familiar example of a 'dragon' to show the difference in symbolic meanings between Chinese and Western cultures. In China, a dragon symbolizes good luck and high status and gives a generally auspicious feeling. In the English tradition and literature, however, a dragon can be the symbol of something unpleasant and evil. Liang rightly observes that the translator must understand the correct symbolic meanings of something where the author is located, not on the basis of the symbolic meaning of the same thing from the translator's own culture; otherwise, misinterpretation can occur. Liang recommends four strategies for handling cultural differences in translating:

1. Understanding the slang and idioms commonly used in Britain and the USA.
2. Strengthening the grasp of the implicit meaning of words behind British and American culture.
3. Mastering the words related to the Anglo-American culture.
4. Paying attention to the effective combination of cultural information with Chinese vocabulary.

Liang offers the case of translating 'Robert Rosenthal effect' into 罗森塔尔影响 ('*luo sen ta* influence') as an example of poor translation; while 罗森塔尔效应 ('*luo sen ta* effect') is a better translation, which caters to the reading habits of the Chinese audience. In addition to the eight areas of possible cultural differences between China and the West proposed by Chen (2018) and Liang (2018) above, Liu (2017) also brought up the issue of allusions in literary works. According to Liu, the allusions in English literature came from three sources: myths and legends, religious tradition, and fables. Yang (2016) further noticed that, in English and American literature, vague language played a uniquely pragmatic and rhetorical aesthetic function. She suggested that the translation of vague language required a deep understanding of the meaning of the source language, as well as strategies and techniques of translation, in order to accurately convey the meaning of the story, and to enrich the inherent meaning of the literary works. The kind of 'vague language' Yang had in mind for literary translation was found in words like *approaching* in the sentence *A Saturday afternoon in November was approaching the time of twilight* which, according to Yang, was better translated as 靠近 ('nearing') rather than 步入 ('stepping into') due to the former's better compatibility with the imagery of the 'time of twilight'. Yang also proposed three translation strategies to deal with vague languages as defined by her in the article:

1. Retaining the artistic conception of literary works by appropriate addition and supplementation.
2. Maintaining the style of literary works by timely transformation.
3. Expressing the meaning of literary works by accurate selections.

Yang gave more examples of her so-called vague language from a verse reproduced below:

> Art is long, and time is fleeting,
> And our hearts, though stout and brave,
> Still, like muffled drums, are beating
> Funeral marches to the grave.
>
> (from *A Psalm of Life* by Henry Wadsworth Longfellow)

According to Yang, the words *long, fleeting, stout, brave* and *muffled* are all examples of vague language in the poem and should be translated into 'equivalently vague' language in Chinese, with 长久 ('long'), 飞逝 ('fleeting'), 英勇 ('brave'), 坚强 ('strong'), 低沉 ('overcast') and so on, ensuring that not only would the vague language be 'accurately translated', but that the beauty of the original work would be preserved. In doing so, a combination of accuracy and beauty was achieved, and the emotions expressed in the original works of literature were adequately presented.

We will end this section with Xiong's (2017) paper, which offered a relatively rare discussion on the application of a linguistics-based translation theory to literary translation. Xiong looked at English literary translation from the perspective of Nida's functional equivalence and approached the problem from four angles: vocabulary, semantics, style and culture. An example Xiong gave at the vocabulary level that illustrated how functional equivalence could be reached in literary translation was based on two existing translations of the English novel Wuthering Heights. The word in question was *catch* in the sentence *When would you catch me wishing to have what Catherine wanted?* where one translator had used the formal equivalent of 抓住 ('catch'); while another had used the functional equivalent of 瞅见 ('saw') to achieve a better result. At the semantic level, Xiong used a sentence from Max Beerbohm's prose *Seeing People Off, Overnight, we had given him a farewell dinner*, and two different translations of *given him a farewell dinner*, namely 为他办告别宴 ('giving him a farewell feast') and 为他设宴饯行 ('organizing a feast to bid him farewell'), to show how the latter translation caters more to the Chinese audience's reading habits and was a better translation. Finally, at the culture level, Xiong reminded us that language has profound social and cultural attributes. As an art form expressed by language, literary works encompass a unique breadth of national culture imprinted in a certain vocabulary. For example, Xiong noted that the moon symbolized homesickness in ancient Chinese, and that a flying canopy symbolized drifting. She concluded that translators should not overemphasize the correspondence between forms in translation, but should start from the perspective of cross-cultural communication, taking effective communication between cultures as being the primary task of translation.

In this section, we have introduced China's literary translation activities in respect of the importation of foreign (notably English) literature via translating. We have also reviewed what Chinese researchers have to say about the problems and strategies involved in translating foreign literature into the Chinese language. Lefevere's assertion that a self-centered and homogenous culture does not care about the Other reverberates at the end of this discussion. Indeed, we have seen very little said by Chinese researchers about the social functions or ideological changes brought about by the introduction of foreign literature. We have also found no detailed or in-depth discussion on the plot, theme, literary value or even the language of any translated foreign literature in China, in line with Lefevere's claim. Conversely, we will see in the next section how such a culture is centrally concerned with a great novel it produced and how the remarkable classic work is translated into English. The huge amount of literature produced in this strand not only indirectly proves Lefevere's point but also gives a good sense of what Chinese literary translation is intimately concerned with.

The translation of Hong Lou Meng

Chinese classical literature has a long history and is profound and captivating (although it also becomes increasingly abstruse after classical Chinese was replaced by vernacular Chinese some 100 years ago). In the 2000 year-long recorded Chinese history of China, we have observed foreign literature and philosophy being introduced into China on only three occasions (the Buddhist and the Christian religious texts and the scientific, literary and philosophical translations) following Lefevere's (1998) reasoning, who also claimed that such a self-centered and homogenous culture as the Chinese one did not care too much about the Other. Therefore, as noted by Lefevere, Daoist terms were used to ease the introduction of exotic Buddhist concepts when the sutras were translated. In the same vein, when Yan Fu translated those influential books from the West to enlighten the Chinese people, he also had a particular readership in mind and freely adapted the source texts in order to suit his audience and purposes. Against this background, for hundreds of years, on the basis of friendly contacts with the external world, Chinese classical literature somehow made its way into the Western culture and seized opportunities to promote its own development: the prose of Chinese pre-Qin philosophers was brought to the West by missionaries during the tide of East to West (东学西渐) in the 17th century. In Europe thereafter, from the 18th century French Enlightenment thinker Voltaire to the Russian great writer Tolstoy, from the German philosophical revolution to German classicism, Western thought and literature were all influenced by the pre-Qin philosophers, especially Confucianism, to a greater or lesser degree. At the end of the 19th century and the beginning of the 20th century, Taoist thought was evident in the French symbolic poetry and the post-war German spirit. Among the symbolism movements in France, the Taoist philosophy inspired the symbolist poets to think that there was an inherent fit between the mind and the outside world. Exploring the use of individual symbols to express the rich connotations of poetry had a huge impact throughout the European literary world.

The narrow meaning of Chinese classical literature may refer to Chinese classical literary works. According to the research conventions of Chinese literary history, these can be divided into pre-Qin literature (先秦文学); Qin-Han literature (秦汉文学); Wei-Jin Southern and Northern dynasties literature (魏晋南北朝文学); Sui Tang and Five dynasties literature (隋唐五代文学); Song and Yuan dynasties literature (宋元文学); and Ming and Qing dynasties literature (明清文学). Representative literary works include poems, Song poetry, songs, as well as essays and novels and so on. Among them, the novels of the Ming and Qing dynasties are the most inclusive of the essence of traditional culture in terms of ideological connotation and subject matter. The unprecedented breadth and depth of these novels reflect the various aspects of social life at that time so that they become the main literary style to reveal social and recreational life in those eras. Some excellent works have been translated into more than a dozen languages, making an important contribution to global cultural exchanges.

On April 23, 2014, the British media *The Daily Telegraph* released its Ten Best Asian Novels of All Time, with *The Dream of the Red Chamber* ranked first. The title of the novel, 红楼梦 (literally 'red building dream'), was also translated into *The Story of the Stone* based on the plot of the story, but in this chapter we mainly use Pinyin to refer to this novel, that is, *Hong Lou Meng* or *Hongloumeng*. Foreign sinologists call the novel a monument to Chinese literature and the most fascinating treasure of world literature. They believe that the writer Cao Xueqin, who was comparable to Balzac, Shakespeare, Tolstoy, and Cervantes, was a genius in the world of literature. The translation history of *The Dream of the Red Chamber* in the English-speaking world dated back to 1830, when John Francis Davis published a long article entitled 'On the Chinese Poetry in The Royal Asiatic Transaction'. Zhao and Fu (2009) roughly divided the history of the translation of Hong Long Meng into four periods: the beginning period, the unfinished period, the compilation and translation period, and the full translation period.

1. The beginning period (1830–1846). Two fragmental English translations of *Hongloumeng* appeared in this period. The first one was published in the Journal of the Royal Asiatic Society in 1830. The translator, John Davis, also a member of the Royal Society, translated two poems from the third chapter of the novel allegedly written by Jia Baoyu (贾宝玉) and gave these an overall title of *Chinese Poetry*. The two poems were originally written by the author following a specific Song poetic style of Xi Jiang Yue (西江月 'West River moon'). The second fragment of *Hongloumeng* to be translated into English was the sixth chapter of the novel and the translator was Robert

Thom, the British Consul in Ningbo in 1846. This piece, with 27 pages, was published in a book Thom compiled: *The Chinese speaker or extracts from works written in the Mandarin language, as spoken in Peking* (Thom, 1846). In the same year, it was republished by the Presbyterian Church Press, entitled *Dream of the Red Chamber*, which was the first English title given to the novel.

2. The unfinished period (1868–1893). Two incomplete translations appeared. The first eight chapters of Dream of *Hongloumeng* were translated by an Englishman working as the Inspector General of Qing Dynasty (清朝海关税务司) named Edward Charles MacIntosh Bowra (1841–1874) from 1868 to 1869, and serialized in The Chinese Magazine (中国杂志) entitled *Dream of the Red Chamber*. The other was done by the British vice-Consul in Macao, Henry Bencraft Joly (1857–1898), who translated the first 56 chapters of *Hongloumeng* from 1892 to 1893, altogether in two volumes each with 378 pages and 583 pages, respectively. The first volume was published by Kelly and Walsh in Hong Kong and the second was published by Typographia Commercial in Macao.

3. The compilation and translation period (1927–1958). There are a total of three compilations. The first was translated by Wang Liangzhi (王良志), a teacher of Chinese ancient literature at New York University in 1927. The book was entitled *Dream of the Red Chamber* with 95 chapters and 600,000 words; it was published as a standalone edition. The second compilation was translated by Chi-chen Wang (王际真), a staff of the Department of Oriental Affairs at the New York Museum of Art and also a part-time faculty member of the Chinese language department at Columbia University. The first edition of the book, entitled *Dream of the Red Chamber,* with 39 chapters was issued by Doubleday, Doran and Co in 1929, and the second edition with 60 chapters was published by Routledge in 1958. The two books were translated/compiled mainly based on the love affair between Baoyu (宝玉) and Daiyu (黛玉). The third compilation, based on the German sinologist Franz Kubn's German version, was translated in 1958 by the British translators Florence McHugh and Isabel McHugh. The book, containing only one-fifth of the 120 chapters of the original novel, was entitled *The Dream of the Red Chamber*, and published as a stand-alone edition by Routledge and Kegan Paul Ltd.

4. The full translation period (1973–1986). After the founding of the People's Republic of China, the power of the nation continued to grow, and the cultural flow between China and the West gradually entered an equal and mutually beneficial period. Under this historical condition, the selected translation of *Hongloumeng* produced as a language textbook in the 19th century and the translation of excerpts produced in the 1920s only concerned with the love affairs in the novel were far from being able to meet the needs of the new generation of readers. Thus, the full translation era of *Hongloumeng* began. The first full version, entitled *A Dream of Red Mansions*, was translated by the Chinese-British translator couple Yang Hsien-yi (杨宪益) and Gladys Yang (戴乃迭), and published by Foreign Languages Press, Peking

in 1978 in three volumes. The other full version was provided by the British sinologist David Hawkes and the translator John Minford, entitled *The Story of the Stone*, which came in five volumes each with a subtitle: *The Golden Days, The Crab-Flower Club, The Warning Voice, The Debt of Tears* and *The Dreamer Wakes*. This full translation came with no notes, but had long prefaces and a variety of appendices and was first published by the British Penguin Group in 1982.

Chen and Jiang (2003) examined and analyzed nine translations shown in Table 5.2, most of which appeared in one of the above mentioned four stages, using a comprehensive diachronic description method. As the relative strengths of Chinese and Anglo-American cultures shifted over the years in different historical periods, translators' intentions and tendencies had been influenced to different degrees, which was directly reflected in the differences between the translations.

The first four translations were not in the true sense of translation. With the growing number of Westerners in China at that time, the main purpose of translation was to help those foreigners learn the Chinese language. Readers of these excerpts or fragments of translation did not really care about the integrity of the novel. The form of presentation was just partial translation adapted into many Chinese language teaching textbooks. That being said, the translation of this period had its own value of existence, that is, it served as a prelude to the English translation of *Hongloumeng*, and to use the translations as materials for foreigners to learn Chinese. The textbook that David Hawkes, one of the translators of the full translation, chose as a graduate student to study Chinese at Peking University from 1948 to 1951, for example, was *Dream of Red Mansions*.

Table 5.2 Nine versions of *Hongloumeng* translation (adapted from Chen & Jiang, 2003)

Version	Year of publication	Translator(s)	Title of translation
1	1830	John Davis	Chinese Poetry
2	1846	Robert Thom	Dream of Red Chamber
3	1868–1869	E. C. Bowra	Dream of Red Chamber
4	1892–1893	Bencraft Joly	Dream of Red Chamber
5	1927	Liangzhi Wang	Dream of the Red Chamber
6	1929–1958	Chi-chen Wang	Dream of Red Chamber
7	1958	Florence Mchugh and Isabel Mchugh	The Dream of Red Chamber
8	1973–1980 1982–1986	David Hawkes and John Minford	The Story of the Stone
9	1978–1980	Yang Hsien-yi and Gladys Yang	A Dream of Red Mansions

Around the time of the May Fourth Movement in 1919, the New Culture Movement was launched in China. The scientific and systematic methodology introduced during this period opened up a new world for the study of *Hongloumeng*. Many scholars began to realize that the great artistic charm of *Dream of Red Mansions* was comparable to that of Western novels and philosophical works. At the same time, they acquired a more comprehensive and indepth understanding of this great novel and its creative background in Chinese history. Wang Liangzhi (王良志) and Chi-chen Wang (王际真) were among such scholars. Both of their translations were carried out in the United States at a time when it became the most powerful nation in the world. During the period when Western Centralism prevailed, what attracted readers in the West for such English translations of Chinese literature was only the 'exotic ingredients' and the 'legendary plot'. Thus the American publishers required the translators to adapt and transform the novel into a simple love story. Even though the length of the translations was significantly longer than previous versions and the contents were much richer, the two translations mainly focused on the love tragedy between Baoyu and Daiyu. Also, the names of the characters in the two translations each had a unique style of English translation. In the translation of Wang Liangzhi, the names were all translated based on the semantic content of the words; for example, *Daiyu* was translated as Black Jade. Chi-chen Wang, on the other hand, translated the names of male characters with transliteration, and the female names on the basis of their extended meanings. Among these compilations, Chi-chen Wang's translation had the greatest impact and was the most popular. The view that *Dream of Red Mansions* was a love story taken by many Western readers was mainly because of Chi-chen Wang's translation. At the same time, the original artistic charm of the novel began to attract the attention of English readers.

The translation of *Hongloumeng* as a research genre itself can be traced back to Li (1993), which discussed the history of the translation of *Hongloumeng* into various languages like Russian, Mongolian, Korean, Tibetan, Thai, Vietnamese and so on, the cultural implication of the translating of Hongloumeng as 'the crystallization of Chinese traditional culture' covering all walks of life from the court culture down to the customs of the people and touching upon all corners of the feudal dynasty in China, and the translation of the rich contents of *Hongloumeng* including the book title, character names, poetry and drama, house architecture, utensils and crafts, medicine and health, apparels, garden design, etiquette, music and art, religion and philosophy, official titles and positions and so on and so forth. Li also wrote about the translation theory for *Hongloumeng* by referring to Yan Fu's *xin-da-ya* theory and the traditional concepts like 'direct translation' (直译), 'free translation' (意译), 'hard translation' (硬译), *shenxi* (神似), etc. – understandable as the importation of and enlightenment from Western translation theory was not in full swing yet at the beginning of the 1990s, and gave some personal opinions about the ideal skills and strategies for translating *Hongloumeng*.

Wang (2004) suggested that the study of the translation of *Hongloumeng* fell within the broad area of Chinese translation studies recently being constructed in China. At the same time, it could also be subsumed under the study of *Hongloumeng* or the Redology (红学), which had been established for several decades. According to Wang, the study of the translation of *Hongloumeng* should be an independent subject, but it could help with further development of both the Chinese translations studies and the Redology. In the meantime, it could also benefit from existing research results of Chinese translation studies and Redology. Wang claimed that if there were no comparative translation studies based on the world's top masterpiece *Hongloumeng,* the field of comparative literature would be 'incomplete and pale' (Wang, 2004, p. 487, my translation). Similarly, Wang thought that the field of translation studies would be 'empty and powerless' (ibid.) if there were no research on the translation of *Hongloumeng.*

Feng (2015) proposed the standardized use of the term 红楼译学 ('red mansion translation studies') to refer to the research on the translation of *Hongloumeng* itself, as well as related topics such as the study of the translation history of *Hongloumeng* or the dissemination and the influence of *Hongloumeng* translation overseas. In the face of the burgeoning research efforts and results surrounding the translation of this classic Chinese novel, Feng proposed a classification of nine research areas regarding the translation of *Hongloumeng* based on his long-term observation of relevant research activities. These are: 1. history of *Hongloumeng* translation, 2. history of *Hongloumeng* translation research, 3. contents of *Hongloumeng* translation, 4. *Hongloumeng* translation theory and strategies, 5. comparative literature or overseas *Hongloumeng* studies, 6. textual criticism, 7. controversy and debates, 8. introductory work with research, 9. other kinds of research. In the following analysis and discussion, we adopt Feng's model (excluding the ninth category) to examine the current status of *Hongloumeng* translation studies in China.

1. The study of the translation history of Hongloumeng. This line of research focuses on the organizing of diachronic translations and the excavating of early translations. For example, Dr. Fanz Kuhn's German version of Hongloumeng had been reprinted more than 20 times since its first publication in 1932 and the total number of books printed were well over 100,000 copies. Since it was an abridged version, the translator only selected important chapters and key characters' stories and cut down a lot of artistic conception, poetry, songs and ode (赋) which could only be expressed in Chinese. Overall, the number of words deleted amounted to almost half of the original book. Despite the fact, this translation had accurately reproduced the main plot of the original book with its elegant language and well-balanced abridgement techniques. This creative transformation appealed to the tastes of Western readers and won the favor of thousands of European readers. Therefore, Fanz Kuhn's translation has been continuously translated into other languages. There are currently 6 languages known: Dutch translation (1946), Finnish translation (1957), French translation (1957, 1964), English translation (1958), Italian translation (1958), and Hungarian translation (1959).

Wang (2016) used first-hand literature and combined quantitative analysis and qualitative evaluation methods to reveal the dissemination and acceptance of Fanz Kuhn's version in the German-speaking world from 1932 to 2015 in the following ways:

- Issues and collections

Wang found that the release of Kuhn's *Dream of Red Mansions* and its library collections made use of the OCLC (Online Computer Library Center) Global Joint Catalogue (Worldcat) database, and obtained 88 records of Kuhn's translations from there. After double-checking each item, he found that this version was available not only in the German major libraries but also in the state, city, university library of German-speaking countries such as Austria, Switzerland, Liechtenstein, Belgium and the Netherlands and Denmark, which were heavily influenced by German culture. Although limited by data, the information accessed cannot truthfully reflect when the libraries (how long after the version was published) and how they (through purchasing, exchanging or donating) acquired the version, the translation of the public library still to some extent explains its impact and reputation.

- Used book transaction

The collection of the OCLC special database showed the literary value, ideological significance and cultural taste of the book. The online second-hand book trading market is another reliable way to discover the spread of classic texts in the public. Most of the used books in online bookstores are personal items, which largely reflects the spread of books among ordinary readers. Wang searched for the world's largest online book market at www.booklooker.de and located 112 items of information on the translated *Hongloumeng* books. The transaction pattern of the used book was highly consistent with the above-mentioned library collections. It covered all representative versions of each period in the 64 years since the first edition of 1932–1995. Of the 112 translations, 82 are from Germany and the rest were from other German-speaking countries. In terms of translation literature, the above data showed that this version performs well in the second-hand book trading market and was widely spread in the German-speaking world.

- Professional evaluation

Professionals refers to elites who are well-educated, have a say in reading and can influence the acceptance and dissemination of works, usually including famous writers, critics, literature professors, editors, translators, etc. Wang (2016) cited about 18 famous writers and critics who highly praised Kuhn's translation from the perspective of comparative literature and literary history. For example, Hermann Hesse, author of the Nobel Prize for Literature; Ottomar Enking, the German writer and professor of literature; the Austrian sinologist, E. Votl Zach; German Nobel Prize winner, Gunther Debon; and the German writer, Erwin Laaths. They generally believed that this more complete translation was faithful to the original in details and spirit, and suitable for European readers in terms of structure and scale. They also affirmed Kuhn's contribution to popularizing Chinese classical literature overseas.

- Ordinary readers' response

In addition to professionals, the audience of literary works also includes ordinary readers. Wang believed that only by winning the broad acceptance of ordinary readers could literary translation be truly successful. He selected and analyzed 15 comments from customers of the German Amazon website, including nine for a five-star rating, three for four-star, and three for three-star. The overall evaluation was very high. Wang believed that Fanz Kuhn's translation conveyed the essence of *Hongloumeng* to European readers and achieved great success in general. Translated *Hongloumeng* accompanied generations of German sinologists by providing reading experiences when they were students and opened the door to sinology for them, which indirectly gave birth to the full German translations. The first 80 chapters translated by Dr. Rainer Schwarz were published in 2007, and the last 40 chapters translated by Martin Woesler were issued in 2009. In the meantime, the spread of this classic text in the German-speaking world also has implications for the current 'Chinese literature going out' initiative.

The original version of Kuhn's translation remains intact from the first edition of 1932 to the latest edition of 2014, which means any possible mistranslations have never been corrected. Wang (2017) identified all the mistranslations in Fanz Kuhn's translation and analyzed them one by one. These alleged mistranslations were classified into eight types: location, person, number, title, plant, medicine, cultural background and misreading. Wang considered the nature of mistranslation and found some mistakes were quite serious. For example, the name of a bird 画眉 *hua mei* ('thrush' or literally 'pain brow') was mistakenly translated into 'penciling the eyebrows'. Although the word is polysemous, the meaning was translated by Kuhn out of context. Some mistakes concerned trivial details, such as a pine being mistranslated into a cypress. Wang thought that the main reason for the errors was lack of time. The overall time Fanz Kuhn spent on translating *Hongloumeng* was only about a year. Also, at the beginning of the 20th century, China's domestic research on Redology was still in its infancy; while in Germany and even the entire western world, the study of Redology was a blank. Very few resources and references were accessible to Kuhn in 1932. In contrast, another *Hongloumeng* translator, David Hawks, was able to use the help of many Redologists by absorbing useful ideas from their works, as clearly stated in the preamble of his 1973, 1977 and 1980 translations. Fanz Kuhn had no access to such help. In general, however, there were not many mistranslations in Kuhn's translation. Considering it was an incomplete and varied translation (i.e. 变译), the overall impact of these errors on the acceptance of the translation was minimal, not least because it was difficult or impossible for readers of the German-speaking world who did not understand the original to find these flaws.

As a *Hongloumeng* translation researcher, Tang Jun (唐均) has made substantial contributions to the study of multilingual translations of the novel. Tang himself is fluent in English, French, Russian, Arabic and other foreign languages, and also masters Manchu, Sanskrit, Xixia (西夏文), Jurchen (女真文) and other minority languages, even some dying ones. His notable contributions to the research of multilingual translations and dissemination of *Hongloumeng* are summarized below.

Tang (2016) counted that there were 155 different translations in 34 languages of *Hongloumeng* in the world as of 2016. Among them, 36 full translations were distributed in 18 languages. The most translated language of *Hongloumeng* in the East was Japanese, and Japan was one of the earliest strongholds of the translation of *Hongloumeng*. There were 28 Japanese translations counted by Tang, three of which were full translations, one consisted of the first 80 chapters, and the rest were summarized or excerpted translations. The most translated language for *Hongloumeng* in the West was English, and the number of English translations published was almost the same as that of the Japanese versions, which also proved that the closest cultural exchanges with China are Britain and the United States in the west and Japan in the east. However, the language that offered the largest number of versions that collectively translated all 120 chapters of the book was Korean, amounting to a total of 21 versions, 10 of which were full translations. Other languages that offered a high percentage of fully translated books included Kazakh, Burmese, Swedish, Czech, and Esperanto. In some cases, there was only one translation which happened to be a complete translation. This may have reflected some occasional trends in the cultural exchanges between China and foreign countries (for example, government behaviors, translators' personal interests, etc.)

Tang also offered some preliminary analyses of non-mainstream language translations of *Hongloumeng* in Finnish, Swedish, Norwegian, Danish, Icelandic, Greek, Slovak, Polish, etc. For example, Tang (2011) introduced a Finnish abridged version translated by Jorma Partanen and published in 1957, which was an indirect translation from the Franz Kuhn German version, rather than directly translated from the original Chinese text. The Finnish translation had a total of 50 chapters with 672 pages, which basically contained the entire contents of the text of Franz Kuhn's translation. Tang believed that because Finnish language resembled Eastern languages in structure more than other Indo-European languages, the Finnish translation either closely followed or transcended the translation strategies of the German version and became closer to the ultimate source of the translation – the Chinese original. Tang (2012) studied the hitherto unique version of Greek translation, translated by Helly Lamplitti and published in 1963, and found the book more loosely structured than that of Chi-chen Wang's 1959 translation, from which the Greek version was indirectly derived. In terms of translation, when translating the famous name of *Dream of Red Mansions* by Greek transliteration, the translator mechanically applied the simple correspondence between the Wade–Giles System and the Greek alphabets. Thus, there had been many signs of confusion and it was difficult to show the original delicacy of the novel. In addition, a large number of typographical errors had greatly increased the reading burden for Greek readers and correspondingly weakened the acceptance of the exotic beauty of the novel.

Besides Tang Jun, there were other scholars discussing multilingual translations and distributions of *Hongloumeng*. Xia (2008) introduced the version translated by Nguyen Duc Van and Nguyen Van Huyen and published in Hanoi, Vietnam in 1963. This appeared to be a very rare translation and there were almost no relevant introductions and comments on it to be found. In the preface of the book, the famous Vietnam sinologist Peiqi gave a general introduction to the content, art and value of *Hongloumeng* and evaluated the artistic features of this novel from the aspects of characters, events and language. Another Vietnamese version of *Hongloumeng* was translated by Wu Peihuang, Yan Shou, and Yin Yindi and published in 1962 by the Cultural Publishing House (Hanoi). Today, the library of Peking University has the full translation of a total of six volumes.

Qin (2016) introduced part of the first volume of the translation of *Hongloumeng* produced by the Bulgarian sinologist Petko T. Hinov (Chinese name Han Yu 韩裴). As the first Bulgarian translation to be published and amounting to a total of 600 pages, this book added a new language to the worldwide translations of *Hongloumeng*. In the paper, Qin first introduced the context of the translator, the publisher and the base text. She believed that the 60 illustrations in this translation were an important feature which helped express the meanings that were difficult to express with words. The useful pictures helped the reader to understand the contents of the book; that is to say, the illustrations became an essential part of the translation. Qin also offered a partial analysis of the preface written by the translator. For example, the translator helped the Bulgarian readers to understand the background of the novel by referring to the symbolic meaning of the Second Bulgarian Empire. In all, however, Qin's introduction was just an overview and listed the most basic information. It did not elaborate on the translator's style, translation quality or translation techniques.

Research on multilanguage translations of *Hongloumeng* broke through the limitations imposed by previous research patterns based solely on English translations. It was especially important for the translation and dissemination of many excellent Chinese classical novels represented by *Hongloumeng* in non-mainstream world languages. In addition to various foreign language translations, *Hongloumeng* has also been translated into various Chinese ethnic minority languages. Exploring the research status of minority language translations, we can understand the interactive relationship between ethnic minority creative literature and their cultures, which was conducive to the development of the grand cause of Chinese literature. Lack of research on the translation of *Hongloumeng* into minority languages will not only make the translation studies of *Hongloumeng* incomplete but let go of a significant contribution to the overall Chinese translation studies.

Zhang (2012), for one, studied research on the translated versions of *Hongloumeng* in Chinese ethnic minority languages. She collected 20 research papers published between 1979 and 2010 focusing on partial or full translations of *Hongloumeng* into seven minority languages (Korean, Mongolian, Kazakh, Tibetan, Uighur, Sibe and Manchu) and analyzed the contents of their research. Zhang identified five research themes running through these 20 articles: translation criticism, translator studies, influence of translation, subject building (referring to Li's 1993 and 1995 advocacies for establishing translation studies as an independent discipline) and research data availability (which could be difficult for the relatively rare ethnic minority translations). Zhang found the translation criticism research mainly based on the 'faithfulness' standard in Chinese traditional translation theory and focused on the effects, gains and losses of translation. The study on translators, on the other hand, was mainly descriptive, describing the translator's life, translation process, translation thoughts and insights into *Hongloumeng*, and commenting on the translator's translation contribution. The impact study focused on the influence of translation on minority literature and the literary value of the translation, which reflected the literary exchange and cultural integration among different ethnic groups within China, according to Zhang. On the topic of building *Hongloumeng* studies as an academic discipline, there were two papers calling for the recognition of *Hongloumeng*-based translation studies and the identification of its academic status and research content. The only paper in Zhang's study that dwelled on the topic of research data referred to the Manchu translation of *Hongloumeng* accessed via the national library of Berlin, Germany, which was of great value for the study of *Hongloumeng's* translation into minority languages abroad. At the end of the paper, Zhang also commented on the inadequacies of research on minority language translations of *Hongloumeng* in four ways: insufficient research volume, lack of theoretical support, limitation of research paradigm and research methodology, and the confinement of research topics. Some of Zhang's research findings can be generalized to the study of the translation of *Hongloumeng* into foreign languages, for example, the desirability of theoretical support for *Hongloumeng* translation studies. Overall, the study of the translation of *Hongloumeng* into minority languages seems to stay at the level of phenomena description, a relatively superficial empirical kind of research without support from serious translation theory, thus lacking in depth and breadth in its current form.

2. History of Translation Studies in *Hongloumeng*. The history of *Hongloumeng* translation studies is a meta-research that analyzes research on the translation of *Hongloumeng* itself and related topics. The research objects include all the results of the *Hongloumeng*-based translation studies. We start this section by first looking at the history of *Hongloumeng* translation studies for a

specific language. Wen and Ren (2012) analyzed 782 papers on the research of English translation of *Hongloumeng* from the CNKI database published between 1979 and 2010 in China from three aspects: research periods, research themes and research angles. They regarded 1979–1999 as the initial stage of research on the English translation of *Hongloumeng*, which included only 39 papers showing a relatively slow development of the research theme. Then entered the development stage between 2000 and 2005, with an average of 24 papers published each year. Since 2006, the number of papers soared with remarkable growth, amounting to over 70 articles per year and, in 2008, the number of publications was up to 154. Since then the translation studies of *Hongloumeng* entered a period of real prosperity. Among the 782 papers Wen and Ren collected, the percentage of papers focusing on the issue of translators and versions was 15.7%, that on the issue of cultural translation was 16%, with another 17% focusing on the translation of vocabulary. Only 1% of research touched upon the publication business of *Hongloumeng* translation and the translation of couplets in the novel; while less than 1% of the sampled research investigated the translation of household utensils and character image in *Hongloumeng*. Wen and Ren also found that the study of *Hongloumeng* translations mainly concentrated in Hawks' translation (29 articles) and Yang's translation (19 articles). The number of research papers dwelling on other translations was very small. There were two pieces of research on Chi-chen Wang's translation, two on Bencraft Joly's translation, and only one introduction to Wang Liangzhi's translation. In terms of translation comparison, domestic research mainly focused on the comparative analysis of Hawks' translation and Yang's translation, and the number of papers in this area was as large as 60. As these two full translations have distinct characteristics and different styles, they enjoy a good reputation in the translation industry at home and abroad. Consequently, Chinese scholars have made substantial progress in advancing *Hongloumeng* translation studies on the basis of these two versions.

Liu (2013a) collected and analyzed 211 major journal articles on the translations of *Hongloumeng* from 1979 to 2011 in respect of research topics, research perspectives and research methods, and found that the most investigated research themes were culture (34 papers) and poetry (27 papers), accounting for 29% of the log. There were 18 articles on the translation of certain types of words, for example, color words. In addition, there were 14 papers on rhetorical themes, 11 papers on the subject of criticism, and 10 papers on metacriticism, which were all written by Hong Tao (洪涛). With the research rigor of textual criticism, Hong exonerated those translators of *Hongloumeng* from researchers' criticisms one by one, and reminded readers of the dangers of applying western concepts and theory such as ideology (Hong, 2008), skopos theory and polysystem theory (Hong, 2010), deconstruction theory (Hong, 2006) and cultural hegemony (Hong, 2011a) to *Hongloumeng* translation studies. As for research angles taken by these 211 articles, Liu found the researchers mostly approached the issues from cultural and aesthetic perspectives. Among them, the qualitative analyses based on cultural translation strategies arrived at very similar conclusions. In terms of research methods, the 211 papers mainly used qualitative methods. Only 18 out of the 211 papers, or 91%, used a quantitative research method. Liu believed that some aspects of the English translation of *Hongloumeng* have not been studied, such as the garden architecture, food, calendar and seasons, music, etiquette and customs and so on.

Ran et al. (2016) used CiteSpace as a scientometric tool to analyze articles published in China on English translation of *Hongloumeng* extracted from the CNKI database covering the period 1979–2015, and explored the status quo and the hotspots of research in the field. They used 红楼梦英译 ('English translation of *Hongloumeng*') or 红楼梦翻译 ('the translation of *Hongloumeng*') as the search phrase in the 'topic' field, removed irrelevant results and obtained 2,583 items of relevant literature. From 1979 to 2000, there were only a few research papers on the English translation of *Hongloumeng*, totaling 64 papers. Since 2000, the number of papers published each year has soared, reaching a peak of 319 in 2012, followed by a significant decline in the number of papers published in subsequent years. At the same time, Ran et al. also listed the top 50 keywords extracted from these papers: 翻译策略 ('translation strategies') appeared 221 times, 异化 ('foreignization') and 归化 ('domestication') 177 and 170 times, respectively, and *Hongloumeng* translators Hawkes and 杨宪益 ('Yang Xianyi') 102 and 100 times, respectively. As far as translated versions and translators are concerned, Yang Xianyi and Hawkes were the most frequently mentioned names. Also, Ran et al. claimed that most of the studies they looked at were based on existing Western translation theories such as skopos theory and relevance theory and, as such, were lacking in innovation. In terms of research methods, Ran et al. found that the majority of research was based on traditional contrastive linguistic analysis; while a newly emerging keyword having to do with research methodology was *corpus*. As a representative work of Chinese culture, *Hongloumeng* includes a rich amount of cultural information and, accordingly, there were many keywords related to culture in the literature Ran et al. analyzed. However, they found that research mainly focused on the study of language and culture. There were relatively few in-depth studies on the Yi Jing culture, traditional Chinese medicine culture, architectural culture and feng shui (风水) embodied in *Hongloumeng*. In the context of today's 'Chinese culture going out' movement, the keywords 世界文化交流 ('world cultural exchange'), 汉语热 ('Chinese language fever'), 美国红学 ('American Redology'), 国外读者 ('foreign readers'), 海外传播 ('overseas communication'), etc. were highly related to the topic. However, Ran et al. found only one article making the connection between *Hongloumeng* and 'Chinese culture going out'.

The second strand of research on the history of *Hongloumeng* translation studies is to explore research occurring in a particular period of time. Feng (2011), for example, collected 132 papers published in 16 academic journals from 2000 to 2010 as a corpus, and discussed the status quo of the translation of *Hongloumeng* from the following aspects: research focus, research methods and languages involved in the research. In respect of research focus, Feng found 19 articles on the translation of poetry and 19 on the translation of cultural contents; ten papers on the translation of certain types of words, such as the translation of various soups and the translation of *fengyue* (风月 'nice scenery or love affairs'); eight papers each on the translation history of *Hongloumeng* and on the translation of idioms and proverbs; six papers each on the translation of book titles and the verification of original Chinese texts, names or character titles. In terms of research methods, among the 132 papers selected, qualitative research still accounted for the majority with 123 articles or 93% of the papers accessed; while only 9 papers used a quantitative methodology. All the quantitative studies examined by Feng were claimed to be backed by specific data support to establish the objectivity of the analysis, such as the compilation of parallel corpora in Chinese and English. As regards the kinds of language used for translation, a total of 11 languages were found among the 132 papers, 106 of which were on English translations, accounting for 80%. The articles in other languages mainly involved the translation's history, the dissemination of the translation, the preface and the postscript, the cultural content of the translation, and the base text (底本) verification research. Feng believed that the problem of translating language and culture was the core research objects in *Hongloumeng* translation studies, which was also the main concern of the majority of research articles sampled. Feng thought that the breadth of the research could be further strengthened and suggested that rational increase in interdisciplinary research can produce powerful discourse power, such as from semiotics, philosophy and so on. Finally, Feng noted that research on the translation of a certain linguistic or cultural phenomenon in *Hongloumeng* had a tendency to dwell on superficial descriptions, so the depth of research also needed to be increased.

3. Translation of specific contents of *Hongloumeng*. As a classic masterpiece, *Hongloumeng* involves culture, history, politics, religion, art, food and many other aspects of China. It can be described as an encyclopedia of the people and life of the official feudal age of China. It has a very high value for appreciation and value. Wen and Ren (2012) analyzed the 782 papers they collected on the English translation of idioms in *Hongloumeng* and found the research results to be very rich and diversified. They found 59 research papers in this area, covering the main types of idioms, proverbs and sayings. On content of research, Wen and Ren found 29 articles focusing on idiom translation of Yang's *Hongloumeng* translation, and only two on Hawkes' translation. To some extent, Yang's translation seems more prominent in providing raw materials for idiom research in *Hongloumeng* translation. Meanwhile, the Chinese translation research community has made some explorations in the translation of specific words in *Hongloumeng*. The most researched words were the translations of *xiao* (笑 'laugh') and *xiaodao* (笑道 'say with chuckle'). There were three articles on the English translation of 'red' (红)

and two papers on the translation of *ban* (半 'half'), *men* (门 'door'), *chi* (痴 'silly') and *lianzu* (莲足 'lotus foot'), respectively. There are many poems in *Hongloumeng,* which is a real challenge for the translator, and the translation of poetry is another highlight in *Hongloumeng* translation studies. Wen and Ren found 16 papers on the overview of English translation of poetry in *Hongloumeng*, and 77 articles on the translation of specific poems. In terms of research topic, the papers could be divided into two kinds. On one hand, there were papers which selected several poems to investigate from different angles and, on the other hand, there were papers targeting specific poems, for example, the Chrysanthemum Poetry (菊花诗), Funeral Flowers Chant (葬花吟), All Good Things Must End (好了歌) and so on. Being a literary masterpiece, a lot of rhetorical devices can be found in *Hongloumeng* that come in many varieties. Among them, Wen and Ren found research on metaphors (25 articles), euphemisms (15) and puns (10). The contents of these papers were mainly concentrated on the translation techniques and methods of the rhetorical devices in question. Nearly 33 research papers were on name translation, mainly focusing on three aspects: person name (25 articles), book title (5) and translation of architectural names. Only seven articles touched on the study of characters in the novel. Among them, two studies focused on character image translation in general, and the rest on the case study of certain characters. Yan et al. (2017) searched the CNKI database and found 72 articles from 2005 to 2015 investigating the translation of poems in *Hongloumeng*. The papers were found to be mainly focused on investigating poetry translation in one *Hongloumeng* version or comparing poem translation between two versions from the perspectives of translation aesthetics, rhetoric, skopos theory, cultural empathy and other theories. While identifying the similarities and differences and analyzing the translation strategies adopted by translators in different cultures and their motivations, most of these papers were found to be comparative studies or independent studies from a certain perspective or theory without combining sociology, history, philosophy and other interdisciplinary views, according to Wen and Ren. Researchers tended to study the imagery in the poetry translation and conduct a comparative analysis from the perspective of culture. The research mainly consisted of subjective comparative analysis, in Wen and Ren's opinion, and did not adopt objective quantitative research methods. Moreover, Wen and Ren found that few scholars had conducted long-term and consistent research in this field.

The author of *Hongloumeng*, Cao Xueqin, was apparently an expert in Chinese historical relics. The selection and depiction of a wide variety of ancient artifacts mentioned in *Hongloumeng* were very detailed and faithful to historical objects. Today, we still can find many ancient artifacts in their physical forms. Cao Xueqin skillfully arranged various ancient artifacts at different scenes in *Hongloumeng*, whether to show off the richness of Ning Rong Er Fu (宁荣二府 'The Ning Residence and the Rong Residence') or to reveal the attributes of a certain character, or to use it in a metaphorical sense to describe people or a state of things. To accurately translate these ancient artifacts, translators need to have a wealth of knowledge in historical artifacts and the mastery of foreign language vocabulary in this field. There were currently only four articles focusing the translation of artifacts in *Hongloumeng*. Zuo (2008) discussed the translation of *ruyao da huanang* (汝窑大花囊 'potpourri container from Ru kiln'), *jian tong* (剪筒 'a wick trimmer with cup-shaped blades'), *chengyao chabei* (成窑茶杯 'small lidded cup from Cheng kiln'). Zuo (2010) explained in great detail how to translate *Tu ding ping* (土定瓶 'a graceful Ding-ware vase, white with a brownish tint'), *Xun long* (薰笼 'a bed shaped wooden furniture with openwork on its top and four sides, placed over a censer for scenting clothes'), *Layou dong foshou* (蜡油冻佛手 'precious Qintian stone, yellow and unctuous like lard fingered citron known as Buddha's-hand'). These two core journal articles by the same author approached the issue by first explaining the specific form and use of the utensils, then consulting the translations in relevant foreign museums, and finally by providing a more appropriate translation than a direct translation based on the ST. It is a pity though that the author did not provide the corresponding translation model or strategies.

Zeng and Zhu (2013) focused on the descriptions of the Qing dynasty official system repeatedly mentioned in *Hongloumeng*. Using data-driven research methodology and corpus technology as a backbone of their research, they analyzed the original *Hongloumeng* text and the translations of Hawkes and Yang, respectively. Data statistics were obtained which showed that the word 吏部 ('Ministry of Civil Service') appeared eight times in the original work, 户部 ('Ministry of Finance and Civil Affairs') three times, 礼部 ('Ministry of Rites and Education') nine times, 兵部 ('Ministry of Military Affairs') four times, 刑部 ('Ministry of Legal Affairs') 14 times and 工部 ('Ministry of Works, Measurement and Taxation') 15 times. After further comparison, Zeng and Zhu found two major problems in the translation of these six official terms between these two versions. First, the translation of the same official name was quite different. For example, in translating the word *bu* (部), Hawkes mainly used the word *Board*, while Yang used both *Ministry* and *Board*. Secondly, the English translations of the same official name were inconsistent in the same book. For instance, Yang sometimes translated *li bu* (礼部) into The Ministry of Rites and sometimes as The Board of Ceremony. Zeng and Zhu suggested that the word *bu* in *liu bu* (六部) should be unanimously translated into Ministry (and for all six ministries in question) by future translators. They argued that *bu* was the name for a state agency and, unlike ordinary vocabulary, should have a fixed translation.

4. *Hongloumeng* translation theory/strategy/skills research. This research category mainly refers to the theory and strategies summarized from the study of (single or multiple) *Hongloumeng* translations. It can also refer to the use of *Hongloumeng* translation(s) as a corpus to confirm a certain translation theory or viewpoint. Zhang (2012) distinguished five categories of theories

mentioned in the papers they extracted from the CNKI database from 1979 to 2010 on *Hongloumeng* translations of any language. They were: 1. translation theories including equivalence theory, communicative translation theory, semantic translation theory, functional translation theory, translatability theory, translation ethics, translation process and polysystem theory; 2. linguistic theories including markedness theory, conversational implicature, implicit grammar, semiotics, vague language theory, discourse and power, text linguistics, systemic functional linguistics, cognitive linguistics, register theory, relevance theory, adaptation theory, theory of theme and rheme and pragmatic discourse ideology; 3. literary theories including intertextuality, literary stylistics, acceptance aesthetics, feminism, narrative theory, postcolonialism, reader response theory and so on; 4. Philosophical theories mainly including hermeneutics, deconstructionism, phenomenology, translator's subjectivity and intersubjectivity; 5. other theories, such as communication studies and psychology. From different theoretical levels, these research papers generated new meanings, expounded the value of *Hongloumeng*, and subsequently enriched its literary content and promoted the dialogues between *Hongloumeng* and world literature, heading in an overall positive direction. But at the same time, there were some potential worries and shortcomings: the applicability and fitness of western theory and philosophy in the study of Chinese classical literature may cause a fragmentation of overall meaning of *Hongloumeng* in the process of reasoning. Excessive use of Western literary theory may also cause a certain degree of distortion in interpreting research results, Zhang suggested.

5. Comparative Literature Studies in *Hongloumeng*. The discipline of comparative literature studies is generally cross-language and transnational, and one of the texts being compared is normally based on existing translations. Redology has become a prominent school in the past century, and with the development of overseas studies via translation, it has increasingly become a cross-cultural, cross-language, cross-border world cultural phenomenon, which is in line with the characteristics of comparative literature research. By 2010, more than 100 Chinese papers have compared *Hongloumeng* with a specific piece of world literature, including *The Tale of Genji*, *One Hundred Years of Solitude*, *Pride and Prejudice*, *Wuthering Heights*, *Tess of d'Urbervilles*, *Hamlet*, *Vanity Fair*, *Living Elsewhere*, *Anna Karenina*, *Jane Eyre*, *Notre-Dame de Paris* and so on. Almost all of them are classics of world literature. These comparative studies explore the worldwide influence of the aesthetic value of *Hongloumeng* and provide a new opportunity for the novel to represent Chinese literature in the dialogues of world literature. The earliest comparative studies published in China involving was 'The review of Hongloumeng' (红楼梦评论) written by Wang Guowei (王国维) in 1904, which drew from Schopenhauer's voluntarism philosophy, proposed three paradigms of Chinese and Western tragedies for the world literature, and compared *Hongloumeng* with Goethe's *Faust*. In this way, Wang's work promoted the status of *Hongloumeng* in worldwide literary discourse (Shen 2010).

The current author queried the CNKI database for journal papers on comparative literature research involving *Hongloumeng* and found that, since the publication of *The Tale of Genji* translated by Feng Zikai (丰子恺) from 1980 to 1983, comparative research between *Hongloumeng* and *The Tale of Genji* has become a hot topic. The number and variety of comparative literature studies based on *Hongloumeng* and other literary works are shown in Table 5.3. Interestingly, the author analyzed the 57 articles collected as of April 2019 and found that the number of comparative studies was increasing but the quality was not improving too much. These Chinese papers basically adopt a single parallel research paradigm, mostly comparing people, themes, ideas, styles, structures and techniques. The comparative research was basically carried out according to very similar paradigms, that is, exploring the difference of essence, identifying the profound cultural roots, and analyzing and discussing the similarities or differences between the two novels. The translation study of *Hongloumeng* in the comparative literature strand should, in principle, follow a medio-translatology (译介学) approach *Hongloumeng*, not dwelling on the language conversion of specific words in the translation process but focusing on the creative treason (创造性叛逆) in translation. In other words, research should be diverted from pure linguistic study to literature study and cross-cultural studies.

6. Research on the versions of *Hongloumeng* Translation. Version (版本) is the basis of text (文本). Different versions always engender different texts; therefore, it is important to clarify the base version of a certain (translated) text. The study of versions has special significance for *Hongloumeng* as the novel was initially spread in the form of handwritten manuscripts. Due to the different literary accomplishments and different social experiences of the copywriters who

Table 5.3 Number and variety of comparative literature studies involving *Hongloumeng*

Contrasted title (with Hongloumeng appearing in Chinese)	Publication date	Number of articles
The Tale of Genji (红楼梦与源氏物语)	1985–2015	57
Pride and Prejudice (红楼梦和傲慢与偏见)	1986–2019	25
The Scarlet Letter (红楼梦与红字)	1992–2018	18
One Hundred Years of Solitude (红楼梦与百年孤独)	1992–2017	16
Wuthering Heights (红楼梦与呼啸山庄)	1984–2016	10
Gone with the Wind (红楼梦与飘)	1996–2016	9
Jane Eyre (红楼梦与简爱)	2001–2017	4
Tess of the d'Urbervilles (红楼梦与苔丝)	2003–2010	4
Notre-Dame de Paris (红楼梦与巴黎圣母院)	1995–2010	3
Living Elsewhere (红楼梦与生活在别处)	2004	1

reproduced and passed on the manuscript, it was very likely that the texts will be modified to varying degrees intentionally or unintentionally. For example, a later copywriter might have changed the speaker or composer of certain words or poems from A to B at a key point where the novel gave hints about plot development or characters' fates, thus misleading the reader. If we know the evolution of the version of *Hongloumeng*, we can approach the original author Cao Xueqin to the greatest extent and know his original intention.

The versions of *Hongloumeng* are very complicated. There are at least 13 kinds of versions, which are divided into two systems. One version contains only the first 80 chapters, which retains the evaluation of Zhi Yanzhai (脂砚斋), which is called Zhiping system (脂评系统) or Zhiping version (脂评本). The other is the Cheng–Gao version (程高本) which was finished by Cheng Weiyuan (程伟元) and Gao E (高鄂) as a continuation of the first eighty chapters, with all comments removed. There are multiple versions under each system, and there are differences between each version. For example, Cheng Weiyuan and Gao E printed the 120-chapter version in wooded type printing, commonly known as Cheng Jiaben (程甲本). 70 or more days after the release of Cheng Jiaben, the book was reprinted in movable type printing, called Cheng Yiben (程乙本). Illustrations in these two versions are exactly the same, but there are over 20,000 word differences in the text between the two versions. Given this diversity of versions, the translator needs to make a decision before the translation officially begins as to whether the work is based entirely on one version or on the synthesis of multiple versions. If the translator has not left a reliable description concerning this issue, it is much more difficult to clarify which version has been used. Therefore, to study the translation of *Hongloumeng*, we must first verify the base text used for translation as the first step towards an objective and fair evaluation of the outcome of translation. Wang (2007) compared several ST versions and translations in two aspects (preface and main text) and found that Bencraft Joly's translation was produced in the heyday of Wang Xilian's (王希廉) commented version, and his English translation was identical to Wang's version. Therefore, it was proven that the base text for Joly's English translation was the original Chinese version by Wang Xilian, which was in turn based on the Cheng Jiaben version. This finding provided an important reference for the in-depth study of Joly's translation. The English translations by Edward Charles Macintosh Bowra (1841–1874) of the first eight chapters of *Hongloumeng* were published in The China Magazine, an English-language journal, in the mid-19th century. The remaining copies of this periodical were very few and this was one of the rare translations of *Hongloumeng* from early on. Ren (2010) made a complete discovery of the first eight chapters of Bowra's English translations and did a literature examination and general research on that basis. By reorganizing the literature and investigation the texts from four aspects: the title of the novel, the table of contents of the first eight chapters, the body of the text and the variant texts (特殊异文), Ren concluded that

Bowra's translation was also based on Wang Xilian's commented version of *Hongloumeng*.

The fact that Hawkes synthesized multiple versions of *Hongloumeng* as its Chinese base text has become a consensus in the field of Redology, but research on which versions Hawkes adopted and why he did so is still fairly limited, and any arguments put forward so far are short of reliable evidence. Based on a careful examination of relevant literature including Hawkes (1973), and Hawkes (1989), Liu (2013b) arrived at the conclusion that Hawkes' English translation was mainly based on the third edition of *Hongloumeng* published by People's Literature Publishing House in 1964. From time to time, however, Hawks referred to nine other *Hongloumeng* versions (all limited to the first volume) or made revision of his own intuition to improve the consistency of events and time or to achieve better artistic effect. In doing so, Hawkes created a proofread version of *Hongloumeng*, or the Hawkes' Collated Edition. Therefore, Hawkes' translation has an independent text value that is not equivalent to any version of *Hongloumeng*.

7. Research debates on the Translation of *Hongloumeng*. The debates on *Hongloumeng* translation mainly occur in two forms: different views researchers take or different research results in textual criticism. The former refers to rational debates among scholars on the description and verification of issues raised in the research history of *Hongloumeng* translation, which overlaps to a large extent with the research on the translation history of *Hongloumeng*. The latter mainly refers to the discussion and debates on the historical facts revolving around *Hongloumeng* and its translations, where the excavation and discovery of new historical materials would be most convincing. The current author entered '红楼梦'into the CNKI database, retrieved 70 journal articles, manually removed research papers of a non-contentious nature, and obtained 51 relevant articles between 1965 and 2018, which either contained the word 争鸣 ('contention'), 商榷 ('deliberation') or the like in their title or showed a controversial nature in their main text. Most of the discussions center on the issues of base text and translation versions and there is quite a variety of novel topics surrounding these issues. For example, Hong (2011b) studied the problem of 'native language culture' (母语文化) in translation activities using a Chinese and English parallel corpus of *Hongloumeng* and its translation. The subject of controversy and the target for investigation was Feng Qinghua's book titled *Translator's Style in Native Language Culture* (2008). Hong analyzed the problem from two points: content and technology. In terms of content, Hong believed that Feng's native language culture only focused on English culture and had nothing to do with the Chinese translator's home culture. On the technology side, Hong found some missing parts out of the results presented in Feng's study using computer retrieval techniques, such as the neglected present of 'lisping' (咬舌音) in chapters 21, 22, 31, 32, 49 and 56. Hong also pointed out Feng's mistake in misinterpreting some statistical results. For example, Hong claimed that among the first 80 chapters of *Hongloumeng*, only the 61st chapter mentioned *fu ling shuang*

(茯苓霜). However, Feng mistakenly stated in his book that 'in the first 80 chapters, people often mentioned *fu ling* (茯苓)'.

8. Introductory study of *Hongloumeng* translation. Introductory research mainly provides relevant information, including introductions to versions and translators, historical materials related to translation of *Hongloumeng*, and other forms of cross-cultural communication such as film, television, drama, etc. Liu et al. (2011) compiled a Chinese–English parallel corpus of *Hongloumeng* consisting of 2.74 million words out of four English translations: Bencroft Joly, Reverend Bramwell Seaton Bonsall, David Hawkes and John Minford and Hsien-yi Yang and Gladys Yang. The styles of these translators were investigated from the lexical level and the sentence level. Liu et al. found that Hawkes and Minford's translation was characterized by the use of rich vocabulary, low vocabulary density, large number of sentences, and the use of more than one English sentence to translate a Chinese sentence. Accordingly, Liu et al. inferred that Hawkes' translation obviously leaned toward the narrative style and discourse strategies of English, allowing readers to read and understand easily and obtain abundant information. In Bonsall's translation, the vocabulary density was relatively low, the average word length was short, and a lot of sentences were used to interpret a Chinese sentence in the ST. It would appear that the translator consciously reduced the difficulty of the TT to make it more readable. Yang's translation demonstrated a greater variety of words, but the overall volume of vocabulary was low. Compared with the other three versions, Yang's translation was obviously shorter than the other three. In addition, Yang's translation strictly followed the Chinese sentence segmentation and its paragraph developmental patterns, so that the readers should clearly feel the text being a result of translation. The most obvious feature of Bencroft Joly's translation was that he used longer sentences. Compared with the other three versions, he more frequently combined several Chinese sentences into a complex or compound English sentence, which may have to do with the English style of the times in which he lived. That being the case, contemporary readers of Joly's work may feel a sense of distance.

Liu and Zhang (2012) found that the most commonly used Chinese–English dictionaries were mainly interpretative, meaning-based translations. Due to the lack of support from corpora with authentic language and context, word translations listed in these dictionaries provided little reference value for the translation of literary works. To demonstrate their point, Liu and Zhang located 103 cases of *chi* (吃 'eat') from the *Hongloumeng* translation of Hawkes, Yang, Bonsall and Joly, respectively. They then adopted the Chinese–English literary translation study methodology based on parallel corpora analysis of many established translations and extracted the word *chi kui* (吃亏 'suffer losses') as an example to reflect the actual usage patterns of the word in synchronic and diachronic settings. Liu and Zhang thought that the translators' common choices can help to correct the subjective judgment and empirical bias of the traditional dictionary in determining the meaning selection of entries, and provide a flexible choice between literal translation and free translation for the compilation of new Chinese–English dictionaries and meet the needs of translators and language learners with different translation purposes.

On 4th December 2014, at the Monaco International Film Festival, the international premiere of a film adaptation of the Chinese Kun Opera (昆曲) *Hongloumeng* directed by Gong Yingtian (龚应恬) won the festival's top award, the Angel Trophy Award. This was the first time a Chinese film was accorded the honor. The adaptation, selected to open the film festival, also won the Best Original Music and Best Costume Design awards. 'The Kun Opera film, A Dream of the Red Mansions, uses modern film technique to perfectly fuse the over 600-year-old Chinese Kun Opera with the Chinese classic *Hongloumeng* written 200 years ago,' said the festival's jury president, Zeudi Araya Cristaldi. On October 15, 2017, the show was also unveiled at the British Film Institute Cinema in Thames, London. The film was two hours and 40 minutes long with English subtitles. However, there is still no research on how *Hongloumeng* was adapted into plays or movies to spread abroad. Further development and in-depth study of this art form will help Chinese literature go global in many directions, not just literature in book form.

Hongloumeng *in the West*

In recent decades, Redology studies in Europe have been booming, and two Redology forums were held in 1992 and 2014, respectively. Europe organized many activities to celebrate the 300th anniversary of Cao Xueqin's birth in 2015, such as exhibitions and dance performances, and held the third Redology Forum in Germany. Ge (2007) did the statistics which indicated that there had been 15 books, more than 150 articles, and almost 30 doctoral theses published on Redology in the West as of 2007. The first Western scholar to publish an English related paper was the German missionary Karl Gutzlaf. The title of the article was 'Hung Lau Mung, or Dreams in the Red Chamber' in Chinese Repository in 1842 which gave the novel a somewhat critical evaluation. In 1919, W. Arthur Cornaby published 'The Secret of the Red Chamber' in The New China Review, which gave a positive review of *Hongloumeng* including its popularity, the length, its various sequels and the tragic ending. Cornaby also speculated on the real historical archetypes of the characters in this novel and provided a brief outline of the story. In 1952, the renowned Swedish researcher on Chinese literature, Bernhard Karlgren, published the paper 'New Excursions in Chinese Grammar'. Through detailed grammatical analysis, he found the amazing similarity in syntactic structure between the controversial last 40 chapters of *Hongloumeng* and the established first 80 chapters. In 1956, American scholar Jerome B. Grieder published the paper 'The Communist Critique of Hung Lou Meng', which introduced China's controversy over the reevaluation of the novel in the early 1950s. The first golden period of Western *Hongloumeng* studies was from the 1970s to the early 1980s. During this period, Western sinology, especially the field of

Chinese literature, began to attract more and more scholars' interest. China's reform and opening up policy has made it easier for Western scholars to obtain research materials from mainland China. At this time, there were also English journals specializing in Chinese literature, such as CLEAR (Chinese Literature: Essays, Articles, Reviews) and Tamkang Review. Both magazines published a large number of excellent papers on *Hongloumeng* in the 1980s and 1990s. In the late 1980s and 1990s, some famous journals on Asian studies such as The Harvard Journal of Asiatic Studies, Journal of Asian Studies, T'oung Pao, Late Imperial China, etc. began to publish Redology papers. In 2005, the international journal of comparative literature *Tamkang Review* released a special issue on Redology.

Ge (2007) distinguished contemporary western Redology research into nine categories: 1. Studies of the philosophical thoughts reflected in *Hongloumeng*, including Buddhist thoughts and Taoist thoughts; 2. Points for comments on *Hongloumeng*; 3. Feminist literature (or feminist literature), gender, sex and female studies; 4. Narrative structure and skills of *Hongloumeng* such as the organization of materials, the plot framework and how the author Cao Xueqin used a variety of writing skills to keep the narrative coherent and vivid; 5. Whether or not *Hongloumeng* should be treated as a purely fictional work; 6. The topic of 'love' where Western scholars put the meaning of love manifested in *Hongloumeng* into the historical background of the Ming and early Qing literature, and studied the perspective of love demonstrated in the novel; 7. Studies of the specific characters in *Hongloumeng* and comparing *Hongloumeng* with other novels in the West, East Asia or China itself, such as comparing *Hongloumeng* with *The Tale of Genji*, or the comparison between Kim Man-chung's *Jiusun Dream* (九云梦 or 'The Cloud Dream of the Nine') and *Hongloumeng*. Western researchers also compared *Hongloumeng* with *Water Margin*, *Journey to the West*, *Peach Blossom Spring*, *West Chamber*, *The History of Confucianism*, *Mirror Flower* and so on; 8. Research on the sequel and imitation works of *Hongloumeng* in the late Qing dynasty; 9. Special research topics, including how the facial features of the characters reveal their personalities, their mental states and emotions, the important role of costume description, as well as the analysis of views on aesthetics of ceramic art in Qing dynasty through the porcelain described in *Hongloumeng*. Understanding the feedback on Chinese classical literature from abroad and studying the comments of foreign sinologists will broaden our horizons and enrich and deepen our studies in classical literature. The field of Chinese translation is on a mission to translate more influential Western studies on *Hongloumeng* into Chinese to open up new horizons for Redology. In 2006, the first Chinese monograph was published as a compiled translation based on essays originally written in English by the late Professor Anthony C. Yu (余国藩) entitled 《红楼梦》、《西游记》与其他 ('*Hongloumeng, Xiyouji* and Others'). Similarly, we expect more Chinese works in Redology to be translated into English, so that Western researchers can gain an updated and fuller understanding of the Chinese results on *Hongloumeng* research and enter into constructive dialogues.

We will conclude our review and discussion of *Hongloumeng* translation by offering the following observations. First, we noted that there is a substantial number of Chinese papers using qualitative analysis to examine the English translations of *Hongloumeng*. For example, segments of translation from different English versions have been isolated for comparative analysis, targeting translation techniques used for certain kinds of literary genres or cultural phenomena. These qualitative studies were mainly based on the analysis of individual cases and were fairly subjective and easy for researchers to overgeneralize. Second, there seems a large proportion of papers of an 'appreciative' (rather than, say, critical) nature for the English translations of *Hongloumeng*. Such articles appear to have no serious theoretical basis and their aim was mainly to show the appreciation for the outstanding features and the aesthetic values of the translation. Accumulating large volumes of research in this fashion, consisting of repetitive studies residing at the same intellectual level, only increases the overall quantity and not the quality of research. Thirdly, the discussion of translation strategies and methods is relatively simple and narrow, mainly from the perspective of foreignization vs. domestication and referring to Western translation theories such as skopos theory, translator's subjectivity and relevance theory. Although the range of research topic is relatively broad, the analysis is mainly based on traditional contrastive linguistic and cultural studies, or on some minor aspects of the translations such as individuals' costumes or a specific cultural phenomenon. There are few in-depth studies on the more significant Yijing culture, architectural culture and Fengshui (风水) embodied in *Hongloumeng*, for example, and studies on prominent translators are limited to Yang Xianyi and Hawkes, lacking in research findings for other translators. Finally, from the perspective of mainstream languages in the contemporary world, the Portuguese-speaking world so far has no full translation of *Hongloumeng*, and the same goes for the Indian cultural circle including India, Pakistan, Bangladesh, Nepal, etc. This shows that the world's most populated regions outside China have no contact with China regarding such core cultural elements as *Hongloumeng* literature, which is a major weakness in China's current cultural dissemination policy. In Sub-Saharan Africa, the diplomatic relations between China and African countries have been good with frequent official and civilian interactions. However, the complete lack of *Hongloumeng* translations in these regions signals the lack of a decisive influence at the cultural level between China and the African people. There is a burning need for the core and high-end elements of Chinese culture to be introduced into Africa with the help of an excellent a piece of literature as *Hongloumeng*.

Conclusion

We started this chapter by alluding to the indecisive nature of literary translation, especially in light of the current lack of literary translation theories to guide the formulation of consensus and the concentrated development of the field. The assumption being made, we went on to explore the practical side of Chinese literary translation first by examining its socio-political conditions in recent years, then by reviewing some discussions on linguistic and cultural issues involved in translating Anglo-American literature into Chinese, and finally through some detailed introduction and analysis of the abundant literature produced by Chinese researchers surrounding the translation of the classic Chinese novel *Hongloumeng*.

By the end of the chapter, we have had some ideas as to what form or forms literary translation studies takes in the Chinese context when we put together all these impressions gained from the long discussion. The above picture we have painted for Chinese literary translation, however, was far from complete. There are other equally interesting areas of Chinese literary translation that are not mentioned in the limited scope of this book. For example, in terms of research on translating between Chinese and languages other than English, there is research on translating Japanese (Wang & Jiang, 2019), French (Liang, 2019), and Russian literature (Jin, 2019). There is also a small amount of research on literary translation theory. For example, Liu (2019) discusses the aesthetic value in English literary translation by analyzing the linguistic, artistic, structural, humanistic and tragic beauty of literary works, expounding the aesthetic value in English and American literary translation, and explaining the application of aesthetic value in such translation from the angles of image translation, emotional translation and artistic translation. Hu and Zhu (2018) also explored the connection between translation theory and Chinese ethnic minority literature from the aesthetic point of view. Fu (2019) thinks that deconstructive translation theory applies well to the translation of literary works as the theory advocates open thinking, pluralism and creativity, which coincide with the characteristics of literary language (openness, polysemy, ambiguity, implicitness and uncertainty). For Fu, deconstructionism is a key to unlocking the untranslatability issue of literary works. On the more practical side, Qian (2019) analyzes the status quo and inadequacies of Chinese literary translation and puts forward suggestions for improvement to promote the spread of Chinese literature overseas and better serve the 'One Belt One Road' initiative. Rong and Fang (2019) discuss the mingling of dialects in Chinese literary translation, suggesting that dialect and literature are the concentrated expressions of the dual characteristics of literary locality and dialect regionality, an important topic not to be ignored in the 'Chinese literature going out' movement. Ma (2019) notes that children's literature has unique linguistic features and that, when translating children's literary works, one should consider the aspects of education, imagery and interest, and translate them with the strategies of visualization, simplification and musical supplement. Liu (2019) thinks that, at present, children's picture books in China are mainly imported from abroad and the quality of their translations is uneven, there being a lack of uniform standards. Liu analyzes the current translation status of children's picture books and summarizes the principles and rules that should be followed in the translation process of children's picture books. Overall, it looks like Chinese literary translation is a fertile area that stands to be further cultivated to produce highly promising results.

References

Chinese references

Chen, Jiaming 陈嘉铭 (2018) 语境文化对英美文学翻译的影响及其翻译策略 (The influence of contextual culture on English and American literary translation and its translation strategies). 齐齐哈尔师范高等专科学校学报 (*Journal of Qiqihar Junior Teachers' College*). 164: 131–133.

Cheng, Hongwei and Jiang, Fan 陈宏薇, 江帆 (2003) 难忘的历程--《红楼梦》英译事业的描写性研究 (Tanslation of *Hongloumeng* into English – a descriptive study). 中国翻译 (*Chinese Translator Journal*). 24(5): 46–52.

Feng, Qinghua 冯庆华 (2008) 母语文化下的译者风格：《红楼梦》霍克斯闵福德英译本特色研究 (*Translators' Style as a Product of the Native Language Culture: A Survey of the English Version of Hong Lou Meng by David Hawkes and John Minford*). 上海:上海外语教育出版社 (Shanghai: Shanghai Foreign Language Education Press).

Feng, Quangong 冯全功 (2011) 新世纪《红楼》译学的发展现状及未来展望——基于国内学术期刊的数据分析 (2000–2010) (The current situation and future prospect of *Hongloumeng* translation studies in the new century: based on data analysis of domestic academic journals (2000–2010)). 红楼梦学刊 (*Studies on 'A Dream of Red Mansions'*). 2011(4): 135–153.

Feng, Quangong 冯全功 (2015) 《红楼》译学的研究领域与研究模式 (The research field and model of the translatology of Hong Lou). 红楼梦学刊 (*Studies on 'A Dream of Red Mansions'*). 2015(4): 140–161.

Fu, Qiaoyu 付巧玉 (2019) 解构主义翻译观视域下文学作品不可译性探究 (A probe into the untranslatability of literary works from the perspective of deconstructionist translation). 东北师大学报(哲学社会科学版) (*Journal of Northeast Normal University (Philosophy and Social Sciences)*. 2019(02): 55–60.

Ge, Rui 葛锐 (2007) 《英语红学研究纵览》 (An overview of the study of English Redology). 红楼梦学刊 (*Studies on 'A Dream of Red Mansions'*). 2007(3): 181–226.

Hong, Tao 洪涛 (2006) 《红楼梦》译评与期望规范、解构主义翻译观——以 Nibbansday 为中心 (The translation criticism on *Hongloumeng* and the expected norm from the perspective of deconstructivism: centering around Nibbansday). 红楼梦学刊 (*Studies on 'A Dream of Red Mansions'*). 2006(06): 238–265.

Hong, Tao 洪涛 (2008) 《翻译规范、意识形态论与《红楼梦》杨译本的评价问题——兼论《红楼梦》译评与套用西方翻译理论的风险 (On translation norm and ideology and the assessment of Yang's *Hongloumeng* translation: extending to the translation criticism of *Hongloumeng* and the risks of applying western translation theory). 红楼梦学刊 (*Studies on 'A Dream of Red Mansions'*). 2008(01): 228–259.

Hong, Tao 洪涛 (2010) 《红楼梦》翻译研究与套用"目的论"、"多元系统论"的隐患——以《红译艺坛》为论析中心 (The translation study of *Hongloumeng* and the caveats in applying skopos and polysystem theories: with analysis centering around the book 'On the Translation of Hong Lou Meng). 红楼梦学刊 (*Studies on 'A Dream of Red Mansions'*). 2010(02): 283–305.

Hong, Tao 洪涛 (2011a) 《红楼梦》译论中的孤立取义现象和"西方霸权"观念——兼谈霍译本的连贯和杂合 (The phenomenon of isolated meaning extraction in *Hongloumeng* translation criticism and the concept of western hegemony: also on the coherence and hybridity of Hawkes translation). 红楼梦学刊 (*Studies on 'A Dream of Red Mansions'*). 2011(06): 290–311.

Hong, Tao 洪涛 (2011b) 《红楼梦》双语语料库、"母语文化"影响论的各种疑点---与冯庆华先生商榷 (Bilingual corpus of A Dream of Red Mansions, various doubts about the influence theory of 'mother tongue culture' – a discussion with Mr. Feng Qinghua). 《中国文化研究》 (*Chinese Culture Research*). 2011(3): 186–194.

Hu, Yanqin and Zhu, Qi 胡燕琴, 祝琦 (2018) 民族文学翻译的美学研究 (The aesthetic study of ethnic minority literature translation). 湖南工程学院学报(社会科学版) (*Journal of Hunan Institute of Engineering (Social Science Edition)*). 2018(04): 64–67.

Ji, Xianlin 季羡林 (1998) 翻译的危机 (The crisis of translation). 语文建设 (*Language Planning*). 1998(10): 45–46.

Jin, Fang 靳芳 (2019) 俄苏文艺学派翻译思想中的文学观念 (Literary concepts in the translation thoughts of Russian and Soviet literature schools). 攀枝花学院学报 (*Journal of Panzhihua University*). 2019(01): 55–61.

Li, Shaonian 李绍年 (1993) 《红楼梦》翻译学刍议 (The dispute of Hongloumeng translation studies). 语言与翻译 (*Language and Translation*). 1993(01): 30–36.

Li, Shaonian 李绍年 (1995) 红楼梦翻译学概说 (A general remark on the translation studies of Hongloumeng). 语言与翻译 (*Language and Translation*). 1995(02): 62–71.

Liang, Haijun 梁海军 (2019) 沈宝基与法国文学翻译 (Shen Baoji and French literature translation). 三峡论坛(三峡文学·理论版) (*China Three Gorges Tribune*). 2019(02): 40–42.

Liang, Hui 梁慧 (2018) 文化差异对英美文学翻译的影响研究 (The influence of cultural differences on the translation of British and American literature). 襄阳职业技术学院学报 (*Journal of Xiang Yang Vocational and Technical College*). 17(6): 137–140.

Liu, Jingjing 刘晶晶 (2017) 翻译英美文学典故需注意的问题及策略 (Problems and strategies in translating the allusions in Anglo-American literature). 语文建设 (*Language Planning*). 2017(23): 76–76.

Liu, Yingjiao 刘迎姣 (2013a) 《红楼梦》英译研究回顾与展望 (A survey and prospect of researches on English versions of Hongloumeng). 湖南科技大学学报: 社会科学版 (*Journal of Hunan University of Science & Technology (Social Science Edition)*). 2013(3): 150–154.

Liu, Yingjiao 刘迎姣 (2013b) 《红楼梦》霍译本第一卷底本析疑 (A study of the source texts of David Hawkes's The Story of the Stone). 外语教学与研究（外国语文双月刊）(*Foreign Language Teaching and Research (bimonthly)*). 45(5): 766–775.

Liu, Yue 刘悦 (2019) 我国儿童绘本译作现状及启示 (The status quo and implication of Chinese children's picture book translation). 智库时代 (*Think Tank Era*). 2019(11): 267+269.

Liu, Zequan, Liu, Chaopeng and Zhu, Hong 刘泽权, 刘超朋, 朱虹 (2011) 《红楼梦》四个英译本的译者风格初探——基于语料库的统计与分析 (A study of the translator's style in the four English versions of A Dream of Red Mansions – based on corpus statistics and analysis). 中国翻译 (*Chinese Translator Journal*). 2011(1): 60–64.

Ma, Yetong 马叶彤 (2019) 儿童文学作品特点及翻译策略—以《爱丽丝漫游奇境》为例 (The characteristics of children's literature and its translation strategies: using Alice in Wonderland as example). 泰山学院学报 (*Journal of Taishan University*). 2019(02): 135–139.

Qian, Qingbin 钱庆斌 (2019) 一带一路背景下的中国文学翻译出版 (The publication of Chinese literary translation in the context of 'One Belt One Road'). 文学教育 (*Literature Education*) 2019(01): 142–145.

Qin, Xiaolan 秦晓岚 (2016) 《红楼梦》第一个保译本述略—以 "译者序" 为研究中心 (A Brief Introduction to the first Bulgarian translation of A Dream of Red Mansions). 曹雪芹研究 (*Studies of Caoxueqin*). 2016(4): 119–132.

Ran, Shiyang, Li, Defeng and Yang, Qin 冉诗洋, 李德凤, 杨青 (2016) 国内《红楼梦》英译研究论文知识图谱分析 (CiteSpace-based knowledge analysis of CNKI papers on English translation of Hongloumeng). 中国外语 (*Foreign Languages in China*). (13)5: 98–105.

Ren, Xiankai 任显楷 (2010) 包腊《红楼梦》前八回英译本考释 (An examination of the first eight chapters of Bowra's translation of Dream of the Red Mension). 红楼梦学刊 (*Studies on 'A Dream of Red Mansions'*) 2010(06): 10–59.

Rong, Liyu and Cui, Kai 荣立宇，崔凯 (2019) 方言·文学·翻译 (Dialect, literature, translation). 西华大学学报(哲学社会科学版) (*Journal of Xihua University (Philosophy & Social Sciences)*). 2019(02): 13–18.

Shen, Zhijun 沈治钧 (2010) 王国维红学语境述要 (A summary of linguistic context in Wang Guowei's Redology). 红楼梦学刊 (*Studies on 'A Dream of Red Mansions'*). 2010(04): 67–103.

Sun, Huijun and Zheng, Qingzhu 孙会军，郑庆珠 (2010) 新时期英美文学在中国大陆的翻译(1976–2008) (The new era of Anglo-American literature in China: 1976–2008). 解放军外国语学院学报 (*Journal of PLA University of Foreign Languages*). 33(2): 73–77+88.

Sun, Zhili 孙致礼 (2008) 新时期我国英美文学翻译水平之我见 (On the level of translation of Anglo-American literature in China's new era). 中国翻译 (*Chinese Translators Journal*). 2008(03): 47–51.

Tang, Jun 唐均 (2011) 《红楼梦》芬兰文译本述略 (A brief account of Finnish translation of A Dream of Red Mansions). 红楼梦学刊 (*Studies on 'A Dream of Red Mansions'*). 2011(4): 53–70.

Tang, Jun 唐均 (2012) 《红楼梦》希腊文译本述略 (A brief account of Greek translation of *Hongloumeng*). 明清小说研究 (*The Journal of Ming-Qing Fiction Studies*). 2012(2): 88–100.

Tang, Jun 唐均 (2016) 《红楼梦》译介世界地图 (World map of translation of A Dream of Red Mansions). 曹雪芹研究 (*Studies of Caoxueqin*). 2016(2): 31–46.

Wang, Hongyin 王宏印 (2004) 《精诚所至，金石为开——为建立"〈红楼〉译评"的宏伟目标而努力》 (To achieve the goal of Redology translation). 刘士聪主编 (in Liu, Shicong ed.) 《红楼译评--〈红楼梦〉翻译研究论文集》 (*A Collection of Essays on Hongloumeng Translation Studies*). 天津：南开大学出版社 (Tianjin: Nankai University Press), p. 486-487.

Wang, Jinbo 王金波 (2007) 乔利《红楼梦》英译本的底本考证 (Textual research on the English version of Jolly's A Dream of Red Mansions). 明清小说研究 (*The Journal of Ming-Qing Fiction Studies*). 2007(1):277–287.

Wang, Jinbo 王金波 (2016) 库恩《红楼梦》德文译本的流传与接受——以德语世界为例 (The dissemination and acceptance of Kuhn's German translation of A Dream of Red Mansions: a case study of the German world). 《红楼梦学刊》 (*Studies on 'A Dream of Red Mansions'*). 2016(2): 282–315.

Wang, Jinbo 王金波 (2017) 库恩《红楼梦》德文译本误译分析 (An analysis of the mistranslation of A Dream of Red Mansions in German). 《红楼梦学刊》 (*Studies on 'A Dream of Red Mansions'*). 2017(2): 245–271.

Wang, Mengyu and Jiang, Weiei 王梦雨，蒋莘莘 (2019) 日本文学作品中文译本翻译方式对比研究 (Contrastive analysis of translation methods in the Chinese translations of Japanese literature). 文学教育 (*Literature Education*). 2019(04): 7–9.

Wen, Jun and Ren, Yan 文军，任艳 (2012) 国内《红楼梦》英译研究回眸 (1979—2010) (*Hongloumeng*: review of English translation research in China (1979—2010)). 中国外语 (*Foreign Languages in China*). 9(1): 84–93.

Xia, Lu 夏露 (2008) 《红楼梦》在越南的传播述略 (A brief account of the spread of A Dream of Red Mansions in Vietnam). 红楼梦学刊 (*Studies on 'A Dream of Red Mansions'*). 2008(4): 46–67.

Xiong, Ying 熊英 (2017) 功能对等视角下的英美文学翻译研究 (Research on the translation of English and American literature based on the functional equivalence).

信阳农林学院学报 (*Journal of Xinyang College of Agriculture and Forestry*). 27(1): 45–51.

Yan, Li, Zhou, Li and Lei, Xiaoling 严丽, 周利, 雷晓玲 (2017) 近10年来国内关于《红楼梦》诗词翻译研究述评 (A review of domestic studies on poetry translation of A Dream of Red Mansions in recent 10 years). 重庆科技学院学报（社会科学版） (*Journal of Chongqing University of Science and Technology（Social Sciences Edition*)). 2017(12): 78–80.

Yang, Hui 杨慧 (2016) 英美文学作品中的模糊语言及其翻译策略探究 (A study of fussy language in English literary works and translation strategies). 绵阳师范学院学报 (*Journal of Mianyang Teachers College*). 35(12): 91–93.

Zeng, Guoxou and Zhu, Xiaoming 曾国秀, 朱晓敏 (2013) 《红楼梦》霍译与杨译对"六部"官制之翻译考辨 (On the translation of 'liubu' official system by Hawks and Yang in *Hongloumeng*). 明清小说研究 (*The Journal of Ming-Qing Fiction Studies*). 109: 236–248.

Zhang, Huiqin and Xu, Jun 张慧琴, 徐珺 (2014) 《红楼梦》服饰文化英译策略探索 (A study on translation strategy of dress culture in A Dream of Red Mansions). 中国翻译 (*Chinese Translator Journal*). 4: 111–115.

Zhang, Ruie 张瑞娥 (2012) 《红楼梦》中国少数民语种译本研究探析 (Reflections on previous studies of the translated versions of *Hongloumeng* in Chinese ethnic minority language). 广西民族大学学报（哲学社会科学版） (*Journal of Guangxi University for Nationalities (Philosophy and Social Science Edition*)). 34(6): 159–162.

Zhao, Changjing and Fu, Tianjun 赵长江, 付天军 (2009) 《红楼梦》英译与中国文化传递 (The English translation of Dream of the Red Chamber and the Transmission of Chinese culture). 河北学刊 (*Hebei Academic Journal*). 29(2): 199–202.

Zuo, Yaokun 左耀琨 (2008) 《红楼梦》中若干古器物的汉英翻译问题 (English translation of several old articles of daily use mentioned in A Dream of Red Mansions). 外语学刊 (*Foreign Language Research*). 2008(1): 134–136.

Zuo, Yaokun 左耀琨 (2010) 再谈《红楼梦》中古器物的汉英翻译问题 (English translation of several old articles of daily use mentioned in A Dream of Red Mansions). 中国翻译 (*Chinese Translator Journal*), 2010(3): 77–79.

Other references

France, P. and Gillespie, S. (2008) General editors' foreword. In R. Ellis (ed.) *The Oxford History of Literary Translation in English: Volume 1: To 1550*. Oxford: Oxford University Press.

Hawkes, D. (1973) An introduction. In X. Cao and E. Gao (eds) *The Story of the Stone, also known as The Dream of the Red Chamber (Vol. I The Golden Days)*, London: Penguin Classics. pp. 15–46.

Hawkes, D. (1989) The translation, the mirror and the dream. In J. Minford and S. -K. Wong (eds) *Classical, Modern and Humane: Essays in Chinese Literature*. Hong Kong: The Chinese University Press, pp. 159–179.

Lefevere, A. (1998) Chinese and western thinking on translation. In S. Bassnett and A. Lefevere (eds) *Constructing Cultures: Essays on Literary Translation*. Clevedon: Multilingual Matters.

Munday, J. (2016) *Introducing Translation Studies: Theories and Applications*, 4th edition. Oxon: Routledge.

Thom, R. (1846) *The Chinese Speaker or Extracts from Works Written in the Mandarin Language, as Spoken in Peking*. Ningpo: Presbyterian Mission Press.

6 Chinese translation

From research to teaching

In the process of researching the various aspects of Chinese translation studies, we have come across many authors extending their research results to the didactic dimension. Liu and Mu (2017), for one, concluded their three stages of historical development of Chinese translation research (i.e. summarization of experiences, formulation of hypotheses and founding of the subject) with an expectation for a good educational system for translators as an ultimate aim for the establishment of the discipline. Yan (2017) introduced the German functionalist approach and noted its pedagogical value of guiding students toward considerations beyond the linguistic level, helping students understand the role of translator, revising translation teaching models and reforming the standard and method of translation assessment. Gao (2019) not only associates Sperber and Wilson's relevance theory with translating but also extends it to pedagogical application, noting that relevance theory helps draw students' attention to the context and the communicative intention of the author, so as to achieve the purpose of translation teaching. In view of the perceived key role played by translation theory in translation teaching, many Chinese researchers have emphasized and explained the functions of translation theory in a pedagogical setting. Wang (2019), after noticing the negligence of translation theory in many translation teaching programs, suggests that the teaching of translation theory can inspire students to consciously apply the principles and methods learned in theoretical classes to actual translating and improve their skills. Wang further advises that translation theory can help elevate trainee translator's cognitive level, enhance their executive ability and improve their ability to self-correct. Sun (2018) had the same idea that translation theory had not been systematically applied to translation teaching so that the effect of instruction had been compromised. He also advised the further strengthening of research and analysis of translation theory and clarification of its critical role in teaching, thereby improving the quality and effect of translation instruction.

In this chapter, we first introduce the status quo of research in translation teaching, in particular, as that evidenced by scholarly outputs in China in the form of journal papers. Then we return to address the fundamental issue of the nature of translation competence and translation process in an attempt to reveal their relevance to translation pedagogy. We then find ourselves at the core of translation teaching where issues regarding materials, methodology and curriculum occupy a central place. Then we move on to the increasingly important topic of the use of language technology in translating and its pedagogical implications before concluding the discussion.

Research in translation teaching

We start this section with Zhang and Wen's (2017) review of English publications on translation teaching based on CiteSpace analysis of some 2,214 papers extracted from Translation Studies Bibliography (TSB) database covering the period 1975–2016 using the search words 'teaching', 'education', 'training', pedagogy' and 'didactics' (the word 'translation' is unnecessary as the database is inherently about translation). The first six higher frequency keywords they found were *teaching, curriculum, competence, professionalism, evaluation* and *theory*. Three of this set of words (*teaching, curriculum, evaluation*) are directly relevant to classroom teaching activities. The word *competence* represents a background concept opposite to the translator's *performance* and must be well researched in order to guide the formulation of a teaching hypothesis. The other two words, *professionalism* and *theory*, represent the two poles of translators' education – one in the practical direction and the other in forming translator's knowledge base about translation. Through a complicated procedure of keyword, publication, citation and author analysis, Zhang & Wen summarized three research trends on translation as a result of scientometric analyses based on 40 years of published literature in English. Firstly, they noted that the mainstream topics in foreign research on translation teaching were curriculum provision, assessment, teaching concepts and methods, translation competence, translation and language teaching, and professionalism. Secondly, with the moving of times and accelerated speed of globalization, the field of translation teaching manifested finer distinction within the discipline, further development and application of technology and an emphasis on professional translation. Thirdly, Zhang & Wen believed that human and sociological factors in translating are increasingly being emphasized. Toward the end of their analysis, Zhang and Wen made the following suggestions to the research on translation teaching in China. 1. Adopt an international perspective and follow closely the mainstream research in the West. 2. Take a humanistic approach in directing student learning and teacher training. 3. Emphasize research and survey results of translation markets and demands of society. 4. Increase the volume of Chinese researchers' publications on international journals and their numbers of citation. Jiao (2018) did exactly what Zhang and Wen (2017) recommended by introducing Venuti's 2017 edited book, *Teaching Translation: Programs, Courses, Pedagogies*, to readers in the Chinese translation field. Jiao reviewed Venuti's book from three perspectives: main contents, editing method and post-reading reflections. He thought that Chinese and Western translation teaching were heterogeneous in nature but isomorphic in structure. Thus, this academic work summarizing the research results of translation teaching in major

Western countries would help domestic scholars to understand the latest translation teaching plans, curriculum and teaching methods in the West and to promote the development of translation teaching in China. However, Jiao also noted some weaknesses, such as there being few studies about interpreting in the book, lacking the mention of Chinese translation studies and no comprehensive application of new technologies such as multimedia to translation teaching. Like Zhang and Wen, Jiao also advised Chinese researchers in translation teaching to draw from this book useful ideas for their own area of expertise and go out and exchange ideas with Western academic circles.

Translation teaching as a research genre itself can be seen as a subfield of translation studies. In this subfield, it is essential not only to explore issues like programs, curricula and teaching methodologies but perhaps more importantly, to establish connections between translation research and translation teaching and to translate findings in translation theory into teaching materials and methodologies usable in the classroom. Venuti himself pointed out the important connection between theory and practice at the pedagogical level in his edited book that Jiao (2018) introduced to the Chinese audience:

> In the current configuration, mandatory courses… focus on theory and practice, joining the study of theoretical concepts and research methods with the acquisition of practical skills in translating and interpreting.
>
> (Venuti, 2017, p. 1)

It is not a straightforward thing, however, to encode results found in translation theory research in pedagogical terms. Colina and Venuti (2017) gave a survey of translation pedagogies and conveyed a general impression that translation teaching had moved from a 'positivist' epistemology to a 'constructivist' one. In essence, this means a shift from teacher-oriented to student-oriented approaches and from an emphasis on the ST–TT correspondence to the discovery of the translator and the translation process (to which we should add the translation's purpose and the context of translating at least). Colina and Venuti then went on to introduce a number of translation teaching methods, new and old. The positivist epistemology to them represents a 'transmissionist view' of learning and teaching where knowledge is passed down from teacher to students in class through lecturing and the correction of assignments. This is perhaps the oldest existing translation teaching method, which Colina and Venuti called 'read-and-translate' method, where the emphasis is put on the text and not on the students. The constructivist epistemology then gave birth to student-centered approaches in which the teacher becomes a facilitator and created environments for the students to construct knowledge. Here, however, practices diverged according to which translation theory the practitioners followed. Because translation draws upon concepts and theories from other disciplines, according to Colina and Venuti, 'these interdisciplinary syntheses have resulted in useful approaches, but they have also displayed the fragmentation that besets the field of translation studies' (p. 208). After introducing such constructivist teaching methods as González-Davies's task-based pedagogy, Sonia Colina's 'communicative translation', Joanna Drugan and Chris Megone's argument to teach students translation ethics, and the general 'workshop' approach where literary and aesthetic recognition is the goal, Colina and Venuti concluded:

> The research that has transformed translation studies since the 1980s, approaches that have brought it closer to developments in literary and cultural studies by pursuing sociological and political orientations, has yet to make a significant contribution to teaching the practice of translation.
> (Colina & Venuti, p. 213)

Thus, one of the most important jobs to be done in future research on translation teaching would be how to harvest research findings in translation theory and how to incorporate them into pedagogical models in an informed and useful fashion. To this end, we turn to an overview of China's research on translation teaching and see what has been achieved so far in respect of the formulation of pedagogical theory and the application of Chinese translation theory to teaching. Again, we searched the CNKI database with the phrase 翻译教学 'translation teaching' in the topic area and retrieved a bibliography corpus consisting of some 12,000 journal articles published between 1979 and 2018. A scientometric analysis using CiteSpace produced a set of keywords from the literature as visualized in Figure 6.1 and listed in Table 6.1, respectively.

A tally of keywords in Table 6.1 produced the following concept groups surrounding the research theme of translation teaching:

- Programs and curricula: 'college English', 'translation major', 'MTI', etc.
- Translation theory: 'constructivism', 'Eco-translatology', etc.
- Translation practice: 'business English translation', 'translation strategy', etc.
- Teaching perspective: 'teaching model', 'teaching reform', etc.
- Translation technology: 'corpus', 'Computer-assisted translation', etc.

In respect of the above-mentioned connection between translation theory and translation teaching, it might seem that Chinese researchers have so far not dwelled too much on it, as there are only two theories brought up as keywords in Table 6.1, i.e. 'constructivism' (note how Colina and Venuti, 2017 mentioned this as a backbone of new approaches to translation teaching) and 'Eco-translatology' (an increasingly popular Chinese translation theory or paradigm). Recall that Zhang and Wen (2017) found a set of keywords out of 2,214 papers centering around the research of translation teaching in Western literature, which were: *teaching, curriculum, competence, professionalism, evaluation* and *theory*. A significant overlap is the word 'competence', which also appears as the second top keyword in our list in Table 6.1. 'Translation competence' is a cognitive and psycholinguistic term that has strong theoretical and pedagogical implications

Chinese translation 199

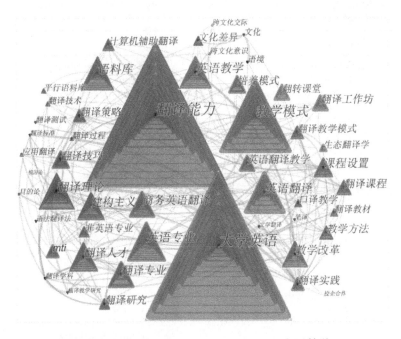

Figure 6.1 Keywords from scientometric analysis of 翻译教学 'translation teaching' literature in visualization form (see this image in color at www.routledge.com/9780367209872).

which we will investigate in some detail in the next section. The fact that 'college English' appears as the top keyword in the Chinese context is due to the fact that translation is traditionally an indispensable module for foreign language students in Chinese universities. Many translation tutors and researchers teach in translation modules that belong to a foreign language (notably English) program. They therefore publish papers on translation teaching in the context of university English teaching; hence the highest frequency keyword in Table 6.1, signifying an intersection between translation and English language teaching at the program level. Another interesting research strand that can be gathered from keywords in Table 6.1 and Figure 6.1 is the connection between translation teaching and language technology, illustrated by such keywords as 'corpus', 'parallel corpus' and 'computer-assisted translation'. This shows Chinese researchers in translation studies and pedagogy are probably very aware of the advancement of computer technology and its implication to a translator's education. We will then include a section on the implication of language technology for translation teaching in the following discussions after a proper look at the curricular and pedagogical matters, which are represented by keywords like 'teaching model', 'teaching reform', 'translation curriculum' and so on in Table 6.1.

Table 6.1 A list of top 50 keywords from scientometric analysis of 翻译教学 'translation teaching' literature

Frequency	Keyword	Frequency	Keyword
712	大学英语 (college English)	119	翻译技巧 (translation techniques)
701	翻译能力 (translation competence)	118	人才培养 (talent training)
380	教学 (teaching)	117	现状 (a status quo)
364	教学模式 (teaching model)	110	教学方法 (teaching method)
229	问题 (problem)	107	培养模式 (cultivating model)
228	英语翻译 (English translation)	105	翻译研究 (translation studies)
227	翻译理论 (translation theory)	99	翻译课程 (translation curriculum)
212	对策 (countermeasures)	97	翻译策略 (translation strategy)
209	英语专业 (English specialty)	96	英语翻译教学 (English translation teaching)
205	英语教学 (English teaching)	95	翻译工作坊 (translation workshop)
187	语料库 (corpus)	91	大学英语翻译教学 (college English translation teaching)
183	大学英语教学 (college English teaching)	86	高职 (vocational college)
165	翻译人才 (translation talents)	84	计算机辅助翻译 (Computer-assisted translation)
161	建构主义 (constructivism)	82	翻转课堂 (flipped classroom)
153	教学改革 (teaching reform)	82	MTI (Master of Translation and Interpreting)
152	翻译专业 (translation major)	80	翻译教学模式 (translation teaching model)
151	商务英语翻译 (business English translation)	74	文化差异 (cultural differences)
150	商务英语 (Business English)	72	口译教学 (interpretation teaching)
137	课程设置 (curriculum provisions)	71	外语教学 (foreign language teaching)
136	英语 (English)	70	非英语专业 (non-English majors)
132	应用 (applied)	63	教学翻译 (translating teaching)
127	改革 (reform)	61	翻译教材 (translation textbook)
124	策略 (strategy)	61	翻译学 (translatology)
122	翻译实践 (translation practice)	54	高职院校 (higher vocational college)
120	培养 (cultivate)	53	生态翻译学 (eco-translatology)

Translation competence

The term 'translation competence' surfaces as the second prominent keyword from some 12,000 papers published between 1979 and 2018 on China's translation or foreign language journals. Contents of research and discussion surrounding this topic include what constitutes translation competence, how these ingredients interact with one another, how they are supposed to work together to finish the job and how instruction can help develop students' translation competence. In terms of the first question, i.e. what constitutes translation competence, the Spanish team PACTE (Process in the Acquisition of Translation and Evaluation Competence) is highly recognized in the field, and many Chinese authors publishing in this area refer to their work, for example, Tong (2010), Li (2011), Tan (2016), Hu and Wang (2018), Yu (2018) and so on. Among them, Tong seemed to give the most comprehensive and useful review. He first distinguished between the early PACTE translation competence model put forth in 1998 consisting of six kinds of competence:

- Communicative competence in the two languages
- Extra-linguistic competence
- Transference competence
- Psycho-physiological competence
- Professional instrumental competence
- Strategic competence

and the later revised model consisting of five subcompetences (bilingual, extra-linguistic, strategic, instrumental, and knowledge about translation) with strategic subcompetence at the center and a psycho-physiological component outside the five subcompetences. As regarding the acquisition of this translation competence, Tong reported that the process was thought to be dynamic and spiral, moving the learning from novice to expert through the use of learning strategies and interaction between different subcompetences. Tong noted that there were also some problems in PACTE's translation competence research. Firstly, it is questionable whether the sub-competences included in the PACTE model were sufficient to cover all aspects of translation ability. Secondly, studies through the think aloud protocols (TAPs) and questionnaire method mainly covered the horizontal and synchronic factors, at the expense of the vertical, developmental aspect. Thirdly, PACTE's division of the development stage of translation competence was too simple. The theoretical hypothesis distinguished only the novice phase and the expert phase, and there were no detailed divisions between the transition phase from the novice to the expert. Nevertheless, Tong thought that, although there were certain problems in the PACTE model, it was undoubtedly the most complicated and comprehensive translation competence model to date, which had profound enlightenment value for Chinese translation studies, mainly in respect of how to cultivate and improve translators' translation skills, and how to evaluate such skills. Yang and Wang (2010) further proposed to divide the five subcompetences of the PACTE model into three groups: 1. basic competence (bilingual and extra-linguistic subcompetences), 2. core competence (knowledge about translation and strategic subcompetence) and 3. peripheral competence (instrumental subcompetence). They thought that by doing so, researchers can decide which level of competence to focus on at different stages, for example, working from the basic to the core competence. Other Chinese authors also introduced additional translation competence models from the West. For example, Fu (2015) investigated Albrecht Neubert's model of translation competence comprising language, subject, cultural, textual and transfer competence and collating it with Wang's (2013) and Wen's (2005) model. Fu emphasized that translation competence was one of the main factors that determined the quality of translation. People's understanding of translation skills changes with the times. Faced with the new normal of translation today, the understanding of translation competence has changed greatly in many aspects compared with the traditional concept. The translation competence under the new translation norms has many characteristics. Understanding these new characteristics and adjusting the corresponding translation teaching strategies is crucial for the development of translation talents.

There are Chinese researchers who independently worked out models of translation competence outside of the established PACTE model or other Western models. Qian (2012) for example, created a translation competence model consisting of five primary components and 28 secondary components including the 'driving relations' (驱动关系) among the five key components. The five main components were: internal driving force (内驱动力), knowledge (知识能力), cognitive ability (认知能力), linguistic competence (语言能力) and operational competence (操作能力). Each of the five main components broke down into 4–8 secondary components. For example, the 'internal driving force' was defined by Qian to include responsibility, passion, psychological quality, curiosity and confidence; the knowledge component includes culture, social knowledge, time knowledge and aesthetics; operation competence breaks down into subcompetences of countermeasures, planning, skills, resource use, processing and refining. As for the 'driving relations' between these components of translation competence, Qian advised that the internal driving force positively influenced all the other components, and the operational competence, at the final receiving end of all the other forces, were positively influenced by the other four components. Qian (2011) modified her 2012 model slightly, now using Charmaz's (2006) 'grounded theory' (扎根理论) as the theoretical foundation for her model and calling it the 'Translation competence system pyramid model' (翻译能力体系金字塔模型). Qian's 2011 revised model now consisted only of four components (from the bottom of the 'pyramid' to the top): internal driving force, cognitive ability, linguistic competence and operational skill – the 'knowledge' component previously included in the 2012 model was now gone. Qian explained that translation competence was composed of the internal driving force, cognitive ability, language competence and operational competence. Among them, internal drive was the translator's internal factors such as psychology, physiology and knowledge. It was the fundamental competence and had a positive influence on the other components. Cognitive ability was the translator's ability to recognize and grasp the characteristics and laws of translation activities, and had a positive influence on linguistic competence and operational competence. Linguistic competence was the translator's ability to master and use language, which positively affected operational competence. Operational competence was the ability to perform language conversion in an efficient manner and was positively affected by the other three translation capabilities.

Hu and Wang (2018) proposed a metacognitive model for translation competence from a problem-solving perspective. In their model, the 'translation metacompetence' (翻译元能力) controls and coordinates between three subcompetences of translation competence to solve translation problems: orienting subcompetence (导向能力), analyzing subcompetence (分析能力) and evaluating subcompetence (评估能力). According to Hu and Wang, translation metacompetence is the manifestation of translation competence under the control of metacognition during the dynamic process of translation problem solving. Translation metacompetence is a fundamental ability working at a deep level in the cognitive process of translation activities. Under the regulation of translation metacognition and a series of guidance, planning, monitoring and evaluation processes, problems are identified, analyzed and solved based on bilingual abilities. Meanwhile, the metacompetence module effectively incubates, develops and coordinates other translation capabilities, plans the entire translation process, and optimizes the allocation of translation capabilities according to the needs for solving translation problems. Also included in the metacognitive model are, orienting subcompetence, which means a translator's ability to enter a controlled processing program to build problem space; analyzing subcompetence, the ability of the translator to propose various options through multi-planning and real-time monitoring to solve translation problems; and evaluating subcompetence, the translator's ability to evaluate the alternatives from multiple angles and make the final decision. Hu and Wang divided the translation problem-solving process into three stages: the problem-identification phase, the problem-analysis phase, and the problem-solving phase. In the process of translation problem solving, after the translation metacompetence is activated, each subcompetence will mobilize other translation subcompetences as needed to complete the translation task. No matter which translation subcompetence is mobilized, it is realized under the command and control of translation metacompetence. Translation metacompetence is the core of translation competence. In a different work, Feng (2010) also proposed a cognitive model for translation competence comprising a 'translational schemata' module and a 'cognitive mechanism' module with the latter regulating the former. There were eight translation schemata in Feng's model, the contents of which seemed obvious from their names.

- Culture translation scheme
- Language translation scheme
- Text translation scheme
- Style translation scheme

- Aesthetics translation scheme
- Topic translation scheme
- Tool translation scheme
- Profession translation scheme

The 'cognitive mechanism' in Feng's model is a function of the brain and an organic system composed of a series of cognitive components. It performs its function under the coordination of thinking, including the identification and acquisition of information, and the processing and storage of information. The cognitive mechanism is innate, but it can also be cultivated and developed. According to Feng, in the process of translation, various cognitive components perform their own functions and interactions, and jointly complete highly complex translation tasks. The translator's strategic application ability runs through the entire translation process and plays a dominant role. Overall, Feng's model says that translation schemata can refer to both concrete internalized knowledge and the abstract ability to manipulate knowledge. Both layers of meaning are closely related to translation competence, and both perform their functions under the control of the cognitive mechanism. The translator's accumulation and storage of knowledge constitutes the most important and direct source of translation schemata. The more abundant the knowledge reserve, the easier it is to form high-quality translation schemata, so that the problems in the translation process can be more effectively solved under the control of the cognitive mechanism.

In addition to the cognitive approach, Chinese researchers also explored the issue of translation competence from the sociological perspective. Notably, Yu (2018) investigated the issues of constitution, development and assessment of translation competence using Pierre Bourdieu's field theory. Yu thought that the goal of translation competence research was to examine the translator's ability to perform in translation activities, and translation competence was the core *cultural capital* in the translation field (the other two capitals were social capital and economic capital). The translator uses his capital/capabilities to participate in the competition of the translation field, weighs the field status and capital of himself and others, internalizes the field specification, and makes translation decisions to maintain his position and even obtain a better position. Translation competence is the translator's most important ability, that is, 'field competitiveness'. Yu suggested the cultivation of this ability could be done in the following ways:

- Simulating translation field competition activities to cultivate students' field competition awareness.
- Analyze the translation field to help students understand the field rules, field structure and field capital composition.
- Provide various ways to help students complete the initial capital accumulation and production required to enter the translation field.
- Help students master the rules and methods of capital conversion and borrowing.
- Provide internships and practical opportunities to consolidate students' field competitiveness.

These methods can effectively help students to have initial field competitiveness when they leave the ivory tower and enter the arena of the translation market by quickly adapting to the rules of the translation field and actively responding to field competition.

Other Chinese researchers also suggested models for developing translation competence leading to its application in the field work. Liu (2011) argued that a teaching model with the development of translation competence at its core was an effective model for cultivating professional translators needed by the market. However, the development of translation competence should be staged, and it is necessary to select teaching methods and content according to different teaching tasks at different stages. In this way, the final stage of automation of translation skills can be reached as the trainee translator enters the professional translation industry. More specifically, Liu proposed a set of five teaching methods as key pedagogical means and paths for translation talents training aimed at developing their translation competence:

- Introspective teaching (自省式教学): training students' self-evaluation of translation competence.
- Interactive teaching (互动式教学): student-centered approach.
- Simulated teaching (模拟式教学): teaching in the form of workshops.
- Practical teaching (实战式教学): taking the 'project' as the leading activity.
- Team-based teaching (团队式教学): based on interaction between students in teams.

Li (2011) proposed an integrated model of translation competence and translation teaching built on the idea of a 'dynamic view of translation competence' and the concept of 'literacy development' as the ultimate aim for translator education. Li's model consisted of three layers or stages: translator quality (译者素质), translator competence (译者能力) and translator's literacy development (译者素养). Translator quality refers to the subjective conditions of the translator's physical, psychological and linguistic activities necessary for translation activities. It is mainly composed of declarative knowledge and procedural knowledge expressed in the form of statements. It is the premise and basis for the formation and development of the translator's ability. Translator competence is the externalization of the translator's quality, which is mainly reflected in the translator's application of knowledge to solve the thinking and behavioral process of translation problems. It is also a process in which the translator transforms static knowledge into dynamic knowledge, and the translator gradually forms the translation ideology. It is also a process of accumulating translation experiences. Translator's ability is a dynamic structure, not a static structure. It has a direct relationship with the translation process. The translator's ability with the core of thinking should be the core issue of translation teaching. Translator's literacy is the result of the comprehensive development of translator's quality and translator's ability. It is mainly reflected in the translator's autonomy, flexibility and creativity in constructing translation according to the translation context and purpose. It is the main ability of the translator to form expert ability and sustainable development ability. According to Li, translator literacy refers to the translator's creative awareness and practice in solving translation problems and generating translation products in specific social and cultural contexts, including learners' language literacy, knowledge literacy, strategic literacy, digital literacy, critical literacy and social literacy. Li notes that the translator's literacy education is a complicated systematic project. It not only needs the transformation of translation education concept, but also requires the support of a series of environmental factors. It draws from the basic principles of learning science followed by an in-depth and meticulous discussion on its application. In view of the practical level of translation teaching, Li advised that empirical research be carried out from the perspectives of theoretical foundation, goal orientation, realization conditions, operational procedures, and effect evaluation, in order to generate a result that can be used for further reference, and then positively promote the cultivation of translation talents. Li thought that the translator's literacy development model described above echoed the National Medium- and Long-Term Programme for Education Reform and Development (国家中长期教育改革和发展规划纲要) officially released in 2010 in four ways:

- Focusing on cultivating learners' ability to adapt to the development of the times alongside personal development.
- Emphasizing the subjectivity of learners and turning learning into a process of continuous generation and development of human autonomy, initiative, and independence.
- Advocating inquiry-based learning, cultivating learners' problem consciousness, critical consciousness and innovation consciousness.
- Building a multi-learning environment and cultivating learners' social ability and compatibility.

Our discussion on translation competence is well concluded with Wu's work which referred back to the PACTE model and pondered such questions as: what kind of local translators are required to complete the mission of introducing Chinese culture abroad? What kind of translation competence is in question? and how do we improve the quality of education for Chinese to foreign language translation? Wu studied the PACTE model and other Western works on translation competence, such as Campbell (1998) and Pym (2003), and concluded that they were all multi-component models with multiple modules. Wu noted several problems in the fostering of translation talents under the Chinese culture 'going out' initiative in China, including: 1. the lack of authoritative mechanisms for the selection of translation talents, 2. lack of awareness of the translation industry and translation norms, 3. lack of translation talents in professional fields, insufficient training of humanities and literal qualities (This echoes Li's (2011) literacy development educational needs discussed above), 4. ignorance of the use and training of translation tools, and 5. less consideration given to the cultural psychology and reading experience of Western readers when selecting and developing translation strategies. In response to these alleged problems, Wu proposed six countermeasures in translator training to address the perceived problems: 1. developing standards and specifications for the translation industry and introducing market access mechanisms, 2. setting up a diversified and systematic translation program system, 3. strengthening bonds with advanced-level translators overseas, 4. understanding all aspects of translation and adjusting translation strategies, 5. establishing a sound assessment and evaluation system and finally, 6. gathering and guiding civil society and overseas resources. By implementing the above translation teaching policies, Wu believed that China could bring together academic forces from the private, higher education institutions and the translation industry to grasp development opportunities, meet the needs of the market, form a global vision, and demonstrate a truly diversified Chinese culture overseas.

Thus, we saw how Chinese researchers have been actively engaged in the discussion of translation competence, exploring its nature, components, practical concerns and pedagogical implications. As we continue to explore the Chinese discourses on translation curriculum and teaching, we will find a lot of academic works and thinking firmly grounded in a fundamental theory about the nature and functions of translation competence.

Translation curriculum and pedagogy

Research in translation curriculum and pedagogy is intimately connected to research in translation competence. This can be seen in many publications linking between the two stands in the research of translation teaching. Likewise, in the following review and discussion, we can see some authors referring back to the findings of translation competence research while dwelling on translation curriculum and pedagogy. Chai (2015) offered a quite unique perspective from which to look at translation competence to derive corresponding teaching methods. Targeting China's translation programs at both the MTI (Master of Translation and Interpreting) and BTI (Bachelor of Translation and Interpreting) level and citing no particular references, Chai claimed that a professional translator's overall competence can be characterized by the following seven traits: complexity (叠加复合性), heterogeneity (多样性), approximation (近似性), open-endedness (终端开放性), creativity (创新性), situationality (场合性) and historicity (历史性) as a result of speculating on internationally recognized translation competence models (Chai, 2015, p. 6). By 'complexity' Chai meant the translator needed to possess a highly complicated system of skills, each of which was made up of multiple subskills. Chai put forth six sets of complex skills:

- Skill complex: The translator's skills are multifaceted, including language skills, professional knowledge and translation skills.
- Expertise complex: Translators are constantly providing translation services for different areas of expertise.
- Knowledge complex: In order to be competent in translation work in various professional fields, the knowledge that translators need to master requires a certain degree of overlap and compounding.

- Cultural complex: Translators must face a complex combination of cultures in their work.
- Context complex: Translators are always faced with ever-changing contexts and need to have the processing power of different texts in different contexts.
- Target complex: The target of translation services is people, from different backgrounds. Translators must realize the composite characteristics of the service objects and adopt effective coordination and communication strategies to successfully complete the translation tasks.

Chai advised that all aspects of translation competence detailed above should be implemented throughout the training and practicing processes of professional translators' education. Another property Chai associated with translation competence was the 'heterogeneity' aspect of expected translator ability. Translating itself as a social act is characterized by diversity. Professional translators must recognize the diversified nature of the industries they work in, and they must also have the characteristics of diversity. It is not possible for a translator to engage in only one kind of translation, and translations in different professional fields have different characteristics. There are various translation activities and translation methods for different texts and different contexts. The next property Chai associated with translation competence was 'approximation', which seemed motivated by a pedagogical concern rather than a research interest (in the true nature of translation competence). Chai first pointed out that 'approximation' was the goal that the translator strived to achieve in translation practice. It was also the translator's rational understanding of the actual translation effect that could realistically be achieved. Chai criticized that such consciousness was common among professional translators but, in actual teaching, many teachers who had no practical experience in translation were constantly pursuing the 'standard answer' of a translation problem (i.e. a perfect TT). Chai suggested that such classroom teaching and homework correction methods not only misled students' understanding of translation, but also failed to provide real and effective help for students' problems in the translation process. The 'open-endedness' property associated with translation competence in Chai's scheme referred to the fact that in the actual process of translating, much of the work was not carried out in the translation process itself, but in preparation or follow-up work beyond translation. Therefore, the translator must have the ability to prepare and finalize the translation by literature research, liaising with commissioners, editing and proofreading and so on. The 'creativity' feature of translation competence referred to the translator's ability to adjust to the change of the times and the invention of new media and vocabulary. As new industry sectors continued to emerge, new discourse systems also emerge, and many expressions demand new translation strategies once they are used in newly created domains. 'Situationality' referred to the translator's ability to properly control and adjust discourse and texts in different contexts. Finally, by 'historicity' Chai meant the translator's ability to follow the norms established in history and adopt the conventional expressions or fixed terms used in translation. In addition to the above-mentioned seven properties integrated in translation competence as suggested by Chai (2015), the same author also regarded the more conventional subcompetences such as *linguistic* competence, *textual* competence, *subject* competence, *cultural* competence and *transfer* competence as 'related competences' that impose restrictions on the translator's translation behavior and results. He advised that in the process of professional translation training, it was necessary to set up a translation-oriented course to train students' ability to transform at different levels of language. As a skill base for translation training of different topics, texts and occasions, students would be required to practice repeatedly to achieve proficiency.

From the perspective of the curriculum, Chinese researchers have studied the national standards for translation programs and considered how they should be translated into a curriculum and pedagogy of translation classes. Zhong and Zhao (2015), for example, explained that the National Standards of Teaching Quality for Undergraduate Translation Majors (翻译本科专业教学质量国家标准) was designed on the basis of 'a center' (一个中心) and 'four persistence' (四个坚持). The one center referred to taking the 'people-oriented' concept as the central idea, promoting the all-round development of people and adapting to the needs of society as the fundamental criterion for measuring the quality of education. The 'four persistence', on the other hand, embodied the following thoughts: adhering to the scientific quality requirement and highlighting the professional training objectives, adhering to the normalization of standards and conforming to the 'three in one' (quality, knowledge, capacity) training protocol; adhering to the subjectivity of teachers and students and building a three-module curriculum system (linguistic, translational and related competence); and adhering to the unification of principality and heterogeneity, as well as adapting to the needs of diversified talent development models. At the program level, researchers have also given useful analyses of current and prospective translation programs in China. Mu (2008), for example, advocated building a 'complete translation educational system' for China. He insisted that in order for the discipline to develop in a steady and healthy fashion, translation teaching must first have a comprehensive vision of the structure of the teaching system, accurately position translation teaching at all levels, make it as close as possible to the international translation teaching system, and then formulate and implement their respective cultivated goals and teaching plans so that the talents we train meet international standards and are recognized by international peers. Mu offered a then current translation program structure in China which included a PhD (and an MA) in Translation Studies and Interpreting, up to nine MTI (Master of Translation and Interpreting) programs in literary, legal, business, media, computer-aided, science and technology translation/interpreting and so on, and one BA in Translation. Mu also called for the strict regulation and standardization of the many (graduate) Certificates in Translation and Interpreting programs existing in the private translator training organizations. Wang (2018) examined the curricula of 31 colleges and universities with BTI (Bachelor of Translation and Interpreting) programs in China according to five competence modules: *linguistic* knowledge and competence, *translation* knowledge and competence, (translation-related) *general* knowledge and competence, *vocational* knowledge and competence and *professional* knowledge and competence. Through an SPSS 19.0 data analysis and a Kruskal-Walllis H test, Wang hoped to find out the rules and characteristics of the current undergraduate curriculum setting for a translation major in China, and provide references and suggestions for the curricular research on the development of a translator's competence. The results showed that all institutions studied focused mostly on the linguistic knowledge and competence module, followed by the translation knowledge and competency module. Most institutions did not have courses related to vocational knowledge and competency modules or did not allocate teaching hours. Moreover, the professional knowledge and ability modules have hardly attracted the attention of colleges and universities. Wang recommended that undergraduate translation programs should pay more attention to practical teaching modules and provide more practical opportunities for students, add computer-assisted translation courses and emphasize the cultivation of vocational and professional knowledge and competence. In addition, Wang thought that Chinese universities could draw on the 'pre-service education' model from foreign countries at undergraduate level and advocate multi-lingual teaching, and at the same time focus on cultivating students' ability in 'terminology', 'technical competency', 'document research' and 'professional writing'. Finally, Wang would like to see in translation curriculum design the strengthening of students' general literacy skills, critical thinking abilities and information retrieval skills, as these were very important in cultivating students to become qualified translation professionals.

Beyond the macro levels of translation program and curriculum, Chinese researchers have also been studying what actually happened or should happen in the translation classroom, that is, issues regarding teaching models, methods, materials, strategies and so on. Liu (2013) discussed the theory and application of translation teaching models. He thought that a pedagogical model should consist of five elements: theoretical basis, teaching objectives, operating procedures, implementation conditions and teaching evaluation. In particular, Liu believed that teaching objectives were at the core of the structure and imposed restrictions on other components that constituted the teaching model. He quoted from Translation Master's Degree Admission Test National Joint Test Guide (翻译硕士专业学位入学考试全国联考指南) compiled by China National Committee for Translation & Interpreting Education which said that the MTI programs should aim to cultivate high-level, applied and professional translators who are capable of meeting the needs of the country's social, economic, cultural and social construction needs to adapt to the global economic integration and the need to improve the country's international competitiveness. Most importantly, for Liu, translation teaching models and methods must be based on translation theory and related theories, embody the rules and characteristics of the profession, reflect the development of rules and requirements of translation ability, place students at the center, take 'practice' as the starting point and focus on tasks and achievements. Ma (2015) classified MTI teaching materials used by translation courses in China into three categories. Firstly, there were the teaching materials purely used for foreign language instruction. Then there were dedicated translation teaching materials used in foreign language programs. A third type were teaching materials used in translation programs, which was the focus of Ma's paper. According to Ma, the MTI teaching materials at the time of her writing were plagued with a host of problems. Quoting another author, Ma pointed out that most translation teachers shared the traits of subjectiveness, randomness and blindness when selecting textbooks. Ma thought this could be attributed to three factors. First, teachers paid scant attention to textbook selection. Second, teachers lacked scientific understanding of the process of textbook selection. And finally, Ma accused some teachers of forcing students to purchase the textbooks they had written for class use, regardless of the syllabus requirements or the degree of acceptance and learning outcome of the students. There were even 'teaching materials for personal relationship and favor' (人情教材) running rampant on university campuses, according to Ma. In addition to the above-mentioned phenomena, Ma mentioned some intrinsic problems in MTI materials selection in China: 1. Existing textbooks did not exactly match the expected needs. 2. There was a shortage of teaching materials to choose from. 3. The comprehensive evaluation and highlights of textbooks were not easy to reconcile (i.e. some texts had overall good rating but were mediocre in quality; some were rated low overall but had good highlights). 4. Those responsible for choosing materials lack discriminative ability. Ma insisted that the selection of textbooks is not a unilateral issue from the teacher's perspective, but an interactive process. She thought that the textbook selectors (practicing teachers and the readers) did not only have a relationship with the textbook; they were also closely related to the editors and publishers. The latter provided guidance and training to the former, while the former provided feedback to the latter for further improvement of the teaching materials, forming a virtuous cycle. Ma also proposed some guiding principles for selecting MTI materials:

- Textbook attributes match the needs of the selector.
- The difficulty of the textbook is consistent with the level of the user.
- Comprehensive analysis well balanced with highlights of the textbook.
- Practicality integrated with trend of time.
- Combination of theory and practice.
- Phased selection at different stages of teaching goal.
- Combination of paper textbooks and electronic textbooks.

Although dedicated Translation and Interpreting programs are now prevalent in China since the first establishment of BTI programs in three universities (Guangdong University of Foreign Studies, Fudan University and Hebei Normal University) in 2006, translation courses affiliated to BA programs as a means of learning foreign languages are still a mainstream practice in the Chinese regions. Li (2007) discussed the then current situation of translation teaching to non-English majors in China by analyzing different versions of the College English Teaching Syllabus. He found several problems inherent in the translation modules of college English teaching. First of all, the setting of the translation course in

English programs created an awkward situation. Since translation was an elective module available to all undergraduate students, classes were often large (often consisting of 200–300 students, according to Li) and it was extremely difficult to achieve teaching goals and teaching quality. Students were at uneven levels of language proficiency and poorly motivated, many only wanting to get the credits. Moreover, Li noted that the college English syllabus only imposed certain requirements on the ability of students to translate, and did not offer a holistic teaching plan. In addition, college English translation teaching was still stuck in the traditional teaching mode. The model was teacher-centered and knowledge transfer was unidirectional from the teacher to the students. Although there were many official textbooks for college English, a nationally recognized translation textbook was almost non-existent. In response to the predicament the teaching of translation was caught in, Li proposed some solutions for improving translation teaching in China's BA programs. Firstly, the marginalization status of translation teaching in college English teaching should be changed. Under the premise of the lack of national syllabus for college English translation, each region or university should formulate a suitable 'college English translation syllabus' according to the actual situation of the region or university to guide the translation teaching affiliated to college English. After the development of the translation syllabus, qualified translation teaching staff must be recruited who can complete the teaching objectives and tasks specified in the syllabus. Moreover, in the process of college English translation teaching, Li advised that teachers should abandon the past teaching methods of emphasizing knowledge and belittling skills. Translation teaching should focus on the cognitive and metacognitive strategies used in the process of student translation practice, in order to cultivate students' translation competence and skills, creative thinking ability and bilingual ability in English and Chinese. Liu (2009), speaking about the same issue of BA translation modules, argued that whether it was a translation course for foreign language majors or a translation course on translation programs, it was necessary to highlight the professional quality of the course and to fully understand the significance of translation process training in the formation of translation competence, and the impact of automation of translation-related cognition on the different stages of training. Liu thought that undergraduate translation teaching should focus on the training of translation-oriented thinking, supplemented by the provision and analysis of different genres of text and speech. Skill training and language improvement should go hand in hand as dual teaching objectives, gradually forming the student-centered approach assisted by the teacher; while learning takes place in both classroom and after-school settings in both knowledge acquisition and practical activities. The integrated teaching model of undergraduate translation should also make full use of modern language and network technology, insisted Liu.

Innovative translation teaching models have been proposed by Chinese researchers drawing from existing linguistic or educational theories. Ding (2013) explained a translation teaching model based on Charles J. Fillmore's frame theory. The idea was to introduce frame theory in the process of translation theory teaching, to broaden students' research horizons and promote the construction of their professional translation knowledge. Specifically, in the teaching of translation theory, teachers could guide students to describe the translation process from the perspective of context-frame semantics, and reinterpret the role of the translator, that is, the translators started from the established frame and inferred the scene described in the original text with cognitive experience. Eventually, they found the corresponding frame of expression in the target language and reproduced the original scene. Ding suggested that in the actual translation practice, this model broke through the limitations of traditional translation teaching focusing only on vocabulary and syntactic domains, guiding students to further explore the culture and contextual factors involved in the frame and emphasizing the interrelationship between semantics and cognition. It encouraged intuitive and graphical ways of discussing translation problems to develop translation competence and skills. Wu (2019), on the other hand, suggested a 'flipped classroom' model for teaching literary translation. According to her, literary translation is a complex process of code-switching and aesthetic reproduction. It is not only communication at the level of lexis, phrase, sentence and texts, but also the transmission of aesthetic experience between different ethnic groups and the exchange of cultural information. The translation theory and translation skills taught in the literary translation course are relatively rich in quantity, and the information coverage is relatively wide. Things like original author introduction, their writing style, background of the work, the central idea of the work, analysis of the characters, and the translation methods and skills involved in the translating process, all require students understanding to some extent beforehand. As in most flipped classroom models, Wu proposed three stages of instruction. Before class, the teacher produces micro-lectures (微课), PPTs, lecture notes and exercises related to the content of instruction. The teacher sends these materials to students through the online platforms (WeChat group, QQ group). The students send the completed translations to the teacher in groups. The teacher returns the preliminary review results to students. During the class, the teacher displays with PPT the translations of each group. Students hold discussions within groups. Student groups comment on works between the groups. Each group makes a summary report. The teacher provides overall feedback and summarizes the translation practice. After class, the teacher makes a general review of the completion of the teaching objectives within the student group and the completion of the evaluation tasks between the groups. The students prepare a written summary report in groups. Wu concludes that a flipped classroom optimizes the teaching opportunities, realizes the transformation of the teaching role, makes full use of teaching resources and teaching environment, and brings new ideas to the construction of new teaching models for literary translation courses. Some researchers explicitly advocated market-oriented translation teaching. Hu and Wang (2009), for example, insisted that translation teachers must not neglect professional quality training and translation teaching should be geared to meet both learners' and market needs. That is, in translation teaching, learner needs should be in harmony with market demand. On one hand, learners can enhance job-seeking competitiveness and market adaptability through learning knowledge and training skills according to market demand. The market, on the other hand, puts higher demands on teaching through the use of translation talents.

We can see from the above review and discussion how Chinese translation researchers and educationists have explored the interconnections between translation competence, professional skills, translation curriculum, national standards and classroom teaching, and how they have pointed out current problems (e.g. in textbook selection) and future directions for translation programs and pedagogy. We will now turn to an important aspect of current and future translator training processes, that is, the use of language technology in professional translating and translator training.

Translation technology

Since the introduction of Google Neural Machine Translation (GNMT) in 2016, machine translation (MT) has entered a new era in its practical application, none the less in the great enterprise of translator education. As the quality of MT output improves dramatically, it is the translator trainer's responsibility to consider how MT can be (or cannot be) used in classroom and assessment settings, and how students can be best trained to make correct and full use of this cutting-edge translation technology. In addition to MT, language and translation technology also brought in the computer-aided translation (CAT) facility and protocol, which translation educationists also need to take into consideration regarding its usefulness, cost factor and instruction methods. Apart from MT and CAT, the use of the internet (for web-based research) and social media, especially through mobile devices, is also highly important and implicational in the use of technology for translating and translator's training programs. In this section we will review and discuss some important works in the area of translation technology and its implications for Chinese translation teaching programs and methodologies.

Li and Chen (2018) did a scientometric analysis on 77 papers from linguistics journals and 318 papers from journals of computer science published in China between 2007 and 2016 writing on the topic of MT. In addition to the difference in quantity of papers published between the broad linguistics and the computer science categories (that is, there was much more of the former than there was of the latter), Li and Chen also found both disciplines placed different foci on their issues in question. That is, the linguistic (including language teaching and translation) community pays more attention to the field of 'computer-aided translation', which aims to use machine translation to help human translation and use this technology for translation teaching. The computer science community, on the other hand, pays more attention on how to improve machine translation to obtain more accurate translations and make the user experience more enjoyable. Feng (2018) offered a concise and accessible explanation of what the most recent MT system was about especially on its connection with AI (artificial intelligence) while 'demystifying' the true capacity of AI and MT in their current form. Feng advises that Google's GNMT is a 'big data'-based neural machine translation system. When the computer is translating, it requires the input of large quantities of authentic data from a large-scale corpus for deep learning, and automatically obtains language features and rules from the corpus. The results of training and learning through the use of large corpora then produce 'weights' allocated to connections between nodes that exist in a multi-layer neural network. A well-trained neural network can automatically translate a text from the source language to the target language. However, Feng noted that AI systems may exceed human capabilities in specific application areas and for specific scenarios. However, at the current level of technology, it is far from being able to fully meet or surpass human intelligence. Currently, all industrial intelligence systems are fully dedicated AI system with strict scene restrictions, rather than a general AI system. Once the scene or field is changed, the performance of the system will decrease. The current neuro-machine translation system is only effective in daily conversations, news translation, etc. Once the topic area is changed, the neuro-machine translation system immediately appears stretched and its output is full of errors. Qin (2018) also introduced the neural network MT and extends the discussion to the translation teaching domain. According to Qin, the neural network MT systems are characterized by the following traits. Firstly, the translation of the sentence as a unit and the fluency of the whole translation are significantly improved. Thus, the neural network MT gives the overall impression that the translation is highly readable. Secondly, there is an internal mechanism to the neural network MT that is a shared multilingual translation module to achieve zero-shot translation (零训翻译) by transferring learning without having to repeat the deep learning procedure for multiple languages. That is, Google's GNMT can translate between dozens of languages and, more importantly, translation between different languages can be implemented using the same translation model, saving time and workload. The third characteristic of neural network MT, according to Qin, is its 'black box' machinery based on a simulation of the human brain that is beyond explanation and comprehension. Qin commented that the rules-based MT principle is transparent and the translation results are interpretable. Statistical MT is also statistically interpretable because the machine always chooses the translation output with the greatest probability. But the results of neural network MT are hard to explain. Although the neural network design claims to simulate the human brain nervous system structurally speaking, in essence, its information processing mechanism is different from the human brain. The weights ultimately stored between the nodes of the neural network are closely related to the data and network structure used for training, but the meaning of the connection weight is difficult to explain. The translation mechanism of neural network machine translation remains mysterious. Qin concluded that the neural network MT uses a deep neural network to implement an end-to-end translation method, which significantly improves the fluency and accuracy of the translation, but its translation mechanism is more difficult to explain. Although machine translation based on deep learning has made great progress, it does not mean that neural network is the only way to solve the problem of MT. In particular, Qin believed that the development of machine translation will not deprive human translators of their job opportunities, and high-level translators will still be in short supply in the future.

In that light, Qin proposed the following translation teaching principles for the future generation of technology informed translators:

- Clarifying human–machine division and realizing human–computer collaborative translation: We need to clarify the usage scenarios and translation features of MT and consider the focus of language and translation teaching. Building an efficient collaborative work environment is a requirement for high-level, high-efficiency translation in the future.
- Expanding the new field of translation: The popularity of MT has produced a new type of language service industry – post-editing. Post-editing refers to improving the quality and applicability of MT through manual review and editing. Translation teaching in colleges and universities has begun to set up post-editing courses, which should be encouraged.
- Improving traditional teaching methods and software application skills: Machine translation, machine-assisted translation and translation management systems provide a more efficient translation work environment for human translators. Learning courses on tool software should be added to translation teaching as skilled use of translation software has quickly become one of the skills that high-end translators must master.

In sum, Qin firmly believed that as a translation technology, MT will not only NOT replace human translators, but will create new service areas. Translation teaching should also follow technological progress, effectively use the latest technology to enhance teaching content and improve teaching methods. The problem of how to incorporate MT skills into translation pedagogy was taken on by Liu (2018), who proposed three components to be included in an MT-based translation course design: contrastive analysis between MT and human outputs, pre-editing and post-editing. Liu suggested that in the initial stage of the course, students can be arranged to compare machine translations and manual translations, present sentences with problems in MT, compare them with the original text, classify MT errors and analyze the causes of these errors. The main purpose of this part is to help students understand how MT systems work and be familiar with the types and possible causes of their errors in order to lay the foundation for subsequent pre-editing work. At the next stage, pre-translation editing techniques such as syntactic structural adjustment, addition, early translation of terminology and the addition of punctuation are taught to students. Finally, post-editing focuses on the modification of proper nouns, tenses, terms, etc. to perfect the MT output. Liu advised that, following this teaching model, students can become efficient in using machine translation and meet the basic requirements of translation companies.

Alongside but distinct from MT are the computer-aided translation (CAT) tools which also received some attention in technology-oriented translation practice and teaching. We can start from Sun and Lin's (2016) questionnaire-based investigation of 152 undergraduate students regarding their needs, evaluation and application of CAT tools. Results showed, firstly, although students had systematically studied through CAT technology, they still had a strong demand for technological capabilities. Secondly, although they thought that CAT technology was powerful and relatively easy to operate and they would like to continue using CAT in future work, they still encountered great difficulties in acquiring these technologies. Finally, although they often used the CAT-based collaborative translation mode in the classroom learning process, the use was significantly reduced after class. In practice, students had to build their own translation memories from scratch. The point of translation memory seems a crucial factor in determining the usefulness and efficiency of CAT tools in the pedagogical setting. Zhu and Chen (2013), for example, did a comparative study between four brands of CAT tools: SDL Trados, Déjà vu, Wordfast and Yaxin (北京东方雅信软件). They found SDL powerful and able to handle the increasingly widely used PDF files. However, because of its complicated modular structure, it was not easy for beginners to quickly get started. They thought it more suitable for high-level translators in large companies or translation agencies that had high requirements for software localization. For Zhu and Chen, the functionality of Déjà vu was complete, the terminology management tools were distinctive, and the translation memory and terminology libraries were highly portable, suitable for teamwork and freelance translators. As for Wordfast, its classic version was simple in function. Although there was no Chinese interface to it, the software was small, easy to operate and fast, suitable for translators who often translated Word documents. Yaxin CAT 3.5 was found to have the main functions of CAT tools and came with its own terminology database consisting of 74 terms, eliminating the long process of accumulating terminology. Zhu and Chen emphasized that the overall development trend of CAT was that the functions of various brands of software gradually converged. To meet the increasing needs of clients, the most radical demand to satisfy was the translation memory and terminology problems that come with the software, because the construction of these databases was a time-consuming and laborious process. If there were no rich examples of the CAT software's translation memory and terminology related to the material to be translated, CAT software would not be able to fully realize its function of improving translation efficiency. In addition to the most well-known translation memory and terminology management software commented on in Zhu and Chen above, Zhou (2015) expanded the types of CAT tools to include four varieties: stand-alone CAT software (This would include the four brands of software compared in Zhu and Chen, 2013), server version CAT software, free online CAT software, and cloud translation software. According to Zhou, the server version CAT software was specially customized for project management and real-time team collaboration. This solution enabled the sharing of translation memory and terminology in real time, improved translation efficiency and ensured accuracy and consistency of the translation. However, the routine maintenance required special technical staff which could not be undertaken by ordinary teachers of translation technology. Google Translator Toolkit (GTT) is a free web application designed to allow translators to edit the translations that Google Translate automatically generates. The main problems with GTT, Zhou noted, were it being greatly affected by the network environment, and the functions of project management and terminology were weak. In terms of the implementation of CAT teaching in translation classrooms, Wen and Ren (2011) proposed three guidelines:

- Perfection of teaching systems: Domestic research at the master's level is more comprehensive, but the research on undergraduate and doctoral levels is still relatively lacking. There is no systematic coverage of CAT teaching across all levels of translation programs.
- Development of teacher competency: Teachers of CAT courses not only require foreign language proficiency, but they also need to learn CAT technology and master a variety of tools. Therefore, research on how to improve the overall quality of CAT teachers needs to be strengthened.
- Compilation of teaching materials: Although there are many publications on computer and translation in China, research on CAT teaching materials is relatively weak. This blank in this area desperately needs to be filled.

Despite the enthusiasm and the promising outlook of CAT tools in Chinese translation programs, some authors issued warnings about this trend. Wang and Sun (2009), for example, cautioned that computer-assisted translation had little effect on the mastery of students' translation skills and the improvement of translation competence. Moreover, if students relied too much on a translation memory system, it might cause bad translation habits to be formed which would affect the quality of translation. Secondly, Wang and Sun noted that the training and learning of translation memory systems were quite time-consuming and labor intensive. Even if the learner had good computer literacy, it would take a long time for students to master the use of the translation memory system. All in all, Wang and Sun insisted that the value and practicality of computer-aided translation technology was beyond doubt, but in translation teaching, how to correctly guide students to learn and use this technology was worthy of consideration for every translation teacher. If one pursued the advanced technology and neglected the cultivation of translation ability, then the result would be 'cart before the horse'.

Crowdsourcing translation has become increasingly popular with the coming of cloud computing, more capable neural network MT and so on. Wang et al. (2018) note that the translation industry has seen new changes in the context of 'big data'. The open source concept of freedom and sharing, Web 2.0 technology, and the application of emerging elements such as cloud computing and artificial intelligence have contributed to the transformation and innovation of translation models. The emergence of new translation models such as crowdsourcing translation, cloud translation and network MT has attracted the active participation of the public, enabling collaborative translation and collective intelligence to be fully realized, bringing translation into the public and non-professional setting. Wang et al. think that crowdsourcing translation fully demonstrates the user's active participation and group wisdom; cloud translation integrates translation resources and technology and improves management efficiency, satisfying customers' demands for low-cost, high-efficiency and high-quality translation products; neural network MT has greatly improved the quality of output and users' dependence on translation technology has been increasing. As of now, translators need to adapt to the results of MT and modify as appropriate. Human–computer collaboration and human–machine dialogue have become a new dimension in translation studies in the future. However, Wang et al. also caution that internet-based translation does suffer from some weaknesses and poses some problems in the context of big data in its current form. Firstly, there exist confrontations among crowdsourcing translation, official authority and mainstream discourses, which require a solution through dialogue and negotiation. In addition, there are the ethical paradoxes amid scenes of utter chaos in crowdsourcing translation. Quality control and evaluation of translation in the networked environment is also a big problem. Last but not least, 'What exactly is the place of human translator in the context of big data?' is a question worth pondering in the years to come. Methodologically, Zhou (2007) offered a partial solution to some of the above-mentioned problems by proposing a series of actions for a human translator to trawl the web for good solutions to translation problems. According to Zhou, 'Internet search engine assisted translation' could be a form of computer-assisted translation that facilitated translators in finding resources and helped translators improve the accuracy and efficiency of translation. How to use internet search engines in practice is a problem translators should pay attention to. Zhou proposed a series of three steps in making use of search engines to solve translation problems. Step 1: List the words or knowledge points that one needs to find or search, that is, keywords, and type them into the search engine. Translators should learn the basics of how to use search engines to better assist them in translation. There are many ways to query, and different methods yield different results. Step 2: After the search results are revealed, one should carefully check the web pages containing the keywords, try to screen useful web pages, learn to identify the source of the data, and find a more appropriate translation method. Step 3: Retype the selected one or more translations into the search bar to determine whether the translation is truly appropriate in the TT context. The final step is indispensable in helping to decide whether the hypothesis of the translator is correct in producing their best translation after the initial web search. Another important method for improving translation quality is the use of translation corpora, which is highly relevant in both translating and translator's training. Liu and Chang (2018) did a CiteSpace analysis of nearly 2,000 papers published in China between 1998–2007 writing about bilingual corpora or 'corpus-based translation studies' (语料库翻译学). They found four areas of research in this field which they called 'research hotspots' after studying 20 years of publications. These were: corpus construction, features of translated language, translator style and translation teaching. Wang (2004) provided some thoughts on how parallel corpora could help with translation teaching by serving as reference tools or working platforms. Firstly, parallel corpora can provide rich and varied bilingual translation examples for a search term or phrase. In addition, they also provide a variety of bilingual examples for common structures for explanation and simulation in translation teaching and practice. Finally, parallel corpora can provide rich and randomly extractable multiple translations for a given text for contrastive studies. Wang concluded that the use of bilingual parallel corpora and search tools in translation teaching is very beneficial to students' rich translation experience, improving translation ability and multi-channel translation. It is irreplaceable by other textbooks and reference books.

Conclusion

We started the discussion in this chapter by looking at Chinese and Western research on the teaching of translation and found several concepts and ideas that authors are concerned about in this field. Translation competence: what does it mean? What are its functions and how to develop it on the part of the trainee translators? Theory and practice: most researchers emphasized the importance of professional elements in translator training but also insisted on the inclusion of both theory and practice in translation teaching. It is not a straightforward matter though, to translate the results of theoretical research into pedagogically accessible terms. However, as more and more investigations on the nature and components of translation competence are published with encouraging results, the prospect of designing the best translation curricula and teaching materials incorporating both theory and practice is looking good. More promisingly, we have seen how neural network MT, CAT tools, cloud-based translation and crowdsourcing, and corpus-based translation have revolutionized the practice (and soon the theory) of translating and how Chinese researchers are already prioritizing their work in these new domains. Translation research and teaching will move forward in tandem as the 21st century unfolds in a way that is facilitated by advanced translation technology, but also inherently dependent on human intervention, with the two working seamlessly together to achieve perfect intercultural communication.

References

Chinese references

Chai, Mingyin 柴明颎 (2015) 本科翻译专业教学思考 (Reflections on the teaching of translation major for undergraduate students). 东方翻译 (*East Journal of Translation*). 2015(5): 4–10.

Ding, Weiguo 丁卫国 (2013) 基于框架理论的翻译教学模式研究 (Research on translation teaching model based on frame theory). 外语界 (*Foreign Language World*). 2013(6): 72–76.

Fu, Jingming 傅敬民 (2015) 翻译能力研究: 回顾与展望 (Research on translation competence: review and prospect). 外语教学理论与实践 (*Foreign Language Learning Theory and Practice*). 2015(4): 80–86.

Feng, Quangong 冯全功 (2010) 从认知视角试论翻译能力的构成 (On the constitution of translation competence from a cognitive perspective). 外语教学(*Foreign Language Education*). 2010(6): 110–113.

Feng, Zhiwei 冯志伟 (2018) 机器翻译与人工智能的平行发展 (The parallel development of machine translation and artificial intelligence). 外国语 (*Journal of Foreign Languages*). 2018(6): 35–48.

Gao, Lvbin 高吕斌 (2019) 论关联理论视角下大学英语翻译教学 (On college English translation teaching from the perspective of relevance theory). 福建茶叶 (*Tea In Fujian*). 2019(1): 253–254.

Hu, Dongping and Wang, Jianhui 胡东平，王建辉 (2009) 基于市场需求的翻译教学的混沌认识及其应对方略 (Chaotic understanding of translation teaching based on market demand and its countermeasures). 外语界 (*Foreign Language World*). 2009(4): 43–47.

Hu, Zhenming and Wang, Xiangling 胡珍铭，王湘玲 (2018) 翻译能力本质的元认知研究 (Metacognitive study on the nature of translation competence). 外语教学理论与实践 (*Foreign Language Learning Theory and Practice*). 2018(3): 91–96.

Jiao, Pengshuai 焦鹏帅 (2018) 西方翻译教学研究及中国翻译教学成果国际化—韦努蒂编著《翻译教学：教学计划、课程设置和教学法》(2017) 介评 (Research on translation teaching in the west and internationalization of translation teaching achievements in China-venuti, translation teaching: teaching plans, curriculum and pedagogy (2017)). 上海翻译 (*Shanghai Journal of Translators*). 2018(6): 89–92.

Li, Hanji and Chen, Haiqing 李晗佶，陈海庆 (2018) 国内机器翻译研究动态科学知识图谱分析 (2007—2016)—基于语言学类与计算机科学类期刊的词频对比统计 (Dynamic knowledge map analysis of machine translation research in China (2007–2016)—word frequency statistics based on linguistic and computer science journals). 西安外国语大学学报 (*Journal of Xi'an Foreign Languages University*). 2018(2): 99–103.

Li, Ruilin 李瑞林 (2011) 从翻译能力到译者素养：翻译教学的目标转向 (From translation ability to translator quality: the goal of translation teaching turns). 中国翻译 (*Chinese Translators Journal*). 2011(1): 46–51.

Li, Zhonghua 李忠华 (2007) 大学英语翻译教学：现状与对策 (College English translation teaching: current situation and countermeasures). 外语与外语教学 (*Foreign Language and Their Teaching*). 2007(9): 47–49.

Liu, Guobin and Chang, Fangling 刘国兵，常芳玲 (2018) 基于 CiteSpace 的国内语料库翻译学研究知识图谱分析 (Emerging trends in corpus-based translation studies in China: A Scientometric analysis in CiteSpace). 河南师范大学学报 (自然科学版) (*Journal of Henan Normal University (Natural Science)*). 2018(6): 111–120.

Liu, Heping 刘和平 (2009) 论本科翻译教学的原则与方法 (On the principles and methods of undergraduate translation teaching). 中国翻译 (*Chinese Translators Journal*). 2009(6): 34–41.

Liu, Heping 刘和平 (2011) 翻译能力发展的阶段性及其教学法研究 (A study on the stages of translation competence development and its pedagogy). 中国翻译 (*Chinese Translators Journal*). 2011(1): 37–45.

Liu, Heping 刘和平 (2013) 翻译教学模式：理论与应用 (Translation teaching model: theory and application). 中国翻译 (*Chinese Translators Journal*). 2013(2): 50–55.

Liu, Jianzhu and Mu, Lei 刘建珠，穆雷 (2017) 中国翻译理论话语体系的构建及其划界 (On the construction and demarcation of discourse system for China's translation theory). 上海翻译 (*Shanghai Journal of Translators*). 2017(2): 1–5.

Liu, Yong 刘勇 (2018) 机器翻译融入翻译教学的模式探究 (Research on the mode of integrating machine translation into translation teaching). 科学大众(科学教育) (*Popular Science*). 2018(12): 150.

Ma, Yili 马义莉 (2015) 翻译硕士专业教材选用现状，问题及对策 (The present situation, problems and countermeasures of the selection of specialized textbooks for the master of translation). 东方翻译 (*East Journal of Translation*). 2015(4): 22–26.

Mu, Lei 穆雷 (2008) 建设完整的翻译教学体系 (Build a complete translation teaching system). 中国翻译 (*Chinese Translators Journal*). 2008(1): 41–45.

Qian, Chunhua 钱春花 (2012) 翻译能力构成要素及其驱动关系分析 (An analysis of the components of translation competence and their driving relationships). 外语界 (*Foreign Language World*). 2012(3): 59–65.

Qin, Yin 秦颖 (2018) 基于神经网络的机器翻译质量评析及对翻译教学的影响 (Quality evaluation of machine translation based on neural network and its influence on translation teaching). 外语电化教学 (*Computer-Assisted Foreign Language Education*). 2018(2): 51–56.

Sun, Bin 孙斌 (2018) 分析翻译理论在翻译教学中的作用 (Analyze the function of translation theory in translation teaching). 文化创新比较研究 (*Comparative Study of Cultural Innovation*). 2018(17): 67+70.

Sun, Li and Lin, Zonghao 孙利, 林宗豪 (2016) 计算机辅助翻译技术的应用现状—基于翻译方向本科生的调查 (Application status of computer-aided translation technology – based on the survey of undergraduates majoring in translation). 外语学刊 (*Foreign Language Research*). 2016(3): 141–145.

Tan, Yesheng 谭业升 (2016) 翻译能力的认知观: 以识解为中心 (Cognitive view of translation competence: it centers on construal). 中国翻译 (*Chinese Translators Journal*). 2016(5): 15–22.

Tong, Yahui 仝亚辉 (2010) PACTE翻译能力模式研究 (Studying the PACTE translation competence model). 解放军外国语学院学报 (*Journal of PLA University of Foreign Languages*). 2010(05): 88–93.

Wang, Jiayi, Li, Defeng and Li, Liqing 王家义, 李德凤, 李丽青 (2018) 大数据背景下的互联网翻译—开源理念与模式创新 (Internet translation in the context of big data – open source concept and model innovation). 中国翻译 (*Chinese Translators Journal*). 2018(2): 78–82.

Wang, Kefei 王克非 (2004) 双语平行语料库在翻译教学上的用途 (The application of bilingual parallel corpus in translation teaching). 外语电化教学 (*Computer-Assisted Foreign Language Education*). 2004(6): 27–32.

Wang, Saise 王赛瑟 (2019) 翻译理论在英语翻译教学中的重要性研究 (Research on the importance of translation theory in English translation teaching). 学周刊(*Learning Weekly*). 2019(3): 10–14.

Wang, Shuhuai 王树槐 (2013) 翻译教学论 (*On Translation Teaching*). Shanghai: Shanghai Foreign Language Education Press.

Wang, Tianyu 王天予 (2018) 我国本科翻译专业课程设置现状研究 (Research on the current situation of undergraduate translation curriculum in China). 外语学刊(*Foreign Language Research*). 2018(2): 110–114.

Wang, Zheng and Sun, Dongyun 王正, 孙东云 (2009) 翻译记忆在翻译教学中的优势与局限性 (The advantages and limitations of translation memory in translation teaching). 外语界 (*Foreign Language World*). 2009(2): 16–22.

Wen, Jun 文军 (2005) 翻译课程模式研究—以发展翻译能力为中心的方法 (A study on the model of translation curriculum: translation-competence centered approach). Beijing: Chinese Literature and History Press.

Wen, Jun and Ren, Yan 文军, 任艳 (2011) 国内计算机辅助翻译研究述评 (A review of domestic computer-aided translation studies). 外语电化教学 (*Computer-Assisted Foreign Language Education*). 2011(3): 58–62.

Wu, Liru 武利茹 (2019) 基于翻转课堂的文学作品翻译课程教学模式构建研究 (A study on the construction of teaching mode of literary works translation in the flipped classroom). 吉林省教育学院学报 (*Journal of Educational Institute of Jilin Province*). 2019(4): 82–85.

Yu, Jing 余静 (2018) 从象牙塔到竞技场—翻译能力的社会学研究 (From the Ivory tower to the Arena: a sociological study of translation competence). 外国语(*Journal of Foreign Languages*). 2018(2): 101–107.

Yan, Jiaxin 闫佳馨 (2017) 功能派翻译理论对英语专业翻译教学的启示 (Implications of functionalist translation theory for translation teaching in English majors). 黑龙江教育（理论与实践） (*Heilongjiang Education (Theory & Practice)*). 2017(11): 68–69.

Yang, Zhihong and Wang, Kefei 杨志红，王克非 (2010) 翻译能力及其研究 (Translation competence and its research). 外语教学 (*Foreign Language Education*). 2010(6): 91–95.

Zhang, Wenhe and Wen, Jun 张文鹤，文军 (2017) 国外翻译教学研究: 热点, 趋势与启示 (Research on translation teaching abroad: hot spots, trends and implications). 外语界 (*Foreign Language World*). 2017(1): 46–54.

Zhong, Weihe and Zhao, Junfeng 仲伟合，赵军峰 (2015) 翻译本科专业教学质量国家标准要点解读 (Interpretation of key points of national standards on teaching quality of undergraduate majors in translation). 外语教学与研究: 外国语文双月刊 (*Foreign Language Teaching and Research*). 2015(2): 289–296.

Zhou, Jie 周杰 (2007) 互联网搜索引擎辅助翻译研究 (Research on translation assisted by Internet search engines). 外语电化教学 (*Computer-Assisted Foreign Language Education*). 2007(5): 62–65.

Zhu, Yubin and Chen, Xiaoqing 朱玉彬，陈晓倩 (2013) 国内外四种常见计算机辅助翻译软件比较研究 (A comparative study of four common computer-aided translation software at home and abroad). 外语电化教学 (*Computer-Assisted Foreign Language Education*). 2013(1): 69–75.

Zhou, Xinhua 周兴华 (2015) 计算机辅助翻译协作模式探究 (Research on the cooperative mode of computer aided translation). 中国翻译 (*Chinese Translators Journal*). 2015(2): 77–80.

Other references

Campbell, S. (1998) *Translation into the Second Language*. London and New York: Longman.

Charmaz, K. (2006) *Constructing Grounded Theory: A Practical Guide Through Qualitative Analysis*. Thousand Oaks, CA: Sage Publications.

Pym, A. (2003) Redefining translation competence in an electronic age: in defence of a minimalist approach. *Meta* 48(4): 481–497.

Venuti, L. (2017) Introduction: translation, interpretation, and the humanities. In L. Venuti (ed.) *Teaching Translation: Programs, Courses, Pedagogies*. Abingdon, Oxon: Routledge, pp. 1–14.

7 Conclusion

Chinese translation officially started from the Eastern Han dynasty (25–220 CE) and became an organized activity commission by the government when Dao'an (312–385 AD) was enlisted by the pre-Qin emperor Fujian to head a Buddhist Scripture translating team ('fojing fanyi' 2019). 150 years ago, these highly proficient and intelligent translators not only transformed the memorized Sanskrit sutras into Chinese words in large quantities, but they also managed to put forward some kind of translation theory in their highly limited intellectual environment. Dao'an, for example, was said to have proposed the 'five lost originals' (五失本) and the 'three not easy' (三不易) characteristics (or inherent restrictions) of translating.

Five lost originals:

- Sanskrit syntax differed dramatically from Chinese syntax which caused meaning to be lost when translated into Chinese sentences.
- Sanskrit was concise and simple; Han language favors decoration. Some textual elements were lost in translation.
- Sanskrit Scriptures had repeated signs and slogans, some of which were deleted in the Chinese texts to the detriment of the original message.
- Sanskrit Scripture often narrated in prose and then summarized the same thing in verses. The repetitions were deleted in translation and meaning was lost.
- Sanskrit Scriptures often repeated the previous text before new narrations. The repeated parts were deleted in translation and the original intention was lost.

Three not easy:

- The scripture comprised what Buddha said at a particular point in time. It is not easy to recover the original meaning and examples at the current time.
- The supreme beings of Buddha had higher intelligence than ordinary people. It is not easy to use ordinary language to express what Buddha meant.
- The anthology of Buddhist Scriptures was the result of painstaking work from 500 learned monks. It is not easy for ordinary people to translate ('Shi Daoan' 2019).

Throughout the book, especially in Chapter 3, we have seen other brilliant Chinese translators with or without names in the Chinese history jointly establishing, maintaining and handing down the tradition of Chinese translation in respect of both practice and theory. Many researchers and thinkers wondered why the 2000 years of translating experience in China had not boiled down to a formidable Chinese translation theory to enable Chinese researchers and practitioners to lead the trend in global translation discourse. Ma (2019) explores the issue and offers some viable explanations. She notes that China's translation studies, especially theoretical research, have long been influenced by Western translation studies (It is fair to say that the length of this influence, as manifested by previous discussions in this book, can be more accurately pinpointed at around 40 years (i.e. from 1979–2019) when the beginning of modern Chinese translation studies coincided with the introduction of Western translation theory starting from Nida). Ma further notices that almost all translation theory courses in China's universities are based on Western translation theory. She also claims that there is little or no original theory in the field in China, and no internationally recognized Chinese translation theorists so far. This leads to the commonly alluded to the fact that Chinese translation studies is in a state of 'aphasia' (失语) on the global stage. This status is not commensurate with China's status as a major translation country (in the sense that it has a long translation history and that it has a lot of universities with translation programs – possibly as many as 270 at the time of writing). In view of the current low status of Chinese translation studies, Ma sets out to answer two questions: why does Western Centralism appear prominently in Western and Chinese translation studies? How can contemporary Chinese translation studies get rid of Western Centralism? For the first question, Ma thinks that there are two obvious reasons for the emergence of Western Centralism in the field of translation studies worldwide. One is the rapid development of contemporary European translation studies, and the other is the strong position of English as an international lingua franca. Apart from that, Ma also brings up a less noticed factor regarding the identity of translation teachers. According to Ma, in China, translation courses are generally set in foreign language departments of universities and translation teaching is closely related to foreign language teaching. Teachers from a foreign language (mainly English) background usually choose Western translation theory as the main content of lectures, which contributes to the emergence of Western Centralism in the academic setting. An additional factor contributing to the scarcity of Chinese translation theory, Ma says, is the emphasis on *applied* research in China in translation studies, which sees to it that the majority of papers published by leading journals such as the Chinese Translation Journal (中国翻译) and the Shanghai Journal of Translators (上海翻译) are applied research in nature. To reverse the trend of overemphasis on Western translation theory, Ma proposes four future directions for Chinese translation studies:

- Conducting in-depth research on the practice of translation in China and producing original results of translation theory accordingly.

- Introducing the results of contemporary oriental translation theories and carrying out a comparative study of Eastern and Western translation theories.
- Strengthening critical thinking and applicability research on Western translation theories.
- Disseminating the research results of Chinese researchers based on their study of Chinese translation phenomena.

The first suggestion is most important, and the word *in-depth* is critical as many papers currently published in Chinese journals do tend to be 'short and shallow' (probably due to their being 'applied' in nature). Most of the papers published in China's translation-related journals range from 1 to 10 pages in length and have between 2400 and 12000 characters (roughly equivalent to about 1600–8000 English words, as about half of the Chinese characters in the word count will consist of disyllabic words, that is, two Chinese characters translating into one English word, e.g. the two Chinese characters *wen zhang* (文章) translating to the one English word *article*). To produce substantial research in Chinese translation theory, it seems advisable to extend the length of papers published in Chinese journals in the first place with a corresponding increase in the analysis of empirical data and extended, well-informed discussions that eventually contribute to the formulation of Chinese translation theory.

In terms of comparative studies, some researchers have worked out potential differences (and seminaries) between Chinese and Western translation theories. Meng (2018), for example, concisely suggested that Western translation studies was more nuanced although failing to provide an overall picture; Chinese translation studies, in contrast, was good at providing overall pictures but lacking in detail. Wang (2009) alleged that Chinese translation theory had the characteristics of being 'simplified and concise, succinct and subtle' and strong in practicality; however, it was mostly based on subjective experience and lacking in systematic and scientific analysis. Western translation theory, conversely, emphasized rational analysis, science and systematicity, but its practicality value may be slightly lower. Wu (1998) noted that the Chinese translation theory was relatively vague but 'savvy', embodying a strong humanistic approach; the Western translation theory was clearer and more rational, reflecting a stronger spirit of scientificism. He thought that the Chinese translation theory was more suitable for the translation of literature as the literary language was rich in originality and semantics and strong in visualization. The equivalence-based methods in Western translation theory, Wu thought, were not suitable for literary translation but could be applied to scientific translation with transparent formal features and clearer semantics. Tan (2000) observed that the main feature of the Chinese translation tradition was that it had always emphasized the practical value of translation theory, highlighted the normative role of translation experience, and stressed the translator's 'spiritual' comprehension of the translation. The main feature of the Western translation convention, on the other hand, was the emphasis on the regularity and systematicity of translation theory; the focus on the rational description of the translation process and the constant updating of translation concepts. While a lot of studies found differences between Chinese and Western translation theories, one researcher, Siqin (1997) put forth a cogent argumentation trying to prove the identical developmental trajectory of translation theory between China and the West before World War II. According to her, China's translation theory was mostly generated from translators' own practice in response to the specific problems encountered in translating. The translators and translation theorists par excellence worked out solutions from the perspective of philosophy and aesthetics, rather than establishing theories from linguistics. This was true with Kumārajīva, Xuan Zang, Yan Fu, Lu Xun and so on. In the West, on the other hand, Siqin felt that the translation theory output before the World War II was almost the same as that in China from the perspectives of research scope, problems investigated and methods adopted. For example, the Italian idealist philosopher Benedetto Croce (1866–1952) thought that translation could not reproduce the original work perfectly. Language was generated by intuition and translation was a recreational activity. Translation itself should have original artistic value and become an independent artwork. This was very similar to the intuitive approach of the Chinese translation theory. The other Western translation theorists Siqin mentioned included Walter Benjamin (1892–1940), the German philosopher, cultural critic and essayist; Paul Valéry (1871–1945), the French poet, essayist, and philosopher and others. Siqin found that, in this period, Western thinkers also approached translation theory from the perspective of literary translation, especially from the perspective of classical literature translation. Therefore, much like the Chinese counterpart, translation theory in this period was a by-product of literary translation practice. The translators contrived theories either from their translation experience or from the aesthetic point of philosophy, not a scientific approach. Therefore, Siqin concluded that both China's translation theory and the Western translation theory before World War II were both generated from experience and speculation. Incorporating translation into the category of (applied) linguistics, as well as making translation theory a kind of comparative linguistics and scientific enquiry, was something that happened after World War II.

So where are Chinese translation studies now? Wang (2017) divided the history of Chinese translation thinking into three periods: 1. The ancient period of Buddhist Scripture translation from Dao'an to Xuan Zang; 2. The modern period from Yan Fu to Qian Zhongshu (1910–1998); and 3. The current period from 1990 to the present. He noted that, in the past three decades, Chinese translation thought has become transdisciplinary and cross-cultural. The expression of thought on translation has transcended the translator's personal experience and feelings. Academic papers written in scholarly methods are now the main form of expression. Translation studies has become a scientific discipline. Due to the formation of different ideological camps and academic paradigms, the tendency and germination of different schools of thought in translation studies have emerged. This indicates a bright prospect for the further development of Chinese translation studies in the future. Some scholars did not hesitate to point out new directions for future Chinese translation studies. Li (2013), for example, suggested the 'Sinicization of Western translation theory' and the 'Internationalization of Chinese translation theory'. That is, on one hand, transplanting Western translation theory into the soil of Chinese translation studies and combining it with Chinese translation theory and practice to enrich the latter's translation studies. On the other hand, establishing a dialogue mechanism with Western translation studies, and gradually transforming passive acceptance into active discourse making. For the second point, initiating dialogue with the West, Zhang (2005) offered three concrete suggestions after having a conversation with Dirk Delabastita, editor of the Target journal: improving the quality of academic output in the Chinese translation studies circle, especially journal papers at the international level, actively contributing to the publication of special issues of international journals, and actively recommending relevant scholars to join the editorial board of international journals and to participate in multilingual platform construction to promote Chinese translation. Jiang's (2016) research uncovered an encouraging trend to make the future prospect possible when Chinese researchers can bring something different and inspiring to the global translation studies arena. After studying 125 papers from the Chinese Translators Journal published between 2008 and 2015, Jiang distinguished four types of research: foreign theories, domestic theories, traditional theories and empirical studies. Importantly, Jiang found that the number of studies on foreign theories was decreasing while that on domestic translation theories was increasing, signifying a shift of focus and a higher possibility of engendering 'translation theory of Chinese characteristics', so to speak. In formulating the new generation of Chinese translation theory, an important approach is making the theory 'problem oriented', as included in Zeng's (2017) suggestions for future directions and cogently argued in Lan (2018), who commented that, in recent years, China's translation theory research had departed from the useful problem-based approach. Lan highly recommended a return to identifying problems, persistence in pursuing solutions to problems, and the promotion of awareness to problems as the right way to develop translation theory in the new era.

The past four decades have witnessed a large amount of one-way communication and, increasingly, two-way communication between Western and Chinese translation studies. Yu (2008) commented that Chinese research tended to emphasize historical facts and general descriptions; while Western studies liked to highlight differences. Interestingly, Yu made the bold suggestion that when comparing Chinese and Western translation theories (referring to a certain Western scholar's work), one should avoid overemphasizing similarities or differences. Instead, Yu recommended that authors should try to achieve the goal of mutual understanding, mutual authentication and complementarity through the integration of ancient and modern translation theories and dialogues between Chinese and Western translations. This book, I would argue, is one of those efforts to make Chinese translation studies known in the West and to help smoothen out the undesirable differences while keeping the useful differences. Better, if they could be enlightening to both parties in some ways.

Chinese references

'fojing fanyi' 佛经翻译 (2019) *Wikipedia*. Available at https://zh.wikipedia.org/wiki/佛经翻译 (Accessed: 9 May 2019).

Jiang, Wengan 蒋文干 (2016) 中国翻译理论构建现状与趋势--基于《中国翻译》的一项统计研究 (The current situation and trend of translation theory construction in China – based on a statistical study of Chinese Translators Journal). 山东农业工程学院学报 (*The Journal of Shandong Agriculture and Engineering University*). 2016(7): 137–142.

Lan, Hongjun 蓝红军 (2018) 面向问题的翻译理论研究 (Problem-oriented translation theory). 上海翻译 (*Shanghai Journal of Translators*). 2018(3): 1–6.

Li, Chunguang 李春光 (2013) 中国当代译论研究模式的转型与流变 (The transformation and evolution of the research mode of contemporary translation theory in China). 天津师范大学学报:社会科学版 (*Journal of Tianjin Normal University (Social Science)*). 2013(5): 61–64.

Ma, Huijuan 马会娟 (2019) 走出"西方中心主义"基于中国经验的翻译理论研究 (Exloping the feasibility of decentering Eurocentrism in Chinese translation studies). 上海大学学报社会科学版 (*Journal of Shanghai University (Social Science)*). 2019(2): 104–113.

Meng, Fanjun 孟凡君 (2018) 论翻译研究本土化趋势下的译学体系构建 (On the construction of translation studies under the trend of localization of translation studies). 上海翻译 (*Shanghai Journal of Translators*). 2018(6): 10–14.

'Shi Daoan' 释道安 (2019) *Wikipedia*. Available at https://zh.wikipedia.org/wiki/释道安 (Accessed: 9 May 2019).

Siqin, Gaowa 斯琴高娃 (1997) 我国翻译理论与二战前西方翻译理论的异同及其成因 (Similarities and differences between Chinese translation theories and western translation theories before World War II and their causes). 语言与翻译 (*Language and Translation*). 1997(3): 47–48.

Tan, Zaixi 谭载喜 (2000) 中西译论的相异性 (The opposites between Chinese and western translation theories). 中国翻译 (*Chinese Translators Journal*). 2000(1): 15–21.

Wang, Xiangyuan 王向远 (2017) 中国翻译思想的历史积淀与今年来翻译思想的诸种形态 (The historical accumulation of Chinese translation thoughts and the various forms of translation thoughts in recent years). 海外华文教育动态 (*Overseas Chinese Education*). 2017(8): 29–34.

Wang, Xiaoqin 王小琴 (2009) 中西译论对比研究 (A comparative study of Chinese and western translation theories). 语文学刊:外语教育与教学 (*Journal of Language and Literature*). 2009(2): 85–87.

Wu, Yingcheng 吴义诚 (1998) 中西翻译理论的比较 (A comparison between Chinese and western translation theories). 外国语 (*Journal of Foreign Languages*). 1998(3): 48–52.

Yu, Deying 于德英 (2008) 中西译论比较在异同间寻求文化对话互动的空间 (Chinese and western translation studies seek space for cultural dialogue and interaction between similarities and differences). 外语与外语教学 (*Foreign Languages and Their Teaching*). 2008(1): 56–59.

Zeng, Lisha 曾利沙 (2017) 论翻译学理论研究范畴体系的拓展 (On the extension of the category system of translation studies). 中国外语 (*Foreign Languages in China*). 2017(1): 90–96.

Zhang, Chunbiao 张传彪 (2005) 对西方语言学理论与翻译理论的再思考 (Rethinking western linguistic theory and translation theory). 上海翻译 (*Shanghai Journal of Translators*). 2005(4): 9–14.

Index

aesthetic point 190, 227
aesthetic reproduction 137, 213
aesthetics 9, 10, 15, 34, 35, 39, 45, 54, 57, 122, 137, 139, 155, 160, 180, 182, 188, 202, 204, 227
androgyny 83, 88
Anglo-American 160–164, 169, 189, 192, 193
anthropology 3, 4, 136, 163
assessment 65, 70, 91, 107, 162, 191, 195, 196, 204, 207, 214
audiovisual 3, 4
authenticity 109, 130
author-centered 48, 81
automation 205, 212
autonomy 143, 205, 206
axiology 37

background information 74, 102, 108
background knowledge 72, 135, 139, 153
balanced 75, 76, 115, 163, 211
bibliographic 2, 7, 59, 60, 101
bidirectional 99
bilingual 146, 148, 153, 191, 201–203, 212, 219, 222
Buddhist Scripture 24, 61, 101, 102, 129, 227
buzzwords 138, 139

canons 98–100, 130
Chinese culture 14, 21, 24, 28, 31, 37, 55, 77, 78, 93, 96, 97, 100, 109, 112, 113, 116, 117, 120, 131–133, 135, 138–145, 149, 150, 152, 153, 155, 156, 159, 161, 178, 189, 191, 206, 207
Chinese discourse 12–14, 16, 19, 20, 23, 24, 26, 28, 38, 39, 79
Chinese literature 14, 52, 77, 142, 143, 154, 157, 158, 167, 170, 173, 175, 182, 187, 188, 190, 194, 222

Chinese philosophy 28–30, 32–37, 57, 114, 121, 145
CiteSpace 2, 7, 26, 59, 63, 91, 146, 178, 196, 198, 219, 221
classics 24, 96–100, 105, 116, 121, 126, 130, 131, 142–145, 149, 154, 156, 182, 194
cloud-based 220
cognitive 5, 50, 66, 80, 84–87, 149, 152, 182, 195, 198, 202–204, 212, 213, 220, 222
coherence 69–71, 138, 191
cohesion 66, 69, 91
colonialism 76, 136
commentary 33, 76, 109
communicative functions 64, 65
communicative intention 71, 85, 86, 195
communicative translation 20, 182, 198
Communist Party 84, 95, 155, 162
competence, translation 196, 209
computer-aided translation 214, 216, 218, 222
computer-assisted translation 198–200, 218, 219
conceptual level 51, 119, 144
consciousness 29, 52, 70, 80, 82, 143, 149, 206, 208
contemporary Chinese 11, 63, 67, 75, 138, 141
contextual effects 85, 86
contextual factors 81, 101, 136, 213
contrastive linguistics 2, 4, 6
corpus-based 4, 219–221
correspondence 63, 145, 166, 175, 197
cosmopolitanism 16, 98–100
crowdsourcing 25, 218–220
culturally loaded 77, 132, 133, 146, 148
curriculum 196–200, 207, 209, 210, 214, 221, 222
customs 76, 135, 163, 164, 170, 178

Index

Daoism 24, 30, 31, 35, 36, 105
debate 18, 38, 79, 130, 157
deconstruction 78–81, 86, 88, 89, 91, 100, 177
diachronic 169, 171, 186
dialectical 10, 32, 34, 50, 116, 121
dichotomy 21, 114
dictionaries 138, 139, 162, 186, 187
discourse analysis 4, 44, 47
discourse hegemony 76, 78, 83
dissemination 16, 41, 56, 89, 99, 132, 133, 135, 138, 155, 171, 172, 174, 175, 179, 189, 193
domestication 4, 9, 21, 22, 50, 61, 64, 106, 134, 140, 159, 160, 163, 178, 189
dynamic equivalence 59, 62, 63, 67, 86
dynasty 15, 16, 93, 94, 96, 99, 101, 106, 107, 109, 110, 117, 138, 144, 168, 170, 181, 188, 224

Eastern 93, 174, 224, 226
eco-translatology 54, 61, 121–130, 198, 200
emotion 33, 35, 89, 136
empathy 29, 82, 122, 180
English translations 107, 108, 116, 118, 130, 139, 167, 170, 174, 179, 181, 184, 186, 189
equivalence 2, 4, 9, 11, 12, 24, 38, 45, 47, 50, 59–71, 75, 86–92, 132, 134, 165, 182, 193
ethics 4, 12, 49, 61, 94, 107, 109, 124–126, 156, 158, 182, 198
eurocentrism 4, 6, 27, 49, 50, 52, 229
extralinguistic 201, 202

faithfulness 14, 15, 49, 64, 70, 85, 107–109, 111, 116, 159, 160, 176
feminism 24, 59, 60, 81–83, 86, 88, 182
foreignization 9, 21, 22, 50, 53, 61, 81, 105, 106, 134, 143, 160, 163, 178, 189
frequency 4, 7, 9, 10, 60, 134, 160, 196, 199, 200, 221
functionalist 24, 61, 63, 69–72, 80, 81, 83, 86–90, 195, 223

geographical 6, 78
globalization 4, 49, 53, 112, 131, 132, 134, 137, 196
government 49, 84, 95, 97, 142, 155, 161, 174, 224
grammar 5, 27, 45, 62, 63, 65, 67, 70, 106, 115, 182, 187

hegemony 49, 52, 75–78, 81, 83, 99, 138, 177, 191
historical background 82, 109, 163, 188
holistic 34, 35, 69, 121, 122, 124, 149, 212
Holmes 13, 15, 22, 27, 53, 58
humanistic 145, 190, 196, 226
hybridity 4, 77, 137, 191

ideology 4, 10, 13, 20, 21, 23, 52, 61, 65, 75, 76, 82, 83, 94, 96, 97, 114, 117–119, 138, 145, 160, 177, 182, 191, 205
idiomatic 20, 106
imported 13, 20, 41, 43, 51, 59, 62, 83, 94, 95, 100, 110, 190
interpreting 3, 4, 10, 17, 18, 102, 103, 125, 129, 139, 159, 182, 197, 200, 207, 209–211

Japanese 125, 174, 190, 193

Kumārajīva 101–106, 129, 227

language teaching 42, 129, 163, 169, 192, 196, 199, 214, 223, 225
legitimation 96, 97
lexical 66, 146, 150, 186
linguistic 2, 3, 5, 7, 13, 23, 32, 43, 46, 54, 55, 62, 64, 65, 67, 75, 83, 88, 113, 123, 124, 126, 133–136, 139, 159, 178, 179, 182, 183, 189, 190, 193, 195, 202, 203, 205, 209, 210, 212, 214, 221, 230
literal translation 9, 13, 16, 20, 36, 38, 47, 52, 53, 60, 64, 65, 116, 148, 187
localization 4, 217, 229

machine translation 4, 41, 214–216, 220–222
Marxism 95
metacognitive 203, 212, 221
mistranslation 173, 193
multilingual 156, 174, 175, 194, 215, 228
Munday 6, 74, 75, 78, 84, 91, 158, 194

nationalism 16, 75, 76, 78
naturalization 138, 159
neologisms 138, 148
Nida 45, 46, 48, 56, 59, 61–63, 89, 92, 108, 130, 225
non-equivalence 133, 139

ontology 32, 37, 40, 114, 125, 135
original text 6, 104, 111, 140, 150, 152, 213, 216
over-translation 65

patronage 13, 20
pedagogy 61, 195, 196, 198, 199, 207, 209, 214, 216, 221
plagiarism 18
pluralism 162, 190
political 37, 50, 64, 76, 81–83, 90, 94, 96–100, 107, 113, 117, 118, 137, 154, 158, 162, 198
polysemy 190
polysystem 13, 136, 160, 177, 182, 191
postcolonialism 74–78, 80–82, 182
professional 12, 42, 172, 196, 201, 205–210, 212–214, 220
psycholinguistic 3, 198
psychology 6, 15, 34, 35, 44, 153, 182, 202, 206

qualitative 172, 178, 179, 188, 189, 223
quantitative 172, 178–180

readership 13, 48, 64, 65, 70–72, 81, 82, 85, 93, 108, 112, 138, 139, 142, 143, 159, 160, 163, 166
register 67, 182
relevance theory 2, 60, 83–87, 91, 132, 178, 182, 189, 195, 221
religion 94, 117, 164, 170, 179
revolutionary 53, 70, 84
rhetoric 18, 33, 35, 69, 149, 180

Sanskrit 17, 102–106, 127, 159, 174, 224
Saussure 30, 79
scientometric analysis 3, 4, 7–9, 83, 134, 160, 198–200, 214, 221
semantic 9, 12, 20, 21, 35, 52, 55, 61, 63, 66, 67, 69, 90, 106, 149, 165, 170, 182
semi-colonialism 74, 75
sinology 173, 187
skopos 9, 11, 12, 25, 47, 48, 60, 70–72, 132, 134, 160, 177, 178, 180, 189, 191
sociological 12, 118, 196, 198, 204, 223
standardization 146, 209
syntactic 5, 12, 26, 35, 66, 85, 147, 187, 213, 216

target language 20, 35, 66, 68, 116, 120, 124, 133, 137, 213, 215
technical translation 39, 94, 97, 101
terminology 1, 4, 14, 63, 124, 130, 145–150, 152–155, 210, 216, 217
textbooks 113, 125, 148, 169, 211, 212, 220, 221
text types 7, 19, 68, 91, 99

traditional Chinese medicine 24, 108, 133, 144–147, 149, 153–155, 178
traditional culture 29, 109, 113, 138, 167, 170
trainee 195, 205, 220
translatability 9, 15, 17, 18, 53, 79, 85, 103, 124, 125, 182
translation competence 24, 195, 196, 198, 201–208, 212, 213, 220–223
translation criticism 6, 15, 41, 61, 70, 71, 87, 112, 125, 143, 176, 191
translation method 17, 38, 53, 88, 103–106, 116, 119–121, 123, 143, 146, 151, 215, 219
translation problems 5, 13, 15, 19, 23, 41, 45, 68, 72, 75, 84, 122, 124–126, 129, 133, 137, 139, 203, 205, 206, 213, 219
translation process 4, 15, 29, 45, 61, 123, 150, 153, 176, 182, 190, 195, 197, 203–205, 208, 212, 213, 227
translation strategies 7, 64, 68, 71, 72, 76, 80, 82, 89, 101, 108, 109, 119, 127, 137–140, 144, 154, 161, 165, 174, 178, 180, 189, 190, 192, 194, 206–208
translation teaching 4, 15, 60, 70, 90, 125, 143, 195–200, 202, 205–207, 209–216, 218–223, 225
translation technology 7, 198, 214, 216–220, 222
translation theory 3, 4, 6–8, 10–16, 18–28, 30–32, 35–46, 48–63, 67–84, 86–91, 93, 101, 106, 108–110, 113–125, 127–132, 136, 146, 157, 159, 165, 170, 171, 176, 181, 182, 190, 195, 197, 198, 210, 212, 213, 222–230

universal theory 5, 84
untranslatability 17, 18, 33, 34, 79, 103, 190, 191

variation 10, 19, 20, 25, 108, 109, 118–120, 128
Vietnamese 170, 175
visualization 2, 3, 7, 8, 59, 60, 89, 132, 154, 190, 199, 226
vocabulary 9, 84, 90, 108, 111, 115, 123, 139, 148, 149, 151, 153, 164–166, 177, 181, 186, 208, 213

Western Centralism 170, 225
Western literature 24, 63, 121, 198
Western philosophy 28, 29, 57, 95

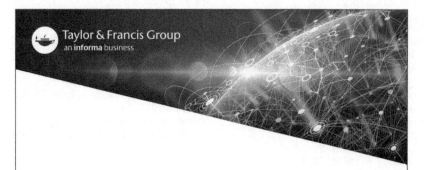